# Ripped, torn and cut

MANCHESTER
1824

Manchester University Press

# Ripped, torn and cut

## Pop, politics and punk fanzines from 1976

EDITED BY
THE SUBCULTURES NETWORK

Manchester University Press

Published by Manchester University Press
Altrincham Street, Manchester M1 7JA, UK
www.manchesteruniversitypress.co.uk


British Library Cataloguing-in-Publication Data is available


ISBN 978 1 5261 2059 5 hardback

ISBN 978 1 5261 3907 8 paperback


First published by Manchester University Press in hardback 2018

This edition first published 2019


The publisher has no responsibility for the persistence or accuracy of URLs for any external or third-party internet websites referred to in this book, and does not guarantee that any content on such websites is, or will remain, accurate or appropriate.


Typeset
by Toppan Best-set Premedia Limited

Printed in Great Britain
by TJ International Ltd, Padstow

# Contents

# Figures

# Contributors

**Jess Baines** is a senior lecturer in contextual and theoretical studies at the Design School, London College of Communication (LCC). For the last few years she has been researching and writing about the UK's alternative radical printshops (in which she was once an active participant) culminating in her Ph.D. thesis, 'Democratising Print? The Field and Practices of Radical and Community Printshops in Britain, 1968–98' (London School of Economics, 2016). Publications include 'Engaging (Past) Participants: The Case of radicalprintshops.org', in S. Kubitschko and A. Kaun (eds), *Innovative Methods in Media & Communication Research* (2016) and 'Nurturing Dissent? Community Printshops in 1970s London', in J. Uldam and A. Vestergaard (eds), *Civic Engagement and Social Media: Political Participation Beyond Protest* (2015). With other ex-workshop members Pru Stevenson, Suzy Mackie and Anne Robinson she also co-authored the monograph *Red Women's Workshop: Feminist Posters, 1974–90* (2016). Along with Tony Credland, she is part of LCC's Design Activist Research Hub.

**Russ Bestley** is reader in graphic design at the London College of Communication. He has written and designed a number of books including *Visual Research* (2004, 2011, 2015), *Up Against the Wall: International Poster Design* (2002) and *Experimental Layout* (2001), and has contributed articles to *Punk & Post Punk, Eye, Zed, Emigré, The National Grid, 360°, Street Sounds* and *Vive Le Rock*. His book *The Art of Punk* was published 2012. He is also editor of the journal *Punk & Post Punk* and a member of the Punk Scholars Network.

**Rebecca Binns** is currently researching a Ph.D. on the work of Gee Vaucher at LCC. Her recent work includes contributing a catalogue essay for a major retrospective of Gee's work at FIRSTSITE, Colchester, and participating in round table discussions on zines and art and anarchism at the British Library and Anarchist Book Fair respectively. She has written more widely on punk graphics, photography, fine art, architecture and squatting for both commercial and academic publications.

**Benjamin Bland** is currently completing an AHRC-funded Ph.D. in the Department of History at Royal Holloway, University of London. He is a historian of modern and contemporary Britain, whose doctoral research focuses around subcultural iterations of neo-fascism in the UK since the 1970s. He has wider interests in the political culture of the right, and in ideas of cultural and political extremism in the post-war period.

**Nicholas Bullen** is an artist and composer. His creative life began at the age of 12, writing fanzines and forming the group Napalm Death who invented the grindcore genre of extreme music. Described as 'still one of the most exciting extreme artists working today', his musical compositions have been made available on over 40 releases and he makes regular performances at an international level. Developed across a range of media and inter-disciplinary in approach, his artworks have been presented at Tate Britain, Art Basel, Institute of Contemporary Arts, Hayward Gallery, White Columns, Schirn Kunsthalle, Casino Luxembourg, Kunsthall Oslo and others. He is currently researching anarcho-punk fanzines during the period 1978 to 1984.

**Cazz Blase** is the music review editor at *The F-Word* website www.thefword.org.uk. She blogs about music at www.cazzblase.blogspot.com and about Manchester and Greater Manchester at http://toolateforcake.wordpress.com. She also works as a library assistant at the University of Manchester and is working on a book about women and the UK punk scene.

**Richard Cabut** is the co-editor of and contributor to the anthology *Punk is Dead: Modernity Killed Every Night* (2017). His journalism has featured in the *NME* (pen name Richard North), *Zigzag*, the *Guardian*, the *Daily Telegraph*, *Big Issue*, *Time Out* and more. He was a Pushcart Prize nominee in 2016 for his fiction. Richard's plays have been performed at various theatres in London and nationwide, including the Arts Theatre, Covent Garden, London. He published the fanzine *Kick* and played bass for the punk band Brigandage.

**Laura Cofield** is an AHRC-funded doctoral researcher in the Department of History, University of Sussex. In 2014 she was awarded a grant from the Santander Mobility Fund to visit the Riot Grrrl Collection at the Fales Library, New York. Her previous publication, co-authored with Professor Lucy Robinson, was entitled, '"The Opposite of the Band": Fangrrrling, Feminism and Sexual Dissidence', *Textual Practice*, 30:6 (2016).

**Tony Credland** is a senior lecturer on MA Graphic Media Design at the London College of Communication. A graduate of Chelsea College of Art and the Jan van Eyck Academie in Maastricht, he was co-founder of the Cactus Network, which manifested itself as a mail-art magazine, and co-editor of the poster magazine *Feeding Squirrels to the Nuts*. He was involved in radical media projects such as London Indymedia and Reclaim the Streets and continues to be active in grassroots politics. He is a co-editor of the book *We Are Everywhere: The Irresistible Rise of Global Anticapitalism* (2003). Along with other LCC staff, he set up the Design Activist Research Hub focusing on the visual and material culture practices and artefacts of social movements and other formations of resistance and agitation.

**Pete Dale** studied at Sunderland Polytechnic. On graduating, he played in several indie/punk underground bands (Pussycat Trash, Red Monkey, Milky Wimpshake) and set up the cult DIY label/distributor Slampt, which ran very successfully between 1992 and 2000. Pete completed an MA in Music (2005) and then a Ph.D. at Newcastle University (2010) while simultaneously working as a teacher. He took an early career fellowship at Oxford Brookes in 2012, subsequently becoming senior lecturer in popular Music at Manchester Metropolitan University in 2013. His monographs include *Anyone Can Do It: Tradition, Empowerment and the Punk Underground* (2012), *Popular Music and the Politics of Novelty* (2016) and *Engaging Students with Music Education: DJ Decks, Urban Music and Child-centred Learning* (2017). Pete is associate editor of the *Punk and Post-Punk* journal and a founding member of the Punk Scholars Network.

**Mike Diboll** was active in the early UK anarcho-punk scene, producing the *Toxic Graffiti* anarcho-zine (1978–82) and various other writing and graphic projects. He earned a Ph.D. in Comparative Literature in 2000, before working overseas in comparative literature and related fields in the Middle and Far Easts between 2001 and 2011 and was an eyewitness to the Bahrain revolution of 2011 and its murderous suppression. Struggling against PTSD and major depression he took an MA in the anthropology of violence to make sense of his experiences. He is a research associate at the UCL Institute of Education and a Fellow of the Higher Education Academy. He researches progressive education in a changing Middle East and writes creatively and autoethnographically as therapy.

**Tony Drayton** produced the seminal fanzine *Ripped & Torn* in November 1976, featuring the first ever interviews with Adam and the Ants and Crass. He started *Kill Your Pet Puppy* in 1979, the first issue going on sale at the Ants' New Year's Eve concert at Camden's Electric Ballroom. In 1984 Tony stopped producing fanzines and began busking around Europe with a fire-eating and juggling act; this developed into a circus-skills based career which saw him perform around the world. In 2007, he started the *Kill Your Pet Puppy* web site in order to document anarcho-punk. This has proven very popular, making available hard-to-find cassette-only releases from the era plus many other interesting sounds and pieces of ephemera.

**Keith Gildart** is professor of labour and social history at the University of Wolver-hampton and author of *Images of England through Popular Music: Class, Youth and Rock 'n' Roll, 1955–76* (2013).

**Anna Gough-Yates** is head of the Department of Media, Culture and Language at Roehampton University. Her research has focused mainly on the magazine and television industries, and has examined the ways in which the economic processes and practices of production are also phenomena with cultural meanings and effects. She has published a number of articles in this area, and is also the author of two books: *Understanding Women's Magazines: Publishing Markets and Readerships* (2003), and *Action TV: Tough Guys, Smooth Operators and Foxy Chicks* (2001), co-edited with Bill Osgerby.

**Sian Lincoln** is senior lecturer in media studies at Liverpool John Moores University. Her research interests are in youth culture, private space and identity, and young people's uses of social media. Her book *Youth Culture and Private Space* was published in 2012. Her work has also been published in anthologies and journals such as *New Media & Society, Journal of Youth Studies, Social Media + Society* and *Qualitative*

*Research*. She is co-editor of the Cinema and Youth Cultures series with Yannis Tzioumakis.

**Kirsty Lohman** is a Leverhulme Early Career Fellow at the University of Surrey working on feminist and queer punk in the UK. Her research interests include DIY musical/cultural participation, gender and political/community activism. Her Ph.D. thesis was an ethnography of the punk scene in The Netherlands and has been published as a monograph: *The Connected Lives of Dutch Punks: Contesting Subcultural Boundaries* (2017).

**Claire Nally** is a senior lecturer in twentieth-century English Literature at Northumbria University, and has published widely on Irish Studies, subcultures and gender. Her first book was *Envisioning Ireland: W. B. Yeats's Occult Nationalism* (2009), followed by *Selling Ireland: Advertising, Literature and Irish Print Culture 1891–1922*, written with John Strachan (2012). With Angela Smith she has co-edited two volumes on gender, as well as the library series Gender and Popular Culture. Her next book is *Steampunk: Gender, Subculture, and the Neo-Victorian* (2018).

**Bill Osgerby** is professor in media, culture and communications at London Metropolitan University. His research interests focus on modern American and British media and cultural history; he has published widely with particular regard to the areas of gender, sexuality, youth culture, consumption, print media, popular television, film and music. His books include *Youth in Britain Since 1945* (1998), *Playboys in Paradise: Youth, Masculinity and Leisure Style in Modern America* (2001), *Youth Media* (2004) and an anthology, *Action TV: Tough-Guys, Smooth Operators and Foxy Chicks* (2001), co-edited with Anna Gough-Yates.

**Mark Pawson** is an artist, bookseller, self-publisher and visiting lecturer based in East London. In 1994, he co-curated the 'Counter Intelligence' exhibition of self-produced zines, comics, pamphlets and flyers at the squatted 121 Centre in Brixton, which also travelled to Gavin Brown's Enterprise, New York. Between 1998 and 2012 he wrote a reviews column for *Variant*, covering comics, zines and other publications, now archived online at www.variant.org.uk. In 2012, his personal collection of independent, autonomous print creations was displayed at UNBOXING, a reading room installation at xero, kline & coma, London.

**S. Alexander Reed** is the author of *Assimilate: A Critical History of Industrial Music* (2013) and co-author of a 33⅓ book *They Might Be Giants' Flood* (2014). He has taught at New York University, the University of Florida, William & Mary, and Ithaca College. With his bands Seeming and ThouShaltNot, Dr Reed has made many albums and toured internationally.

**Lucy Robinson** is professor of collaborative history at the University of Sussex. She writes on popular music, politics and identity, feminism and punk pedagogy. As well as co-ordinating the Subcultures Network, and the open access digital project 'Observing the 80s', she has recently advised on an exhibition on Jersey in the 1980s and on a new documentary project funded by the BFI, *Queerama*.

**Karl Siebengartner** studied history, English literature, language and educational studies at the Ludwig-Maximilians-Universität (LMU) Munich, and contemporary history at the University of Sussex. His Ph.D. project is a transnational history of the punk scenes in the Federal Republic of Germany from the mid-1970s until the mid-1990s. His main research interests are post-Second World War history, youth and subcultures, popular culture, history of historiography and media history.

**John Street** is a professor of politics at the University of East Anglia. He is the author of several books, of which the most recent are *Music and Politics* (2012) and (with Sanna Inthorn and Martin Scott) *From Entertainment to Citizenship: Politics and Popular Culture* (2013).

**Tom Vague** was the editor/designer of *Vague*, one of the first post-punk fanzines, founded at Salisbury College of Art and Technology (now Wiltshire College) in 1979. Through the 1980s, *Vague* went from featuring the Ants, Banshees, Joy Division, the Pop Group, PIL and the Slits, to become a cyber-punk manual covering TG/Psychic TV, the Baader-Meinhof gang, situationist and conspiracy theories. He has since worked on his London psychogeography project in Notting Hill, including the Clash 'London Calling' box set booklet and www.colvillecom.com.

**Clare Wadd** produced six issues of her fanzine *Kvatch* between the ages of 16 and 19, before setting up Sarah Records with Matt Haynes from *Are You Scared to Get Happy?*. Sarah Records operated from 1987 to 1995, when it reached catalogue number 100 – a landmark they celebrated with a big party and by shutting the label down. Sarah's 100 catalogue numbers included four fanzines, which Clare and Matt saw as their contribution to the label's output. Clare is now director of finance at a climate change charity.

**Peter Webb** is a writer, lecturer and musician who specialises in research into popular and contemporary music, subcultures, globalisation, new media, politics and social theory. He is a senior lecturer and programme leader for sociology at the University of the West of England, Bristol.

**David Wilkinson** is lecturer in English at Manchester Metropolitan University. He is the author of *Post-Punk, Politics and Pleasure in Britain* (2016) and member of the Subcultures Network. He has also worked with the Manchester Digital Music Archive on an online archive of *City Fun*, which can be accessed at www.mdmarchive.co.uk/exhibition/id/78/CITY_FUN.html.

**Matthew Worley** is professor of modern history at the University of Reading. He has written widely on British labour and political history, including books on the Communist Party of Great Britain, the Labour Party and Sir Oswald Mosley's New Party. His more recent work has concentrated on the relationship between youth culture and politics in Britain, primarily in the 1970s and 1980s. Articles have been published in such journals as *History Workshop, Twentieth Century British History, Contemporary British History, Journal for the Study of Radicalism, Journalism, Media and Cultural Studies, Punk & Post-Punk* and chapters in collections such as the Subcultures Network's *Fight Back: Punk, Politics and Resistance* (2015). A monograph, *No Future: Punk, Politics and British Youth Culture, 1976–84*, was published in 2017.

# Foreword

Tony Drayton

Jimmy Pursey of Sham 69 tears up a copy of *Ripped & Torn* number seven which contains a bad review of his band's performance at the Acklam Hall, explaining that 'I started writing on it so they made me buy it'. Pursey scatters the ripped-up copy of the fanzine and storms out the room, which is also the Step Forward record label office in Dryden Chambers. Danny Baker, Kris Needs and Mark Perry are among others in there, and they all look at me and ask the same question: 'What was that about?' They expected it to be a jokey set-up between me and Jimmy, but they laughed even harder when I said I was terrified one of them would point me out as the author. I laughed their laughter off and got back to typing up my interview with Adam Ant, his first ever which I'd taped two days earlier to provide the main feature for *Ripped & Torn* number eight.

Fanzines meant a lot to everyone in that room, not just Pursey. The people gathered there were so because of fanzines; they saw fanzines as both an integral part of the music media of the time and springboards for their own future careers. Even the room itself, Mark Perry's office, would not have been there was it not for fanzines! This, after all, was the summer of 1977. Pursey's Sham 69 were signed to *Sniffin' Glue*'s record label; Baker was still a writer for the fanzine; Needs was there to steal Baker away to his *Zigzag* magazine and I was using the typewriter because I didn't have one back at my squat. Perry was helping me out while also using me as a route to get one of my squat-mates, Alex Fergusson, to form a band with him, which would turn out to be Alternative TV.

For me, being in that room was living the dream (even if Pursey was a potential nightmare). And I was there because of starting *Ripped & Torn* in Scotland less than a year previously. I'd escaped my boring life, which was what starting the fanzine was all about. Equally, the concept of me creating a fanzine wouldn't have been possible without *Sniffin' Glue*, and I mean that most literally.

In October 1976, I'd travelled to London from Scotland to see if this punk thing was as exciting as the music press was making it out to be. On my first night, I went to see The Damned at the Hope & Anchor and experienced punk at first hand for the first time, experiencing not just the band but the crowd and the energy. I got very excited, and when I met Mark Perry at the gig I said I wanted to write about it for *Sniffin' Glue*. Mark told me to go back to Scotland and turn my enthusiasm into a fanzine of my own.

Rather than treat Perry's words as a rebuttal I took them as an inspiration. Back in Cumbernauld a day or so later, I thrashed around listening to my old punk records like the Velvets, Jonathan Richman and the Ramones wondering how to turn my feelings about everything into, well, not just writing but ten pages of single-sided A4 paper stapled in the top left-hand corner just like *Sniffin' Glue*. That'll show him, I thought.

*Ripped & Torn* was produced, to cut a long story short, and as that first issue got orders from shops in London like Rough Trade and Compendium it became less of two fingers in Mark's face and more a sign of how I could escape my dead-end life. It became a one-way ticket for my return to London; the cover stars of *Sniffin' Glue* number five were Eddie & The Hot Rods, and I took their song 'Get Out Of Denver' to heart and got out of Scotland, baby.

Fast forward to the early 1980s. A new punk scene is developing from the Wapping Anarchy Centre, by which time I am producing the fanzine *Kill Your Pet Puppy*. Now I find myself in the same position as Mark Perry in 1976, with people wanting to write for me about how they feel about what is happening to them. I say to them what he said to me, 'go and make your own fanzine'. By coincidence or influence, the great anarcho-punk fanzine industry erupts; but that's another story for different kitchen.

Fanzines, then, mean everything to me. I owe them my life and how it has been lived the past forty-odd years. Every fanzine tells a story between the printed lines, of how important doing it meant to the person concerned. Some of those stories appear in this book, as the writers piece together a culture from the scraps we fanzine producers left behind. I can't wait to read it to see what we got up to … and what it meant.

# Acknowledgements

Special thanks to the archives, archivists and private collectors who helped facilitate the research for this collection. Thanks also to those who gave permission for the use of images.

# Introduction: adventures in reality: why (punk) fanzines matter

MATTHEW WORLEY, KEITH GILDART,
ANNA GOUGH-YATES, SIAN LINCOLN,
BILL OSGERBY, LUCY ROBINSON,
JOHN STREET, PETE WEBB

*I'm scribbling this down at work so I can't let the prose flow but I couldn't care.
There's only one way to defeat the two evils (boring established groups & straight
record shops) and that is to ignore them completely.*

Tony D., *Ripped & Torn*, no. 1 (1976)

It may seem strange that something so ephemeral should warrant historical
attention. Typically made with wilful irreverence and designed, often, to capture
but a fleeting cultural moment, the archetypal punk fanzine could be dismissed
as little more than pop detritus. Indeed, many of the homemade zines that
flowered as a result of punk's impetus to 'do-it-yourself' were parochial in
their focus and concern. Most were short lived; some were one-offs. They
were often bought and discarded in a matter of days, their contents comprising
adolescent obsessions and subjective musings presented in hard-to-comprehend
scribble, one-finger type or slap-dash collage. The inaugural issue of *Sniffin'
Glue*, produced by Mark Perry in 1976 and generally recognised to be Britain's
first self-defined punk fanzine, even denied that it was meant to be read. It
was 'chucked together' and best used for 'soaking in glue and sniffin'. On one
page, a large gap was filled only by Perry's thick black marker-pen scrawl: 'I
didn't no what to put here so I wrote this!' [*sic*].[1]

   And yet, look harder, think deeper, and fanzines become far more than
just cast-off copies of yesterday's teenage news. Not only do they provide

portals to a particular time and place, with parochialism transformed into resonant snapshots of cultures beyond the hubbub of London's media, but they also offer glimpses of the interests, concerns and opinions of youthful milieux. Most obviously, they help us understand what it is to be a 'fan' (or a 'punk' or a 'skinhead' or a 'riot grrrl'). Yet they further allow insight into cultural preoccupations and socio-political understandings. Flick through their yellowing, stapled pages and alternative cultural narratives are recovered, hidden voices are heard, cultural networks are pieced together and formative political awakenings discovered.[2] For all their immediacy, fanzines serve as residues of youthful agency; 'visual and verbal rants' freed from the pressures of censorship, editorial dictates, subbing and deadlines.[3]

As this suggests, punk-informed fanzines developed in myriad ways. Most early zines – be it *48 Thrills*, *Bondage*, *Shy Talk* from Manchester, *Gun Rubber* from Sheffield or any of the literally hundreds of titles that emerged from towns, cities and suburbs across the UK from 1976–77[4] – followed the *Sniffin' Glue* template: fervid text with cut 'n' paste imagery that was Roneo-stencilled or Xeroxed to be sold for minimal cost at gigs, school, college or in local record shops.[5] Over time, however, some of these – and countless others – began to broaden their scope, taking in politics, as with Lucy Whitman's *JOLT* (1977), or committing towards critical analyses of punk's cultural advance. Tony Drayton first produced *Ripped & Torn* as an 18-year-old living on the outskirts of Glasgow in late 1976, before moving to London to provide a three-year running commentary on punk's dissipation. By 1980, after eighteen issues, *Ripped & Torn* had morphed into *Kill Your Pet Puppy*, debating anarchist politics and esoterica. Not dissimilarly, *Vague* began as a fairly conventional fanzine from Wiltshire in 1979 before transforming through in-depth analyses of punk's socio-cultural relevance to expanded essays on situationist practice, cyber-punk and the Red Army Faction.[6] *Rapid Eye Movement*, too, evolved from a punk zine to a book-length compendium exploring what its founder, Simon Dwyer, called 'occulture'.[7]

Culturally, zines opened up enquiry into everything from surrealism (*The Eklektik*) to situationist excursions through urban space (*Adventures in Reality*) to the writings of Wilhelm Reich, Henry Miller and Austin Osman Spare (*White Stuff*).[8] Poetry and short stories began to mingle amidst the gig and record reviews.[9] Politically, progressive causes were aligned to music coverage in zines such as Manchester's *City Fun*, while the influence of Crass, a band formed in 1977 and credited with transforming punk's rhetorical anarchy into coherent practice, led to a groundswell of overtly anarchist zines into the 1980s.[10] Beyond Gee Vaucher of Crass's own *International Anthem* and Poison Girls's *The Impossible Dream*, titles such as *Acts of Defiance*, *Anathema*,

*Enigma, New Crimes, Pigs for Slaughter, Scum* and *Toxic Graffitti* [*sic*][11] mixed limited music coverage with political tracts on subjects that included militarism, squatting, feminism, vivisection and the various structural props of 'the system'.[12]

The presentation of punk-informed fanzines also brokered experimentation. Where the first edition of Jon Savage's *London's Outrage* (1976) interspersed media clippings with pop cultural references and an essay forewarning Britain's descent into fascism, the second (1977) compiled photographs of desolate London landscapes that reflected punk's dystopian vision of 'No Future'.[13] A year later, in 1978, Savage co-produced *The Secret Public* with Linder (Linda Mulvey), comprising photomontages that spliced together pornographic images, household appliances and advert-speak to expose the gendered false promises of the media spectacle.[14] More generally, the graphic design of punk zines advanced to incorporate homemade collage, illustration and a wider colour palette. Paper sizes varied, while the layout of text pushed against convention to forge distinct aesthetics. Simultaneously, zines such as *Guttersnipe* (from Telford) began to combine social commentary with social-realist imagery, striving – as did others in their collages of urban decay, National Front marches, police mobilisations, newspaper headlines, domestic ordinariness and media clichés – to capture what Raymond Williams defined as a 'structure of feeling'.[15] By the 1980s, as the Cold War reignited, so images of domesticity, militarism and nuclear devastation were juxtaposed to evoke a 'sense of the quality of life at a particular place and time'.[16]

Given all this, the premise of the current collection rests on the notion that fanzines help the historian trace and better understand the shifting contours of British youth culture. With regard to punk, they map the contested nature of its cultural evolution away from the *moment* of 1976–77 and on through its various and often overlapping subdivisions (subsequently recognised as 'post-punk', 'Oi!', 'anarcho', 'goth' etc.) into the 1980s. Fanzines documented punk in the provinces; they collated debates over the meanings attributed to punk's varied forms and practice; they revealed continuities and distinctions between pre-punk and post-punk cultures. In the process, fanzines also demonstrate the extent to which (youth) cultures are not simply produced and consumed but constructed and utilised. If punk's fanzines first claimed to emerge in lieu of informed media coverage, then they later offered counter-narratives to dominant media perspectives; an alternative press to the music weeklies (*NME*, *Sounds* and *Melody Maker*) and commercial media. To this end, fanzines enabled the formation of what Nancy Fraser has called a 'subaltern counterpublic', formulating alternate and sometimes oppositional 'interpretations of … identities, interests and needs'.[17]

Punk fanzines were more than just pieces of paper: they staked a claim to cultural identity and autonomy. 'I don't wanna see the [Sex] Pistols, the Clash etc. turned into more AC/DCs and Doctors of Madness', Perry wrote in September 1976, referring to two bands then being fêted in the music press and peddled as the 'next big thing'. 'This "new wave" has got to take in everything, including posters, record-covers, stage presentation, the lot!'[18] Two months later he went further: 'I hope that with the new young music will come new writers who have got the right to vent their ideas and opinions ... I used to enjoy reading about the Pistols, the Clash and the other bands in *Sounds* etc, but not anymore. [They] should stick to writing about the established artists. Leave our music to us, if anything needs to be written, us kids will do it ... '.[19] Fanzines, then, became an integral part of punk's challenge; the literary and visual embodiment of 'do it yourself'. To recognise their importance is to recover cultures in the making, grass-roots complements to the pervasive simplicity of mediated narratives.

## Kid's stuff: writing about fanzines

The history of fanzines has been well told.[20] Their origin can be traced back to the home-made magazines produced by science fiction fans in the US and Britain from the 1930s; labours of love that enabled stories and critical commentaries to be shared among enthusiasts. Thereafter, non-commercial and non-professional publications emerged across a range of cultural spheres, from comics, sport and cinema to sexuality and religion. Not surprisingly, music provided – and continues to provide – a particularly fruitful site of fanzine activity, with publications concentrated on specific genres or artists dating back to at least the 1950s. To this extent, many of the early punk fanzines followed in a set tradition, providing celebratory coverage of the 'new wave' for the appreciation of like-minded 'fans'.

And yet, the sheer number of punk-informed fanzines that appeared from 1976 to 1977 suggests they signalled more than a simple by-product of musical consumption.[21] Already, by the 1960s, the distinction between fanzines, countercultural publications (such as *Frendz, International Times, Oz*) and samizdat-style pamphlets rooted in a longer radical tradition had become blurred.[22] In fact, these three points of connection were conjoined via Jamie Reid, whose artwork for the Sex Pistols used détourned media graphics and concepts cultivated during his time at Croydon Art School (with Malcolm McLaren and Helen Wallington-Lloyd) and disseminated through the Suburban Press he co-founded in 1970. The Sex Pistols' own fanzine, *Anarchy in the UK* (1976), displayed such a pedigree, featuring pictures of the band's early coterie with politically charged skits that subscribed to one criterion: 'Does it threaten the status quo?'[23] Crass, too, issued the first of Gee Vaucher's three *International Anthem* zines in late 1977, juxtaposing artwork with collages, lyrics and extended essays by Penny Rimbaud that revealed the band's countercultural heritage. As a result, punk and its associated fanzines came imbued with a subversive aesthetic that helped tender broader political potential and provide space to debate and determine the wider implications of youth cultural politics.

This was recognised at the time. Just as Jon Savage extolled fanzines for providing a graphic complement to punk's musical and stylistic assault, so Tony Parsons insisted they represented 'the largest, nastiest, funniest and healthiest selection of alternative music press in the history of rock 'n' roll'.[24] Scholarly analyses of British punk fanzines also picked up on related themes. Teal Triggs, in particular, has done much to commend the graphic innovations of punk zines, demonstrating how their visual language formed an essential part of punk's cultural revolt and helped forge a unique aesthetic that has since been absorbed into conventional design.[25] More broadly, sociological accounts of British punk have – like Savage before them – noted how a fanzine's cut 'n' paste assemblage reflected the culture's early sartorial bricolage and sense of agency. Dick Hebdige, for example, pointed to the jumbled pagination, spelling mistakes and cheap production values of punk fanzines as an indication of their 'urgency and immediacy … memos from the front line'.[26] Dave Laing, meanwhile, emphasized how the language and imagery used by fanzines helped define punk's boundaries within (and against) the music industry and society generally.[27] If the abiding legacy of punk was to provide a cultural process that transformed the passive observer into active participant, then fanzines deserve their place alongside the independent labels and self-released records that came in its wake.[28] For Steve Duncombe, whose *Notes from the Underground* (1997) provides the most extensive study of fanzine cultural politics, zines formed part of the 'long line of media for the misbegotten': amateur, non-commercial, counter-hegemonic.[29]

The *content* of British punk fanzines has warranted less attention. Beyond Matthew Worley's survey of their varied political approaches and Matt Grimes and Tim Wall's comparative study of early and contemporary anarcho zines, the focus has tended to be on the form rather than the substance of fanzine production.[30] Even the *Punk & Post-Punk* journal has to date published just two fanzine-related articles – Brett Lashua and Sara Cohen's mapping of Liverpool's post-punk 'musicscape' and Paula Guerra and Pedro Quintela's study of Portuguese punk zines – even though zines increasingly form part of the reservoir of resources drawn upon for the study of punk.[31] A notable exception to the rule is riot grrrl, a culture named after a fanzine and for which zines proved integral to its development and dissemination.[32] Subsequently, fanzines have provided much of the core material for those seeking to trace the meanings and objectives of the 'revolution'. As a result, riot grrrl literature – both original and academic – has revealed the important role played by zines in terms of constructing cultural-political networks and providing space for personal empowerment.[33] Or, as Laura Cofield and Lucy Robinson have argued, fanzines forged communities and facilitated a discourse that 'built, reflected on and critiqued the possibilities of a feminist DIY community across geographical boundaries.'[34]

There is much to learn from this. More to the point, the collation of riot grrrl material – such as that housed at Fales Library in New York – is now complemented by a wider and growing number of catalogued zine collections, both archival and digital. Some of these, as in London's British Library or Victoria and Albert Museum, sit alongside prestigious national deposits. Others, such as the Manchester District Music Archive or Bristol Archive Records, are grass-roots digital resources compiling music, zines, memories and ephemera to map the specifics of place.[35] Taken all together, they provide researchers and anyone involved in a particular culture with a valuable historical record.[36] They also offer opportunity to facilitate collaborations between the two, enabling histories to be assembled and written in conjunction with those actively materialising their own experiences and expertise. It is in such a spirit that the current collection has been conceived – scholars, archivists and cultural practitioners combining towards *our* history rather than 'mine', 'yours' or 'theirs'.

## Protesting children minus the bondage: contents, rationale and limits

The book is divided into four Parts, with each one designed to provide distinct but overlapping insights into the politics and practice of punk-related fanzines. Part I, 'Going Underground', will reassert the fanzine's historical importance, recognising zines not simply as a historical resource but as historical writings in themselves. Firstly, Jess Baines, Tony Credland and Mark Pawson place punk's fanzines in the wider context of radical publishing, looking back to the 1960s counterculture in order to trace the practices, techniques and infra-structures that fed into and helped enable punk's fanzine culture. Thereafter, Lucy Robinson and Matthew Worley develop one of the book's core themes: the role of fanzines in constructing historical narratives and identities. For Robinson, fanzines offer far more than just a historical record; they serve also to create and articulate competing cultural and historical canons. Worley, meanwhile, uses three case studies to examine how zines forge and offset the meanings associated with youth cultural practice. Where *JOLT* provides an example of a leftist claim for punk's possibilities, *Anathema* filters punk through an anarchist lens to make sense of its oppositionism. By contrast, *Hard as Nails* was a skinhead zine established, in part, to counter the prevailing media narrative of skins as racist neo-Nazis. Finally, Cazz Blase examines how zines can help make political sense of the youth cultures of which they were part. Concentrating on female fanzine writers, Blase considers why women were so well placed to sustain punk and post-punk's zine culture in the mid-1970s and after.

Part II, 'Communiqués and Sellotape', focuses on the construction of cultural identity and cultural politics. Each of the five chapters picks up on a strand of punk's cultural evolution to explore how fanzines gave meaning to their respective practices and processes. David Wilkinson hones in on Manchester's vibrant post-punk milieu via the long-running *City Fun* (1978–84), tracing countercultural roots that fed into and thereby informed a discourse that one of the zine's writers, Liz Naylor, defined as being about 'how to recreate [Manchester]'. Claire Nally examines goth's long evolution through two zines integral to the culture's form and dissemination, one British (*Panache*) and one American (*Propaganda*). By so doing, Nally reveals the contested and continually evolving nature of youth cultural practice while also demonstrating how zines offered space to debate and construct the meanings ascribed to their particular form. Punk's anarchism is next discussed by Russ Bestley and Rebecca Binns, primarily in relation to the symbiotic relationship between the bands (especially Crass) and the wider anarcho-punk culture that emerged into the 1980s. In particular, Bestley and Binns consider the aesthetics of anarcho-punk, using fanzines to trace the visual conventions used to communicate values, ideas and political positions. Not dissimilarly, Benjamin Bland uncovers how fanzines became an integral part of the industrial culture that emerged parallel (and often overlapped) with punk from the mid-1970s. Often drawn from avant garde performance art and cultural theories designed to challenge, deconstruct and demystify the forces of 'control' (media, government, religion, language, ritual) that shape 'reality', industrial bands such as Throbbing Gristle and zines such as *Stabmental* committed to recovering lost knowledge and disseminating information. Lastly in this section, Pete Dale returns to punk's DIY ethos to demonstrate how such values continued to inform the development of 'indie pop' through the 1980s. Even as the sound, content and aesthetic of 'indie' moved away from the iconoclasm of punk's initial revolt, so its position as a perceived alternative to the corporately owned media and music establishment remained and was sustained within a zine culture aware of its punk roots.

In Part III, 'Memos from the Frontline', those who helped forge punk's and post-punk's fanzine culture are invited to reflect back on their experiences and motivations. As noted earlier in the Introduction, *Vague* passed through a major transformation over the 1980s, from a punk zine to a countercultural, psychogeographical annual. Tom Vague here explains such an evolution, reaffirming his commitment to punk's DIY principles while tracing a hidden history of the 1970s and 1980s. By contrast, Mike Diboll's *Toxic Grafity* chartered a personal journey of political discovery. Suitably, therefore, such reflexivity continues through Diboll's chapter, musing on how the ideas and experiences that shaped *Toxic Grafity* were rekindled later in life. Both Vague and Diboll make connections between punk and the pre-existing counterculture. For Nicholas Bullen, however, punk initially appeared as the proverbial 'year zero', with fanzines providing him the means to find like minds and experiment with ideas. By the time he had left school, Bullen had produced and co-produced a number of fanzines, formulating an aesthetic that he transferred to the musical onslaught of Napalm Death. As for Richard Cabut, his fanzine – *Kick* (1979–82) – proved integral to developing a 'positive punk' based on a premise of 'individuality, creativity, rebellion'.[37] In time, such ideas fed into what became 'goth'. Here, however, Cabut explains why such a conception of punk seemed necessary in the context of the early 1980s. Finally, Clare Wadd reflects on punk's influence on an 'indie culture' that held fast to notions of doing it yourself. Wadd's own fanzine (*Kvatch*) covered the gamut of mid-1980s post-punk culture, providing a 'way in' to the local scene and informing the modus operandi that later helped forge Sarah Records.

The objective of these five chapters is to maintain a dialogue between scholars and practitioners, to cross the lines and develop a history that transcends any divide between practice, experience and interpretation. As with the more analytical chapters, the contributions of Vague, Diboll *et al.* should be read in conjunction with each other: part of a historical mosaic designed to bring clarity of understanding from a range of experiences and contexts.

Lastly, Part IV – 'Global Communications' – looks beyond the UK to consider zine cultures in the USA, Germany and the Netherlands. S. Alexander Reed examines the influence and development of *RE/Search* from San Francisco, a publication that branded itself a subcultural archive and reference guide. As with Britain's *Vague* and *Rapid Eye Movement*, the zine evolved into a compendium, casting its founders V. Vale and Andrea Juno as subcultural archivists, recording and collating hidden cultures and alternative practices in ways that legitimised and informed participants while simultaneously documenting a subterranean history. By contrast, Kirsty Lohman and Karl Siebengartner concentrate on Europe. Where Lohman uses *Raket*, produced in Rotterdam between 1979 and 1980, to expose the contested nature of punk's cultural politics, Siebengartner demonstrates the extent to which Munich's fanzines were integral to the formation of punk identities and the maintenance of local punk scenes. To finish, Laura Cofield moves us forward to riot grrrl, delving into the Fales Library collection to examine how the movement's fanzines negotiated and challenged issues of body politics in a way that collapsed boundaries between the personal and political. Beyond the music, the word and the practice was essential, allowing zines to provide a perfect medium for criticism, self-examination, self-expression and communication.

Taken all together, and in keeping with the Subcultures Network's aim to broker cross-disciplinary discussion, the chapters included here bring varied perspectives to the practice, process and politics of punk-related fanzines. There are limitations: questions of class and race are but touched upon and warrant far greater attention. Part IV, 'Global Communications', is but the proverbial tip of the iceberg. Non-punk scenes also generated fanzines of equal and distinct interest. But despite this, and although a historical outlook predominates, the book hopes to provide context for a wider zine culture that continues to be vibrant and transnational.[38] The aim is to reveal the value of cultural agency and to demonstrate how youth cultures provide space for formative political expression. While scholars have long discussed what youth cultures signify or suggest from the outside, fanzines allow us to discover cultural meanings engendered from within. Historians, in particular, have not yet shown willing to tap into such a valuable resource. In the spirit of our subject, therefore, we decided to do it ourselves.

## Notes

1  *Sniffin' Glue*, 1 (1976).
2  Matthew Worley, 'Punk, Politics and British (Fan)zines, 1976–84: "While the world was dying, did you wonder why?"', *History Workshop Journal*, 79:1 (2015), 76–106.
3  Jon Savage, 'Diary entry', 8 December 1976, *England's Dreaming: Sex Pistols and Punk Rock* (London: Faber & Faber, 1991), pp. 279–80.
4  *48 Thrills* was produced by Adrian Thrills, *Bondage* by Shane McGowan, *Shy Talk* by Steve Burke, *Gun Rubber* by Paul Bower and Adi Newton.
5  In *Gun Rubber*, 5 (1977), p. 20, Rat Scabies of The Damned called London's *Rock On* the 'W.H. Smith of punk rock'. Some zines were given away free, but most sold at a low cost of between 5p and 50p.

6  For extracts, see Tom Vague, *The Great British Mistake: Vague, 1977–92* (Edinburgh: AK Press, 1994).

7  See Simon Dwyer (ed.), *Rapid Eye*, vols 1–2 (London: Annihilation Press, 1989–92). A third volume was published by Creation Books in 1995.

8  *The Eklektik*, 2 (1982); *Adventures in Reality*, G (1981); *White Stuff*, 4 and 6 (1977). These were produced, respectively, by Andy Palmer, Alan Rider and Sandy Robertson.

9  Some poetry zines included *Another Day Another Word* (Mick Turpinl), *Blaze* (Janine Booth), *Cool Notes* (Richard Edwards), *Molotov Comics* (Steven Wells), *Stand Up and Spit* (Tim Wells) and *Tirana Thrash* (John Baine).

10 For Crass, see Richard Cross, 'The Hippies Now Wear Black: Crass and the Anarcho-Punk Movement, 1977–84', *Socialist History*, 26 (2004), 25–44; George Berger, *The Story of Crass* (London: Omnibus, 2006).

11 The spelling of 'graffiti' changed with each issue – e.g. Graffitti, Grafitty, Grafity and Graffity.

12 Those zines listed were produced by Russell Dunbar, Lee Gibson, Rob Challice, Graham Burnett, Ian Rawes, Andy Martin and Mike Diboll.

13 *London's Outrage*, 1 and 2 (1976–77).

14 *The Secret Public*, 1 (1978).

15 Raymond Williams, *The Long Revolution* (London: Pelican, 1961); *Marxism and Literature* (Oxford: Oxford University Press, 1977); *Guttersnipe*, 1–7 (1978–79) and 2:1 (1980). A BBC *Open Door* documentary was broadcast about the fanzine in 1980.

16 Williams, *The Long Revolution*, pp. 63–5.

17 Nancy Fraser, 'Rethinking the Public Sphere: A Contribution to the Critique of Actually Existing Democracy', *Social Text*, 25–6 (1990), 56–80.

18 *Sniffin' Glue*, 3½, 1976, p. 4.

19 *Sniffin' Glue*, 5, 1976, p. 2.

20 Teal Triggs, *Fanzines* (London: Thames & Hudson, 2010), p. 18; Stephen Duncombe, *Notes from the Underground: Zines and the Politics of Alternative Culture* (Bloomington, IN: Microcosm Publishing, 2008 edn), pp. 15–17; Roger Sabin and Teal Triggs (eds), *Below Critical Radar: Fanzines and Alternative Comics from 1976 to Now* (Hove: Slab-O-Concrete, 2000); Chris Atton, *Alternative Media* (London: Sage, 2002); Fredric Wertham, *The World of Fanzines* (Carbondale, IL: Southern Illinois Press, 1973).

21 This is not to suggest punk-related fanzines were the *only* zines to reflect this. Such an observation could be made in relation to fanzines across a range of subject areas and timescales.

22 Nigel Fountain, *Underground – London's Alternative Press, 1966–74* (London: Comedia, 1988); Jeff Nuttall, *Bomb Culture* (London: Paladin, [1968] 1970); Peter Stansill and David Zane Mairowitz (eds), *BAMN (By Any Means Necessary): Outlaw Manifestos and Ephemera, 1965–70* (London: Penguin, 1971).

23 *Anarchy in the UK*, 1, 1976.

24  Jon Savage, 'Every Home Should Print One', *Sounds*, 10 September 1977, pp. 26–7; Tony Parsons, 'Glue Scribe Speaks Out', *NME*, 12 February 1977, p. 12. Parsons' early support for fanzines was short-lived, see Julie Burchill and Tony Parsons, *The Boy Looked at Johnny: The Obituary of Rock 'n' Roll* (London: Faber & Faber, 1987 edn), pp. 36–7.

25  Triggs, *Fanzines*, pp. 16–17; 'Alphabet Soup: Reading British Fanzines', *Visible Language*, 29:1 (1995), 72–87; 'Scissors and Glue: Punk Fanzines and the Creation of a DIY Aesthetic', *Journal of Design History*, 19:1 (2006), 69–83. See also Tricia Henry, 'Punk and Avant Garde Art', *Journal of Popular Culture*, 17:4 (1984), 30–6; Russ Bestley and Alex Ogg, *The Art of Punk* (London: Omnibus Press, 2012); Johan Kugelberg and Jon Savage (eds), *Punk: An Aesthetic* (New York: Rizzoli, 2012); Jon Savage, *Punk 45: Original Punk Rock Singles Cover Art* (London: Soul Jazz, 2013).

26  Dick Hebdige, *Subcultures: The Meaning of Style* (London: Routledge, 2007 edn), pp. 111–12.

27  Dave Laing, *One Chord Wonders: Power and Meaning in Punk Rock* (Milton Keynes: Open University Press, 1985), pp. 14–15.

28  David Hesmondhalgh, 'Post-Punk's Attempt to Democratise the Music Industry: The Success and Failure of Rough Trade', *Popular Music*, 16:3 (1998), 25–74; Alex Ogg, *Independent Days: The Story of UK Independent Record Labels* (London: Cherry Red, 2009).

29  Duncombe, *Notes From the Underground*, pp. 6–21.

30  Worley, 'Punk, Politics and British (Fan)zines', 76–106; Matt Grimes and Tim Wall, 'Punk Zines: Symbols of Defiance From the Print to the Digital Age', in Subcultures Network (ed.), *Fight Back: Punk, Politics and Resistance* (Manchester: Manchester University Press, 2015), pp. 287–303.

31  Brett Lashua and Sara Cohen, '"A Fanzine of Record": Merseysound and Mapping Liverpool's Post-Punk Popular Musicscapes', *Punk & Post-Punk*, 1:1 (2012), 87–104; Paula Guerra and Pedro Quintela, 'Spreading the Message! Fanzines and the Punk Scene in Portugal', *Punk & Post-Punk*, 3:3 (2014), 203–24.

32  Lisa Darm (ed.), *The Riot Grrrl Collection* (New York: City University of New York, 2013).

33  Jessica Rosenberg and Gitana Garofalo, 'Riot Grrrl: Revolutions From Within', *Signs: Journal of Women in Culture and Society*, 23:3 (1998), 809–41; Ellen Riordan, 'Commodified Agents and Empowered Girls: Consuming and Producing Feminism', *Journal of Communication Inquiry*, 25:3 (2001), 279–97; Anita Harris, 'gURL Scenes and Grrrl Zines: The Regulation and Resistance of Girls in Late Modernity', *Identities*, 75 (2003), 38–56; Jennifer Sinor, 'Another Form of Crying: Girl Zines as Life Writing', *Prose Studies: History, Theory, Criticism*, 26:1 (2003), 240–64; Feona Attwood, 'Sluts and Riot Grrrls: Female Identity and Sexual Agency', *Journal of Gender Studies*, 16:3 (2007), 233–47; Sara Marcus, *Girls to the Front: The True Story of the Riot Grrrl Revolution* (London: Harper Perennial, 2010); Kevin Dunn and May Summer Farnsworth, '"We are the Revolution": Riot Grrrl Press Girl Empowerment and DIY Self-Publishing', *Women's Studies* 41:2 (2012), 136–57; Mimi Thi Nguyen,

'Riot Grrrl, Race and Revival', *Women and Performance: a Journal of Feminist Theory*, 22:2–3 (2012), 173–96.

34 Laura Cofield and Lucy Robinson, '"The Opposite of the Band": Fangrrrling, Feminism and Sexual Dissidence', *Textual Practice*, 30:6 (2016), 1071–88. See also Anna Feigenbaum, 'Written in the Mud: (Proto)Zine-Making and Autonomous Media at the Greenham Common Women's Peace Camp', *Feminist Media Studies*, 13:1 (2013), 1–13.

35 There are too many zine archives or archival deposits to list here, but to give a sense we can point to the Birmingham Music Archive, the University of Iowa, Washington Provisions Library and Olympia Zine Library, the Archiv der Jugendkulturen (Berlin), the Fanzinothèque de Poitiers and the Forgotten Zine Archive in Dublin. But see also fanzine deposits at the Liverpool John Moores University and the London College of Communication.

36 Sarah Baker (ed.), *Preserving Popular Music Heritage: Do-it-yourself, Do-it-together* (New York: Routledge, 2015); Catherine Strong, 'Shaping the Past of Popular Music: Memory, Forgetting and Documenting', in Andy Bennett and Steve Waksman (eds), *The SAGE Book of Popular Music* (London: Sage, 2015), pp. 418–34; Sarah Barker and Alison Huber, 'Saving "Rubbish": Preserving Popular Music's Material Culture in Amateur Archives and Museums', in Sara Cohen, Robert Knifton, Marion Leonard and Les Roberts (eds), *Sites of Popular Music Heritage: Memories, Histories, Places* (London: Routledge, 2014), pp. 112–24.

37 *Kick*, 3, 1980, p. 2.

38 See, for example, Red Chidgey, 'Reassess Your Weapons: The Making of Feminist Memory in Young Women's 'Zines', *Women's History Review*, 22:4 (2013), 658–72. See also www.thedebrief.co.uk/things-to-do/books/girls-zines-20160262294.

**- I -**

# Going underground: process and place

# - 1 -

# Doing it ourselves: countercultural and alternative radical publishing in the decade before punk

JESS BAINES, TONY CREDLAND AND MARK PAWSON

Alternative do-it-yourself (DIY) publishing in the UK is often assumed to have started with photocopiers and punks. However, counterculture and grass-roots movements from the mid-1960s onwards generated an explosion of alternative 'not for profit' print and publications, frequently produced by amateurs using basic technologies. Much of this was consciously infused with notions of autonomy and anti-specialism, themes that were to continue or to re-materialise through punk. We do not mean to deny the sheer creativity and distinctiveness of punk culture; but by drawing attention to examples of alternative DIY print cultures that preceded, co-existed with and, at times, intermingled with punk, we hope to constructively complicate the history of fanzine production and the DIY narrative associated with it. We do this by examining three aspects of these 'other' DIY print cultures: the production practices of a range of grass-roots and radical publications; the processes of various artists' publications and activities; and the development of community or 'self-help' radical printshops. Firstly, however, we shall outline the wider cultural, technological and discursive context that enabled these publishing activities to take place.

The counterculture of the 1960s and early 1970s is typically associated with what Michelle Rau has called the 'aboveground underground press', exemplified by such papers as *International Times*, *Friends/Frendz*, *Oz* and, perhaps, *Black Dwarf*.[1] Numerous other marginal and ephemeral publications also proliferated, covering a wide range of 'alternative' positions and interests, from *Gandalf's Garden*, to *Hapt, Hustler* and *Moul/Mole Express*, to name just a few.[2] Most of those involved in this new wave of publishing were amateurs with little if any experience in newspaper or magazine production.[3] While amateurs have long produced small publications, we hope here to locate these publications within particular cultural contexts and emergent 'structures of feeling'.[4] In turn, the publications and the ways in which they were produced significantly contributed to the making of those cultures.

The experimental and creative energies generated by the counterculture stimulated DIY or self-sufficient activity across the expanding field of the alternative left: from 'happenings' to free schools and communes. Within the pages of the underground/alternative press there is clear evidence of how DIY or 'self-help' activities provided a significant component of countercultural sensibilities and practice. 'How To' articles, sharing and 'demystifying' uncommon knowledge were a regular feature and all manner of self-help handbooks could be obtained by mail order or found in alternative bookshops; how to build things, grow things, fix things, take or make drugs, meditate, print and squat.[5] There were also articles and handbooks about how to navigate the unavoidable parts of 'the system', notably the law and the welfare state. It was not just that people could do it for themselves, where possible outside of 'the system' of experts and institutions, but that others could also do it to build 'the alternative society'.

While the reasons for any type of DIY activity can often be cast as necessity (costs, access), there were cultural and political resonances to do-it-yourself, from the individualistic hippy-shtick of 'freedom to do your own thing' to the more collectivist understanding better characterised as doing it (for) ourselves – both of which, in different ways, linked to notions of autonomy and self-determination. Politically, the do-it-yourself/ourselves impetus connected to the rallying cry of May 1968, 'autogestion' (self-management), and Kristin Ross's point that one of central themes of 1968 was 'to contest the domain of the expert, to disrupt the system of naturalised spheres of competence'.[6] This especially related to the distinction between intellectual and manual labour: who has to dig and who gets to decide. We can see this as another element contributing towards a countercultural negation of 'separations', for example between work and play, between the amateur and professional, between art and life. Creatively, it contributed towards new kinds of artistic democracy through the deployment of certain rules, arbitrary orderings or systems of 'chance'.

In his book *Alternative Media*, Chris Atton contrasted the once conventional 'communications circuit'[7] – comprising distinct stages or silos of author, publisher, printer, distributor, bookseller and reader – with that of 'alternative media', whereby these functions are frequently conflated. This is a given for fanzines of course, part of their distinction, but the disruption of discrete roles was also characteristic of earlier countercultural publishing.

At this point, though covered in other publications, we should note that some methods of shared/collective editorship and rotating production were previously a feature of a rather different type of much earlier amateur self-publishing; namely the science fiction and fantasy fanzines that emerged in the 1930s.[8] Aficionados of these genres created their own fanzines as a forum for discussion, directly communicating with each other, sharing opinions and information. They were active fans, not just passive consumers; writing, indexing, publishing and attending conventions.[9] They also developed novel, practical methods of making and distributing publications. *Fantasy Rotator*, for example, started in 1954, was published every three weeks and had a board of thirteen editors who took turns in compiling the fanzine, sharing the workload, creating a community and avoiding a dominant editorial voice.[10] Many fanzines clustered together in 'Amateur Press Associations' (APAs) coordinated by a 'Central Mailer' (CM). Each member would send in their contributions for numbered APA mailings, fanzines, articles or 'Letters of Comment', which would then be collated by the CM into a single package and sent to everyone on the mailing list. Participation was essential, members who failed to contribute regularly would be cautioned and face expulsion.[11] Similar methods of working emerged in the quite distinct realms of radical artistic and social movement self-publishing. Needless to say, the adoption of certain practices means different things at different times, in different contexts and inevitably for different participants.

A word about our choices here: we have not selected on the basis of pre-established 'significance' but our own interests, biographies and personal collections. This may seem idiosyncratic, or run the risk of being unrepresenta-tive, yet we feel that between these diverse examples many relevant bases are covered. Our examples tend to fit within the realm of 'oppositional culture'. We do not address the self-publishing activity associated with music fan cultures that were also part of the wider alternative mêlée of the period. Our chapter is but *one* pre-history for readers to consider, albeit one we believe offers more than a few salient connections.

## Provocations for change

The Provo movement that emerged in Amsterdam in the mid-1960s brought together a refreshed form of anarchic politics with humour and art-inspired happenings that aimed to gather maximum publicity through a profusion of non-violent 'provocations'. The explosion of self-publishing that occurred under the wider banner of Provo was vast, with over 40 publications between 1965 and 1968, among them *Image*, *Ontbijt op Bed* and *Lynx*. Another 15 publications came out of Belgium (including *Revo*); yet more were produced in Germany, Sweden, Italy and the USA.[12] These often mimicked the leading Amsterdam magazine *Provo*, an A4 vertically folded (30 × 10.5 cm) format. They similarly satirised the authorities, covered anarchist politics and shared radical news from across Europe, as well as showcasing experimental poetry and writing. Provo attempted to break out of conventional political networks, creating 'situations'. In issue 12 of their magazine, they described themselves and their intended audiences as follows:

> PROVO is a monthly sheet for anarchists, provos, beatniks, pleiners, scissors-grinders, jailbirds, simple simon stylites, magicians, pacifists, potato-chip chaps, charlatans, philosophers, germ-carriers, grand masters of the queen's horse, happeners, vegetarians, syndicalists, santy clauses, kindergarten teachers, agitators, pyromaniacs, assistant assistants, scratchers and syphilitics, secret police, and other riff-raff.

> PROVO has something against capitalism, communism, fascism, bureaucracy, militarism, professionalism, dogmatism, and authoritarianism.[13]

In 1965, as a precursor to their magazine, Amsterdam Provo distributed single-sheet *PROVOcations*. These attacked the police, the royal family, criticised the traditional left, invited participation in 'happenings' and promoted direct action more generally.[14] Through their instigation of large gatherings and media attention, the movement attracted anarchists, students and Nozems (a working class subculture similar to Teddy Boys).[15] The first issue of the *Provo* magazine was immediately confiscated by police as it included an article from 1900 called 'The Practical Anarchist' that encouraged the use of dynamite as social reform, accompanied by toy gun 'caps' to emphasise the point.[16] This intervention by the state increased the notoriety of the movement and it saw a dramatic increase in numbers attending their gatherings, thereby re-enforcing the provocation intended.

Amsterdam *Provo* magazines were initially printed on a stencil duplicator for issues 1 to 6, in runs of 450–5,000. These were sold cheaply on the streets, enabling the group to buy more paper and possibly contribute small amounts towards the court fines of those arrested at their many pranks.[17] Written contributions in the main came from Roel van Duyn, Robert Jasper Grootveld, Constant Nieuwenhuys, Hans Tuynman and Peter Bronkhorst. Later issues were offset litho-printed and had runs of up to 20,000, finishing with issue 15 in May 1967. The magazine was laid out by amateur designer Rob Stolk. It included basic photographs and illustrations, with the text hand typed, bound and self-distributed at 'happenings'. Commenting on the aesthetics of the magazine, Stolk described how this was shaped by the available technology and their limited resources and skills: 'Swiftly setting text is a difficult task. You always had to search for the right type with the best typewriter. You always wanted to act quickly, so you didn't want to rely on suppliers of professional typography. On the other hand, this is exactly what made it the design of a certain culture. It went against the commercial design of mainstream printed matter that was quite boring and annoying.'[18]

Alongside the magazine, the group continued to produce *PROVOcations*, including the 'White bicycle plan' that aimed to rid Amsterdam of all cars

**1.1**  *Provo*, 2 (1965)

and pollution, replacing them with free bicycles and electric powered cars.[19] Other 'White plans' focused on the squatting of empty buildings, sharing childcare, the legalisation of marijuana and the building of contraception clinics aimed at improving women's health. Although often confrontationally introduced at the time, the ideas of the Provo movement went on to influence Dutch society throughout the 1970s. This happened directly via the Kabouter electoral movement (an offshoot of Provo) that aimed to bring many of the 'White plans' to fruition through local government.[20] As Stolk remarked, 'Provo stopped but the ideas were still there, the newspapers took notice, there was a voice that wasn't there before.'[21] Conversely, of course, it may be argued that through incorporation into the mainstream, counter-hegemonic ideas and culture become politically neutralised and 'sold back' to the public.

By the time Provo ceased to exist as a movement, a flourishing counterculture had become established in many parts of Western Europe and the USA. In the UK, influenced to a degree by Provo and other radical networks in Europe and North America, a small collective connected to the English Diggers started a DIY hand-printed magazine called *Hapt*.[22] This was produced between December 1967 and May 1971, running for 27 issues. It was legal-sized, stencil duplicated, with silk-screened covers and centrespread, printed on rough paper in editions of up to 400. *Hapt* came out every five to six weeks and was distributed for free by post, at alternative bookshops like Compendium, and in radical spaces like the Bit Information Service in London.

The UK edition was written and coordinated by a small team of seven, initially based in London before later moving to set up communes in Bournemouth and Stroud. They described themselves in the 1970 Bitman *Directory of Communes* as a 'decentralised, mobile printing collective at present operating from addresses in Hampshire and Gloucestershire. Functions through close contact with associate brothers and sisters living separate from the tribe or out of the country ... The tribe's project is expansion and contribution to the emergence of a unified revolutionary people who will come together, live together and fight together for the creation of an alternative.'[23] There were sister Hapt communes in Holland (where the magazine made a point of not crediting the editors),[24] Argentina, Belgium and Switzerland. At the Cambridge Digger Conference of 1968, the network of Hapt collectives also proposed a 'postal commune' of publications, collectively written and produced by readers.[25]

*Hapt* (along with *IT, OZ and Friends*) was an early member of the Underground Press Syndicate (UPS),[26] later known as the Alternative Press Syndicate (APS) and described as 'a coalition of independent papers growing out of the mushrooming underground communities in the USA, Canada and England.

**1.2** *Hapt*, 27 (1971)

[Their] purpose is to experiment with new forms of news media or with expanding old forms.'[27] The syndicate provided some of the content and broadened the scope of *Hapt* beyond its own political thoughts and interviews, reprinting texts on the Situationist International, the Black Panthers, the Dutch Kabouter and Provo movements, as well as the original Diggers Manifesto of 1649. It also covered issues such as 'the female orgasm', parent and child relationships, LSD trips and personal recollections of the Roundhouse Gathering of Communes (2 August 1970).[28] The magazine was described by King Mob as 'exceptionally articulate' in terms of its theories, while noting that attempts at living in communes 'ha[d] not been conspicuously successful.'[29]

*Hapt* promoted a DIY culture synonymous with their commune lifestyle, encouraging writing from their readership and sharing knowledge about their means of production through a comprehensive description of the screen print-making process. A spread in issue 26 stated: 'Free Press: How to make a cheap expendable paper (like this one) to give out free in the street. You need: access to a typer, duplicator, stencils, ink and paper. A screen to run off the colour work – make this yourself.'[30] They went on to list all the products needed, describing in detail and illustrating with images the process of making a small print run. Their letters pages show how readers were then inspired to produce their own. For example, *Hapt* offered David Webster of *Street Comix* 'the vision that people could run off cheap comic strips on duplicators and say things to each other that they could not express otherwise.'[31] The collective were also explicit in why political movements needed their own media, espousing a clear DIY ethic:

> The only way to know what other people are doing in the world is to act in it yourself ... The best motivated communication/information sources deflect [*sic*] real feeling and movement and expression – Communication is not a consumer wordmash – ads, newstories, reports, pictures – but SELF EXPRESSION ... AND THE FREEDOM OF EXPRESSION OF EVERYBODY IS REVOLUTION ... make your own!'[32]

Although limited in distribution, publications like *Hapt* aimed to have a wider influence on underground culture, be it through UPS distribution of stories or by emphasising the simplicity and therefore possibility of self-production. The magazine's run ended at issue 27 with a disappointed sense that the radical underground movement had failed to effect significant social change. The collective announced they would be 'dropping the idea of a settled, communal base for the tribe and become a nomadic Earth People.'[33]

But while *Hapt*'s demise was partly indicative of shrinking optimism and ambition for the 'alternatives' of the countercultural imagination, it by no means signalled the end of experiments in self-production. The autonomous living that *Hapt* espoused and practiced continued to be the subject of various countercultural publications, including discussion about alternative technologies. The *Survival Scrapbooks*, for example, were a series of six books published by the Unicorn Bookshop in Brighton between 1972 and 1974.[34] The series was initiated by Stefan Szczelkun. Dissatisfied with his experience at architecture school and inspired by Buckminster Fuller and John Cage, Szczelkun resolved to 'start from scratch', creating three *Scrapbooks* on 'basic life supports': shelter, food and energy.[35] *Survival Scrapbook 5: Energy*, is clearly self-produced and prepared by the original cut-and-paste method of scissors and glue. The text is in the author's handwriting, diagrams are hand-drawn and illustrations liberally borrowed from other books. Pages are unnumbered and chapter titles are replaced with 'information areas' identified by symbols.[36] The book examines how renewable energy sources – sun, wind, fire, water – were used in earlier societies and could currently be harnessed. There is information on low-tech equipment with detailed construction plans, and sections on muscle power, both animal and human, meditation, and maps showing the location and extent of renewable energy sources in the UK. This content is interspersed with extracts from Raoul Vaneigem's *Revolution of Everyday Life*, Guy Debord's *Society of the Spectacle*, a William Burroughs essay, the 'Whoever you voted for … The Government got in' poster, and a detailed illustration by Clifford Harper – a utopian vision of a self-sufficient, off-grid house. The scrapbook concept extends to the physical construction of the book. Pages can easily be removed from the perfect (glued) binding, they are hole-punched ready to be put into a ring-binder and blank pages are included for the reader's additions. The normally passive reader is encouraged to become an active user, to edit and rearrange the contents to suit themselves, liberating the information confined between the covers. 'Publish your own sources of inspiration', Szczelkun writes. 'A network of freely associating, investigating, experimenting groups is difficult to hit. Keep it moving.'[37]

Probably more familiar to a punk audience, Suburban Press was set up in Croydon, South London, by Jeremy Brook, Nigel Edwards and Jamie Reid in 1970. It operated as a community printshop and produced a magazine, also called *Suburban Press*. The publication was one of a number of locally orientated countercultural and radical magazines produced in that period. These included *Mother Grumble* in the North East, *Grass Eye* in Manchester, *Ned/Nell Gate* in West London, *Islington Gutter Press* in North London, *Alarm* in Swansea, *Fapto* in Margate, *Ops Veda* in Sheffield, *Aberdeen People's Press* and *Leeds Other Paper*, to name a few.

**1.3** *Survival Scrapbook 5: Energy* (1974) © Stefan Szczelkun

The front cover of *Suburban Press* issue 6 (1974) shows the towering office blocks of Croydon town centre, surrounded by hundreds of Letraset arrows which appear modern and purposeful, but closer inspection reveals them to be fractured and disintegrating.[38] Inside, 'The complete sordid story of small town politics and business ... THE DEMOCRATIC CHARADE EXPOSED' is a well-researched 16-page diatribe examining the web of connections between councillors, council officers, developers, Rotary Club members and local businessmen. The lengthy article is punctuated on every alternate page by imagery, the sequencing of which is deliberate. 'I was trying to use visuals to make a lot of what was quite turgid text, but full of great ideas, much more simplistic', Reid recalled.[39] These visuals included montages of press clippings and images taken from council brochures, some unaltered, others recaptioned. An aerial photograph of the town centre is ominously labelled an 'Urban Control Zone', détournement *n'est-ce pas*? There's also some artful drawings and carefully composed collages – for example, Delacroix's armed Figure of Liberty on a barricade is relocated from the 1830 July Revolution in France to 1970s South London, leading the people against a backdrop of towering office blocks. Some of these images, created by an uncredited Jamie Reid, would later be reused and reworked for his college friend Malcolm McLaren's company Glitterbest on record sleeves and publicity materials for the Sex Pistols.[40] Suburban Press sold up in 1975. A book collecting all six issues of *Suburban Press* (which reached a circulation of 5,000 copies) was planned but never materialised, partly because of concerns over libel. As they said ironically in the final issue: 'Still never mind. There's better things to do than write and print pamphlets.'[41]

Suburban Press's statement would probably have been contested by at least some participants of our next example. For them, autonomous publishing was a form of activism.[42] *Shrew* was a magazine born of the early Women's Liberation Movement (WLM) in London. Small publications, giving voice to concerns and experiences disavowed or invisible in both mainstream women's magazines and the counterculture, were a central component of the emergent WLM, part of creating a feminist counter-public sphere.[43] The movement, which began to form in the late 1960s and early 1970s in the UK, had a DIY ethos at its core. Feminists set up their own women's centres, refuges and helplines in squats and backrooms, attempted to wrest women's health issues away from experts (and men), and much more besides.[44] For women seeking to define themselves and their struggles in their own right, on their own terms, 'doing it ourselves' was in many ways a political and practical necessity as well as a source of autonomy and empowerment. *Shrew* exemplified this.

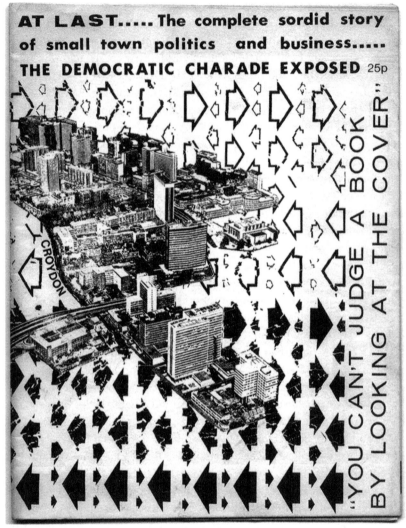

**1.4**  *Suburban Press*, 6 (1974)

The magazine ran regularly between 1969 and 1974, had a circulation of about 5,000 and sold very cheaply either by mail order or in women's centres and sympathetic bookshops. It was the magazine of the London Women's Liberation Workshop, a collectivist federation made up of smaller autonomous local women's liberation groups. Many were 'consciousness-raising' groups, with their own character, agendas and affiliations. Each issue of the magazine was produced by a different local or special interest group that had total freedom in all aspects: content, layout, images and overall design. There was a *Shrew* collective of representatives committed to helping with the production. Their meetings were open to 'anyone who is interested and prepared to learn about the way *Shrew* functions'.[45] As the production of each issue was rotated, the contents and aesthetics of the magazine were incredibly diverse. An issue might contain unsigned personal testimonials about housework, motherhood, sex and relationships or cover wider global topics, as can be seen with subtitles such as 'Under The Gun: Third World Women'. A 1974 edition includes individual narratives about 'early consciousness of oppression', diary-type entries about daily life, the psychological experience of getting a sexually transmitted disease and a piece about going back to work.[46] An issue in 1973, the most colourful yet, with a yellow and red cover, consisted almost entirely of cartoons. The sole (short) article was called 'myths about women', with the subtitles 'how oppressive is cinderella' and 'what are the political intentions of snow white'. The back cover was given over to a 'Pig Identification Chart' showing ten types of male chauvinist, including 'the revolutionary runt (porcus tedius)' and 'the shrink pig (psychoporcus)'.[47]

The appearance of most of the magazines is distinctly amateurish and all of the issues of the first year of *Shrew* are stencil duplicated. While production was a shared task within the groups responsible, it is notable that an early issue contains the plea: 'Please could all WLM women learn to type if they don't know already. Otherwise the few who can become the typists'.[48] From the end of 1970, *Shrew* started to be printed at various left-wing offset litho presses. However, in the summer issue of 1974, a notice stated: 'Let's print *Shrew* ourselves next time. A feminist press is forming. Send money and willing hands to … '[49] In fact, the next issue (Autumn) was printed at another left press. The new feminist press was not yet up and running and *Shrew* briefly halted after this, with a two-year gap followed by single issues over the next three years. These three were printed at women's printshops that had started in the interim (Women in Print and Moss Side Women's Press), the last printed and produced by the Feminism and Non-Violence Study Group. One woman described the rationale: 'we found that there was hardly any material to study, so we decided to write our own magazine *Shrew*. It was written, edited, typed, pasted up, printed, marketed and distributed by our group. It seemed like the more we tried the more we could do'.[50] *Shrew*, as a title known within the women's movement, provided a vehicle for the group to disseminate their ideas and information.[51] The above quote reinforces the sense of empowerment associated by feminists in 'doing it for themselves'.

## Assembling, collating, mailing

Avant-garde art and experimental literature grew exponentially in the 1960s.[52] If the above examples existed on the radical fringes of the wider political field, then those that followed existed in the equivalent space of the cultural field. Artists and writers whose work was too challenging for commercial galleries and publishing houses frequently worked together to create their own autonomous publications. These, in turn, allowed unconstrained freedom of expression. In the late 1960s, a particular type of publication emerged, known as collective or assembling magazines. Although these were distinctly non-fan literature, and in some ways remote from ostensibly popular culture, the way in which they were produced echoed that of the sci-fi/fantasy fanzines mentioned in the introduction.

Assembling publications were initiated when an editor/compiler chose a title, decided a theme, regularity, page size and number of copies, then posted invitations to friends, co-conspirators, cultural workers, inspirational writers, artists and like-minded small publications, inviting them to send, for example, 150 printed copies of their original work and giving them complete freedom to decide on content, layout, printing method and paper type. Once all contributions were received, the editor would design a cover, bind the pages together and send out finished copies to all participants. Everything was included, nothing was rejected. This method of creating a publication dismantled the traditional hierarchical structure of publishing, challenging the need for separate, specialised roles for publishers, editors, contributors and writers. Assembling publications rethought how a publication is made and established a more democratic model where the creative work, physical labour and production costs were shared between everyone involved.[53]

*Assembling, a collection of otherwise unpublishable manuscripts* (1970) was initiated by Richard Kostelanetz and Henry Korn in New York as a repository for avant garde art and literature which the 'editorial-industrial complex' would never invest in.[54] Contributors were invited to send 1,000 copies of their work, on 1–4 sheets of $11 \times 8\frac{1}{2}$ inch paper. The contributions – including fiction, poetry, drawings, sign language, performance scores, visual poetry, sculpture plans, a full page hand-typed manuscript and a chocolate smear – were bound in alphabetical order. The editors added an introduction outlining the purpose of the publication together with biographies and addresses of participants. All 42 contributors received three copies of the finished publication, creating an instant audience. *Assembling* was an ambitious, pioneering project that appeared annually until 1981. Assembling publications show their workings and expose the process of their creation; anyone who has seen one or read the above explanation would, if so inclined, have enough knowledge to start one.

The NYCS Weekly Breeder (New York Correspondence School) was a magazine that sometimes appeared regularly, sometimes erratically, to showcase a tight-knit group of artists. Fluxus artist Ken Friedman began The NYCS Weekly Breeder in San Francisco in 1971 as a couple of quirky, playful pages of collaged information and images mailed to other artists. It was passed on to new editors several times and evolved into a small stapled magazine for participants active in the mail art network.[55] With a strong Dada influence and attitude, pseudonyms were de rigueur and dating of issues unreliable. Buster Cleveland compiled The NYCS Weekly Breeder, Vol. 1 No. 1, 1968 from 1976 and published it in 1978 as an edition of 100 copies.[56] The cover image of an insouciant William S. Burroughs had a real safety pin stuck through his cheek, establishing a counterculture connection between the 1950s beats and 1970s punks. The contents included high-quality offset black-and-white reproductions of collages, drawings, photographs and rubber stamps. Two contributors from the UK provided provocative, controversial work. One of these was an impression from the ADOLf Hitler fan CluB rubber stamp, which Pauline Smith had used on her envelopes since 1974 and intended as 'an analogy for pre-Thatcher British Governments'.[57] The other UK contribution was a costly full-colour photocopied page reproducing a collage by Genesis P-Orridge comprising a postcard of the Queen and Prince Phillip with an added detail from a porn magazine. It's similar to the five postcards with 'indecent designs or images' for which P-Orridge was successfully prosecuted and fined £100 for sending through the British postal system in 1976.[58] Of course, Nazi symbols, collaged photographs of the Queen and porn imagery were also used on some early punk clothes, record sleeves and advertising posters. Deliberately intended to shock, challenging social norms and confronting authority, punk's images reached a much larger audience than The NYCS Weekly Breeder, not least because they were also widely covered in the national mainstream media.

## Printing it (for) ourselves

Having ranged across various publications, we now turn to the radical printshops of the period, many of which actively invited their users to get involved in the process. The explosion of the countercultural press of the 1960s and early 1970s has been associated with combined developments in reprographic technology: Letraset, typesetting, electric typewriters and especially offset litho. 'Offset was freedom', declared Nigel Fountain in his history of Britain's underground press.[59] Offset made production cheaper, faster, more flexible and thus amenable to the amateur creative. However, as we have seen – and is clearly evident in Greg Kaplan's survey of the underground press – many publications were produced using old stencil duplicators.[60] Furthermore, in the UK at least, rarely did any of the new countercultural publications produced by litho actually have their own printing press. If they wanted litho printing they often had to use 'straight' printers and ran into numerous financial, legal and cultural problem; problems often reported in those same publications.[61] At a 1970 alternative press national conference in Manchester, the focus was explicitly on the difficulties of printers and distribution.[62]

There had been some alternative possibilities for 'getting it printed', usually short-lived, such as Open Design in Liverpool.[63] The new Arts Labs occasionally had a printing press, often belonging to an individual, though what they could do was limited. The organised left, from anarchists to Trotskyists and the Communist Party, had by necessity their own presses, and were used to a degree, as were the old printers of the pacifist movement. There were also short-lived presses set up by the more radical elements of the peace movement, such as Stanhope Press and Pirate Press. Screen-printed poster-making aside, which has its own story, it seems that DIY printing – beyond duplicating – was only occasionally folded into the countercultural activities of the 1960s, at least in the UK. It would be another emergent wing of 1960s contestatory culture that began to set up printshops with the express aim of opening access to the means of production: urban community activism.

The above mentioned *Suburban Press* is frequently noted in histories of punk's cultural production, with reference to Jamie Reid's graphic style, situationist influences and so forth. But the publication and printshop of the same name were also part of a loose urban community network.[64] Urban community politics began to attract increasing numbers of usually left-libertarian radicals in the late 1960s and 1970s. It is beyond the remit of this chapter to explore why this was the case, other than to say it was indicative of a rejection of the increasingly narrow and authoritarian agendas of the 'revolutionary left' and, instead, an embrace of what Jim Radford (a key force in the squatting movement of the 1960s) called 'do it yourself politics'.[65] It was DIY because it was about people self-organising and taking matters into their own hands, frequently using varieties of direct action to do so.

The first community printshop was probably Notting Hill Press (NHP) in London, set up in 1968 by two Irish nursing students who abandoned their training to 'join the revolution'; which, for them, was located in the confrontational and creative forces of 'new' urban community activism. Local struggles about housing conditions, redevelopment, police harassment and play space needed a 'community' printing press to communicate; cheap, politically sympathetic and accessible.[66] An ancient A3 offset press from the short-lived Pirate Press was therefore acquired, which the two women learned to use in a 'loaned' space under a homeless hostel, from where NHP was born. Local alternative papers were printed, including *Peoples' News*, the newssheet of the Notting Hill People's Association, as well as *The Hustler*, a radical black paper organised by Courtney Tulloch and Naseem Khan. Numerous other newssheets, leaflets and pamphlets were published, with subjects ranging from single mothers and social security to strikes, squatting, claimants' action and programmes for the new Electric Cinema Club. Local skinheads even came round to do cartoons for leaflets supporting the dustmen's strike.[67] By using the basic resources of the press, people learnt how to do their own artwork and layout, if not the actual printing. Binding and stapling was usually done by hand in the printshop.[68]

Resources of this kind were scarce and NHP soon found itself printing for further afield groups, including *Suburban Press* which, as an ex-member recalled, 'got us into a bit of bother with the police – they advocated blowing up Centrepoint'.[69] NHP supported other groups to start their own local alternative printshop. One of these was Moss Side Press (1970–76) in Manchester, set up on a similar model to provide resources for grass-roots political groups and various strands of the local alternative culture.[70] Although, at both these presses, the idea was to enable local activists to produce their own materials, they were not generally encouraged to actually run the printing press. That came later, as more community printshops started appearing and more ambitious social ideas formed about the empowering value of DIY. Islington Community Press (1972–87), for example, stated: 'we do not do printing for people, we ask them to come and help and learn how to use the equipment themselves ... we want [the press] to be used by local groups who are pushing for more control over their lives and situation'.[71]

There were several such printshops across the country by the mid1970s, usually collectively self-managed, run on a shoestring and loosely aligned to some kind of leftish community activism advocating DIY publishing and printing as part of 'taking control of our lives'. DIY politics, DIY organisation, DIY publishing and printing were all linked together. Significantly, this expanded notion of DIY was also seen as collective; do it ourselves and do it together. In 1974, the first community printshop manual appeared, *Print: How You Can Do It Yourself*, written by Jonathan Zeitlyn. This, the first of several editions (1974, 1975, 1980, 1986, 1992), used each of the printing processes described in the manual and was stapled together by hand. Zeitlyn stressed the social case for printing it yourself: 'we no longer just have to consume we can create what we need ... we can all be writers, printers, publishers as well as readers, in our own neighbourhood, our living rooms or garages'.[72] There was Crest Press, Tyneside Free Press Workshop, Paddington Printshop, Bath Printshop, Lenthall Road Workshop, Union Place Resource Centre, among others. Some, such as Aberdeen People's Press, were was set up in order to produce radical local papers. Material printed included not just the publications of activist and radical groups, but also poetry, comics, gig flyers, local history, even church newsletters – and sometimes zines.[73]

Apart from those with an art school background, the people who joined and even set up these community printshops rarely had prior printing experience; nor did they see it as part of a career. Internally, 'job' functions were loose and tasks shared. The aim was that everyone should learn to do everything.[74] Technology was typically low grade and often acquired through radical networks; second-hand offset presses, dilapidated duplicators and basic screen-printing equipment. The availability of small offset presses was crucial. Although using the same process as the larger machines, they had gained popularity in the 1960s as an 'inplant' printing technology, marketed as an extension of office equipment. Other bits and pieces could be homemade with reclaimed materials from skips and junk shops. For example, printshops often built their own lightboxes and screen-printing tables. Old vacuum cleaners might be stuffed under the latter to create suction to hold the paper in place and the lightboxes doubled as improvised alternatives to make printing plates and stencils.[75] The photocopier did not feature much; they were expensive to acquire and often only through cumbersome lease agreements. At the time, their quality was variable and limited in terms of what could be reproduced. It was also more expensive per copy than small offset litho for longer runs. So while the photocopier is indelibly linked to the advent of DIY printing, these printshops, which mostly faded out as copiers became more genuinely accessible, mediated a fulsome and dynamic scene of alternative self-publishing and printing.[76]

## Getting it out there

Distribution, 'getting it out there', is always contingent on some idea of who and where the audience are. In *Assembling*, distribution was part of the recursive movement between authors and 'compilers'. This publication and *The NYCS Weekly Breeder* were linked to small artistic subcultures, partly defined by their 'mailing' practices. Methods of distribution were shaped by the intent of the publications, but also the available channels. *Provo* was sold on the streets, as were many radical papers and magazines. Alternative/countercultural book-shops, which began popping up in towns and cities during the 1960s and 1970s, were especially crucial for distribution. *Shrew* was distributed via the ad-hoc 'women's centres' of the WLM and its grass-roots conferences and events. Mail order was a persistent method, with small ads placed in other alternative publications. Reaching audiences, especially for those publications that wanted to spread 'messages', was difficult, however, and various groups attempted to address this perennial issue. London's Agitprop collective (formed in 1968) collected and made available radical pamphlets, posters and publica-tions. In 1973, this was taken over as part of the activities of the Rising Free bookshop collective.[77] In 1975, Feminist Books was set up, mainly to distribute feminist pamphlets[78] and, in 1976, the Publications Distribution Co-operative (PDC) began, specifically with the aim of getting radical pamphlets and magazines into the growing network of alternative bookshops.[79] These groups all provided listings of publications, either as discrete leaflets/pamphlets or as sections within related publications. These, in turn, generated and maintained alternative creative and political cultures. By way of example, we might compare this role within one particular small publication from the mid-1960s to one no doubt more familiar to readers of this book.

Peter Finch established the poetry magazine *Second Aeon* in Cardiff in 1966. The first issue featured six pages of his work; the magazine then grew in size and developed into an anthology. The final issue in 1975 was a 268-page paperback with a print run of 2,500 copies. The contents were eclectic and included 'The Small Press Scene' listings, which aimed towards building and sustaining an international scene and became an important resource for readers and publishers. Every publication received was reviewed together with a contact address and price, enabling readers to purchase directly from the source. The full cover price went to the publisher – 'sell-it-yourself'.[80] In 1974, the 40-page 'Small Press Scene' in *Second Aeon* issue 18 included 325 publications from the UK, USA, Canada, Antipodes, Europe and 'elsewhere'; of these, 168 were from the UK and, if titles from commercial publishers and university presses are discounted, 146 were self-published and small press publications.[81]

Fast forward and stripey-jumpered proto-punk spikey-top Dennis the Menace and his companion, Gnasher, are lying on the floor reading comics and sniggering to themselves. This image introduces the mail-order fanzine list issued by Rough Trade in January 1981, featuring eight pages of UK fanzines from big cities and faraway towns, plus a few European and North American imports.[82] The vast majority cover punk and après-punk, together with a sprinkling of publications about reggae, 1950s/1960s rock 'n' roll, poetry, photography, collage zines, comics (*BIFF, VIZ*) and the Mötorhead fan club.

It is, in effect, a one-stop shop for all your fanzine requirements, saving the effort of sending postal orders to a dozen different addresses.[83] There are 159 titles included (143 from the UK) and 289 issues in total, with many back copies still available.[84]

The *Second Aeon* and Rough Trade listings function slightly differently. Where 'Small Press Scene' facilitated direct contact between readers and publishers, the Rough Trade list is a catalogue of goods for sale that maintained a separation between consumers and producers. Nonetheless, they both acted as a nexus for a specific area of contemporary self-publishing, containing details of a significant number of publications. The creators of the publications included in both had all printed sufficient copies to consider methods of distributing and selling copies to an audience outside their immediate social circle and local outlets.

This connection, through the distribution of self-published materials, exemplifies some of the ethos that travelled into punk fanzine culture. The examples shown here can only briefly reflect the abundance and range of material produced. But they do reveal the seeds sown by disparate collectives and individuals. We have also shown how marginal creative and political cultures deployed aesthetics and adopted practices and techniques that would be repurposed in punk self-publishing. There is much more to be said, particularly in relation to the implicit tensions within DIY publishing. There have been some hints, from the waning of activity when the meaning of DIY publishing dissipates to mention of when the ostensibly democratic distribution of tasks does not quite happen. But other pervasive issues that pit autonomy against skill/competence, quality, technology and economics, for reasons of space and focus, remain undiscussed. The links, from underground press to punk fanzine production, have not been overly stressed, though we hope that the reader – as they continue through the chapters that follow – will do this for themselves.

## Notes

1  Cited in Chris Atton, *Alternative Media* (London: Sage, 2002), p. 56.

2  For a more extensive list, see John Spiers, *The Alternative and Underground Press in Britain* (London: Harvester Press, 1974).

3  This is evident from various publications on the subject: Nigel Fountain, *Underground: The London Alternative Press, 1966–74* (London: Comedia, 1988); Robert Dickinson, *Imprinting the Sticks: the Alternative Press Beyond London* (Aldershot: Arena, 1997); Greg Kaplan (ed.), *Power to the People: The Graphic Design of the Radical Press and*

the *Rise of the Counter-Culture, 1964–74* (Chicago: University of Chicago Press, 2013).

4   Raymond Williams, *Marxism and Literature* (Oxford: Oxford University Press, 1977).

5   See articles and classified sections in the now online archive of *International Times*, www.internationaltimes.it/archive/. Examples of dedicated publications might include the long-running *Squatters Handbook* (Anonymous, produced by various squatting groups, including the Advisory Service for Squatters (ASS) London, 14 editions 1976–2016), or those from Release and the Claimants Union. See Helene Curtis and Mimi Sanderson (eds), *The Unsung Sixties* (London: Whiting & Birch, 2004).

6   Kristin Ross, *May '68 and its Afterlives* (Chicago: University of Chicago Press, 2002), p. 6.

7   Robert Darnton, 'What is the History of Books?', *Daedalus*, 111:3 (1982), 65–83.

8   Teal Triggs, *Fanzines* (London, Thames & Hudson, 2010), pp. 17–19.

9   For more on fanzines of this era, see Fredric Wertham, *The World of Fanzines: A Special Form of Communication* (Carbondale, IL: Southern Illinois University Press, 1973) and Johan Kugelberg, Jack Womack and Michael P. Daley (eds), *The Tattooed Dragon Meets The Wolfman: Lenny Kaye's Science Fiction Fanzines 1941–1970* (New York: Boo-Hooray, 2014).

10  Fred Patten (ed.), *Fantasy Rotator*, 137 (1963).

11  *Ibid.*, final page; Charles Burbee, *SHANGRI-L'AFFAIRES*, 23 (1945), Los Angeles Science Fiction Society, first page.

12  Jan Pen, online documentation of Provo publications, www.provo-images.info, accessed 18 February 2017.

13  *Provo*, 12 (undated).

14  Richard Kempton, *Provo: Amsterdam's Anarchist Revolt* (New York: Autonomedia, 2007), p. 38.

15  *Ibid.*, p. 38.

16  *Delta: A Review of Arts Life and Thought in the Netherlands*, 10:3 (1967), p. 20.

17  Kempton, *Provo*, p. 44.

18  Experimental Jetset, *Two or Three Things I Know About Provo*, pamphlet 3 (Amsterdam: Experimental Jetset, 2012). This is a translation and reprint of an interview with Rob Stolk by Tjebbe van Tijen, originally published in *Jeugd en Samenleving* (1991).

19  Peter Stansill and David Zane Mairowitz (eds), *BAMN (By Any Means Necessary): Outlaw Manifestos and Ephemera, 1965–70* (Harmondsworth: Penguin Books, 1971), pp. 24–35 and 75–7.

20  Roel Van Duyn, *Messages of a Wise Kabouter* (London: Duckworth, 1972).

21  Experimental Jetset, *Two or Three Things I Know About Provo*.

22  Stansill and Mairowitz (eds.), *BAMN*, p. 47.

23  *Directory of Communes and Commune Projects, Tribes, Crash Pads and Related Phenomena in Great Britain and Europe* (London: Bit Information Services, 1970).

24  *Hapt*, 26 (1971), p. 11.

25  *Hapt*, 22 (1970), p. 3.

26  Abbie Hoffman, *Steal This Book* (New York: Pirate Editions, 1971), p. 133.

27  *The Rag*, 7 (1966), p. 10.

28  *Hapt*, 22 (1970), p. 1.

29  King Mob, 'Notting Hill: England's First Ghetto Eruption', http:// revoltagainstplenty.com/index.php/archive-local/41-lost-ones-around-king-mob.html, accessed 14 May 2016. For more, see David and Stuart Wise, *King Mob: A Critical Hidden History* (London: Bread and Circuses, 2014).

30  *Hapt*, 26 (1971), p. 18.

31  *Hapt*, 27 (1971), p. 3.

32  *Hapt*, 26, p. 17.

33  *Hapt*, 27 (1971), p. 1.

34  Stefan Szczelkun, *Survival Scrapbook 1: Shelter* (Brighton: Unicorn Books, 1972); *Survival Scrapbook 2: Food* (Brighton: Unicorn Books, 1972); Dave Williams and Stephanie Munro, *Survival Scrapbook 3: Access to Tools* (Brighton: Unicorn Books, 1973); Pauline Vincent and Ann Winn, *Survival Scrapbook 3½: Play* (Brighton: Unicorn Books, 1973); Roger Sheppard, Richard Threadgill and John Holmes, *Survival Scrapbook 4: Paper Houses* (Brighton: Unicorn Books, 1974); Stefan Szczelkun, *Survival Scrapbook 5: Energy* (Brighton: Unicorn Books, 1974).

35  John Cage, *Diary: How to Improve the World (You Will Only Make Matters Worse) Continued Part Three* (New York: Something Else Press, 1967).

36  Stefan Szczelkun, 'Survival in Print', in Anna Chrystal Stephens and Glen Stoker (eds), *A Sick Logic* (Sheffield: Site Gallery, 2017), p. 101.

37  *Survival Scrapbook 5,* inside front cover.

38  *Suburban Press*, 6 (1974).

39  Jamie Reid on *Pinned*, www.youtube.com/watch?v=XS0zVWJ1U3k, accessed 3 February 2017.

40  Jamie Reid and John Savage, *Up They Rise: Incomplete Works of Jamie Reid* (London: Faber & Faber, 1987).

41  *Suburban Press*, 6, p. 31.

42  Laurel Forster, 'Spreading the Word: Feminist Print Cultures and the Women's Liberation Movement', *Women's History Review*, 25:5 (2016), 812–31.

43  Nancy Fraser, 'Rethinking the Public Sphere: A Contribution to the Critique of Actually Existing Democracy', in Craig Calhoun (ed.), *Habermas and the Public Sphere* (Cambridge, MA: MIT Press, 1992).

44  Anna Coote and Beatrix Campbell, *Sweet Freedom: the Struggle for Women's Liberation* (Oxford: Blackwell, 1987); Christine Faulder, Christine Jackson and Mary Lewis, *The Women's Directory* (London: Virago, 1976); Julia Sudbury, *Other Kinds of Dreams: Black Women's Organisations and the Politics of Transformation* (Abingdon: Routledge, 1998); Sue Bruley, 'Women's Liberation at the Grass Roots: A View from Some English Towns, c.1968–1990', *Women's History Review*, 25: 5 (2016), 723–40.

45  *Shrew*, 3:5 (June 1971), inside back cover.

46  *Shrew* (Summer 1974).

47  *Shrew*, 5:3 (August/September 1973).

48 *Shrew* (November/December 1969), p. 16.

49 *Shrew* (Summer 1974), p. 6.

50 Jo Somerset, 'I was a teenage "Jackie" reader', in Amanda Sebestyen (ed.), '68, '78, '88: From Women's Liberation to Feminism (Bridport: Prism Press, 1988), pp. 224–30.

51 Gail Chester, personal communication, May 2017.

52 Bart Moore-Gilbert and John Seed (eds), *Cultural Revolution? The Challenge of the Arts in the 1960s* (London: Routledge, 1992).

53 Géza Perneczky, *Assembling Magazines 1969–2000* (Budapest: Árnyékkötők Foundation, 2007).

54 Richard Kostelanetz and Henry Korn (eds), *Assembling; A Collection of Otherwise Unpublishable Manuscripts* (New York: Assembling Press, 1970); Richard Kostelanetz, 'Introduction', *Second Assembling* (New York, Assembling Press, 1971).

55 Michael Crane and Mary Stofflet (eds), *Correspondence Art: Source Book for the Network of International Postal Art Activity* (San Francisco: Contemporary Arts Press, 1984); Marie Boivent and Stephen Perkins (eds), *The Territories of Artists' Periodicals* (Rennes: Editions Provisoires and Plagiarist Press, 2015); Stephen Perkins, *Approaching the '80s Zine Scene: a Background Survey and Selected Annotated Bibliography* (Iowa City: Plagiarist Press, 1992).

56 Buster Cleveland (ed.), *NYCS Weekly Breeder, Vol.1 No.1, 1968* (1978).

57 Pauline Smith Artist Biography, http://axisweb.org/p/paulinesmith/#info, accessed 7 February 2017.

58 Genesis P-Orridge, *G.P.O v G.P-O: Mail Action* (Geneva: Ecart, 1976).

59 Fountain, *Underground*, p. 24.

60 Kaplan, *Power to the People*.

61 See, for example, *International Times*, 43 (1968); Nicholas Saunders, *Alternative London* (London: Wildwood, 1974).

62 Dickinson, *Imprinting the Sticks*, p. 33.

63 Interview by Jess Baines with Rick Walker, London, 22 August 2011.

64 See Minority Press Group (MPG), *Here is the Other News: Challenges to the Local Commercial Press* (London: MPG, 1980).

65 Jim Radford, 'Family Squatting Campaign: The Point of the Battle is to Win It', in Helen Curtis and Mimi Sanderson, *The Unsung Sixties: Memoirs of Social Innovation* (London: Whiting & Birch, 2002), pp. 1–18.

66 Jan O' Malley, *The Politics of Community Action* (Nottingham: Spokesman, 1977).

67 Interview by Jess Baines with Beryl Foster, London, 17 April 2013.

68 *Ibid.*

69 *Ibid.*

70 In 1976 the press became women only, providing the base for the next edition of *Shrew*.

71 Jonathan Zeitlyn, *Print: How You Can Do it Yourself* (London: Inter-Action, 1975), p. 50. Original emphasis.

72 *Ibid.*, pp. 2–3. This was not the first 'alternative' print manual. See Clifford Burke, *Printing It* (New York: Ballantine Books, 1972), which drew on his experience at

San Francisco State College; this book circulated beyond the USA. In the UK, the mainstream Teach Yourself Books also produced *Into Print: A Guide to Publishing Non-Commercial Newspapers and Magazines* (1975).

73  Jessica Baines, 'Democratising Print? The Field and Practices of Radical and Community Printshops in Britain 1968–98' (Ph.D. thesis, London School of Economics, 2016).

74  *Ibid.*

75  *Ibid.*

76  For more on photocopiers and photocopying, see Patrick Firpo, Lester Alexander, Claudia Katayanagi and Steve Ditlea, *Copyart: The First Complete Guide to the Copy Machine* (New York: Richard Marek, 1978); Kate Eichhorn, *Adjusted Margin: Xerography, Art, and Activism in the Late Twentieth Century* (Cambridge, MA: MIT Press, 2016).

77  *International Times*, 148 (1973), p. 9.

78  Wendy Collins, Ellen Friedman, Agnes Pivot (eds), *Women: The Directory of Social Change* (London: Wildwood, 1978), pp. 101–2; Lucy Delap, 'Feminist Bookshops, Reading Cultures and the Women's Liberation Movement in Great Britain, c. 1974–2000', *History Workshop Journal*, 81 (2016), 171–96.

79  Dave Berry, Liz Cooper and Charles Landry, *Where is the Other News?* (London: Minority Press, 1980).

80  Jeff Nuttall, *Bomb Culture* (New York: Delacorte Press, 1968), p. 182.

81  Peter Finch (ed.), *Second Aeon, 18* (1974).

82  Sue Donne, *Wotcher Everyone This is a List of Fanzines …* (London: Rough Trade, 1981).

83  And if you ordered a selection of fanzines you might receive a couple of extras thrown in for free, as happened to one of the writers of this chapter.

84  For pre-punk music fanzines, see Jymn Parrett, *Denim Delinquent 1971–76: The Complete Collection* (Chicago: Hozac Books, 2016); Mick Farren, Suzy Shaw and Steve Crist, *BOMP!: Saving the World One Record at a Time* (Los Angeles and New York: AMMO Books, 2007).

# 2

# Zines and history: zines as history

LUCY ROBINSON

As this collection shows, it would be fair to say that people interested in history have begun to take zines seriously. From the mid-1990s onwards, archivists and teachers picked up on the possibilities of using zines in their work.[1] Edited collections extended access to zine content, albeit by removing them from their networks of meaning and reinstating traditional forms of publication.[2] More recently, there has been a growth of work on the history of the zine and using zines as historical sources.[3] Historians recognise them as an invaluable way into the messy traces left by subcultures, DIY and fan cultures, and the politics of identity.[4] Archivists on and off-line continue to build new collections, mapping the specifics of a place, scene or group of zine makers. Whether in the most eminent national collections, or more loosely archived on social networking sites, they construct a bottom-up history; irreverent, both textual and visual, recycled and disseminated beyond profit and funding structures.

Historians also use zines to disseminate research. Punkademics produce (aca)zines rather than conference packs to match form with content in the history of subcultures.[5] The Edmonton Zine fair, for example, launched a collaborative history zine, *The History of Punk*.[6] Zines were utilised at various points during the fortieth anniversary of punk. The British Library used its zine collection to collate a narrative from the Sex Pistols' breakthrough to the wider national punk story, whereas Matthew Worley's community project focused on the local experience of Norwich's punk scene. Worley combined a street exhibition with a zine – *Young Offenders: Punk in Norwich, 1976–84* – designed by fellow-punk academic Russ Bestley.[7] These events, recorded through zines, move away from the set-piece, top-down story of punk based on the careers of the Sex Pistols and shopping habits on the Kings Road. *Young Offenders*, for example, records the often ignored filth and fury of the less metropolitan 'sound of the eastway'.[8]

This recent interest in zines from producers (aca)zinesters and researchers can be understood as a turn to the textual past to try and make sense of the digital present.[9] On the one hand, zines and digital social networks produce similar affective networks and identity work. But zines also haunt our digital presents with the pull of the handmade, holdable, shareable objects. As they are made, shared and read, zines accrue authenticity capital through their emotional credentials of 'honesty, kindness, anger and the beautiful inarticulate articulate-ness'.[10] They are a riposte to centralised corporate media. When we trace the virtual roots of our online forums and social networks back to the tangible, DIY zine, we reclaim our digital heritage from multinational dot coms.

In this chapter I want to move beyond thinking about the history of zines and instead to look at the zines that we access as forms of historical analysis worthy of a place in the history of historical writing. Whether produced by riot grrrls looking for inspiration from suffragettes, or anarcho-punks learning the lessons from a previous generation's activists, or queer activists building community memorials, zines construct their own alternative canons and syllabuses. They list alternative heroes, heroines and watershed moments, and fill in the gaps in traditional teaching and learning. We can read them into the longer history of queer, black, feminist and working-class histories that enact justice in the present by rearming the past. Zinesters have their own role in this historical genealogy and they also bring something new to it. Zines deserve a place alongside some of the founding projects of queer and feminist history. At a time when academic publication is quantifiably impactful, with analytics to demonstrate reach (and therefore value), zines help us situate ourselves in a radical tradition, instead.

All of this does, however, make zines difficult to pin down. After all, the practicalities of production mean that they sometimes verge on illegibility and publication dates can be difficult to identify. The secondary literature shows how difficult they are to define. Zines are either too diverse or too inclusive to easily draw boundaries around as a genre.[11] Some approaches define them by their genealogy from fan work.[12] To others, zines are markers of changing DIY media possibilities. Zines punctuate the development of self-publishing, from Banda copier, to Xerox machine, to public photocopier, to desktop publishing software, to home printer, to screen.[13] Beyond content and context, zines are defined by their commercial position,[14] aesthetic[15] or ethics of production.[16] Chip Rowe combines zines' style with temporality ('cut and paste, sorry if it's late')[17] and Kinko emphasises their invisible networks ('on the sly ... word of mouth').[18] For others, zines are identity work that bridges producer and recipient.[19]

Zines disrupt historians' assumptions that sources sit waiting for prosperity, or for a historian to find and analyse them at some later point in time. Alex Carp values their resistance to simplistic reading of a single moment of production. Regarding undated zines, Carp explained: 'why would you? It's about right now ... it's also a sign of not thinking historically, right? Like, why would I put a date on my zine?'[20] It isn't just the point of production that is difficult to pin down. Their authorship is complicated, and traces layers of recycling of the past. They are scavenger art; make do and mend. They reuse a past found in images and texts. Zine makers unpick historical narratives and chronologies, borrowing images, quotes and texts without concern for referencing, copyright or cultural status. Zine makers leave us a record of their own role in the past. They also show us anyone can DIY a history that is redistributed, re-reproduced and moves across space, place, time and theme.

Yet, from the start of the 'zine explosion' in the early 1990s, archives collected, curated and conserved zines which might otherwise have been lost.[21] Different archival approaches capture different elements of zines' movement from past to present and into imagined futures. Sometimes the same zines are held in a number of different collections, for different reasons. *Factsheet Five* was a zine catalogue zine. It catalogued and summarised a thousand zines.[22] More recent digital collections like zineWiki, Digital Fanzine Preservation Society, Qzap and Open Culture translate zines and replicate the zine form in their online structures. Qzap, for example, is crowdsourced, building a community of donors. Other archives are rooted in the physicality of their social space in contemporary autonomous and anarcho spaces; for example, at The Cowley Club in Brighton or the Canny Little Library, Newcastle. In other archives, zines have been incorporated into national collections, as in the Women's Library and British Library for example. Zines have also been incorporated into historic collections of radical tracts.[23] Fales Library, New York, the Stuart Hall Library, London, the International Institute of Social History in the Netherlands, the Alternative Press Center (APC) Collection, University of Maryland, Baltimore County, all include zines in their wider collections of radical literature, as does the University of Kansas, which includes zines collected by the Solidarity! Revolutionary Center and Radical Library. Others collect them according to their aesthetic form; London's Poetry Library, the London College of Communications, Glasgow School of Art, Browne Popular Culture Library all include zines in their visual collections. Some are collected according to subject or theme. Manchester's LGBT Zine Library, Mobile Menstrual Zine Library in Sheffield, Queer Zine Archive, Berlin, or the Barnard Zine combines their sense of local history with a political theme. Others focus more fully on the importance of the local history of zines. In Salford or York, for example, and in Washington, Atlanta and Arizona, zines are in local history collections. Local collections use them as maps of scenes and to curate community networks. As a result, this chapter draws together zines from open access archives and virtual collections, as well as Fales's Riot grrrl archive, Washington's public and Atlanta's university zine archives, Berlin's youth culture archive, London's Women's Library and my own personal collection.

If zines are indefinable and uncataloguable, then their role as historical work is equally messy. Identity history, through which we collectively write ourselves into the past, is a messy process not least because identities are messy. Zines help us trace the history of how we write our own histories and how we network around the histories of those who share stories with us. Zines pick up a series of problematics well established in identity history. They might not help solve the problems that they throw up, but they might help us to find their creative potential. In particular, zines intersect with and bring something new to tensions around identity and DIY histories.

It is hardly news that groups of people have been excluded or written out of history. When history is fixated on how power functions at the top end of society – the rulers – then the histories written focus on the elites. History in this traditional sense has reinforced or reproduced the political inequalities of the world that it claims to analyse. From the 1960s, the civil rights, black power, women's and gay liberation movements saw 'telling their own stories' as political acts. Making people visible simultaneously sought out the roots of their marginalisation/oppression/exploitation and their agency. Thus, demands to be counted in the historical past were political demands in their here and now. Like academics who blurred the lines between academic/activist identities, zine makers blurred the lines between artist, activist and academic work. In the process, they shared the historical project. They uncovered voices or histories of excluded groups in order to document oppression and record resistance to that oppression in order to inspire further resistance in the present.

Popular culture has long had an important role in identity and DIY histories' mission to both document and resist. Historical analysis of popular culture allows us to dissect dominant narratives and trace resistant agency in audience reception and reminds us to challenge the structures through which we see ourselves represented (or not). Literary and film history have shown us the ways in which uncovering and claiming a text is itself a political act. Claiming status for marginalised texts and icons is a process through which the value of status can itself be addressed. Vito Russo's *Celluloid Closet* (1987) used biographies of icons such as Judy Garland, to uncover the structures and experiences of sexual secrecy in the golden age of Hollywood.[24] As well as offering alternative stories and icons, more significantly, Russo uncovered lesbian and gay audiences' creative work decoding popular culture in order to find a place for themselves in the story. Similarly, Elaine Showalter's work recovered a female literary tradition that broadened narrow definitions of 'a classic'.[25] Both Linda and Dale Spender collected forgotten female novelists and the processes that marginalised and undervalued their work.[26] To have a relationship with these books, to collect them and hold them, was a way to connect with women of the past. Nicci Gerrard saw recovered novelists as a way to 'respond to and reveal the symptoms of an age ... as well as reflect back to the reader' her contemporary world.[27] These recovered stories of the past, in films and books, thereby challenged silences and repurposed the canon as a political act in the now.[28] The point was not that women or gay men's social and economic position stopped them being able to write in the first place, but that husbands, fathers, publishers and reviewers actively blocked them and the education system rejected them from syllabuses.

Historians like Sheila Rowbotham wielded women's agency in the past to make a point in their activist present. In *Hidden from History* (1973), Rowbotham discovered the fore-mothers of her own struggles to bridge feminism with socialism and inject a feminist history into the socialist canon.[29] Similarly, Jeffrey Weeks, founder member of London's Gay Liberation Front in 1971, was the movement's resident historian. His book, *Coming Out* (1977), catalogued gay men acting for themselves.[30] He presented gay men as more than victims of inequality or products of medicalised discourse. They were agents struggling for law reform. His later work with Kevin Porter, *Between the Acts* (1990), added a methodological understanding of the importance of letting people speak of their histories for themselves and the power of weaving together their individual stories: attacks in the present sharpened stories of the past.[31] For example, when Porter and Weeks' interviews were originally done in 1978–79 there was little support for the project, but in the 1980s, in the face of renewed attacks on gay equality and the devastating impact of AIDS, there was a new impetus to hear gay stories. Together, Russo, Weeks and Rowbothom show us that we need to do more than recover lost voices. We need recovery as a way to challenge the structures of the status quo.

Feminist and queer historians do this when they put themselves into their processes. They have reflexively incorporated their personal experiences to rearm the past in the present. For example, Dale Spender included transcripts of patronising mansplaining from male academics to literary feminists in an appendix to *The Writing or the Sex* (1989). The appendix reminds the reader, then and now, that they, like the author, function in the same structures that their work critiques.[32] Similarly, these historians thought about the modes of their own production and how they published their work. Rowbotham, Weeks and Spender all published their work in politically aligned publishing projects.

Printing feminism (and feminist printing) has always been more than a way of getting ideas out there; it is a way of changing the processes of publication and dissemination. As Spender pointed out in 1989, 'historically, those who have controlled the printed medium have also exercised power'.[33] Not only did these writers publish in activist publishers, they situated this within a context of historical resistance to publishing structures. Some feminist researchers worked backwards to uncover the unremembered history of women publishers. For example, Cadman, Chester and Pivot's collection, *Rolling Our Own* (1981), looked back to women publishers in the 1600s.[34] Nicci Gerrard wrote *Into the Mainstream* (1989), an analysis of the newly emerging feminist writing and literary theory, alongside her work founding and editing the short-lived *Women's Review* in the 1980s. Gerrard published with Pandora Press, the feminist press that first published Winterson's *Oranges Are Not the Only Fruit* (1985). Feminist publishing houses, like Pandora, The Women's Press, Sheba, Athene, Battle Axe Books, Kitchen Table and Onlywomen, all worked in different ways, with different approaches, with different categorisations. Just as feminism is built of many strands, feminist publishing had many approaches to both feminism and to the market. Ultimately, however, competition was not between forms of feminist publishing but between small independents and the big international publishers.[35]

Virago Press is an exemplar of both the problems and the legacies of a feminist approach to self-publication. Its outputs and history flag up the importance of production, voice and reception in the historical process of recovery. As such it helps us raise questions about zines, and to use zines to rethink some long-established tensions in identity history practice. Virago Press began in the UK in 1973, publishing *Fen Women* by Mary Chamberlain. The company loosely grew out of the experience that Carmen Callil and Harriet Spicer had handling PR for *Spare Rib*. It saw publishing as a form of political action with its own heritage.[36] Virago had a recognisable brand aesthetic. From 1976 its books all carried a quotation from Rowbotham's *Women,*

*Resistance and Revolution* (1972). It combined a green stripe with their logo, the apple. The apple celebrated Eve refusing to do as she was told and simultaneously foregrounded the sexual blame and double standard associated with female sexuality. The publishing house's title, a synonym for shrew, vixen, dragon, scold, spitfire and fury, picked up on the long literary and feminist tradition of reclamation.

Virago set out to recover and re-equip an obscured female past with their Reprint Library, and with Virago Modern Classics which published older, often-forgotten fiction by women. This series had a considerable impact on the careers of writers like Margaret Atwood, Angela Carter and Antonia White. The series came with introductions linking the context of the writer with the lives of the readers. These textual conversations, between the past and the present, evaluated concepts of progress while acknowledging the need to continue to struggle.

Virago's success also flags up a key tension in the politics of historical recovery. Shifting ideas of gender problematised the idea that there was a universal womanhood to recognise in the past. Gerrard's interviews with feminist writers and publishers in the 1980s present the ambivalence in successful feminist publishing. Spender pointed out that by the time women were afforded their own publishing space, the industry was waning and the exciting future was instead in television.[37] Some were uncomfortable with professionalising their feminism and saw commercial success as a Thatcherite incorporation of their resistance.[38] The 'success' of women's publishing was perhaps 'a hollow victory' after all. For women to occupy a cultural space, the assumption was that men 'vacated it'. A feminised cultural space is a devalued space, or acts as self-marginalisation. Furthermore, the women who did get published were often those who already had a voice. Virago had, however, proved that there was a market for women's writing. In 1995, Virago was sold to a mainstream publishing house, Little Brown.

Textual interventions such as those by Rowbotham, Weeks, Virago and Russo all invested in history as a weapon in their present. Their approaches inspired new generations of activist historians, and have in turn been challenged by more contemporary discussion of identity, of the relationship between sexuality and class, and by historians who need a different set of weapons in their armoury today. Publishing and writing projects help us to put feminist zine history writing in its broader context, and to think about the role of uncovered voices for feminism and identity politics more broadly. Focus on zines and zine culture has often used them to trace the networks of paper they build. The zine, as it passes from hand to hand, acts as a marker buoy for the loose connections, shared spaces and moments of transient recognition that build a subculture or scene. The zine is currency in subcultural capital.[39] But we can also take their content seriously. They respond to the same contradictions as the queer and feminist historians; how to build a collective sense of pride around a collection of individual victims and how to work within but against the market.

Like Rowbotham, Spender, Virago, Russo and Weeks, zines produce their own alternative icons and curriculum. They offer, for example, 'a fantastic chance for oppressed women to get their voices heard. Fast, easy and cheap.'[40] They spread alternative content, and alternative models of knowledge. Zines build a shared memory of cultural icons, particularly around popular culture rather than top-down agents, which 'build[s] and main[tains] both individual and collective identity … [and] plays a vital role in … maintain[ing] or changing … social structure'. [41] In our present, for example, Julie Sheele's *The Heroines Zine* (2013) was 'all about our favourite role models'.[42] *Shape and Situate* (2010) zine was made up of posters by iconic DIY artists of 'inspiration or radical European women'. These collections of feminist heroines 'connect us with the past and the present through a cultural articulation of these women's lives'.[43]

Zinesters have called up memories of the 1969 Stonewall Riots to criticise the commercialisation of Pride events, parades, carnivals and the assimilationist agenda. In Toronto, gay zine activists linked gentrification with the 'mainstreaming of the Gay Movement'. Remembering LGBT (lesbian, gay, bisexual, transgender, queer) struggles of the 1960s and 1970s reminds us that this was not what we fought for.[44] These alternative icons respond to the anxiety that our present may end up recorded according to the power structures of the past. 'I hate to think', wrote one zine creator, 'that in years to come it'll only be the "elite" people on the top of the pile who're remembered, creating a voice and mass forgetting of the great work and lives of so many people within our social, cultural and political makeup, communities, and lives.'[45] Shawn(ta) Smith, an archivist at the Lesbian Herstory Archive in New York, produced zines with an explicit historical purpose. *Black Lesbians in the 70s and Before – An At Home Tour At The Lesbian Herstory Archives* (2010) invited and encouraged engagement with the physical archive. But this was also a manifesto:

- All Lesbian women must have access to all archives, no academic, political or sexual credentials will be required to use the archive
- Archives should be housed within the community, not on an academic campus
- The Community should share in the work of the archives.[46]

The *Black Lesbians* zine built a new list of heroines; a black woman who passed as a man for 15 years in 1969, a timeline of the oppression of black lesbians and their activist responses to it from 1969–80. It also suggested further reading, such as J.R. Roberts's *Black Lesbians: An Annotated Bibliography* and offered a form for readers to fill in with their donations to the archive.[47]

I am positing a shared heritage and process with people's history, queer history and feminist historical practice in the way zines scavenge and repurpose icons, texts and structures of knowledge. Like Russo, the zine *Montgomery Clift was Queer* (1994) used the journal form to memorialise the seventh anniversary of an AIDS-related death, so reclaiming Clift was a way of integrating his loss and the loss of the present.[48] The history of sexuality is reimagined through a new set of heroes and heroines. In *Ablaze!*, for example, sexuality was celebrated through the history of rock 'n' roll, with Little Richard providing a recognition point for queer youth and Suzi Quatro 'strutting her stuff with the best of the boys' showing that 'women could make it too.'[49]

Once the alternative icons are in place, zines record the act of recovery. Icons and everyday encounters, historical players and cultural producers past and present are put on the same level. *Shape and Situate* pulls together Anais Nin, Anne Boleyn, Anne Lister, Tove Jansson, The Raincoats, Hedy Lamarr and collectives like The Red Wheelies, Focus E15 and North Staffs Miners' Wives Action Group.[50] The first issue of *Mint Julip* brought together bell hooks, Seamus Heaney, Derek Jarman and Ani DeFranco, all superimposed on a picture of Ella Fitzgerald.[51] *Pussy Town* celebrated Molly Ringwold and JLo.[52] Valerie Solanas puts in a fairly frequent appearance in feminist zines lists. Her manifesto, which could itself be seen as a zine, was discussed in *Shocking Pink*'s 'Violence by Women' issue.[53] *JOLT* also claimed Solanas as a punk. Where icons could not be so easily identified for reclamation, they could be willed into being. *I ♥ Amy Carter* and *Barbra's Psychic Anus* create and then 'out' their own perfect icons: President Carter's daughter and 'Will's illegitimate half sis' Wilhemina Shakespeare.[54]

In the most obvious way, fanzines record the history of a music scene ignored by the 'mainstream'. Feminist music zines, for example, collate women who were producers of culture; 'musician, journalist, or a photographer', not 'just a groupie', or passive consumer labelled by riot grrrl as the 'opposite of the band'.[55] Lucy Cage looked back on her writing for *Ablaze!* She 'bent over backwards to concentrate on women as musicians: … resisted highlighting kookiness over cleverness; [she] wanted to reclaim skill and competence as virtues for female band members'. Feminist zinesters challenged the idea that every woman who did break through was an exception, novelty or a 'wacky curio'.[56] Lucy Toothpaste knew that if she didn't document punk grrrls in her zine *JOLT,* then chances are no-one would.

Zines, like identity history, move across wide varieties of evidence and resources, and pull them into a new reimagined canon. For example, *Plexiform–Democracy* recommended Orwell's *Homage to Catalonia* as a 'good reminder of what mistakes we need to avoid for the future' and *The Dispossessed* by Ursula Le Guin on the relationship between utopianism and structural negotiation.[57] The *Encyclopaedia of Ecstasy* combined William Blake ('Energy is Eternal Delight') with the *Rocky Horror Show* ('Don't Dream It, Be It').[58] Zines challenge the gatekeepers of knowledge and problematise the lines between teacher, student and institutional structures of learning.[59] They are '[e]xtracurricular writing', in Michelle Comstock's words, but with intellectual and pedagogical intent.

Zines disseminated powerful historical knowledges. A variety of zines made various connections to the Holocaust and its memorialisation by linking battery farming to concentration camps in North Yorkshire, or Hiroshima to HIV and AIDS.[60] This autodidactic drive to know our own history also involves unpicking the existing structures of knowledge. Moving academic content into zine form puts knowledge in the wrong place, utilising and challenging the ivory tower. In 1978, for example, two years after *The History of Sexuality* was published, the zine *Chez Foucault* introduced Foucault's theories in a new form. The zine was organised around an interview between Foucault and zine maker Simeon Wade and was explicitly pedagogical. It was a 'workbook' aimed at teachers and students and structured as a 'syllabus' with suggested topics broken down week by week.[61]

Zines also challenged the premise of didactic exchange. For example, *Judy,* a riot grrrl inspired zine from 1993, simultaneously celebrated and playfully undermined celebrity theorists. The aim was to share Judith Butler's work with the tagline 'Don't be alienated, read Judy'. Butler was a fitting subject. In many ways, riot grrrl responded to the growth of queer post-structuralism that took the self and performativity seriously. But *Judy* also played with status. Because Butler was not a normal celebrity it was 'really hard to find pictures of Judith Butler so [*Judy* included a picture of] ... another Judy [Garland]'. (It was not just Russo who recognised Garland's queered significance.) Academic theories were 'crushes' and rock star fan gossip was replaced with spottings of Julia Kristeva, Butler, Eve Sedgwick and Diana Fuss. *Judy* included multiple-choice quizzes like those in women's and girls' magazines; 'are you a theory-fetishizing biscuithead?' The second issue teased 'dirty pictures of Julia Kristeva'.[62] Similarly, a contemporary Brighton zine, *Fan Girl Fan Club*, puts the affective labour of icon production to the front. *Fan Girl Fan Club* displaced the icons (Kate Bush, Freddie Mercury, Liza Minnelli, Florence and the Machine) with the fan work that put them on their pedestal in the first place.[63]

By working through fandom, these zines catalogued the emotional labour of investment in a usable past. They also foreground the problems of presenting individuals as collective solutions. Lots of zines include stories of being let down by the icons needed for inspiration. For example, *Ablaze!* took down Henry Rollins (who responded); Kathleen Hanna took down Evan Dando. *Barbra's Psychic Anus* took a metaphoric journey to New York to meet heroine Patti Smith.[64] But when the writer arrived, it turned out that Smith 'married a man with a white picket fence, changed her name from Smith to Jones … age does ugly things to people doesn't it?'[65]

Sometimes the movement and displacement of academic knowledge was literal. From the 1990s, zines and other forms of photocopier art were picked up as teaching activities, particularly in girls' work. Zines like *Schnews* and *Homocore* were offered free to prisoners.[66] Academic knowledge could not only be moved to the wrong place, it could be repurposed, and these shifts then reflexively analysed. *The Only Thing Missing is You* included an essay on the 1989 invasion of Panama that had been written for a history class. All it took, according the author, to turn it into a zine piece was to remove the footnotes – it still 'reads like a college term paper because that's exactly what it is'.[67] Harriet Alana's *Why is the Zine so Important Within the Feminist Punk Subculture?* began as an essay for her illustration degree in 2012 and was first published as a zine in November 2015. Karen Blaze's zine, *Made in Manchester*, was produced as a course work project for her Communications Studies A level in the summer of 1987. While the mainstream music media focused on London, Blaze wanted to put Manchester on the map.[68] Her project was well timed. The scene had coalesced and was the new mainstream. At this point based in Leeds, *Ablaze!* republished the Stone Roses interview 'to cash it in … and f'k'n well stamp out the tiresome manch myth once and for all.'[69] This time around, *Ablaze!* came to bury rather than praise Manchester. These zines moved and repurposed academic narratives produced behind the gatekeepers of knowledge, manoeuvred them into new forms, and worked through the implications thereof for themselves.

Zines are, as Kearney notes, a way of writing identities into formation.[70] They are filled with reflexive discussion of how it feels to write an identity into the canon. But more than that, they can teach us as historians to challenge the very processes that we reproduce. Zine makers actively build a history, borrowing images, quotes and texts without concern for referencing, copyright or some work's privileged status. Not only have zine makers left us a record of their role in the past, they show us that anyone can DIY their own histories.

They remind us to do more than fill in the absences on other people's behalf. They remind us that the historical conversation involves collecting, curating, cataloguing and analysing texts in as broad a way as imaginable.

Once we see zines as history, and recognise their power to shift the status of knowledge, we can then start to reverse the gaze. Zines are 'DIY propaganda' that can teach historians a way of working together with the past.[71] If the first stage of the history of zines has been to recognise them as historical, methodological and reflexive labour, then what lessons about history might we learn from the zines? Zines as history teach us to take our own position seriously, to think about our own context of production and the networks that we build with our work. Zine archivists and zine writers can teach us that historical work is simultaneously public and private.[72] They also teach us to make the most of what we've got, to repurpose and rearm our histories, and sometimes to put them where they are not meant to be. As feminist or queer historians we should recognise the zine maker as one of our own. We all rely on the structures surrounding us in order to undermine them. We all strive for a collective endeavour that acknowledges collectivity as an intersectional tactic rather than a universal truth. We are all scavengers. Because what else have we got?

## Notes

Acknowledgements: my thanks to the Santander Mobility Fund for funding the original research and to Laura Cofield, Claire Langhamer and Chris Warne for helping me crystallise these thoughts in the bigger picture. Gratitude also to the Riot Grrrl Archive in Fales Library, New York, Berlin's Archive of Youth Cultures, London's Women's Library, Randy Gue at Rose Library, Atlanta Punk Rock collection, Michele Casto at DC Punk Archive, Washington DC Public Library, and to the independent collectors, curators and scanners who have made access to so many fanzines possible.

1   See, for example, Susan Davis, 'Zines and Libraries', Serials Review, 21:4 (1995), 96; Stephanie Ardito, 'The Alternative Press: Newsweeklies and Zines', Database Magazine, 22:3 (1999), 16; Julie Herrada, 'Zines in Libraries: A Culture Preserved', Serials Review, 21:2 (1995), 79–88.

2   Chip Rowe, The Book of Zines: Readings from the Fringe (New York: Henry Hold & Co, 1997); Seth Friedman, Factsheet Five Zine Reader (New York: Three Rivers Press, 1997).

3   For example, Andy Bennett, Culture and Everyday Life (London: Sage, 1995); Matthew Worley, 'Punk, Politics and British (Fan)zines, 1976–84: "While the world was dying, did you wonder why?"', History Workshop Journal, 79:1 (2015), 76–106.

4   I take a broad understanding of 'history work': archivists, curators, teachers, editors, online collectors, independent scholars and academic historians etc., which is a good match for the breadth of meanings, styles, functions and democratic intent of zines themselves.

5   See for example, Keep It Simple, Make It Fast (Porto, Portugal, 2016), www.kismifconference.com/wp-content/uploads/2016/07/Programme-KISMIF-2016_-14-july-2016_web.pdf, accessed 12 December 2016; Resist Festival of Ideas and Actions (London School of Economics, London, 2016), www.lse.ac.uk/sociology/events/PDF/Resist-Fest-Zine2.pdf, accessed 12 December 2016.

6   Edmonton Zine Fair, *The History of Punk*, https://thepastisunwritten.files.wordpress.com/2016/06/history-of-punk-fanzine-3.pdf, accessed 12 December 2016.

7   Matthew Worley, *Young Offenders: Punk in Norwich, 1976–84* (2016).

8   *Ibid.*, p. 2.

9   Bennett, *Culture and Everyday Life*, p. 94.

10  Stephen Duncombe, *Notes from the Underground: Zines and the Politics of Alternative Culture* (Bloomington: Microcosm Publishing, 2008 edn), pp. 6–7.

11  Rebecca A. Pierson 'Best Practices for Zine Programming with Young Adults in the Public Library' (University of North Carolina at Chapel Hill: Information and Library Science, Master's Paper, 2007).

12  Friedman, *Factsheet Five Zine Reader*, p. 9.

13  Kim, *Office Supply Youth*, 5 (1997).

14  Colleen Hubbard, 'DIY in the Stacks: A Study of Three Public Library Zine Collections', *Chicago-Public Library Association*, 44:6 (2005), p. 351.

15  Karen Gisonny and Jenna Freedman, 'Zines in Libraries: How, What and Why?', *Collection Building*, 25:1 (2006), 26.

16  Julie Bartel, *From A to Zine: Building a Winning Zine Collection in Your Library* (Washington: American Library Association, 2004), p. 22.

17  Rowe, *The Book of Zines*, p. xii.

18  Pierson, 'Best Practices for Zine Programming with Young Adults in the Public Library', p. 4.

19  Richard A. Stoddart and Teresa Kiser, 'Zines and the Library', *Library Resources & Technical Services*, 48:3 (2004), 191–2.

20  Alex Carp, 'Inside the "Riot Grrrl" Archives', *The Awl* (2013), https://theawl.com/inside-the-riot-grrrl-archives-46cb0ef3f1d1#.nk0raouvs, accessed 10 October 2016.

21  Open Culture, 'Download 834 Radical Zines' (2016), www.openculture.com/2016/04/download-834-radical-zines-from-a-new-online-archive.html, accessed October 2016; James Romenesko, 'The Zine Explosion', *American Journalism Review*, 14 (1993), 39–43.

22  Romenesko, 'The Zine Explosion', 39–43.

23  Henry Black, 'Radical Periodicals and their Place in the Library', *Progressive Librarian*, 17:2 (2000), 58–69.

24  Vito Russo, *The Celluloid Closet: Homosexuality in the Movies* (London: Harper Collins, 1987).

25  Elaine Showalter, 'Family Secrets and Domestic Subversion: Rebellion in the Novels of the 1860s', in Anthony S. Wohl (ed.), *The Victorian Family: Structure and Stresses* (London: Routledge, 1978), pp. 101–16.

26  Linda Spender, *Intruders on the Rights of Men: Women's Unpublished Heritage* (London: Harper Collins, 1983); 'The Politics of Publishing: Selection and Rejection of Women's Words in Print', *Women's Studies International Forum*, 6:5 (1983), 469–73; Dale Spender, *The Writing or the Sex? Or Why You Don't Need to Read Women's Writing to Know It's No Good* (Oxford: Pergamon, 1989); Dale Spender, *Mothers of the Novel: 100 Good Women Writers before Jane Austen* (London: Pandora Press, 1986).

27  Nicci Gerrard, *Into the Mainstream: How Feminism Has Changed Women's Writing* (London: Pandora Press, 1989).

28  Dale Spender, 'Past, Present and Future: Sources on Women', *Women's Studies International Forum*, 5:6 (1982), 697–700.

29  Sheila Rowbotham, *Hidden from History: Three Hundred Years of Women's Oppression and the Fight Against it* (London: Pluto, 1973).

30  Jeffrey Weeks, *Coming Out* (London: Quartet Books, 1977).

31  Kevin Porter and Jeffrey Weeks, *Between the Acts: Lives of Homosexual Men, 1885–1967* (London: Routledge, 1990).

32  Spender, *The Writing or the Sex?*, pp. 195–201.

33  *Ibid.*, p. 41.

34  Eileen Cadman, Gail Chester and Agnes Pivot, *Rolling Our Own: Women as Printers, Publishers and Distributors* (London: Minority Press Group, 1981); Catherine Riley, 'The Message Is in the Book: What Virago's Sale in 1995 Means for Feminist Publishing', *Women: A Cultural Review*, 25:3 (2014), 235–55.

35  Gerrard, *Into the Mainstream*, p. 22.

36  Riley, 'The Message Is in the Book', 238.

37  Spender, *The Writing or the Sex?*, p. 41.

38  Gerrard, *Into the Mainstream*, p. 23.

39  Ryan Ciarán, 'Music Fanzine Collecting as Capital Accumulation', *Participations: Journal of Audience & Reception Studies*, 12:2 (2015), 238–54.

40  Harriet Alana, *Why is the Zine so Important within the Feminist Punk Subculture?* (2005).

41  Tia DeNora, *Music in Everyday Life* (Cambridge: Cambridge University Press, 2000), p. 126.

42  Julie Sheele, Julia Scheele, Kieron Gillen, Lizz Lunney *et al.*, *The Heroines Zine* (2013).

43  Shape and Situate, *Posters of Inspirational European Women*, 1 (2010).

44  Abuzar, *Shame On Pride!* (2005), http://archive.qzap.org/index.php/Detail/Object/Show/object_id/143, accessed 10 December 2016.

45  Shape and Situate blogpost (2010), http://remember-who-u-are.blogspot.co.uk/2010/11/shape-and-situate-zine.html, accessed 10 December 2016.

46  Shawn(ta) Smith (2010) *Black Lesbians in the 70s and Before* (New York: Lesbian Herstory Archive, 2010) http://archive.qzap.org/index.php/Detail/Object/Show/object_id/420, accessed 10 December 2016.

47 *Ibid.*

48 Charlie Nash *Montgomery Clift Was Queer* (1994), http://archive.qzap.org/index.php/Detail/Object/Show/object_id/179, accessed 10 December 2016.

49 Terry Downe, 'For the Death of Male Rock', *Ablaze*, 7 (1990), in Karen Ablaze! (ed.), *The City is Ablaze! The Story of a Post-Punk Fanzine 1984–94* (Leeds: Mittens On Publishing, 2013), p. 166.

50 Shape and Situate, *Posters of Inspirational Women*, 1 (2010).

51 Hugh, *One Mint Julep*, 2 (c. 1985), http://archive.qzap.org/index.php/Detail/Object/Show/object_id/495, accessed 10 December 2016.

52 SeeDee and YaYa, *Pussytown* 2 (1990s), http://archive.qzap.org/index.php/Detail/Object/Show/object_id/97, accessed 10 December 2016.

53 *Shocking Pink*, 2: 4 (1988).

54 Tammy Rae Carland, I ♥Amy Carter (1992); Splash and Retro, *Barbra's Psychic Anus*, 2 (1992), http://archive.qzap.org/index.php/Detail/Object/Show/object_id/171, http://archive.qzap.org/index.php/Detail/Object/Show/object_id/107, accessed 10 December 2016.

55 Cheryl Cline, quoted in Mary Celeste Kearney, *Girls Make Media* (London: Routledge, 2013), p. 81.

56 Ablaze!, *The City is Ablaze!*, p. 266.

57 *Plexiform–Democracy*, 6 (2000), https://archive.org/details/Plexiform6, accessed 10 December 2016.

58 *Encyclopaedia of Ecstasy*, 1 (1983), http://greengalloway.blogspot.co.uk/2015/02/enyclopaedia-of-ecstasy-1983.html, accessed 1 October 2015.

59 Michelle Comstock, 'Grrrl Zine Networks: Re-Composing Spaces of Authority, Gender, and Culture', *Journal of Advanced Composition*, 21:2 (2001), 384.

60 Eric Deutsch, *AIDS KILLS Fags Dead!*, 1 (c. 1995), http://archive.qzap.org/index.php/Detail/Object/Show/object_id/346, accessed 10 December 2016; Vince and Dave, *Cardboard Theatre*, 1 (1983), www.mediafire.com/file/3kf1on9n8ae1zbf/cardboard+theatre+1.pdf, accessed 10 December 2016; The Bangarang Collective, *Out Of The Closets and Into The Libraries*, 1 (2005), http://archive.qzap.org/index.php/Detail/Object/Show/object_id/109, accessed 10 December 2016.

61 Simeon Wade, *Chez Foucault* (1978), https://progressivegeographies.files.wordpress.com/2015/02/wade-ed-1978-chez-foucault.pdf, accessed 10 October 2015.

62 Miss Spentyouth, *Judy*, 1:1 (1993) and *Judy*, 1:2 (1994), http://archive.qzap.org/index.php/Detail/Object/Show/object_id/251, accessed 10 December 2016.

63 *Fan Club Zine*, 1 (2016).

64 Splash and Retro, *Barbra's Psychic Anus*, 2 (1992); Kathleen Hanna, *My Life with Evan Dando Popstar*, MSS 271, 2, 17 (Kathleen Hanna Papers, Fales Library and Special Collections, New York University Libraries).

65 Splash and Retro, *Barbra's Psychic Anus*, 2 (1992).

66 Tom Jennings, *Homocore*, 2 (1988), http://archive.qzap.org/index.php/Detail/Object/Show/object_id/279, accessed 10 December 2016.

67  *The Only Thing Missing Is You*, 1 (2002), https://archive.org/details/ TheOnlyThingMissingIsYou1, accessed 1 October 2015.

68  Ablaze!, *The City is Ablaze!*, p. 24.

69  Karen Ablaze!, 'Bored in The North', *Ablaze!*, 7 (1990), Ablaze! (ed.), *The City is Ablaze!*, p. 186.

70  Kearney, *Girls Make Media*, p. 144.

71  Alana Klumbia, Christa Orth and Julia Applegate, *Making History: Documenting and Preserving Drag King Culture* (2008), http://archive.qzap.org/index.php/Detail/ Object/Show/object_id/181, accessed 10 December 2016.

72  Ciarán, 'Music Fanzine Collecting as Capital Accumulation', 12.

# 3

# Whose culture? Fanzines, politics and agency

MATTHEW WORLEY

The impetus for starting a (punk) fanzine was often clear enough. Writing in the first issue of *Sniffin' Glue* (1976), Mark Perry bemoaned the weekly music press's failure to understand 'this thing called "punk rock"'. 'The weeklys [*sic*] are so far away from the kids that they can't possibly say anything of importance', he complained: 'why don't they stick to Queen and all that trash that drive around in expensive cars'.[1] For Tony Drayton, communicating from the edge of Glasgow in November 1976, *Ripped & Torn* afforded him 'the only way to read my views on the punk scene'.[2] Steve Burke, meanwhile, told Granada TV's *Brass Tacks* (1977) that he began making *Shy Talk* to get involved. 'I'm tone deaf', he explained, 'but I wanted to be part of [Manchester punk] so I started a fanzine up'.[3]

Less apparent, perhaps, were the repercussions of such impulse: the effect to the cause. Beyond giving expression to the youthful enthusiasms engendered by pop music – and revealing a healthy disdain for commercial media – how did fanzines contribute to the initiatives filtered through punk? In *Sniffin' Glue*'s case, Perry's eight pages of fervent text served as a catalyst; a stimulus for countless other homemade magazines to flower in London and across the country.[4] Simultaneously, *Sniffin' Glue* and the zines it inspired affirmed the DIY ethos associated with punk, embodying a cut 'n' paste aesthetic that signified qualities of immediacy, dissonance and irreverence.[5] For Perry, as for Drayton and Burke, writing a fanzine enabled access to an emergent culture through which to trace, celebrate and shape its development. While Perry formed a band (Alternative TV) and became a go-to person amidst the media clamour of 1976–77, Drayton navigated punk's trajectory through 18 issues of *Ripped & Torn* and, from 1980, six issues of *Kill Your Pet Puppy*, intervening into subcultural debate and defending punk's potential from deviations both real and imagined. Born of the grass-roots, fanzines covered local and provincial scenes to forge networks and lend support. *Shy Talk* 'builds up everything that's going on around Manchester', Denise Lloyd (a fellow young punk from the city) stated at the time.[6]

As this suggests, punk's fanzines opened up a cultural space. Not only did they allow for creative and political expression, but they also enabled a means of intervention. Most importantly, perhaps, they offered a site to claim, contest and retain a sense of cultural ownership in the face of media distortion or wider disinterest. The three zines considered here – *JOLT*, *Anathema* and *Hard As Nails* – each, in their different ways, sought to inform and (re)direct the cultures of which they formed part. They voiced opinion and contributed to a conversation. Beneath any prevailing cultural narrative, be it defined in newsprint or captured on film to be replayed over and over as disembodied spectacle, lay alternate interpretations scribbled, typed and held together with glue and staples. In fanzines we find cultures recorded from the bottom-up rather than the top-down. A 'truth', so The Clash's Joe Strummer would have it, known only to guttersnipes.[7]

## *JOLT* (1977): 'Well, why aren't there any real girl punk musicians around?'

*JOLT* was put together by Lucy Whitman – writing as Lucy Toothpaste – in January 1977, one of the first wave of punk fanzines inspired by the example of *Sniffin' Glue*. It ran for three issues and conformed visually to a recognisable type: scrawled text enveloped by crudely cut newspaper clippings, photos and, later, drawings pasted at odd angles; a punk focus that doubled as personal commentary. Look closer, however, and *JOLT* carried an agenda beyond simply reporting back from gigs or the record shop. As Jon Savage noted in his fanzine round-up for *Sounds* in January 1978, *JOLT* was one of the few early zines to use the medium's lack of censorship to express a political position: to offer a critique; to engage with punk beyond mere celebration or cliché.[8] More specifically, Whitman brought a feminist eye to punk, concentrating on the possibilities – and challenges – for 'girl bands' forming on the cusp of the new wave. 'I want to do lots of things on girl punks', she wrote in the first issue, 'specially who play the guitar'. *JOLT* was not 'just another punk mag': it was '(Just) Another punk mag for ~~punks~~ girls'.[9]

Whitman's introduction to punk came via a Sex Pistols' performance at Walthamstow's Assembly Hall in June 1976. Finding them 'intriguing' and 'exciting', she recognised in punk a 'space for anybody to do whatever they wanted'.[10] For Whitman, then about to become a third-year English student at University College London, this meant both an opportunity for women to form bands and a chance to inject feminist ideas into rock 'n' roll. *JOLT*, therefore, was born with a particular modus operandi: to shape the politics of punk along suitably progressive lines. 'I brought my feminism with me into punk', Whitman recalled, having already played briefly in an all-female band called The Neons before joining Rock Against Racism (RAR) in 1977 and helping develop Rock Against Sexism (RAS) from 1978.[11]

Feminism and anti-fascism proved central to *JOLT*'s style and content, paving the way for Whitman's later writing in RAR's *Temporary Hoarding* magazine, RAS's *Drastic Measures* bulletin and *Spare Rib*. The cover of *JOLT*'s first issue featured Elli Medeiros from the French band Stinky Toys, with a newspaper strapline running diagonally across the page stating (not aimed towards Medeiros of course): 'How an ugly woman is transformed on stage into the beautiful queen of rock'. Smaller press clippings then peppered the zine's five pages, comprising brief snippets relating to Patti Smith and such fledgling all-girl bands as The Slits and The Castrators.[12] Subsequent issues featured illustrated covers: *JOLT* number two was fronted by a punk Queen Elizabeth II celebrating her jubilee; issue 3 by the moral crusader Mary Whitehouse entwined in a lesbian embrace. Inside, photos of The Slits' Ari-Up (Arianne Foster), The Adverts' Gaye Black and X-Ray Spex's Poly Styrene (Marianne Elliot-Said) complemented typed-up interviews and essays. The contrast to the predominantly male faces staring out from most other punk fanzines was stark.

*JOLT*'s first issue also presented a mission statement of sorts, urging girl bands to form, play and overcome any sense of doubt or self-consciousness. '[It] doesn't matter if we don't know how to play the guitar yet, we can soon learn to play as well as any other punk and I think the punk public is just waiting for more all-girl bands to appear'. For inspiration, Andy Warhol's would-be assassin Valerie Solanas was featured as a 'great punk [from] history', replete with extracts from her SCUM (Society for Cutting Up Men) manifesto.[13] Thereafter, issues two and three built around pieces on The Slits and X-Ray Spex respectively, drawing together punk's female presence to show 'that girl punks have at last got going.'[14]

Whitman's anti-fascism was not so predominant but clear nonetheless, finding expression in concern at punk's swastika-chic and susceptibility to right-wing influence. Issue 3, published on the eve of the National Front's (NF) march through Lewisham on 13 August 1977, called for 'hordes of punks' to support a counter-demonstration and 'smash the idea that punk has anything to do with fascism once & for all'.[15] In the event, the 'Battle of Lewisham' presaged the formation of the Anti-Nazi League and gave stimulus to RAR's efforts to mobilise punk support.[16]

The politics of *JOLT* reflected Whitman's own priorities. But she was not alone. For many young, not-so-young and proto-leftists, punk's oppositional spirit and approach complemented (and soundtracked) their own sense of revolt, with The Clash in particular seeming to provide a socially conscious rock 'n' roll that was avowedly anti-racist.[17] At the same time, Whitman's attempts to channel punk's politics revealed tensions resonant of the 1970s. First, in relation to feminism, her interview with The Slits noted feminist antipathy to punk as but another variant of 'cock rock', to which Whitman argued that 'angry women should make an angry noise'.[18] The pressures felt by women forming bands, especially the preconceptions of male reviewers, musicians and audience members, were relayed in both The Slits and X-Ray Spex articles. Yet Whitman's review of The Runaways and Sharon Dunham's review of a gig by The Slits (in issue two) each criticised, albeit from different angles, the bands for 'playing on' their femininity, as if the foregrounding of gender brokered a collision of critical theory, cultural expectation and subjective taste.[19] Nevertheless, running through all three *JOLT*s were questions relating to such contemporary feminist debate as to whether all-female or mixed-gender groups served best to demonstrate women's cultural legitimacy; whether there was such a thing as 'male' and 'female' music; and how best to engage with and challenge the patriarchal structures of the music industry and everyday sexism.

Secondly, and similarly, the contested politics of punk's cultural assault were explored in an essay on 'Marxism & the Mass Media', during which Whitman contemplated the folk-singer Leon Rosselson's assertion that rock was too much a product of the music industry to be a revolutionary force. Where Rosselson understood rock to emphasise a separation between glam-ourised performers and passive spectators, he claimed folk music and folk clubs bypassed the worst excesses of the industry and broke down the performer–audience divide. Again, the essay – based on a discussion held at the Film Co-op in Chalk Farm – was resonant of the time.[20] Though too shy to join in the debate with those suggesting rock, not folk, was 'the music of the masses', Whitman's subsequent reflections fed into an analysis of punk's importance. Two observations stood out. Punk, as with all cultural forms, was full of contradictions, hence its containing 'tendencies towards both fascism and anarchism, which are polar opposites'. Like culture more generally, punk and rock 'n' roll were sites of struggle that had to be fought for. 'I think it's ridiculous to assume that one special type of music ... is somehow untainted by ruling-class values', Whitman continued, noting that folk could be just as 'fucking sexist' and 'pretentious' as any other music. As importantly, she restated punk's progressive potential: that is, the enabling of assertive action via forming bands or writing fanzines; accessibility via cheap equipment and the rejection of virtuosity; a focus on everyday life rather than 'fantasies'; a popular appeal that meant those appropriated by 'big business' were soon replaced by other bands and other fanzines forming at the grass-roots.[21]

Third, and following on from the notion of punk as a contested culture, *JOLT*'s anti-fascist content stemmed in part from a conversation Whitman had with a young punk at a party. He was wearing a swastika, but not for shock effect. He believed in repatriation, conscription and racial segregation. He was also singing along to The Clash's cover version of Junior Murvin's 'Police and Thieves', a reggae tune produced by Lee Perry in 1976. For Whitman, whose description of the conversation in *JOLT*'s third issue was surrounded by images of NF marches and pertinent newspaper clippings, this served, first and foremost, to prove fascism's irrationality. But it also reinforced her concern as to punk's susceptibility to reactionary influence. There followed a plea to 'fight back' and to 'get off the fence', with photos of Nazi atrocities serving as a reminder of where fascism leads. In such a context, Whitman's engagement with RAR and call for a punk presence to counter the NF in Lewisham marked her own solution.[22] At the same time, her concern that anti-fascist violence was often counter-productive gave hint of differences within the left as to how best to confront the NF; differences that would rumble on into the 1980s while also informing punk-related cultures for which far-right interventions at gigs became a growing problem over the turn of the decade.[23]

Though lasting for just three issues, *JOLT* provided Whitman with a way into and a platform to engage with debates circulating on the left and feeding into popular culture. Having taken her feminism into punk, she then took her punk into feminism via RAS and contributions to *Spare Rib*. By so doing, Whitman contributed to a continuum that fed through RAR, RAS, *Shocking Pink*, riot grrrl and onto the burgeoning feminist punk scenes of the twenty-first century.[24] Having used *JOLT* to access the political and cultural opportunities presented by punk, Whitman helped contest and shape the cultures that formed in the Sex Pistols' wake.

## Anathema (1982): 'People in Britain don't write like this'

The Sex Pistols' 'Anarchy in the UK' (1976) ensured British punk came imbued with a political charge. Be it the 7-inch single wrapped in a sheer black sleeve akin to the anarchist's flag or the promotional images of a ripped-up Union Jack held together by bulldog clips and safety pins, the record looked, sounded and *felt* seditious. Whatever the meaning intended by Johnny Rotten's lyric, Jamie Reid's design or Vivienne Westwood and Malcolm McLaren's provocation, the injection of 'anarchy' into pop's lexicon – not to mention the furore surrounding the Sex Pistols' supposed violence and profanity – ensured debate as to the provenance of punk's politics. 'Anarchy', like 'fascism' and 'boredom', became a buzzword; the circled 'A' fed neatly into punk's semiotic arsenal.[25]

By 1980, punk's connection to notions of anarchy had begun to find deeper expression in bands such as Crass and Poison Girls.[26] Though both groups formed in 1977, they remained relatively obscure prior to releasing their first records in early 1979.[27] Both, too, committed to working wherever possible outside the mechanisms of the culture industry, recoiling from the appropriation of punk's first wave to adopt a resolutely autonomous position in the DIY spaces facilitated by the proliferation of independent labels and fanzines. Both included members with countercultural pasts that predated punk's emergence; both understood anarchy as more than simply a signal of subversion or a symbol of self-rule. Distinct from the binaries of 'left' and 'right', anarchy enabled Crass and Poison Girls to develop a libertarian politics that moved beyond the former's slogan of 'there is no authority but yourself'.[28]

The influence of Crass, in particular, is hard to overestimate. To flick through the independent charts of the early 1980s is to see Crass's records as almost ever-present, their output and performances spawning an array of bands, labels and acolytes inspired by their methods.[29] Crass songs were often like treatises, with lyrics that unpicked, critiqued and attacked the structures of 'the system'. The sound was raw, giving caustic expression to ideas that were further complemented by Gee Vaucher's artwork on record sleeves that doubled as communiqués replete with essays, information and contacts. And though Crass eschewed the music press, their ideas were transmitted through an ever-growing number of interviews for fanzines that, in turn, began to replicate the aesthetic and deliberate on the politics of what eventually became known as anarcho-punk.

*Anathema* was one such fanzine. Created by Lee Gibson, a 19-year-old from Longnewton (County Durham) attuned to punk following exposure to the Sex Pistols' 'God Save the Queen' in 1977, its two issues featured interviews with Crass, Poison Girls and the anarchist poet Andy T (Andrew Thorley) amidst an assortment of overtly political essays and collages. Gibson had already produced zines prior to distributing *Anathema* in 1982, changing their titles regularly to avoid falling into a formula. In many ways, therefore, *Anathema* was a continuation of 1981's *Protesting Children Minus The Bondage*; indeed, Gibson's interview with Poison Girls traversed the two zines. Even so, taken as a pair, *Anathema* provides a pertinent example of how fanzines evolved to allow for formative political opinion to be worked out and communicated. Certainly, the ratio between music and politics tipped towards the latter with *Anathema*.

Gibson's discovery of Crass and Poison Girls brought focus to a critical sensibility already piqued by punk. Looking back, he described punk as a message: 'we were all ready and willing to challenge the status quo and the corrupt powers-that-be and to forge our own paths in life'.[30] But it was only after hearing, seeing, writing to, visiting and interviewing Crass and Poison Girls that Gibson's politics began to cohere. 'I stayed with Crass for a few days', he later recalled, 'half mesmerised; it was like a different world and made quite an impression on me. Crass were very organised and focused on what they were doing, whereas I was still making things up as I went along … It was the first time I actually glimpsed the possibilities of alternate ways of living. Something different from the usual family set up and all the restrictions that invariably come with that package'.[31] The results found expression, first, in interview form; then as essay, poem, short story and collage.

The interviews with Crass and Poison Girls covered overlapping ground.[32] While expected fanzine subjects – music, records, gigs – were touched upon, attention focused mainly on the politics developed in the bands' lyrics and lifestyles. Gibson engaged the bands in debate as to the meaning of anarchy; the dynamics and limits of organised protest; the complexities of class; the socially defined constructs of 'family' and individual identity. 'There's always the thing of how do you see beyond [the system]', Crass's Penny Rimbaud (Jeremy Ratter) mused. 'I think it's very precious working with certain forms of behaviour and certain methods by which people can perceive beyond the definitions that they've been given'.[33] In effect, *Anathema* became Gibson's means of doing just that.

In both issues, the structural foundations of state and society were dissected; their power relations exposed and decried. Attention was given to how distorted realities, forged by media, party-politics and religion, transferred to become the hegemonic values of everyday life. Collages juxtaposed newspaper headlines with images of violence; the gendered clichés of tabloid and TV were rendered ridiculous via saturation or recontextualisation. Essays about the 'clever con' of politics followed almost existential ruminations on the travails of existence and the historic implications of 'church control'. 'These are the lies I see being disguised. People's reliance on labour is based upon the agony or oppression of another human being. Company death. State death. The family feast on pain.'[34]

Ostensibly, the worldview espoused by *Anathema* – alongside such comparable zines as *Acts of Defiance*, *Fack* and *Toxic Grafity* – was bleak, a smorgasbord of violence, oppression and commercialised 'opiates' designed to distract from a life cast in the shadow of the Cold War's impending nuclear apocalypse. Simultaneously, as Chris Low – producer of *Guilty of What?* fanzine and drummer for a series of anarchist bands – noted, the 'all-encompassing ethos and ideology' of Crass *et al.* provided a sense of 'identity and sovereignty'; an explanation and an outlet for the disaffection that stoked punk's ire.[35] Anarchy thereby presented an 'alternative reality', a means of breaking down personal barriers of class, race, gender and sexuality towards what Gibson defined as a world of 'co-operations, not domination, not exploitation … peace not war. Love not hate. Constructive construction not destructive destruction. Care not violence. Intelligence not ignorance … We will work for real needs. For each other, not some smarmy boss … Not for commercial profit'.[36] And while such musings often rested on angsty platitudes that sometimes became as doctrinaire as those they opposed, the process of critical engagement rendered by writing an essay, poem or creating a collage at least served as a form of political rationalisation. The fanzine, moreover, provided the medium of expression; the means of communication.

Looking back, the anarchist zines produced in the early 1980s collated a remarkable historical record. They documented a reimaging of radical politics taking place on the margins of popular culture; revolutionary ideas bound to youth's obsession with music and style. Not only did they capture a process of adolescent questioning, they also revealed fumblings toward new politics and lifestyles distinct from the organisational and ideological mores of the twentieth century. For Gibson, punk combined with anarchist politics to open up new ways of thinking and doing. As well as providing a creative outlet, they paved the way for a life of squatting and intellectual enquiry. As the strapline to his autobiography puts it: 'I'm not sure what messed me up the most; Punk Rock, Anarchy, LSD, Magick or UFOs. I'm just thankful I got messed up.'[37]

## Hard As Nails (1983–85): 'sussed skins against the scum'

Few cultures have been so reviled as skinhead. Emerging from the dissipation of mod in the later 1960s, skinheads embodied an avowedly working-class alternative to the hippie counterculture resonant of the 'swinging sixties'. The style was all: boots, braces and button-down – sometimes collarless – shirts; jeans turned up or Levi's Sta-Prest; cropped hair, short but never cut to the bone. Sheepskin coats were popular before Crombies and Harringtons eased the transition to suedehead; for a night out, mohair suits and brogues were complemented by a touch of Ivy League among the more discerning.[38] Musically, the skinhead soundtrack comprised bluebeat, early reggae and soul, a mix that enabled Jamaican rude-boy influences to infuse the cross-cultural synergy. Equally, however, skinheads retained the territorial proclivities of their forebears, finding an outlet in football and local rivalries that enlivened a Saturday afternoon or night out. Though punch-ups and street-corner gangs were never the sole-preserve of skinheads, it was the 'bovver' that became the media's defining motif, especially if racial overtones could be teased from a story. A monster was born, captured for posterity in Richard Allen's popular novellas of the 1970s and made all too real by the far right's cultivation of skinhead cadres later in the decade.[39] By 1980, 'skinhead' had become synonymous with 'neo-Nazi' in the public/media imagination; a racist yob, lumpen and violent.

There were different narratives, of course. Aspects of skinhead culture could vary across postcodes, let alone the UK. The media's codification of skinhead bore only tenuous relation to the experience of those described, although – as is often the way with youth subcultures – the clichéd caricature provided a template to copy and perpetuate. As a result, the *politics* of skinhead culture were always contested, be it in terms of 'left' and 'right' or the conventions of style. Moreover, by the time the NF and British Movement (BM) had begun to nurture young skins to their cause, so punk too had begun to inform the skinhead 'revival' that gathered around bands such as Sham 69. Both 2-tone and Oi! emerged from the punk diaspora: the first an amalgam with ska that brokered cross-racial groups such as Specials, The Selecter and The Beat; the second a reassertion of punk as 'working-class protest' that included skinheads among its 'loose alliance' of 'tearaways, hooligans [and] rebels'.[40] The aesthetics, soundtrack and politics of being a skinhead were therefore in a state of uneasy flux by the turn of the decade; battlegrounds for those staking a claim to any 'true' skinhead identity.

*Hard As Nails* was very much a rejoinder to all this. Conceived by Ian Hayes-Fry and Paul Barrett in 1983, two telecom and Post Office workers from Canvey Island, the zine was designed to become a 'focal point for sussed skins'; 'a reaction', as Hayes-Fry put it, 'to *The Sun* idea of skins'. Instead of 'scruffs' with 'bald heads, sniffing glue and birds in 18-hole Docs', *Hard As Nails* looked to affirm the 'real '69 skin-ideals'.[41] Attention to detail ensured Ben Sherman shirts, suits and brogues – Trevira skirts and penny loafers for the girls – eclipsed the MA-1 flying jackets, too-tight jeans and battered boots favoured by those mutating into far-right boneheads. Reggae, ska and soul came back to the fore, at least complementing Oi! and correcting what Barrett complained was punk's negative influence. 'Skinheads became just an extension of the punk shock thing with the bald heads and the tattoos on the forehead … bald punks … a real moron element, people who think it's hard to be ignorant'.[42] As this suggests, *Hard As Nails* was an intervention: a means of reclaiming skinhead from the distortions of the media lens and, as importantly, the corrosive effect of punkish idiocy and far-right intrusion.

Ostensibly, the content of *Hard As Nails* was typical fanzine fare: band interviews, record lists and gig reviews. The first issue featured a piece on Oi!, picking out the good from the bad across the various compilation albums issued from 1980 to 1983, and a jokey round-up of 'skinhead love songs'.[43] But it also endeavoured to reassert skinhead's cultural lineage, charting a history that marginalised the 'scummy' skins and 'plastic glueheads' in order to concentrate on those keen to 'stay sharp, stay sussed'.[44] Running through the zines was the tale of 'arry 'arris, a cartoon version of a scruffy, glue-sniffing skinhead sent back in time to meet his forebears in 1970. Given 'arry's facial tattoos, bald head, tatty jeans and jacket, the original skins mistake him for some kind of greaser and have no truck with his 'we're all white ain't we' politics.[45]

Much attention was given to skinhead's roots, with features on the early sounds and styles that defined the culture and interviews with 'originals' celebrating 'traditional … skinheadism'.[46] So, for example, issue 3 traced the transition 'from skin to smooth', explaining the evolution of skinhead fashion over the early 1970s, while issue 7 offered a guide to suitably sharp coats and jackets.[47] Not dissimilarly, *Hard As Nails* emphasised the breadth of skinhead culture, eschewing political loyalties for class-cultural identity. As well as featuring 'scooter skins' and overviews of scenes across the UK and wider world, there were also essays on tattoos, boxing and the Kray Twins. Unusually for skinhead zines, too, space was given to skinhead girls, with 'renees' writing in to offset the male focus. The interview with Janice, 'an original skin-girl from South London', remains a rare insight.[48]

Of course, *Hard As Nails* could not expunge politics altogether. In issue 2, the zines stance was bluntly stated: '[Skins] should be neither Nazi or Red. Skin is enough, the style and the music … '[49] Where the far right's politics were seen to be as shabby as their fashion sense, the far left were regarded as middle-class trendies out-of-touch with the working class. Only Red Action – a grass-roots working-class anti-fascist organisation – received positive mention. Nevertheless, the political ramifications of such a position rumbled throughout all seven issues in some form or other. Features on avowedly socialist bands such as Burial, The Oppressed, Red London and Redskins brought criticism from the 'proud to be white and proud to wear the union jack' brigade gathered in Islington's Agricultural pub, a hang-out for the far right in the early 1980s.[50] Simultaneously, editorial efforts to retain a distance between the fanzine and politics raised concern among those such as Shaz, a skinhead girl from Leeds, who felt 'the SWP and even Labour' were 'the only real way out'. 'The whole skin & oi movement's supposed to be working class', she insisted, 'so when you have to get political, do make it clear where you stand.'[51]

Some punches were not pulled. Skrewdriver, an erstwhile punk band that adopted a skinhead image in 1977 and eventually came out openly for the NF in 1982, were given short shrift. 'What kind of skin would be seen dead with 3 days of stubble and a lumber jacket?' Politically, too, they were portrayed as chancers flirting 'with the sieg-heiling dickheads'. In short, Skrewdriver were the antithesis of everything Hard As Nails regarded as skinhead: Nazi-skins hiding swastikas behind union jacks; 'patriots (ha!) who chant kraut slogans and take their line from Italians'. '[Surely] people can see who the real enemy is? It's not the greasers, the punks, the mods. It's certainly not the blacks. We all know it's Maggie, her and everyone's bloody mindedness.'[52]

It would be ridiculous to suggest that Hard As Nails single-handedly redirected skinheads away from the politics and associated aesthetics of the far right. But it was important, nevertheless, in reasserting the culture's (pre-punk) history and presenting an alternative reading of skinhead's rationale. The zine helped connect and then reinforce links between 'sussed' skinhead milieux across the UK (including the Cardiff Skins, Glasgow's Spy-Kids, Southend's Clockwork Patrol); these, in turn, produced comparable zines (Backs Against the Wall, Bovver Boot, Crophead, Croptop, Spy-Kids, Street Feeling, Suedehead Times, Tell Us the Truth, Tighten Up, Zoot) that both challenged any overly London-centric perception of skinhead and further marginalised those coalescing around the Nazi politics of the NF, BM, Skrewdriver and, ultimately, Blood & Honour.[53] Among references to keeping ideals and not losing sight of the past, Hard As Nails curated a class-cultural history: proud, stylish and sussed.

## Conclusion

JOLT, Anathema and Hard As Nails offer three pertinent examples of processes evident across a fanzine culture given stimulus by punk. Beyond the sense of agency inherent in producing a zine, they offered opportunity to shape, collate

**3.1**  *Hard as Nails*, 4 (1984) © Ian Hayes-Fry

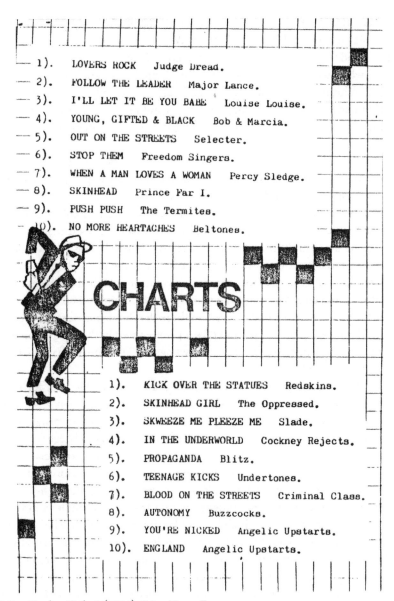

1). LOVERS ROCK    Judge Dread.
2). FOLLOW THE LEADER    Major Lance.
3). I'LL LET IT BE YOU BABE    Louise Louise.
4). YOUNG, GIFTED & BLACK    Bob & Marcia.
5). OUT ON THE STREETS    Selecter.
6). STOP THEM    Freedom Singers.
7). WHEN A MAN LOVES A WOMAN    Percy Sledge.
8). SKINHEAD    Prince Far I.
9). PUSH PUSH    The Termites.
10). NO MORE HEARTACHES    Beltones.

CHARTS

1). KICK OVER THE STATUES    Redskins.
2). SKINHEAD GIRL    The Oppressed.
3). SKWEEZE ME PLEEZE ME    Slade.
4). IN THE UNDERWORLD    Cockney Rejects.
5). PROPAGANDA    Blitz.
6). TEENAGE KICKS    Undertones.
7). BLOOD ON THE STREETS    Criminal Class.
8). AUTONOMY    Buzzcocks.
9). YOU'RE NICKED    Angelic Upstarts.
10). ENGLAND    Angelic Upstarts.

**3.2**   *Hard as Nails,* 3 (1984) © Ian Hayes-Fry

and defend cultural practice in the face of media, commercial and, indeed, academic distortion. With *JOLT*, Lucy Whitman endeavoured to apply a feminist and broadly socialist reading to punk, critiquing aspects of the emergent culture while also denoting the progressive possibilities opened up by notions of DIY. Whitman recognised punk – and culture generally – as a contested site that harboured contradictory tendencies and impulses. *JOLT*, therefore, provided a means of engagement, enabling Whitman to intervene in debate as to punk's political potential.

*Anathema* revealed more existential qualities, allowing Lee Gibson to reflect on, filter and apply the anarchist perspectives developed by Crass and Poison Girls to the world of which he was part. The result was an almost methodical deconstruction of the systems that maintained late twentieth-century society. In effect, Gibson offered articulate expression of his teenage angst, recognising the absurdities and abuses of life itself. Simultaneously, his writings – again inspired by the records he listened to and the bands he saw live – explored alternative lines of investigation: anarchism, political activism, even occultism. Looked at this way, his fanzine(s) enabled him to find a route out of the life he felt was mapped before him through school, marriage, mortgage and work. 'I feel I ought to try and take a positive step in the right direction from poetry and anti-establishment scrawlings ... YOU must change YOU ... For the love of life ... LIVE!!'[54]

Finally, *Hard As Nails* offered reclamation of a subculture. Media distortions and far-right incursions were seen to have faded the 'spirit of traditional, original' skinheads. In response, *Hard As Nails* provided opportunity to restate that original 'spirit' and critique those factors deemed to have caused degeneration. Class pride and the politics of style were reasserted in place of racism and tabloid caricature. A celebration of working-class culture was prioritised over the self-pity of those who wallowed in a 'scummy-gummy induced hell'.[55]

Each of these zines bore influence within the cultural milieux among which they circulated. Though all but hidden from the mainstream media's coverage of pop and youth culture, they nevertheless traced alternative narratives and dialogues resonant of their time. Modern cultural history is all too often defined – contained, even – by whatever was captured in newsprint or on celluloid. Meanwhile, on the ground, people made their own cultures and lived their own lives no less important than those transformed into spectacle.

## Notes

Acknowledgments: my thanks to Ian Hayes-Fry, Chris Low, Lucy Robinson, Toast (Dave Rumsey) and Tim Wells for comments, insights and material.

1 Mark Perry, 'The Last Page', *Sniffin' Glue*, 1, 1976, p. 8; Mark Perry, *Sniffin' Glue: The Essential Punk Accessory* (London: Sanctuary, 2000).

2 Tony Drayton, 'My Excuse For This Self-Indulgent Escapade', *Ripped & Torn*, 1, 1976, p. 3.

3 *Brass Tacks*, Granada TV, 1977.

4 Matthew Worley, 'Punk, Politics and British (Fan)zines, 1976–84: "While the world was dying, did you wonder why?"', *History Workshop Journal*, 79:1 (2015), 76–106.

5 Teal Triggs, *Fanzines* (London: Thames & Hudson, 2010); 'Scissors and Glue: Punk Fanzines and the Creation of a DIY Aesthetic', *Journal of Design History*, 19:1 (2006), pp. 69–83; Stephen Duncombe, *Notes from the Underground: Zines and the Politics of Alternative Culture* (Bloomington: Microcosm Publishing, 2008 edn).

6 *Brass Tacks*, Granada TV, 1977. Other early Manchester fanzines included *Ghast Up*, *Girl Trouble*, *Noisy People*, *Out There* and *Plaything*. As should hardly need to be said, music fanzines – such as *Hot Flash* – existed in Manchester prior to punk's emergence.

7 The Clash, 'Garageland', *The Clash* (CBS, 1977).

8 Jon Savage, 'Pure Pop Art for Now People', *Sounds*, 14 January 1978, pp. 17–18.

9 *JOLT*, 1 (1977), pp. 2–4.

10 Quoted in Cazz Blase, 'A Woman Called Toothpaste: An Interview with Lucy Whitman', *The f-Word*, 20 May 2011, www.thefword.org.uk/features/2011/05/Lucy_Whitman, accessed 15 February 2016.

11 Blase, 'A Woman Called Toothpaste' (unpaginated); Martha Zenfell, 'Love Sex, Hate Sexism?', *NME*, 7 April 1979, p. 15; Daniel Rachel, *Walls Come Tumbling Down: The Music and Politics of Rock Against Racism, 2-Tone and Red Wedge* (London: Picador, 2016); Ian Goodyer, *Crisis Music: The Cultural Politics of Rock Against Racism* (Manchester: Manchester University Press, 2009).

12 The Castrators were a short-lived band that included Tessa Pollitt, later of The Slits. The snippets used in *JOLT* included bits from Carolyn Martin, 'Here Come the Punkesses', *News of the World*, 16 January 1977, p. 3 and Caroline Coon's *Melody Maker* guide to punk, 27 November 1976, pp. 33–9.

13 Solanas quotes also decorated the walls of SEX, the shop run by Vivienne Westwood and Malcolm McLaren that cultivated punk's early attitude and aesthetic.

14 'Editorial', *JOLT*, 2 (1977), p. 4.

15 'Just Another … ', *JOLT*, 1 (1977), p. 4; 'Important Message' and 'Off Your Rocker', *JOLT*, 3 (1977), pp. 6–8.

16 Dave Renton, *When We Touched the Sky: The Anti-Nazi League, 1977–81* (Cheltenham: New Clarion Press, 2006).

17 Matthew Worley, 'Shot By Both Sides: Punk, Politics and the End of "Consensus"', *Contemporary British History*, 26:3 (2012), 333–54.

18 'The Slits', *JOLT*, 2 (1977), p. 2.

19 'Girl Bands', *JOLT*, 1 (1977), p. 3; Sharon Dunham, 'Review', *JOLT*, 2 (1977), pp. 3–4.

20 Matthew Worley, 'Marx–Lenin–Rotten–Strummer: British Marxism and Youth Culture in the 1970s', *Contemporary British History*, 30:4 (2016), 505–21.

21  'Music and the Mass Media', *JOLT*, 2 (1977), p. 5.

22  'Off Your Rocker', *JOLT*, 3 (1977), pp. 7–8.

23  Sean Birchall, *Beating the Fascists: The Untold Story of Anti-Fascist Action* (London: Freedom Press, 2010); *Kill Your Pet Puppy*, 1 (1980); Worley, 'Shot By Both Sides'.

24  Lucy Whitman, 'Women and Popular Music', *Spare Rib*, June 1981, pp. 6–8 and pp. 20–1; Julia Downes, 'Riot Grrrl: The Legacy and Contemporary Landscape of DIY Feminist Cultural Activism', in Nadine Monem (ed.), *Riot Grrrl: Revolution Girl Style Now!* (London: Black Dog Publishing, 2007), pp. 12–49; Anna Gough-Yates, '"A Shock to the System": Feminist Interventions in Youth Culture – The Adventures of *Shocking Pink*', *Contemporary British History*, 26:3 (2012), 375–403; Kevin Dunn and May Summer Farnsworth, '"We are the Revolution": Riot Grrrl Press, Girl Empowerment and DIY Self-publishing', *Women's Studies*, 41:2 (2012), 136–57; Laura Cofield and Lucy Robinson, '"The Opposite of the Band": Fangrrrling, Feminism and Sexual Dissidence', *Textual Practice*, 30:6 (2016), 1071–88.

25  The nod here to Alternative TV's 'How Much Longer' (1977) is obviously deliberate.

26  For a discussion of punk's relationship to anarchy see Russ Bestley, 'Big A Little A: The Graphic Language of Anarchy', in Mike Dines and Matthew Worley (eds), *The Aesthetic of Our Anger: Anarcho-punk, Politics and Music* (Colchester: Minor Composition, 2016), pp. 43–66.

27  Crass's debut EP, *The Feeding of the Five Thousand*, was scheduled to be released in late 1978 but was delayed until 1979 following a dispute at the pressing plant. Objection was taken to the blasphemous content of 'Asylum', the EP's opening track.

28  Richard Cross, 'The Hippies Now Wear Black: Crass and the Anarcho-Punk Movement, 1977–84', *Socialist History*, 26 (2004), 25–44; '"Take the Toys from the Boys": Gender, Generation and the Anarchist Intent in the Work of Poison Girls', *Punk & Post-Punk*, 3:2 (2015), 117–45.

29  Ian Glasper, *The Day the Country Died: A History of Anarcho Punk, 1980–1984* (London: Cherry Red, 2006).

30  'I heard [Sex Pistols' 'God save the Queen'] and bang … I fell in love with this new angry music … the rejects of society were beginning to unite'. Lee G. [Gibson], *A Punk Rock Flashback* (London: Lulu Press, 2013), pp. 13–18.

31  G., *A Punk Rock Flashback*, p. 45.

32  'Poison Girls Interview', *Protesting Children Minus The Bondage*, 2 (1981), pp. 10–12; 'Poison Girls', *Anathema*, 1 (1982), pp. 31–2; 'Crass Interview', *Anathema*, 1 (1982), pp. 11–14.

33  'Crass Interview', p. 14.

34  'The Art of Politics/A Clever Con', *Anathema*, 1 (1982), p. 28; 'Life Today', *Anathema*, 1 (1982), p. 17; 'Church Control', *Anathema*, 1 (1982), p. 19; 'Company Dreams', *Anathema*, 2 (1982), p. 23.

35  Chris Low interview with Russ Bestley (August 2014), quoted in Bestley, 'Big A Little A', pp. 53–4.

36  'Revolution The Pipe Dream', *Anathema*, 2 (1982), p. 32.

37  G., *A Punk Rock Flashback*, cover.

38  'Jim Ferguson's Fashion Notebook', in Nick Knight, *Skinhead* (London: Omnibus Press, 1982), pp. 36–47.

39  Bill Osgerby, '"Bovver" Books of the 1970s: Subcultures, Crisis and "Youth-Sploitation" Novels', *Contemporary British History*, 26:3 (2012), 299–331; Matthew Worley and Nigel Copsey, 'White Youth: The Far Right, Punk and British Youth Culture', *Journalism, Media and Cultural Studies*, 9 (2016), pp. 27–47.

40  Rachel, *Walls Come Tumbling Down*, 231–336; Dave Thompson, *Wheels out of Gear: 2-Tone, The Specials and a World in Flame* (London: Helter Skelter, 2004); sleevenotes to Various Artists, *Oi! The Album* (EMI, 1980); Garry Bushell, 'The New Breed', *Sounds*, 1 November 1980, pp. 32–3; 'Oi! – The Column', *Sounds*, 17 January 1981, 11. For pre-2-Tone reference to multi-racial skinhead gangs, see Garry Bushell's coverage of the second ANL carnival in *Sounds*, 30 September 1978, p. 46.

41  Quoted in Garry Bushell, 'Burial Plot', *Sounds*, 10 November 1984, p. 20.

42  *Ibid.*

43  I have been unable to locate a copy of the first *Hard As Nails*, so my thanks to Ian Hayes-Fry for providing me with an overview of issue 1.

44  Editorial, *Hard As Nails*, 3 (1984), p. 2.

45  There is a nod here, in 'arry's comment, to 'Chubby' Chris Henderson's appearance on the BBC documentary 'Skinheads' (1982), part of the *Arena* series. Henderson was the lead singer with Combat 84 and a British Movement (BM) stalwart. Closer to home, Hayes-Fry also recalled: 'a bunch of BM skins had come down from Basildon to The Grand Hotel in Leigh-on-(pre-gentrification)-Sea to trash a gig, and that confused "but we're all white" line came when their ringleader grabbed a mic and pathetically attempted to justify himself and misguidedly appeal for some sort of racial solidarity from a pissed-off and/or completely bemused audience' (correspondence with author, 7 December 2016).

46  'H.A.N.', *Hard As Nails*, 2 (1984), p. 2; 'Skinhead Remembrance', *Hard As Nails*, 7 (1985), pp. 10–11.

47  'From Skin to Smooth: The End of a Style', *Hard As Nails*, 3 (1984), p. 14.

48  'Class of '69', *Hard As Nails*, 5 (1985), pp. 8–9.

49  The quote is from *Hard As Nails*, 2 (1984), p. 14.

50  Letter from Andy, Paul *et al.*, *Hard As Nails*, 5 (1985), p. 18.

51  Letter from Shaz, *Hard As Nails*, 2 (1984), p. 14. See also Gaz from Darlington's letter in issue 3.

52  'Redskins', *Hard As Nails*, 3 (1984), pp. 8–9.

53  Due mention should be given to *Boots & Braces*, *Chargesheet* and *Skins* as skin-zines that tried to avoid politics and pre-dated *Hard As Nails*. All, however, were (initially) somewhat ambivalent to the scene that eventually coalesced around Skrewdriver.

54  'Revolution The Pipe Dream', *Anathema*, 2 (1982), p. 32.

55  'On the Deck', *Hard As Nails*, 7 (1985), p. 15.

# 4

# Invisible women: the role of women in punk fanzine creation

CAZZ BLASE

The role of women and girls in the creation of 1970s punk fanzines is largely unacknowledged. Because this area of punk fanzine research is so underdeveloped, this chapter will be situated within a much longer time period than is usual, beginning both pre-punk and pre-1970s. This is in order to reflect the contribution women have made towards independent printing and publishing from the nineteenth century onwards.

There are a number of of key moments of pre-punk agitation in print that have a link to punk in the widest sense; that is, those publications that were created to inform and entertain but also to challenge the prevailing authority and/or prevailing print or media culture of the day. Those this chapter will discuss in detail are the unstamped press of the 1830s, the 'Slow Print' movement of the 1880s, and the Wimmins comix of the early 1970s. This chapter also touches on the suffrage papers produced in the UK in the first two decades of the twentieth century, trench newspapers of the First World War, and the 1960s countercultural and underground press.

From here the chapter moves to the punk era and women fanzine editors; the influence of second-wave feminism and the women's liberation movement on some punk fanzines; female fanzine creators within editorial teams and collectives; and the role of female photographers and artists within punk fanzines. Women were also involved in the more technical, backroom aspects of fanzine production, such as publishing, printing and photocopying and had an important role to play in the technical side of the fanzine production process. Due to a number of societal circumstances they were also in a more advantageous position than their male counterparts when it came to having access to the means of fanzine production.

A final note on language: I refer to four different periods of feminist activity throughout this chapter, which I would define thus:

- Period One, 1860–99: Victorian feminism, including the very early suffrage campaigns and also wider concerns such as women's access to education and employment.
- Period Two, 1900–18: the women's suffrage campaign, the First World War, and the extension of the voting franchise to women over thirty.
- Period Three, 1968–89: the women's liberation movement and second-wave feminism.
- Period Four, 1990–2008: third-wave feminism, including cultural moments such as riot grrrl and Ladyfest.

## Poking a fork in the eye of the establishment: in search of pre-punk agitation in print

If punk represented a line in the sand, a year zero in which the past was stripped away and the future was banished, then punk fanzine creation (in its production methods at least) can be seen to represent a reassuring continuum. The punk fanzine as it existed in the UK between 1976 and the 1980s has many literary ancestors. This is especially the case if we include any independently produced publication that was founded with a strong desire to challenge authority and/or the prevailing print or media culture of its time. Whether that media culture was the patchouli and dope-scented culture of the UK music press in the 1970s, the relentlessly cheerful propaganda of UK war reporting during the First World War, or the birth of what would become mainstream newspaper journalism in the latter half of the nineteenth century, there has always been someone on hand to take issue and provide an alternative, often at great personal risk.

Women have been active participants in a number of key moments in printing history, but it requires a certain amount of digging to discover this. Elizabeth Carolyn Miller's history of Victorian small press culture and publications 'Slow Print': Literary Radicalism and Late Victorian Print Culture (2013) refers only in passing to The Torch, an anarchist newspaper produced by sisters Olivia and Helen Rossetti from their parents' basement in 1892.[1] Similarly, Barbara Onslow refers to Emily Faithfull's all-women Victoria Press in the 1860s, which was vital both when it came to training young women in the craft of printing, but also as the main printer of feminist literature at the time.[2]

The unstamped press, which first began to emerge in 1830, fifteen years after the introduction of a fourpenny stamp (or tax) on newspapers, and mere months after the July Revolution in France, can be seen as an early example of anti-establishment publishing, often with radical intent.[3] The unstamped penny newspapers that first began to appear in London in 1830 were within the price range of the poor who, unable to afford books, took what little education they could get from newspapers. It is for this reason that the fourpenny stamp was referred to as a 'tax on knowledge'.[4] The writers, editors and publishers of the unstamped papers were able to charge such low prices because they were illegal. Their publishers and owners had chosen not to pay the fourpenny tax and, as such, lay themselves open to prosecution by the government while at the same time attracting readers who could not afford the legal, stamped newspapers. As Patricia Hollis writes, '740 men, women and children went to prison' for selling papers such as the *Poor Man's Guardian*, *Destructive* and the *Working Man's Friend* on the streets of London.[5] Furthermore, London was not the only city or town to have its own unstamped press; it was just the most prolific. Despite the clear risks of publication, the circulation of such titles as *The Poor Man's Guardian* soared as sales of the stamped press declined, and this ongoing stand-off between the unstamped press and the government led to the reduction of stamp duty to a penny in 1836, and later to the scrapping of stamp duty altogether in 1855.[6]

Another moment of reaction to prevailing developments in the history of printing and journalism was the 'Slow Print', Ruskin-inspired publications of the 1880s. Elizabeth Carolyn Miller uses the phrase 'Slow Print' to describe the methods and ethos of a number of small-scale publications, the number of which surged in the late nineteenth century in the UK. The 'Slow Print' titles existed in parallel to a similar surge in publications for a mass audience, but these mass-audience titles were created using the cutting-edge technologies of increasingly mass production. *The Times* was the forerunner in this: in the first half of the nineteenth century, under owner John Walter II, it pioneered new, faster, more efficient printing methods, installing the first steam press in 1814; 'a new machine with four cylinders that printed 4,000 sheets an hour from flat formes' in 1827; and 'the first rotary press was invented in its office by Applegarth' in 1847.[7] By 1896, production techniques had moved so far, so fast, that the newly launched *Daily Mail* was able to make use of the latest in English and American printing technology to live out its claim to be 'A penny newspaper for a Halfpenny'.[8] They were using a Linotype printing press, which 'can set type – in solid lines – ten times as fast as a hand compositor and does not require stocks of type'.[9] 'Slow Print' titles, by comparison, were created using older, slower technology, on a much smaller scale and were not aimed at mass audiences.[10]

Come the early twentieth century and suffrage papers – such as *The Suffragette* and *Votes For Women* – and trench newspapers – including *The Wipers Times*, which ran from 1916 until 1918 – would attest to the long history of radical DIY printing and publishing in the UK. Much closer to the punk era was the explosion of print that came to be such an integral part of the 1960s counterculture. The underground press was best exemplified by such titles as *Oz* and *International Times* (*IT*), as well as by local papers such as *Mole Express*. These and similar titles proved important because a number of their writers, for example Sheila Rowbotham, Marsha Rowe and Rosie Boycott, would later go on to become involved with the women's liberation movement and/or women's papers such as *Spare Rib*. As we shall see, *Spare Rib*, which launched in June 1972, had an important role to play in the wider story of women and punk. It is also relevant as regards women and punk fanzine writers.

Equally, the early 1970s saw the important emergence of wimmins comix. Created in the context of the women's liberation movement and the tail-end of the 1960s counterculture, wimmins comix were explicitly created in reaction to the male-dominated, male-interest comix of the counterculture. Perhaps the crudest examples of the male comix's sexist content may be found in the work of the US cartoonist Robert Crumb. A cartoon created by Crumb for *East Village Other* (vol. 4, no. 13, 1969), for example, was titled 'FANTASY number 96, 747 Child *molesting* section. You fuck the little girl from the back while she licks grape jam off her fingers!!'. The cartoon depicts a small, passive, female child being anally raped by an adult male.[11]

Trina Robbins has spoken of a clear sense of feeling unwelcome in the late 1960s San Francisco comix scene, in which work on collaborative titles was often commissioned informally by other, male, comix writers via an unofficial boys' network. Robbins could therefore get work as a solo comix artist, or by being commissioned directly by publishers, but she did, nonetheless, lose work because she was excluded from a larger number of collaborative ventures.[12] Intelligent, artistically inclined women of the counterculture, weary of being excluded from working on the alternative comix, and equally weary of the representation of women in those publications, created overtly feminist publications such as *It Ain't Me Babe*, *Tits'n'Clits*, and *Wimmins Comix*. These publications first began to appear in 1970 in the USA, but it was only in 1977 that Suzy Varty, a Newcastle-born comix artist and a member of Birmingham Arts Lab, produced the first UK wimmins comic, *Heroine*.[13]

Both the women's liberation movement and wimmins comix preceded and ran parallel to punk, interacting with it in ways that have only begun to be discussed in recent years.[14] Certainly, the women's liberation movement impacted on punk and punk fanzines, just as certainly as it provided a spur for wimmins comix such as *Heroine*. If we look at fanzines such as Lucy Toothpaste's *JOLT* and the collectively run Birmingham fanzine *Brass Lip*, we can see the language of feminist debates around women in the workplace being mirrored in their debates around the treatment of women in the music industry. This is further enhanced by the scattergun quoting of feminist lyrics by the likes of The Raincoats (whose song 'Off Duty Trip' was based on a true story of a soldier who had raped a woman but was not convicted because the judge didn't want to damage his military career), X Ray Spex (whose 'Oh Bondage Up Yours!' remains something of a feminist call to arms) and The Slits (whose song 'Typical Girls' lampooned stereotypical female mores) alongside the embracing of both Patti Smith and Valerie Solanas as equally valid female role models. In Rock Against Sexism (RAS), the music and feminist organisation born out of Rock Against Racism (RAR), which sought to combat sexism in music and use music to fight sexism in society, we can see the ultimate fusing of punk and feminism a whole generation before the riot grrrl movement of the 1990s.

### I am a creator as well as a consumer: women, punk fanzines and feminism

Lucy Whitman, who wrote under the name Lucy Toothpaste, was introduced to the London punk scene in 1976, when she attended a gig at Walthamstow Town Hall featuring the Sex Pistols, Ian Dury and the Blockheads and The Stranglers. Studying for an English degree at the time, she was suitably excited and energised to launch *JOLT*, a punk fanzine with a feminist heart and anti-fascist sensibility.[15] 'I was already a feminist before I was a punk', she explained; 'I was also very concerned about the flirting with Nazi regalia and Nazi imagery and so on – I just thought that was stupid, but I thought it was dangerous too.'[16]

Stuck together in Lucy's bedroom using cut-up sections of *NME* and *Socialist Worker*, *JOLT* was a one-woman operation from the point of creation to production to distribution: 'I lugged them in carrier bags to Compendium Bookshop in Camden Town, which was where I used to buy all my fanzines, and Rough Trade'.[17] Later, *JOLT* would feature contributions from Sharon Spike, a friend of Lucy's who wrote the fanzine *Apathy in Ilford* (and, like Lucy, became involved with RAR), and Ros Past-it, Lucy's sister, who drew the covers for issues two and three.[18]

While *JOLT* did feature male punk bands, Lucy's central concern was to explore the role that women were playing within the developing London and UK punk scene. 'My fanzine came about from absolute excitement about the music and about the way things seemed to have cracked open. There was space for anybody to do whatever they wanted, including girls. You know, boys could get up on the stage who couldn't play their guitar and that meant that girls could get up onstage who couldn't play guitar either, so it was very, very democratic do it yourself stuff. I loved all of that.'[19] Her female-centred approach and sense of timing led The Slits to her door in their quest for a new girl bassist. This encounter led to an interview with the band, which appeared in issue 2. An interview with X Ray Spex frontwoman Poly Styrene was to follow in issue 3.

Whitman was not uncritical of the women she wrote about. She gave The Runaways short shrift and, when interviewing Siouxsie Sioux for *Spare Rib*, was critical of the Banshees' frontwoman's use of swastikas.[20] Similarly, she expressed disappointment in the first issue of *JOLT* that Siouxsie, Patti Smith and Elli Medeiros (Stinky Toys), while strong women, had all-male backing bands. *JOLT*'s strengths, however, of which there were many, concerned not just Whitman's unique position as a feminist punk fanzine writer, but also the clarity of her writing. Issue 1 of *JOLT* leapt straight to the matter at hand in its first paragraph: 'Well, why aren't there any real girl punk musicians around? I know there's sposed [sic] to be the Slits but all I've ever seen them do is spit at Eater – do they every play any gigs?'[21]

Whitman's writing serves as a vivid and articulate document of the early days of the London punk scene from 1976 through to 1977; the time when, for the inner circle of London punks around the Sex Pistols, everything felt possible, everything felt permissible, and optimism in nihilism was a valid currency.[22] As The Slits' Viv Albertine told me: 'That little crack only opened up in the music industry for almost 18 months [when] you could go in, before it slammed shut behind you.'[23]

Although there were only three issues of *JOLT*, each sold out and the groundwork was laid for Whitman's later work at the feminist magazine *Spare Rib*, at which she was key in bridging the generation gap between the magazine collective and the young punk women coming up. In a continuation of her dual fight against fascism and sexism, Whitman would also become involved with both RAR and RAS as an activist and writer on the publications *Temporary Hoarding* and *Drastic Measures*.

In contrast to Whitman's one-woman bedroom operation, the Birmingham punk fanzine *Brass Lip*, which emerged in 1979 for one issue, had two female editors. Syd Freake and Connie Klassen created the fanzine alongside a small and largely female battalion of writers and photographers. Looking at *Brass Lip* today, it does appear to have picked up the baton first grasped by *JOLT* in 1977, namely that of the questioning female punk fan with a feminist sensibility. RAS was in play by 1979, and *Brass Lip* includes a feature on sexism and the music industry alongside interviews with the Au Pairs and Poison Girls, two explicitly feminist mixed-gender post-punk bands.

In a nod to Ros Past-It's Silver Jubilee-inspired cover image of the Queen as a guitar playing, gobbing punk rocker for *JOLT*'s second issue, *Brass Lip* also opened with a drolly surreal 'Message from the Queen on the opening of *Brass Lip*'. This was purportedly written by the now touring punk Queen, detailing life on the road, with the corgis in the tourbus and 'Land of Hope and Glory' sung ringingly at the end of each show.[24] But whereas *JOLT* was cut up and glued together in a bedroom, *Brass Lip* was designed by the Birmingham Arts Lab's Suzy Varty. The fanzine was also professionally printed – rather than Xeroxed – by the all-female Moss Side Printing Co-Op in Manchester, linking the punk and post-punk women of Birmingham to the feminist wing of the counterculture and the grass-roots of the women's liberation movement.

If this was going to happen anywhere, then Birmingham seemed a more than likely place. The music press was not based in the city, meaning punk had time to breathe and develop in a way that the London scene simply couldn't do. Similarly, the Birmingham scene was not being mythologised and built up in the music press by regional stringers, unlike the scenes in Manchester and Leeds. Nonetheless, Birmingham was a thriving cultural hub in the late 1970s and early 1980s. It combined the Arts Labs' countercultural activists with both a thriving punk scene and an energised reggae scene. There was also the Centre for Contemporary Cultural Studies at Birmingham University (CCCS), from where some youth-interested academics – particularly Angela McRobbie – had a foothold in the world of the Au Pairs. The links from Birmingham's late 1970s punk and reggae scenes to Coventry's 2-tone scene are well documented; the involvement of women such as Suzy Varty and Angela McRobbie in the world of the Au Pairs and *Brass Lip* less so.

## Girls together, girls alone: female fanzine creators in editorial teams and collectives

A fanzine that is created alone in a bedroom is, by implication, a quicker and less complex operation than a fanzine that involves two or more people. The more people involved in creating a fanzine, the more opinions there are to consider, the more points of view and personal polemics to acknowledge and either challenge or incorporate. This can slow things down at the point of creation, but can definitely speed things up when it comes to the production end of things. Different fanzine collectives and editorial teams had their own ways of negotiating this, whether formally or informally, some of which can be gleaned from close reading of the fanzines in question (especially Manchester's *City Fun*). In other cases, the teams were small groups of two or more friends, and the process appears to have been fluid and easy enough to not involve comment.[25]

*More On* was written, edited and printed by two London schoolgirls, Crystal Clear and Vinyl Virgin (also known as Sarah Shoshubi), who also provided The Slits with rehearsal space.[26] Their first issue was created in just two hours at school one day in 1977 and such was the media excitement around the London punk scene that *More On* was soon being discussed by the women's magazine *Honey* and the cultural commentator Peter York in *Harpers & Queen*.[27] Like Lucy Whitman, Crystal and Sarah began their fanzine because they wanted to become more involved with the London punk scene. They wanted to create punk rather than merely consume it. 'The whole feeling at the time was that you had to do something. We felt something special, part of a new thing that was very radical – underground … We wanted (still do) really to be the ones on the stage.'[28] Whereas *JOLT* featured personal polemics intertwined with coverage of the developing punk scene, *More On* was all about the scene and, especially, the music. Issue 3 featured intelligent and penetrating interviews alongside fantastic photography taken up close and marred only by the terrible quality of reproduction meted out by the early Xerox machines of the day. The cover was an off-guard shot of Viv Albertine, engrossed in inspecting a hole in her fishnet tights. The access Crystal and Sarah had to their subjects suggests they were being taken seriously as cultural creators and intermediaries by those they interviewed. They were insiders, but they could also be critical, sifting the good from the bad.

While the most recognised way in which women became involved with punk fanzines was as the lone or co-editor, there were also a number of instances of women taking over the reins as editor at an existing punk fanzine, as Vermillion Sands did for the final issue of Tony Drayton's *Ripped & Torn*, or contributing as writers to collectively run fanzines such as Manchester's *City Fun*. Some women also formed part of more traditional editor-contributor set-ups, as on *Sniffin' Glue* and *Worthless Words*. Future Marine Girls bassist and Everything But The Girl singer Tracey Thorn wrote in her memoir of time spent writing pieces for the Hatfield punk fanzine *The Weekly* Bugle.[29] Indeed, her account underlines the ways by which fanzine writing provided an entry ticket into the heart of punk for many.

The collective who ran Telford's *Guttersnipe* were brought together in 1978 by a teacher and social worker. The fanzine was founded as a creative outlet for the town's youth, comprising young men and women aged between 15 and 18 inspired by the activities of the Anti-Nazi League and RAR. Barney Mokgatle, one of the students involved in the Soweto uprising in South Africa, was living in Britain in 1978 and visited Telford a few weeks prior to the launch of *Guttersnipe*.[30] The meeting that Mokgatle spoke at was cited by *Guttersnipe* as 'The kick-off for the A.N.L. [Anti Nazi League] in Telford' and seems also to have served as a catalyst for the fanzine.[31] Largely anonymous (all contributions to the fanzine were unsigned and collective members and editorial staff were not named in the fanzine), some light is shone onto operations by a 1980 episode of the BBC's *Open Door* programme featuring the collective. An articulate, smartly dressed woman with a Scottish accent and red hair worn in bunches, and a slightly more guarded, but equally articulate, man with close cropped hair, long grey overcoat and scarf, both perhaps in their mid to late twenties, provide the viewer with an overview of *Guttersnipe*. The viewer meets some of the local teens and local bands involved with the collective; a pink-haired punk girl types copy on a typewriter and various teens are shown duplicating, assembling and reading *Guttersnipe* hot off the presses of their local community printshop. The need for *Guttersnipe* is made eloquently by the pink-haired punk girl, who tells the interviewer that she doesn't read the music press because, despite having three A levels, she can't understand a word of it. And if she can't understand it, what chance do people without A levels have?[32]

## Beyond writing: art, photography and aesthetics

Because of quality control issues in regard to the reproduction of punk fanzines, the role of photography has tended to be overlooked. The most brilliant action shot of Joe Strummer would be rendered a toner-flooded mess if it wasn't screened or filtered properly when xeroxed. Those fanzines that made use of the older duplication techniques of the offset litho machine might fare a little better. But by far the best results were those achieved by fanzines printed professionally, from plates, such as *It's Different For Grils* [*sic*] in Sheffield, which achieved staggeringly high-quality resolutions thanks to this technique.

It is perhaps for this reason that the fanzine work of much respected and established photographers such as Sheila Rock, Erica Echenberg and Jill Furmanovsky, all of whom contributed to issue 6 of *Sniffin' Glue*, has largely gone unnoticed. The production qualities of the average fanzine could vary considerably according to which specific machine in the printshop (and its state of repair at the time) and the type of machine it was (linoprint or Xerox, for instance), who was operating it and how experienced they were, not to mention – in the case of Xerox machines – how close the toner was to running out. Photographers, therefore, had very little control over how the image would look when reproduced in a fanzine.

Similarly under-discussed has been the role of fanzine artists and illustrators. Lucy Whitman's sister Ros Past-it hand-drew the distinctive cartoon covers that adorned issues two and three of *JOLT*. As mentioned earlier, the second issue featured the Queen in her Silver Jubilee year as a gobbing, guitar-wielding, leather-trouser-clad punk icon. The image has been much reproduced over the years, making it almost as widely recognised as Jamie Reid's safety-pinned Queen, which adorned the cover of the Sex Pistols' banned number one single 'God Save The Queen.'[33]

Ros's drawing for issue 3, in which the moral campaigner Mary Whitehouse is depicted naked in a seemingly passionate lesbian tryst, is less well known. It can be viewed as being part of a tradition of lampooning public figures in the UK that goes all the way back to the eighteenth century, to the early days of engravings and the printing press, putting Ros in a satirical tradition that began with Cruickshank and Hogarth. While Arthur M. Hind has compared George Cruickshank's work to that of Charles Dickens, Neil MacGregor, writing on William Hogarth's *Marriage A-la-Mode* (c. 1743), believes that the actual technicalities and subtleties of the paintings were 'subordinated to his moral purpose: ridicule fired by anger and sustained by a rare instinct for the eloquent detail.'[34] He adds that Hogarth 'did not preach virtue; instead he satirised vice and folly.'[35] Ros Past-it's depiction of Mary Whitehouse works on a similar level because Past-it is using humour to undermine Whitehouse's position as a moral campaigner who, among other things, frequently targeted homosexuality in her campaigns.

The work that Linder Sterling created for Buzzcocks (particularly the 'Orgasm Addict' sleeve/poster art with Malcolm Garratt), for the Manchester fanzine *City Fun*, and for the art/polemic fanzine *The Secret Public* (a collaboration with Jon Savage, comprised of montages created alternately by Linder

**4.1**  Cover of *JOLT*, 2 (1977). Reproduced by kind permission of Lucy Toothpaste; drawing by Ros Past-it

and Savage), made stark use of montage; clean cut-ups of male and female porn images juxtaposed with everyday household domestic items such as irons, vacuum cleaners and similar appliances. The result was a jarring and unsettling subversion of highly gendered material that was explicitly feminist in nature, foreshadowing the work that Linder would create in the early 1980s with the band Ludus.

The writer Ariella Yedger sees a parallel between Linder's punk-era work and that of the Berlin Dadaist Hannah Höch, also known for using montage. Yedger identifies that both Höch and Linder were women operating in a male-dominated heterosexual cultural scene. (Berlin Dada on one hand, Manchester punk on the other) 'and were aware of their positions as such'.[36] While Linder's role within punk has been more widely recognised than Höch's was in Berlin Dada, the art world was slower to recognise her as an artist.[37] This lengthy wait for recognition highlights the wider issues of recognition for women artists, not just women Dadaists.[38]

A different aspect of Linder's punk-era work is shown through the stark linoprint of Jordan, Malcolm McLaren and Vivienne Westwood's famed shop assistant, which was created in 1977 at the height of the media moral panic surrounding UK punk. The image was created from a photo of the punk icon that had appeared in a punk exposé in one of the tabloids.[48] Printed in black, enhancing the image's starkness and Jordan's confrontational stare, the result is a more nihilistic, unsettling, and powerful version of Warhol's brightly coloured linoprints of Marilyn Monroe: a different icon for a different age.

## Backroom grrrls: women and fanzine production

Birmingham Arts Lab, founded in 1968, was one of a number of Arts Labs to spring up in the wake of the UK's 1960s counterculture. The name was borrowed from the 'Arts Laboratory set up by the American Jim Haynes in London's Drury Lane'. These Arts Labs were 'radical arts centres', and while the counterculture in its late 1960s form may have been in decline by the late 1970s, Birmingham Arts Lab was not.[39] Collaboration was at its heart, so it makes sense that they would work closely with the local punks.

As previously mentioned, Birmingham Arts Lab artist and wimmins comix creator Suzy Varty designed the overall look of Birmingham punk fanzine *Brass Lip*. Varty was the lone woman at the Arts Lab and she had a background in feminist publishing, particularly in relation to the female artist. Alongside her comic *Heroine*, and its micro-comic spin-off *Paper Doll Heroine*, she was also involved with the collaborative magazine *Mama!* ('Women Artists together') and the travelling postal art exhibition *Feministo: Portrait of the Artist as a Young Woman.* First exhibited in 1976, this explicitly feminist art project and exhibition was comprised of small but powerful artworks in a range of artistic media, using a variety of conventional and unconventional materials, by women across the UK. The size of the artworks was decided by the nature of the project: each piece of art had to be delivered on to the next artist via the UK postal system. Speaking of the isolation many of the women as wives and mothers felt, the exhibition included such works as Lyn Austin's 'Bubble Bath Suicide', in which a doll is positioned face down in a bath that has been filled with Styrofoam beads, representing bubble bath. Another piece, by Phil Goodall, was a drawing of a naked woman with butterfly wings, a pin stuck between her breasts. A review of the exhibition by Linda Melvern for the *London Evening Standard* was headed 'Wife is a 4-letter word'.[40]

Given her artistic and feminist background, Varty was perfectly positioned not only to work with Syd Freake and Connie Klassen on *Brass Lip*, but also to understand and appreciate the context that bands such as the Au Pairs were working in. In a less recognised way, women were also instrumental in seeing that both *Ripped & Torn* and *Sniffin' Glue* happened, at least initially. The first *Sniffin' Glue* was typed by editor Mark Perry and the first 50 copies were Xeroxed by his girlfriend on her office photocopier.[41] Similarly, it was a female colleague of Tony Drayton who Xeroxed *Ripped & Torn* on their office photocopier.[42]

There is also the role of at least two female-only printing co-ops to consider: Moss Side Community Press, who printed *Brass Lip*, and Sheffield Women's Printing Group, who provided the plates for *It's Different For Grils*. These co-ops were part of a lineage of UK female printing co-ops, leading all the way back to the Victoria Press, founded by Emily Faithfull in the 1860s.

The predominance of women and girls in the clerical sector has a long lineage. The typewriter was first patented in 1868 by Christopher Lattam Sholes, and Stephen Van Dulken has claimed that its entry into offices marks the point when women began to enter office work. He also claims that this was because women tended to be faster and more accurate typists than the male clerks who they began to replace.[43] Certainly, women had begun to dominate clerical work by the early 1950s.[44] So much so, in fact, that the academic Juliet Webster, reflecting on her time as a secretary in the 1970s, mused that office work was the most frequent workplace destination for the middle-class girl not deemed bright enough to be steered towards one of the professions.[45] By 1985, an OECD study found that in Canada, France, Germany, Italy, the UK and the US, workforce women were most highly concentrated in clerical work.[46]

The ability to type and operate a Xerox machine would have been useful entry-level skills for the average fanzine writer at the time. Because women were so concentrated in clerical work, this would have given young punk women a definite advantage insofar as having a greater opportunity to make subversive use of office equipment to create their punk fanzines or, as we have seen, Xerox the works of others. That more women didn't do so can be put down to a number of factors: lack of inclination and a lack of unsupervised moments connected to, perhaps, the controls placed on them by office politics and office manager regimes. We also only have access to those punk fanzines that were collected and survived to be archived. Nonetheless, the ready access of women to office work and its means of production (typewriters, Xerox machines) and the uses this presented to punk women was acknowledged by the film maker Susan Seidelman in her film *Smithereens*, in which the film's anti-heroine, Wren, makes use of her job in a printshop to produce flyers advertising herself, which she then sticks up in the New York subway and around town as part of her quest to infiltrate and start a band within the New York post-punk scene.[47] This would seem to suggest that for those with nothing to lose, or who simply didn't care about getting sacked, access to typewriters and Xerox machines in the workplace for non-work activities represented something of a potential jackpot. It wouldn't make you rich, but it would be a substantial enhancement to any resourceful punk woman's creative arsenal which, in the pre-internet age, was unlikely to be sniffed at.

## Some of our women are missing: a conclusion

Given that women were actively creating punk fanzines in the UK in the late 1970s and early 1980s, we need to ask: just why has the work of women such as Lucy Whitman, Sharon Spike, Crystal and Sarah, Syd Freake, Connie Klassen and others been so often forgotten? Why are *More On* and *JOLT* not mentioned in the same breath as *Sniffin' Glue* and *London's Outrage*? Ultimately, this particular omission in the history of fanzine production in the UK is symp-tomatic of a wider omission within histories of UK punk itself so far as women are concerned. It has become a matter of record, particularly since 2007 (when Helen Reddington first published her book *The Lost Women of Rock Music*, a book which explicitly set out to address this historical amnesia), that women's cultural creative role within punk is frequently forgotten or misrepresented. This has, in turn, led to women in punk often being viewed through a cultural male gaze that casts them in a supporting role, as 'punkettes' and partners, girlfriends and lovers, rather than as cultural agents in their own right. This is as much the case for female punk fanzine writers as it is for female musicians, music journalists, managers, photographers and writers of the punk era.

The struggle for recognition faced by fanzine writers differs from those of musicians, however, in a number of important ways. Whereas punk musicians performed on stage, in the glare of the spotlight and the critical glare of the press and audiences, fanzine writing by its very nature was at least semi-anonymous. Whereas some fanzine editors, such as Mark Perry and Tony Drayton, went on to become faces on the punk scene, this didn't always happen. Some editors and contributors, such as the entire editorial team and fanzine collective of *Guttersnipe*, operated anonymously. Many writers and editors also used pseudonyms. While some writers wanted a high profile, others were happy to shun the limelight. This approach increased the likelihood of writers being overlooked in histories of punk and punk fanzines, with the loudest voices tending to be the ones that got heard.

It is important to remember as well that many women served as backroom girls, labouring away on the more editorially rigorous fanzines selling advertising, or else typing, Xeroxing and distributing fanzines. They represented an army of unsung heroines, acknowledged only in the small print of the editorial sections of the fanzines in question. Taking the long view, the contribution women made to punk fanzines, whether in the creative or technical sense, is part of a continuum of engagement, one that goes all the way back to the early days of journalism and printing in the nineteenth century. The legacy of the punk fanzine for women creating fanzines after punk is also important because, just as pre-punk publications forged a path for punk women, so *JOLT* and *Brass Lip* forged a path for *Shocking Pink, Bad Attitude, Girl Frenzy* and riot grrrl in the UK.

## Notes

1 Elizabeth Carolyn Miller, *'Slow Print': Literary Radicalism and Late Victorian Print Culture* (Stanford, CA: Stanford University Press, 2013), p. 2.
2 Barbara Onslow, *Women of the Press in Nineteenth-Century Britain* (London: Macmillan Press, 2000), pp. 154–6.
3 Patricia Hollis, *The Pauper Press: A Study in Working-Class Radicalism of the 1830s* (London: Oxford University Press, 1970), p. vii.
4 *Ibid.*
5 *Ibid.*
6 *Ibid.*; Martin Hewitt, *The Dawn of the Cheap Press in Victorian Britain: The End of the 'Taxes on Knowledge', 1849–1869* (London: Bloomsbury, 2014), p. 1.

7 Harold Herd, *The March Of Journalism: The Story of the British Press from 1622 to the Present Day* (London: George Allen & Unwin, 1952), p. 130.

8 *Ibid.*, p. 239.

9 *Ibid.*, p. 239, footnote.

10 Miller, '*Slow Print*', pp. 1–2.

11 Sean Stewart (ed.), *On The Ground: An Illustrated Anecdotal History of The Sixties Underground Press in the U.S.* (Oakland, CA: PM Press, 2011), p. 117. Original emphasis.

12 *Ibid.*, pp. 113–16.

13 Roger Sabin, *Comics, Comix & Graphic Novels* (London: Phaidon Press, 1996), pp. 105–11.

14 Most notably by Lucy O'Brien in her essay 'The Woman Punk Made Me', in Roger Sabin (ed.), *Punk Rock: So What? The Cultural Legacy of Punk* (London: Routledge, 1999); and by Helen Reddington in *The Lost Women of Rock Music: Female Musicians of the Punk Era* (Aldershot: Ashgate Publishing, 2007).

15 Cazz Blase, 'A Woman Called Toothpaste: An Interview with Lucy Whitman', *The f-Word*, 20 May 2011, www.thefword.org.uk/features/2011/05/Lucy_Whitman, accessed 22 May 2011.

16 *Ibid.*

17 *Ibid.*

18 *Ibid.*

19 *Ibid.*

20 Jill Nicholls and Lucy Toothpaste, 'I Play the Vocals', *Spare Rib*, July 1979, pp. 16–18.

21 *JOLT*, 1 (1977), p. 2.

22 Jon Savage, *England's Dreaming: Sex Pistols and Punk Rock* (London: Faber & Faber, 1991), pp. 195–6.

23 Cazz Blase, 'Words, Not Guitar: Viv Albertine on the Book She Never Thought She'd Write', *The f-Word*, 24 September 2015, www.thefword.org.uk/2015/09/viv_albertine_interview/, accessed 25 September 2015.

24 *Brass Lip*, 1 (1979), p. 2.

25 I define a collective as a group of fanzine producers with interchangeable tasks and responsibilities, and an editorial team as running along more traditional journalistic lines, with editors, writers, photographers and advertising staff whose roles are all clearly defined and distinguishable.

26 Caroline Coon, *1988: The New Wave Punk Rock Explosion* (London: Omnibus, 1978).

27 *More On*, 1 (1977), quoted in Virginia Boston, *Shockwave* (London: Plexus, 1978), p. 80. In an interview with The Heartbreakers in *More On*, 3 (1977), the following exchange took place between Johnny Thunders and Sarah: 'You kids from HONEY? (to be read with New York accent). S.S – No – She's from Honey. She is doing us. We're doing you.' See also 'Little Magazines', *Harpers & Queen*, August 1977, in Peter York, *Style Wars* (London: Sidgwick & Jackson, 1980), pp. 145–52.

28 *More On*, 1 (1977), quoted in Boston, *Shockwave*, p. 80.

29  Tracey Thorn, *Bedsit Disco Queen* (London: Virago, 2013), pp. 18–25.

30  The Soweto uprising refers to a series of protests by black students in schools in Soweto in 1976 against the imposition of Afrikaans as the language of instruction for their education. These protests were brutally put down by the South African police, leading to the deaths of a number of the student activists and the exile of many others.

31  *Guttersnipe*, 1 (1978), p. 11.

32  BBC, *Open Door*, 1980, available on YouTube, https://youtu.be/PFwXK4eK6Jk, accessed 17 December 2016.

33  Cover of *JOLT*, 2 (1977) reproduced by kind permission of Lucy Toothpaste; drawing by Ros Past-it.

34  Arthur M. Hind, *A History of Engraving & Etching: From the 15th Century to the Year 1914* (London: Constable & Co., 1963), p. 238; Neil MacGregor, 'Foreword', in Judy Egerton, *Hogarth's Marriage A-la-Mode: Hogarth in the National Gallery* (London: National Gallery Publications, 1997), p. 6.

35  MacGregor, 'Foreword', p. 6.

36  Ariella Yedgar, 'The Exploded Image', in Mark Sladen and Ariella Yedgar (eds.), *Panic Attack! Art in the Punk Years* (London: Merrell, 2007), p. 174.

37  Paul Bayley, 'Introduction', in Philip Hoare, Philip Hoare, Morrissey, *et al.*, *Linder – Works, 1976–2006* (Zürich: JRP/Ringer, 2006), p. 5.

38  Ruth Hemus, *Dada's Women* (New Haven, CT: Yale University Press, 2009).

39  'Introduction', *Birmingham Arts Lab* (exhibition catalogue, Birmingham Museums and Art Gallery, 1998).

40  Linda Melvern, 'Wife is a 4-letter Word', *Evening Standard*, 10 June 1977, p. 5.

41  Mark Perry speaking on *Punk Fiction: 20 Years Of Punk*, Radio 1, 3 November 1996.

42  *Ripped and Torn*, 1 (1976), p. 3.

43  Stephen Van Dulken, *Inventing the 19th Century: The Great Age of Victorian Inventions* (London: British Library, 2001), p. 200.

44  Duncan Gallie, 'The Labour Force' in A.H. Halsey and Josephine Webb (eds), *Twentieth Century British Social Trends* (Basingstoke: Palgrave Macmillan, 2000), p. 287.

45  Juliet Webster, *Shaping Women's Work: Gender, Employment and Information Technology* (London: Longman, 1996), p. 112.

46  OECD, *The Integration of Women in the Economy* (Paris: OECD, 1985), quoted in Isabella Bakker, 'Women's Employment in Comparative Perspective', in Jane Jenson, Elisabeth Hagen and Cellaigh Reddy (eds), *Feminization of the Labour Force: Paradoxes and Promises* (Oxford: Polity Press, 1988), p. 29.

47  Susan Seidelman (dir.), *Smithereens* (1982).

# Communiqués
# and Sellotape:
# constructing cultures

# 5

# 'Pam ponders Paul Morley's cat': *City Fun* and the politics of post-punk

DAVID WILKINSON

Manchester's *City Fun* (1978–83) bears all the hallmarks of punk fanzine media. Early issues in particular feature impulsive anti-authoritarian rants alongside reviews and ruminations on the meaning of punk. *City Fun*'s often striking covers varied in style, though Dada-indebted collages by Linder Sterling and Jon Savage captured a distinctively post-punk structure of feeling; one riven by the crisis of the political conjuncture, which nevertheless offered glimpses of utopia through the joins. It is worth asking how the zine captured the conflicted and evolving politics of the British counterculture as it mutated, fragmented and fed into punk, post-punk and beyond against a backdrop of collapsing post-war welfare-capitalism and the rise of Thatcherite neoliberalism.

Why examine such a development? As I have argued elsewhere, post-punk offers extensive insight into ideological battles fought out in the late 1970s and 1980s over what it might mean to live a liberated and fulfilled life; battles with urgent contemporary relevance. The association of certain strands of post-punk with the post-war libertarian left meant that it often carried through the utopianism of 1960s radicalism into the early days of Thatcherism. This utopianism took muted but nevertheless vital forms during a moment usually characterised by left historiography as bleak, hopeless and even apocalyptic. Post-punk, then, may act as a resource of hope in specifically neoliberal, crisis-ridden conditions. Yet post-punk also marked the incorporation of the counterculture in various ways – not least the aspirational postmodern turn of the 'new pop' – thus teaching harder lessons about the limitations, as well as the possibilities, of countercultural revolt.[1]

Studying *City Fun* reveals that a number of the preoccupations and tensions of post-punk made themselves felt not just in the music but also in its grassroots media. The zine's sustained run, its collective editorial team and its practical function as a nerve centre for the Manchester scene, with eventual national distribution and a relatively high circulation for a publication of its kind, make it an especially significant example of post-punk media through which to examine these issues.[2]

This chapter considers four distinct but interrelated themes. Firstly, debates over the viability of independent, oppositional media production, which in many respects mirrored those taking place in the music weeklies over independent labels. Secondly, debates over the aesthetics and politics of post-punk, which are focused here through two examples: *City Fun's* sometimes fractious relationship with Factory Records, the dominant centre of Manchester's post-punk scene; and the zine's equally fractious attitudes to the London-centric drift of post-punk following the initial regionalist promise of the latter. Both examples disinterred tensions of class and education that were familiar enough given the varied backgrounds of those who participated in post-punk, yet which took quite specific forms here.[3]

In less obvious ways, such tensions animate the third theme, which is the idiosyncratic attitude of *City Fun* toward the sexual and gender politics so captivatingly brought to the fore by post-punk. This attitude was determined in no small part by the central involvement of Liz Naylor and Cath Carroll; a pair who had grown up on the working-class fringes of the Greater Manchester conurbation and who were still teenagers when they began their brilliantly camp, warped and incisive contributions to the zine.

Finally, class also mediated the fourth theme of this chapter: *City Fun's* take on politics with a big 'p', especially the nascent fragmentation of the left into identity-based struggles. These overlapped with post-punk via its countercultural and libertarian left inheritance. More or less self-consciously, the zine associated such politics with a particular fraction of the middle class and ruthlessly satirised them on this basis. Yet, as we will see, it did so without thereby becoming either reactionary or unequivocally pessimistic.

### 'Keeping control': cultural production

As with many strands of punk and post-punk, the origins of *City Fun* can be traced to the counterculture and the post-war libertarian left. Bob Dickinson, who wrote for the zine between 1980 and 1982, refers to its co-founder Andy Zero as a 'short haired punk hippie'. Dickinson notes of a photo of Zero's friend and fellow co-founder Martin X: 'As you can see, he's not that young … I asked him once what his favourite gig was and he said [German beat/psychedelic band] The Rattles at the Twisted Wheel in 1968'.[4]

This lineage was as true of the zine's infrastructure as its founders. For most of its existence *City Fun* used Rochdale Alternative Press as its printer. RAP was a co-operative that began life as the Moss Side Press in 1970, which in turn grew out of a local housing activist group. As well as hippie underground papers *Grass Eye* and *Mole Express*, Moss Side Press/RAP printed a large network of community publications including *Tameside Eye*, *Bury Metro* and *Salford Champion*.[5] The focus of such titles on the neglected concerns of working-class locales alongside critiques of local authorities and businesses reflected libertarian left preoccupations with anti-statism, mutual aid and direct democracy characteristic of the period. One of the last issues of *Mole Express* even featured a symbolic, baton-passing feature on punk.[6] Liz Naylor has called *Mole Express* 'the greatest magazine ever'.[7] The relish with which it engaged in scurrilous dirt-digging was steadfastly maintained by *City Fun* in the continuation of 'gossip' and 'nasty rumours' columns from the earlier paper.

Out of this foment emerged a deeply idealistic endeavour. The first volume of *City Fun* (1978–80) attempted to make good on the democratising, DIY promise of punk. Hierarchy was frowned upon. 'We don't edit', Andy Zero noted in an interview with the *New Manchester Review*, the city's equivalent of *Time Out*. 'We don't cut out anything'.[8] By this Zero meant not simply specific content but also the vast majority of contributions they were sent, as he noted in a pedantic response to accusations of cronyism: 'There are less than six contributions that we have never used.'[9] Few articles featured bylines and those that did were often written under pseudonyms, aiming to discourage egotism and to highlight the zine's collectivist ethos. Just as punk and post-punk bands demystified the recording process by listing costs and 'how to' guides on record sleeves, so *City Fun* featured articles like 'How To Produce A Fanzine' and made some attempt to publicly account for its finances.[10]

This devotion to grass-roots inclusivity did not come without its problems. Early in *City Fun*'s existence, the zine published a number of critical letters noting its uneven quality, including one that began 'Dear Shitty Fun'.[11] While the tone of these letters was petty, their criticisms were often accurate. Print was sometimes blotted or trailed off the edges of pages, which themselves might be duplicated accidentally or stapled in the wrong order. Though much of the content anticipated the sharp wit and diverse concerns that were later to define the zine, it sat alongside mediocre reviews – 'Siouxsie was great I think she's lovely'[12] – and doubtful stabs at creative expression. These included the erratic scansion and bludgeoning rhyme of a poem detailing one man's transformation into a sex doll after a blood donation goes wrong.[13]

Such criticisms anticipated one of the central schisms of post-punk, which could be traced in the pages of the national music weeklies from around the beginning of 1980. As Simon Reynolds notes, key writers and post-punk acts such as Scritti Politti, eager for impact, 'abruptly lost patience' with the 'charming eccentricity' and 'honourable amateurism' of post-punk's more experimental trajectories, uniting around a sensibility of 'mobility' and 'ambition' that has become known as the 'new pop'.[14] Although initially loyal to the independent sector, many of those drawn to new pop began to advocate what Paul Morley called 'an overground brightness' that often entailed strategically signing to a major label. Bob Last, manager of Gang of Four and the Human League (who signed to EMI and Virgin respectively), has opined that the capital reserves of the majors actually made them more 'independent' than post-punk indies like Rough Trade and Last's own label, FAST Product, increasing the likelihood of them being 'a space where different things could happen.'[15]

At stake was an implicit ideological link between economics and aesthetics, which implied that independent productive activity motivated by broadly leftist and democratic values[16] was destined not only to be economically unviable but also to limit the quality and developmental possibilities of cultural production. The same tendency could be noted in the way that Green Gartside, frontman of Scritti Politti, began to scorn the self-released output of his contemporaries as 'failed attempts at music'. By the mid-1980s this division had hardened, as Reynolds observes: 'Most chart pop was glossy ... hi-tech, ultra-modern. Indie made a fetish of the opposite characteristics: scruffy guitars ... lo-fi or Luddite production, and a retro (usually sixties) slant', settling for a 'resentfully impotent opposition' to the mainstream.[17]

The most significant determining pressure on new pop rhetoric was the growing ideological influence of Thatcherite neoliberalism. This was an indirect process; many advocates of new pop retained their leftist commitments. But it is difficult not to observe parallels between their view of the independent sector 'in terms of stagnation'[18] and Thatcher's soundbite summations of the arguments of free market economists such as Friedrich von Hayek: 'socialism is a system [that is] inherently inefficient'.[19] The message was clear – socialism, including co-operative endeavours like Rough Trade – was limiting, undynamic and therefore unfree.

In terms of the specific qualities of cultural production, and thus the kind of pleasure to be derived from it, Paul Morley's advocacy of new pop's 'transient thrill'[20] carried overtones of neoliberalism's colonisation of consumerism as central to human fulfilment ('There are great industries in other people's pleasures', Margaret Thatcher once claimed, ominously).[21] Along with this new pop sensibility went a discourse of 'quality control'[22] and a self-awareness of pop as product inflected with very *du jour* games of postmodern blank parody – visible, for instance, in the way that Scritti Politti singles began to deliberately resemble the packaging of Courvoisier brandy and Dunhill cigarettes.

There were comparable internal critiques of the world of radical publishing to which *City Fun* belonged. These would soon acquire somewhat greater intellectual gravitas than a few snotty letters sent into a zine. The authors of *What a Way To Run a Railroad* included Charles Landry, founder of the think-tank Comedia, and David Morley, a former member of the leftist Birmingham Centre for Contemporary Cultural Studies. The book mounted a stinging takedown of the libertarian left's oppositional enterprises, especially its grass-roots media, arguing that their failure to make headway was a direct consequence of their politically 'prefigurative' forms.[23] Though the authors favoured a mixed economy, their enthusiasm for conventional market mechanisms hinted at the future accommodation the left would make with neoliberalism in the form of New Labour. As with Reynolds's observation of indie's fetishism of 'impotent opposition', so the book's authors accused the left of the belief that 'it doesn't matter if we win, as long as we've played the game in the right spirit.'[24]

A hint of this sensibility is present in Andy Zero's response to *City Fun*'s naysayers – 'sorry, but we are amateurs'[25] – and in the cheerful admission of loose accounting in financial reports: 'what happened to the rest, we don't know.'[26] Overall, though, the zine avoided making a virtue of amateurishness. It rejected the word 'fanzine' as a self-description for itself on this basis and instead aimed for the status of a 'proper magazine'.[27] Furthermore, after around 18 months of existence, it underwent a relaunch in part prompted by an embittered feud with Factory Records, which is discussed in the following section. An exasperated editorial in the final edition of volume 1 acknowledged that *City Fun* had become 'sub-standard'. Its diagnosis, however, was not a lack of conventional professionalism. In fact, attempts at conventionality were seen as part of the problem. It was felt that a fixation on fortnightly production had created a 'treadmill' effect, leading to 'boring' music coverage and content for the sake of content.[28]

The zine's 'caretakers' aimed to learn from this, retaining the commitment to regular publication while looking to print 'more varied, interesting and intelligent' material.[29] *City Fun*'s renewed vision, though, was a far cry from the new pop's quasi-ironic inhabitation of consumer culture and the turn-to-style in magazines like *The Face*, whose launch was concurrent with *City Fun*'s soul-searching. Avoiding predictable market niches such as 'fanzine/music paper', the zine's central collective kicked off volume 2 (1980–82) with a desire to re-establish a broad focus on Manchester's 'sub-world' and to do so through involving particularly gifted writers much more directly – especially Naylor, Carroll and Dickinson.[30] Rather than a turn to marketing, then, the solution to 'having fun in cities'[31] lay in increased co-operation and commitment to a subcultural constituency. As for quality, Zero directly inverted the equation of the new pop: 'if you do sell out you end up with inferior stuff.'[32]

Admittedly, the free-for-all policy of contribution was abandoned, though not without internal conflict. Zero observed regretfully that 'just because somebody hasn't got a good education or isn't particularly literate we don't want to discriminate against them … but we've also got to reject rubbish.'[33] Yet the collective continued to hold open contributor meetings – 'we'd give them tea and biscuits and we'd try and develop ideas and enthusiasms', remembers Dickinson[34] – while commitments to financial transparency and the frequent avoidance of bylines were retained.

*City Fun* was rejuvenated by this reshuffle, with a quantum leap in the variety and quality of its output. Layout improved, and articles now encompassed multiple topics – the Iranian revolution, English eccentricity and gleefully perverse satires of heteronormative children's fiction, to name but a few. Visually, the zine was enhanced by the surreal and frequently hilarious cover art of Brian Mills and the kitsch collage of Naylor and Carroll, which juxtaposed archaic advertising imagery with 'cartoons from old 1960s annuals and comics.'[35] Detailed local listings of gigs, alternative cinema and the like provided a further impetus to purchase, implying activity rather than stagnation.

Ultimately, *City Fun*'s demise three years later was not due to any automatic incompatibility between its oppositional, anti-commercial attitudes and a capacity for enjoyable, professionally assembled output. As Dickinson notes, the zine's cessation was coterminous with the decline of Greater Manchester's alternative media infrastructure more generally. Burnout resulted from 'a time when the sense of community disappeared … with Thatcherism', as Sue Ashby of *Bury Metro* recalls.[36] Such breakdown coincided with the second term of the Thatcher government. This period saw the concerted targeting of the institutional 'nooks and crannies' which the libertarian left had managed to occupy, including left-wing local authorities such as Manchester's with sympathies toward oppositional cultural production.[37]

It is on this score that the true limitations of such cultural production become apparent. In inevitably hostile conditions, small-scale 'prefigurative' initiatives can only go so far. Nick Srnicek and Alex Williams argue much the same of contemporary 'folk politics' on the left – 'the guiding intuition that immediacy is always better and often more authentic' – whose roots they trace to the libertarian and identitarian turn of the 1960s onwards, advocating instead a more coordinated project of 'scale and expansion'.[38]

Nevertheless, what *City Fun*'s six years of existence demonstrated was the possibility that an entertaining, oppositional subcultural media could be sustained – for a time, at least – by collectivist values and practices. The zine's run was by no means harmonious. Internal conflicts saw the gradual loss of its original founders, leaving the third and final volume dominated by Naylor and Carroll. Yet such tension could be productive, as Dickinson observes: 'I think it lasted because of all the arguing! It made people – it toughened everybody's ideas up about what they were writing and why they were writing it. It made you think – you've got to go through with this, you've got to go out and sell it because there's other people doing it as well.'[39]

## 'Fat tories': the aesthetics and politics of post-punk

As might be expected, something of *City Fun*'s attitude to cultural production could be seen in the positions it took on the aesthetics and politics of post-punk itself. Such positions acquire heightened significance when thrown into relief with those of the more dominant Factory Records milieu, which has since absorbed the bulk of popular historical attention to Manchester's post-punk past.

Relations between the two camps were by no means entirely hostile. Factory boss Tony Wilson had funded Naylor and Carroll's first foray into independent publishing, the one-off colour zine *925*.[40] Factory also arranged a benefit gig for *City Fun* early in 1980, although it was the zine's review of this performance that was to be the trigger for open warfare; a war played out in the pages of *City Fun* for some time afterwards.

Objecting to the reviewer's claim that Joy Division's support acts, Section 25 and A Certain Ratio, sounded like 'inferior versions of the main band' due to Factory's 'tightly conceptual approach',[41] Wilson penned a contemptuous response. Accusing the 'City Fun Bored' [*sic*] of 'third rate journalism', a 'turgid level of aesthetic debate' and 'following trends culled from back copies of *NME*', the letter pinpointed *City Fun*'s supposed failing as an 'inability to feel unique qualities in the work of bands still at an early stage of development'. It culminated in the announcement that Factory would henceforth remove the zine from its mailing list.[42]

Aside from a heavy dose of insecurity, what Wilson's letter revealed was the risk of condescension deriving from his Cambridge education. This was an education that also informed the 'tightly conceptual' nature of Factory and which allowed Wilson to pontificate on the 'minutiae' of live rock 'choreography'.[43] Affronted, but nonetheless attempting to ameliorate relations ('FOR FUCKS SAKE we should have more in common than we do in difference'), Andy Zero accepted that there was room for *City Fun* to improve while playing up Wilson's inconsistency. How could the zine be expected to anticipate post-punk's aesthetic evolution if it was to be shut out of the channels of communication? Zero also opined that 'it is far better to acknowledge an influence than deny it', highlighting the Warholian origins of Factory's name.[44] With both gestures, Zero went some way to puncturing the residual modernist arrogance that accompanied Factory's reworking of twentieth-century avant-garde aesthetics.

Martin X elaborated on the educational and classed dimensions of the spat, teasing Wilson over the co-existence of his Granada TV day job with Factory's artistic ambitions. 'It must be so intellectually FRUSTRATING to have to share a television channel with Coronation Street, Crossroads, Mr and Mrs etc.' Defending the 'embarrassing hoy-poloy [*sic*] who hang around Virgin Records and the Underground Market', X upheld their right to voice their opinions freely in print, whether or not they had a 'good job' or had been 'educated to the eyeballs'.[45]

Some insight into *City Fun*'s attitude towards the purpose of post-punk is afforded by X's admission that his grammar school past allowed him to understand Wilson's 'high-blown phraseology'. Similarly telling is the threat that every Factory 'missive' would be printed for the eyes of 'the great uneducated masses that some of us are so busily trying to guide towards the light'.[46] Rather than a competitive race to throw off the formal shackles of rock's past, post-punk was seen as an oppositional, collective and potentially liberating means of fulfilment. This sensibility could be detected, for instance, in stream-of-consciousness opposition to 'trendy minimalism' and the desire for 'honest' bands, 'uniting living human beings bringing we jolly consumer types into that real light [*sic*]'.[47]

In viewing cultural production as key to political struggle and in stressing the responsibility of an educated class fraction to promote the democratisation of culture, X's attitude resembled nothing so much as what Alan Sinfield has called 'left culturism'.[48] This was a prevalent structure of feeling among progressive intellectuals in the post-war period; although its usual focus on appreciation of traditional high arts was replaced here by a stress on grass-roots pop cultural production.

A pessimistic take on this flashpoint might see it as internecine subcultural bickering determined by inequalities of education and class, which could result in vastly exaggerated differences of political position. 'Factory we all just used to call "Fat Tory" records and they were like the mill owners', Naylor recalls.[49] More optimistically, it may well have been Wilson's barbed comments on the quality of *City Fun*'s output that provided the impetus for the zine to rethink its editorial policy a few issues later. Factory, meanwhile, was held to account for the more troubling features of its iconoclasm. Within the confines of Manchester's post-punk scene at least, its tendencies toward monopoly were momentarily challenged as *City Fun* printed letters confirming a wider perception of the label's 'elitist attitudes' and anger about 'the way they dismiss everything else.'[50]

*City Fun*'s take on the post-punk moment was not only visible at a local level. Further from home, its left culturism also prevailed in the stance it took on the London-based weekly music press – especially the *NME*. This was nowhere more evident than in the cartoons of Ray Lowry. In a series of comic strips, Lowry depicted thinly veiled caricatures of new pop ideologue and Greater Manchester export Paul Morley, satirising the postmodern turn that Morley's writing had taken. 'Behind closed blinds', grinning journalists spouted pretentious, pseudo-revolutionary verbiage at one another.[51] The thrust of Lowry's critique was not anti-intellectual populism, however – unlike *Sounds'* Garry Bushell's dubious attempts to rally support to his lumpen 'Oi' punk faction.[52] Rather, Lowry highlighted the potential complicity of 'windy hyperbole' with the dominant culture it appeared to oppose.

Sharply observed strips drew attention to the links between a new pop rhetoric of formal innovation and the pop market's need for new product. Such critique located itself squarely within the broader conjuncture of early Thatcherism by captioning music journalists as 'post-monetarists'.[53] Lowry also caustically observed the way that this call for musical radicalism could become a substitute for political radicalism – one that offered pleasurable compensation for the failure to put 'your principles where your mouth is'. Perched eagerly on a chair, a young journalist declares to a musician: 'I'd like to talk your new album "Flogging the Departed Quadruped" … its wittily imperceptible shifts and falls make me gasp and groan in delight'.[54] Here Lowry's scorn threatened to confirm what Simon Reynolds has characterised as post-punk's 'hair shirt' tendencies,[55] reinforcing new pop's reaction against 'bad-drab' dead ends.[56] Yet the very form of Lowry's work offered its own kind of critical pleasure.

Sharing a similar pedigree to Andy Zero and Martin X, Lowry was working class, born locally and grammar school educated.[57] Despite his London punk connections (Lowry designed the iconic cover of the Clash's *London Calling* and had himself contributed to the *NME*), he remained resident in Lancashire. His jibes at fellow grammar school boy-done-good Morley seem motivated by a belief in the differing paths available to the socially mobile within the world of rock.

On the one hand, you could be geographically mobile too, migrating to the centre of cultural, political and economic power to join the ranks of what one *City Fun* writer dubbed the 'pseudy berks': those whose apparent aim was to become as individually 'successful as the people they slag off', despite their professed political intentions.[58] One Lowry strip featured a journalist declaring: 'we all have our parts to play in the revolutionary struggle ... it's just that I want mine to be on a stage receiving the adulation of thousands and wearing a terrific little New Romantic number.'[59] The alternative, it appeared, was to deploy intelligence and wit to cut through 'whatever the current fashion happens to be',[60] espousing a disenchanted but dogged belief that 'things can be changed'.[61]

No doubt the choice was not so clear-cut in reality. As in the case of Factory, though, what *City Fun* offered here was an alternative perspective to a dominant subcultural discourse, thereby fulfilling its democratic aims.

### 'The joys of oppression': gender and sexuality

It was not only post-punk's overall aesthetic and political direction that *City Fun* writers mapped in geographical and classed terms. This was also true of the way that Naylor and Carroll, especially, approached post-punk negotiations of gender and sexuality. In *The Lost Women of Rock Music*, Helen Reddington deduces from her interview with Naylor that the latter 'felt ... feminists were a middle class confection.'[62] Naylor, who was expelled from school at fifteen, recalls: 'There was a real tension between myself and feminism at the time. In Manchester, Whalley Range and Chorlton and Didsbury, where all the feminists lived, that was everything punk *wasn't*.'[63] This did not mean, though, that *City Fun* avoided engagement with punk and post-punk's interventions on gender and sexuality. Instead it became a focal point for the 'sexual-political dialogue' initiated by Manchester punk pioneers such as the Buzzcocks and Linder Sterling.[64]

The first volume, directed largely by Andy Zero and Martin X, seemed loosely aligned with the mission of post-punk fronts like Rock Against Sexism to challenge unreconstructed attitudes at the level of form as much as content.[65] One local band's performance was dismissed as 'shit, slow macho rock.'[66] Nevertheless, awkward disjunctions arose from the zine's early policy of publishing all contributions. Some live reviews, for instance, evinced a salacious concentration on the attractiveness or otherwise of female musicians rather than on what they were actually doing.

Sexism and homophobia did not go unchallenged by the collective. One response under a review of Motörhead and all-female metal band Girlschool read 'thanks for writing – it patronises women and is down on poofters, but otherwise, ta. The poofters at *City Fun*.'[67] Despite the humour, there was a tinge of sanctimony here that could also be seen elsewhere. Some writers tied themselves in knots, accompanying even passing expressions of desire for women performers with an apologetic tone that was characteristic of the censorious variety of feminism on the ascendant at this time.[68]

A showcase of Manchester's still more or less clandestine gay scene in the second issue of *City Fun* gave an indication of how the zine's approach would change as new voices came to the fore. Signed 'P.N.', the piece was in all likelihood written by Pip Nicholls, the 'androgynous' bass player of The Distractions who lived with Naylor and Carroll.[69] Describing the Picador venue as 'one of those contraception clubs, it could be as reliable as the Pill if used correctly', Nicholls' article displayed hints of the arch humour that would prevail from volume 2 onwards.[70]

This humour was often articulated through a camp inhabitation of existing discourses, generating a less declarative, more subtle and ironic kind of critique, which often relied on visual pleasure for its effect. One issue featured a sex shop advert for a range of dildos, with the head of each one replaced by cut-outs of the faces of A Certain Ratio – or 'A Certain Fellatio', as they were captioned. Significantly, this wind-up was positioned below a kitsch image of a beaming young heterosexual couple gazing into one another's eyes as they picnicked on the beach, which looked like it had been culled from a 1960s magazine. In a classic piece of punk bricolage, the two images fed off one another, making an implicit mockery of commodified heteronormative romance and overly serious male musicians.

The shift in focus was not total, reflecting divergent attitudes within the collective on how to frame issues of gender and sexuality. Throughout volume 2, skits co-existed with serious reflections and exposés. One article aired 'ugly rumours' that Manchester clubs Rotters and Pips operated a 'sexuality ban', noting that the latter's membership rules forbade men from dancing with male partners.[71] Also present, however, was a persistent suspicion of overt political engagement. This is difficult to trace due to the anonymity of many articles. It may sometimes have been the work of Naylor and Carroll though, given Carroll's long-running 'Pam Ponders' satirical diary column of a middle-class feminist and Naylor's take on the stance of the zine at the time: 'Politics are a bit clichéd … nobody takes notice of rantings.'[72]

It is possible that the same mode that lightened the tone of *City Fun*'s interventions on gender and sexuality may at times have undermined them, given the 'disengaged, depoliticised' tendencies of camp.[73] In Britain, the queer sensibility that includes camp carries residual traces of its 1920s adoption by leisure class aesthetes in reaction against 'Victorian seriousness and responsibility'.[74] Though 'twentieth century working class culture defined itself against the middle class queer',[75] this may well account for the transgressive appeal of the latter sensibility to those working-class punks like Naylor who: 'Had a really strong sense of not being in the straight world … my mum would say things like "why don't you go to secretarial college – shorthand is always useful." And I thought, "I want to be Janis Joplin, I don't want to go to fucking secretarial college."'[76] An unattributed article entitled 'Never Mind Dear, We're All Made The Same … Though Some More Than Others' railed against 'the hordes … people frightened by culture/intelligence/sophistication'[77] in a gesture that resonated with the historical elision of queerness and upwardly mobile aestheticism.[78]

That said, this mode was not guaranteed to preclude political commitment, nor did it always imply a sense of outsider superiority generated by exclusion. The author of 'The Joys of Oppression – By Mouth or by Rectum' critiqued those gays and feminists whom they saw as excessively attached to subcultural insularity, viewing this as the elitist desire to be 'something other than your average grotty, unspectacular prole'. Observing the development of ever-narrowing identity-based cliques and the consequent competitive tensions between them, the writer exasperatedly opined: 'wouldn't you think that with … the need for education/liberation that gays could stop fighting amongst themselves for a moment. It's just like a Labour Party into disco and wearing uniforms.'[79]

### 'Meanwhile, back in the jungle': the political conjuncture

As 'The Joys of Oppression' suggested, *City Fun*'s witty hostility towards identitarian fragmentation was not confined to gender and sexuality. For one writer, 'tribalism' had become 'endemic' to British society – from 'the South West Middlesbrough Lesbian Whole-food Commune and Nose-Flute Ensemble Rock Against Sloth Hunting in Guatemala 1984 Committee' to the 'Shetland Liberation Front'. Included in this perspective was 'the current proliferation of quaint youth cults … and their myriad mutations and sub-factions' that had followed in the wake of punk.[80]

While the writer acknowledged the pleasures of subcultural style, they despaired of the way that tribal hostilities could so easily be manipulated 'by those whose games are played on a grander scale', drawing historical parallels with the incorporation of Scottish clans into the service of British imperialism.[81]

The perspective has much in common with Fredric Jameson's diagnosis of the rise of the 'group' in late capitalism – and of postmodern identity politics as being in part a 'properly interminable series of neighbourhood issues ... invested with something of Nietzsche's social Darwinism', at risk of 'disintegrating into the more obscene consumerist pluralisms' of the dominant culture.[82]

On this front, *City Fun* also homed in on the broad left culture of which it was a part. At a time when sections of the British left were retreating from a previously held faith in the centrality of working-class politics, the zine elaborated a nuanced and comical critique of this tendency. Its prophetic qualities were perhaps unique among the post-punk milieu.

From one angle, Cath Carroll's 'Pam Ponders' satire – which ran over the course of seven issues in volume 2 – might be viewed precisely as a form of myopic subcultural 'tribalism'. Dickinson remembers Carroll and Naylor's 'cynical' attitude toward Manchester's post-punk feminist scene, which provided Carroll with material for the feature: 'They thought it was all middle class really.'[83] From another angle, the satire's scope is much broader, chiming with Andrew Milner's argument that the middle-class intelligentsia has overwhelmingly and unrepresentatively led the new social movements of the post-war and postmodern period, thus determining the 'developing preference' of such movements 'for individualist ... as opposed to structural solutions.'[84]

It was exactly this self-conscious individualism that 'Pam Ponders' targeted, mercilessly observing the way that the apparently liberating personal politics of 1960s radicalism were at risk of tipping over into an incoherent blend of moralism and narcissism: 'Pam Bennett, mid-forties and VOCAL when it comes to WHAT MATTERS, has hewn a tiny window into her life for the world to peek thru'. She invites City Funsters to share in her triumphs, frustrations and, above all, her growth as a PERSON.'[85]

From her son's 'nocturnal emissions' to the indiscretions of her social circle, Pam is given to spuriously politicising the minutiae of her daily life, evoking the 'postmodern propensity to represent power as ubiquitous.'[86] Even the family pets – Sitwell the cat, Prentiss the slug and Chloe the communal cannabis plant – are embroiled in the never-ending sequence of psychodramas. Those who fall short of Pam's standards are judged harshly in ways that fuse the moral and the self-regarding. Befriending 'a pair of really great wimmin' on the train, Jan and Trixi, Pam is 'appalled' to learn that Jan's mother cannot tolerate the couple bringing up a child together. 'God, just hope I never get so uptight with Raitch', Pam reflects of her own daughter.[87]

With regard to tribalism, 'Pam Ponders' presciently delineates the class fraction from which such attitudes emanated, noting too the emergent political formation around which the right of this spectrum would coalesce. Dashing about on her moped to media and housing conferences, organising benefit 'bops' played by the 'Wandering Menstruals', Pam is the epitome of the 'new middle class' that Raphael Samuel identified as dominating the membership of the newly formed Social Democratic Party: 'It seems to have a specific appeal to those … who are familiar with the language and procedures of administration, and who like to see things hum.'[88] Sure enough, Pam records in passing: 'Joined SDP. Bloody expensive.'[89]

As the major beneficiaries of post-war consumerism, this class fraction developed what Samuel called a 'new emotional economy': one of 'instant rather than deferred gratification', in which 'sensual pleasures … are the very field on which social claims are established and sexual identities confirmed.'[90] Here there is a hint of the ambiguity of countercultural and libertarian left politicisations of pleasure between the 1960s and the 1980s. As much as such politicisation arose from disaffection with consumerist distortions of social and sexual life, prompting hopes for un-alienated forms of fulfilment, it was also determined by the way that same consumerism melted down collectivism in favour of a particular kind of individual gratification.

André Gorz notes that 'individuals socialised by consumerism … are encouraged to "be themselves" by distinguishing themselves from others.'[91] Something of this ambiguity can be seen in Pam's name-dropping of vegan eateries, her penchant for obscure Norwegian film festivals and her attempted pursuit of exotic extramarital encounters. These are as much self-indulgent distinction as they are opportunities to advocate different ways of life, while fulminating against 'PENILE FASCISM' and the like.[92]

City Fun's lampooning of 'middle class radicalism gone sour'[93] pulls no punches. Pam meets her end Isadora Duncan-style, her husband Cliff recounting how 'that long scarf I knitted for her … got caught in the back wheel' of the moped.[94] Yet it never hardens into opposition to the left per se – even the libertarian left's concentration on the cultural and personal. Instalments of 'Pam Ponders' could co-exist on the same page as articles with titles like 'A Breakdown of Oppression'. This Althusserian tract spelled out the penetration of hegemony to a 'pre-conscious level' and viewed the media, education and family as 'arm[s] of that same octopus that controls the police and the market.'[95] It may well be the case that City Fun's roots in the infrastructure of the libertarian left accounts for this turn of events.

## Conclusion

The long run of City Fun, combined with the sheer scope of its evolving content and its shifting collective of contributors, make it difficult to know where to begin when reflecting upon its long-term significance. If we consider cultural production and the zine's stance on post-punk, we might draw some inspiration from an alternative publication that claimed freedom as the opportunity for those usually denied a public voice to express their perspectives at a point where the right was moving to equate freedom with the capitalist market.[96] Though the internet has democratised communication to some extent, it is worth recalling Raymond Williams's observation that straightfor-wardly capitalist forms of media risk limiting freedom to 'what can profitably be said'.[97]

One of Manchester's most influential contemporary local media outlets is I Love Manchester, a website that proclaims itself 'a way to express our love of the city', recycling countercultural platitudes like 'make love not war' and 'join the movement' in its 'about' section. Along with its coverage of the city's thriving independent cultural scene and the opportunities the site affords for young writers, such manoeuvres appear to position I Love Manchester in the broad lineage of publications like *City Fun*. Yet despite repeatedly pronouncing itself 'incorruptible', the site also claims proudly to have been founded by a group of 'content marketing experts'. The description highlights a contradiction between an apparently democratic desire to 'harness the energy of people' and the site's manipulatively commercial remit, with its clickbait headlines and content that blurs journalism with advertising copy.[98] You are unlikely to find reviews of bands with captions like 'Don't look at my hairstyle – it might fall over', as was the case with *City Fun*'s irreverent commitment to uncensored opinion.[99]

This is not to suggest hypocrisy on the part of I Love Manchester: clearly its *raison d'être* is different to that of *City Fun* and is plainly acknowledged. But in terms of independent media, it does indicate the gap between *City Fun*'s oppositional rhetoric, which was bound up with a subcultural constituency and a broader leftist project – and I Love Manchester's use of oppositional rhetoric as just one more technique of selling us stuff. The phrase 'content marketing experts' also sheds some light on the lasting relevance of *City Fun*'s concern with class, identity and the politics thereof. Evoking something of the new middle class's professional distinction, it is unsurprising that the phrase appears alongside a summary of I Love Manchester's origins. The organisation was founded to 'rise against' the riots of 2011, which erupted a year after a Conservative–Liberal Democrat coalition came to power on a platform of austerity. I Love Manchester's editors reduce the riots to the 'anti-social behaviour' of their presumed inferiors, opposing such behaviour to their own 'unconditional love of the city'. Thus, Pam-like narcissism and moralism combine in an attempted colonisation of 'civic pride' and a 'cool, cultured and cosmopolitan' demeanour, celebrating diversity – except that which uncomfortably draws attention to structural inequality and fractures the city's branding as some utopian creative hub.[100] Tribalism is alive and well.

One of *City Fun*'s proudest achievements was its short-circuiting of the chain of associations that has ideologically coded a desirably 'cool, cultured and cosmopolitan' future as the distinctive consumption patterns of the post-1960s left-liberal middle class, bound up with identitarian tribalism and an eagerness to take the moral high ground. This was not just expressed negatively in jibes at 'pseudy berks' and 'professional gays'.[101] It was also achieved positively. An alliance of renegade grammar school kids, graduates and sharp-witted, wayward drop-outs from the education system was the making of a funny, diverse and more-or-less socialist publication whose own investigative take on the riots of 1981 stands in stark contrast to the indignant reactions on show thirty years later.[102] In this respect, as in so many others, the zine genuinely did things differently, to paraphrase the much-abused words of its one time adversary, Tony Wilson.

## Notes

Acknowledgments: Thanks to the Working Class Movement Library for extensive use of their *City Fun* collection, and to Manchester Digital Music Archive for tirelessly hunting down and digitising the entire run of the zine.

1   David Wilkinson, *Post-Punk, Politics and Pleasure in Britain* (Basingstoke: Palgrave Macmillan, 2016).
2   Bob Dickinson estimates that at its peak, around 2,000 copies of each issue were printed, with a 'high pass-on rate' and the regular purchase of back copies. Author interview with Bob Dickinson, Manchester, 14 January 2017.
3   Wilkinson, *Post-Punk, Politics and Pleasure*, especially pp. 52–3.
4   Author interview with Dickinson, 14 January 2017.
5   Bob Dickinson, *Imprinting the Sticks: The Alternative Press Beyond London* (Aldershot: Ashgate, 1997), pp. 78–82.
6   Mike Rowe, 'Meanwhile Back At The Ranch … ', *Mole Express*, 57, 1977.
7   Dickinson, *Imprinting the Sticks*, p. 150.
8   Bob Dickinson, 'City Fun', *New Manchester Review*, 2 November 1979, p. 15.
9   Andy Zero, 'News', *City Fun*, 1:7, 1978, n.p.
10  'How To Produce A Fanzine', *City Fun*, 1:3, 1978, n.p.; 'City Fun Finance', *City Fun*, 1:2, 1978, n.p.
11  *City Fun*, 1:3, 1978, n.p.
12  S.C. Lowe, review of Siouxsie and the Banshees at Manchester University student's union, *City Fun*, 1:2, 1978, n.p.
13  Bernard Who Did What, 'The Last Laugh', *City Fun*, 1:2, 1978, n.p.

14 Simon Reynolds, *Rip It Up and Start Again: Postpunk 1978–1984* (London: Faber & Faber, 2005), pp. 364–6.

15 Neil Taylor, *Document and Eyewitness: An Intimate History of Rough Trade* (London: Orion, 2010), pp. 214–15.

16 Pete Dale has called this the 'anyone can do it' component of punk and post-punk. See Pete Dale, *Anyone Can Do It: Empowerment, Tradition and the Punk Underground* (London: Routledge, 2012).

17 Reynolds, *Rip It Up and Start Again*, pp. 366 and 519.

18 *Ibid.*, p. 366.

19 Margaret Thatcher, speech to Grantham Conservatives, 4 March 1977, www.margaretthatcher.org/document/103329, accessed 10 May 2017.

20 Paul Morley, review of Scars, *Author! Author!*, NME, 11 April 1981, p. 33.

21 Quoted in Peter Golding and Graham Murdock, 'Privatising Pleasure', *Marxism Today*, October 1983, pp. 32–6.

22 Reynolds, *Rip It Up and Start Again*, p. 366.

23 Charles Landry, David Morley, Russell Southwood and Patrick Wright, *What a Way To Run a Railroad: An Analysis of Radical Failure* (London: Comedia, 1985), p. 13.

24 *Ibid.*, pp. 92–4 and 13.

25 *City Fun*, 1:3, 1978, n.p.

26 'City Fun Finance', *City Fun*, 1:2, 1978, n.p.

27 Andy Zero, 'A Self Indulgence', *City Fun*, 1:10, 1979, n.p.

28 'Charity Stops Here', *City Fun*, 1:25, 1980, n.p.

29 *Ibid.*

30 'Welcome to a New Kind of Magazine! Exclusive Interview With City Fun Staff', *City Fun*, 2:1, 1980, n.p.

31 'Charity Stops Here'.

32 'Welcome to a New Kind of Magazine!'

33 *Ibid.*

34 Author interview with Dickinson, 14 January 2017.

35 *Ibid.*

36 Dickinson, *Imprinting the Sticks*, p. 163.

37 Lynne Segal, *Why Feminism? Gender, Psychology, Politics* (Cambridge: Polity, 1999), p. 21.

38 Nick Srnicek and Alex Williams, *Inventing the Future: Postcapitalism and a World Without Work* (London: Verso, 2015).

39 Author interview with Dickinson, 14 January 2017.

40 James Nice, *Shadowplayers: The Rise and Fall of Factory Records* (London: Aurum, 2010), p. 78.

41 AT, 'City Fun Benefit', *City Fun*, 1:18, 1980, n.p.

42 Tony Wilson, 'Just Another Level of Turgid Aesthetic Debate', *City Fun*, 1:21, 1980, n.p.

43 *Ibid.*

44 Andy Zero, 'Are You Following This? A Classic Case of Overkill: The Turgid Debate … ', *City Fun*, 1:21, 1980, n.p.

45  Martin X, 'Just Another Level of Turgid Aesthetic Debate', *City Fun*, 1:21, 1980, n.p.

46  *Ibid.*

47  Doris Day, 'A Problem', *City Fun*, 1:4, 1979, n.p.

48  Alan Sinfield, *Literature, Politics and Culture in Postwar Britain* (London: Continuum, 2004 third edn). See especially Chapter 11, 'The Rise of Left Culturism'.

49  Justin Toland, 'Factory's Shadow' featured on the website 'Indie Originals: The New Hormones Story', https://newhormonesinfo.com/category/factorys-shadow/, accessed 1 June 2017.

50  Bruce Denning, 'Cynical Betrayal?', *City Fun*, 1:25, 1980, n.p.

51  Ray Lowry [uncredited], untitled, *City Fun*, 2:19, 1981, n.p.

52  Garry Bushell and Dave McCullough, 'Cockney Rejects and the Rise of the New Punk', *Sounds*, 4 August 1979, pp. 16–17.

53  Lowry, untitled, *City Fun*, 2:19, 1981, n.p.

54  Ray Lowry, untitled, *City Fun*, 1:25, 1980, n.p.

55  Reynolds, *Rip It Up and Start Again*, p. 377.

56  Paul Morley, review of The Pop Group, *For How Much Longer Do We Tolerate Mass Murder?*, NME, 22 March 1980, p. 39.

57  'Ray Lowry 1944–2008', *Mojo*, October 2008, www.mojo4music.com/, accessed 2 April 2017.

58  'What's Wrong, Boy?', *City Fun*, 2:17, 1981, n.p.

59  Ray Lowry [uncredited], 'Only Rock 'n' Roll', *City Fun*, 2:14, 1981, n.p.

60  *Ibid.*

61  Lowry, untitled, *City Fun*, 2:19, 1981, n.p.

62  Helen Reddington, *The Lost Women of Rock Music: Female Musicians of the Punk Era* (Sheffield: Equinox, 2012), p. 165.

63  *Ibid.*, p. 187.

64  Dickinson, *Imprinting the Sticks*, p. 146.

65  For a discussion of musical form, gender and post-punk, see Caroline O'Meara, 'The Raincoats: Breaking Down Punk Rock's Masculinities', in *Popular Music*, 22:3 (2003), 299–313.

66  Andy Zero, untitled, *City Fun*, 1:6, 1979, n.p.

67  'Motörhead/Girlschool, Free Trade Hall 11th April', *City Fun*, 1:7, 1979, n.p.

68  Victor Silvester, 'Dance', *City Fun*, 1:20, 1979, n.p. For more on the sexual politics of feminism in the late 1970s and 1980s, see Lynne Segal, *Is The Future Female? Troubled Thoughts on Contemporary Feminism* (London: Virago, 1994).

69  Dickinson, *Imprinting the Sticks*, p. 147.

70  P.N., untitled, *City Fun*, 1:2, 1978, n.p.

71  'Sneak File', *City Fun*, 2:29, 1981, n.p.

72  'Welcome to a New Kind of Magazine!'

73  Susan Sontag, 'Notes on "Camp"', *Against Interpretation and Other Essays* (London: Penguin, [1961] 2009), pp. 275–92: p. 277).

74  Alan Sinfield, *The Wilde Century* (London: Cassell, 1994), p. 132.

75  *Ibid.*, p. 146.
76  Reddington, *The Lost Women of Rock Music*, p. 20.
77  Anonymous, 'Never Mind Dear, We're All Made the Same ... Though Some More Than Others', *City Fun*, 2:9, 1981, n.p.
78  Sinfield, *The Wilde Century*, pp. 147–8.
79  'The Joys of Oppression – By Mouth or by Rectum', *City Fun*, 3:3, 1982, n.p.
80  'Meanwhile Back in the Jungle', *City Fun*, 2:9, 1981, n.p.
81  *Ibid.*
82  Fredric Jameson, *Postmodernism or The Cultural Logic of Late Capitalism* (London: Verso, 1991), pp. 320–2 and 330.
83  Author interview with Dickinson, 14 January 2017.
84  Andrew Milner, *Class* (London: SAGE, 1999), p. 166.
85  Cath Carroll [uncredited], 'Pam Ponders', *City Fun*, 2:11, 1981, n.p.
86  Milner, *Class*, p. 165.
87  Cath Carroll [uncredited], 'Pam Ponders', *City Fun*, 2:15, 1981, n.p.
88  Raphael Samuel, 'The SDP and the New Middle Class', in Alison Light, Sally Alexander and Gareth Stedman Jones (eds), *Island Stories: Unravelling Britain* (London: Verso, [1982] 1998), pp. 256–71: p. 260.
89  Cath Carroll [uncredited], 'Pam Ponders', *City Fun*, 2:13, 1981, n.p.
90  Samuel, 'The SDP and the New Middle Class', p. 259.
91  André Gorz, *Critique of Economic Reason* (London: Verso, 1989), p. 47.
92  Cath Carroll [uncredited], 'Pam Ponders', *City Fun*, 2:11, 1981, n.p.
93  Samuel, 'The SDP and the New Middle Class', p. 270.
94  Cath Carroll [uncredited], 'Pam Ponders', *City Fun*, 2:17, 1981, n.p.
95  'A Breakdown of Oppression', *City Fun*, 2:12, 1981, n.p.
96  Stuart Hall, 'The Great Moving Right Show', in Stuart Hall and Martin Jacques (eds), *The Politics of Thatcherism* (London: Lawrence and Wishart, 1983), pp. 19–39.
97  Raymond Williams, 'Communications and Community' [1961], *Resources of Hope: Culture, Democracy, Socialism* (London: Verso, 1989), pp. 19–31: p. 25.
98  'About Us', http://ilovemanchester.com/about-us, accessed 28 June 2017.
99  'Don't Look At My Hair Style – It Might Fall Over,' *City Fun*, 2:5, 1980.
100  http://ilovemanchester.com/about-us.
101  'The Joys of Oppression', *City Fun*, 3:3, 1982, n.p.
102  The Passage, 'Reading Between the Thin Blue Line', *City Fun*, 2:21, 1981, n.p.

# 6

# Goth zines: writing from the dark underground, 1976–92

CLAIRE NALLY

The period spanning the late 1970s and early 1980s represents the foundational moment in the construction of goth as a subcultural entity. Prior to this moment, the iconography and style of proto-goth culture is visible in a range of zines which situate themselves in film and literature, and more broadly, may be identified as Gothic. Catherine Spooner draws a clear distinction between goth and Gothic in *Fashioning Gothic Bodies*, where she explains: 'The relationship between goth subculture and the Gothic literary tradition is not straightforward … Nevertheless, the two are intimately linked, precisely through the medium of fashion.'[1] Goth as a musical *and* spectacular subculture is frequently foregrounded in these zines, and as such, they can be read as a codification of the goth aesthetic. It becomes apparent that this aesthetic is influential in both Gothic and goth zines: Paul Hodkinson has explained that goth zines played 'a comparatively marginal role' in the 1980s, and affirms such publications were more influential in the 1990s.[2] However, despite the fact that many zines only ran to a few issues, they provide a clear insight into the transition from punk to post-punk and goth, as well as a useful corrective to the focus on the London scene which often characterises academic studies of goth.

This chapter will explore the emergence of goth zine culture through three different zines: *Panache*, *Whippings and Apologies* and *Propaganda*. These zines have been strategically chosen as they represent iterations of early post-punk, goth as it emerged in the 1980s and, finally, the mainstreaming of the culture. They also represent different geographical locations (London, Leeds and the USA), which reveals the tensions and corollaries between different versions of goth, as well as critical lacunae, particularly in the narrative of goth as a London-centric subculture, via the Batcave club, an iconic location for goth culture, and one which is often invoked as central to the origins of goth. The main objective here is to address the ways in which goth subculture evolved from its underground origins in the late 1970s to the early 1990s. Part of this analysis will therefore focus on the ways in which goth zine culture moved from DIY and amateur production to an aesthetic which was much more glossy and mainstream. This trajectory mirrors goth as a music culture, and particularly its incursion into broader cultural representation: we need only think about the Sisters of Mercy's 'Temple of Love' (1992), which reached a number 3 spot in the UK singles charts. This is a re-recording of their 1983 offering which did not even chart. The goth zine culture reveals much about this transition from within the subculture itself, and uncovers the difference in subcultural practice across the UK (Leeds versus London, for instance). The early culture certainly aligns itself (implicitly or explicitly) with political radicalism, particularly with reference to Thatcherite politics and the neo-traditionalist agenda in circulation in the 1980s. However, while much of these early zines do indeed represent a challenge to this mainstream, there is less evidence that such radicalism extends to gender and representations of female performers.

It is important to note at this stage that while punk is commonly associated with working-class dissatisfaction, goth is emphatically white and middle-class.[3] Despite this caveat, the post-industrial North of England was a focal point for 1980s goth, as evinced by *Whippings and Apologies*. This zine was produced in Leeds from 1981 and ran to 11 issues. Richard Rouska describes it as 'the most prolific and glossy of all Leeds zines.'[4] Mick Mercer's fanzine *Panache* (1976–92), which ultimately evolved into Mercer's online zine *The Mick*, represents one of the foremost zines in UK post-punk, articulating both an early goth aesthetic in content and an emphatically DIY ethos in its 'scrapbook' collage design. It was a stapled, A4 production, selling for 20p, with distribution being chiefly confined to London, though coverage of gigs did extend to other parts of the south of England. Mercer's simultaneous writing in *Panache* and the more mainstream *Melody Maker* negotiates the traditional pop culture/subculture divide and might question how far cultural resistance is implicated (and challenged) in this engagement with the mainstream through visual iconography, irony, billingsgate humour, parody, and satire.[5]

By comparison, the US publication *Propaganda*, founded by Fred Berger, emerged from its roots as a punk fanzine with an undeclared but nonetheless emphatically goth and avant-garde agenda. It represented a very different goth zine culture to *Panache* and *Whippings and Apologies*, as it was rooted in the New York underground club scene. While addressing the materiality of the texts in question, this chapter will also evaluate the politics of gender in goth publications, focusing on key examples of gender in goth zines – the representation of Siouxsie Sioux from Siouxsie and the Banshees, Rosie Garland of The March Violets, as well as the iconic status of Andrew Eldritch and The Sisters of Mercy – in order to reveal how gender in the goth scene was represented during its formative years through to its heyday.

The evolution of goth as a music category has been well documented. Martin Hannett famously described Joy Division in 1979 as 'dancing music with Gothic overtones'.[6] These 'Gothic overtones' characterise the content of much proto-goth through BDSM subculture, horror film coverage and, more generally, a dark aesthetic.[7] For instance the zine *Twylight*, published in the late 1960s, had a print run of 500 and was distributed in the UK and the USA by subscription mailing list (53 cents in the USA; 2s 6d in the UK). Common to many zines, *Twylight* was seemingly published quite irregularly, as the February/March 1968 edition claims: 'This is the issue of TWYLIGHT advertised as "out now" in October 1967 ... Pressure of work and lack of money, as usual, beat me.'[8] At this point, the editor (Michael J. Harris) explains he only recouped 50 per cent of the printing costs, which links to Stephen Duncombe's characterisation of zines as not-for-profit.[9] *Twylight* reviewed horror films, including *Torture Garden* (1967), in common with later publications such as *Children of the Night* (1974–85), edited by Derek Jensen and Matthew Le Master. The latter was seemingly published very haphazardly and provided content on films including Gothic icons Christopher Lee and Peter Cushing, vampirism and many staples of what would become goth culture. The Gothic trope of vampirism fed into the later goth subculture: Dave Vanian of The Damned (formed in 1976) was to crystallise this goth/Romantic figure, accompanied by many others. Bauhaus's iconic single 'Bela Lugosi's Dead', with Pete Murphy and the band performing in the opening sequence of the vampire film, *The Hunger* (1983), are obvious examples. The cover of the *Children of the Night* zine (vol. 1, 1974) features Christopher Lee as The Count, preying on a supine female victim. Alongside this image, the cover employs German Blackletter typeface, which would also become a cornerstone of goth iconography. In many instances, such early zines testify to an underground network of the marginalised practices, including the LGBTQ community.[10] Later zines from the 1990s, such as *Marquis' Masquerade Magazine,* which emerged from a fetish club night in Nottingham (and testifies to the intersection of goth and BDSM), and *Bats and Red Velvet*, reveal the intersection of gothic literature with the fetish subculture (which includes poetry as well as music reviews, and hand-drawn adverts for club nights such as those at The Banshee in Manchester). Indeed, Rosie Garland has explained that her outsider status as a lesbian and horror/vampire film aficionado was partially explained and justified by these early publications: 'the zines cover interests I've learnt to conceal in order to limit my bullied isolation: horror movies, vampires, sci-fi, punk, weird illustration, weirder literature. The Gothic, in short. For the first time in my life, I see myself reflected. I encounter an underground community of the imagination. I know I'll never meet any of these fellow-weirdoes, but I am not alone.'[11] While zines are produced for and by 'Freaks, geeks, nerds, and losers', it is also very much the case that they can present social bonding in a pre-internet age.[12] As Alison Piepmeier has suggested, 'Zines instigate intimate, affectionate connections between their creators and readers, not just communities but *embodied* communities, that are made possible by the materiality of the zine medium.'[13] Thus, in many ways, these early 'proto-goth' zines reveal how the subculture drew upon a pre-existing symbolic and cultural iconography from film and literature, as well as how proto-goths would find communal images and solidarity in such zines.

## Panache

In her article on punk fanzines, Teal Triggs characterises *Panache* as a mouthpiece for punk bands specifically, and observes towards the end of her analysis that the publication 'transformed itself into a fanzine for Britain's goths and later established itself as a fanzine for the emerging Indie music scene.'[14] This strictly chronological account tends to overlook the myriad influences and cross-fertilisations which marked the zine and, indeed, the emerging subcultures of the time. Certainly 'indie' as representative of a broadly alternative or 'independent' scene was very much a catch-all term for what became goth, and the transition from punk to goth isn't always so neatly defined in these early publications. With this in mind, *Panache* emerges as a cultural document very much at the forefront of an evolving subculture, which nonetheless bears many of the key characteristics conventionally associated with the medium of zines. 'The Captain's Column' in issue 5 demonstrates this evolution effectively, suggesting the Sex Pistols were the 'first to play punk rock':

> The editions good sense prize goes to the Pistols,In arecent interview with Johnny Rott-en he implied that these people who derided everything that wasn't new wave were just as bad as the establishment that they're rebelling

against.For New Wavers to deny the validity of other forms of rock music is
wrong – after all New Wave was spawned from Rock n'Roll music..So it
would be pointless to deny its own heritage.[15]

As demonstrated above, zines can be delineated as often containing 'a highly
personalised editorial' which then moves to 'opinionated essays or rants
criticizing, describing, or extolling something or other' and conclude with
'reviews of other zines, bands, books, and so forth … Material is also "borrowed": pirated from other zines and the mainstream press, sometimes without
credit, often without permission.'[16] There are elements which are handwritten,
as well as a chaotic layout and often illegible material. This accords very closely
with the aesthetics of *Panache*, which has as its hallmark a wry self-awareness,
acerbic wit and satire, exposure of the editorial process including blacked-out
text and amendments, and a cut-and-paste, DIY aesthetic. We have acerbic
pastiches of the fashion industry (issue 14) and a satirical 'Reader's Wives'
feature which seeks to position itself firmly against the mainstream. Issue 5
offers an interesting example in several respects. The front cover presents
photographic film reproduced as a header and handwritten band names signify-
ing those who are showcased inside. There is also an 'amateurish' layout which
runs out of room on the page and crams the band name 'Penetration' into
the remaining space. The witty, satirical element of the zine is obvious in a
small footer placed on the left of the cover: 'Law Enforcement Agencies: Write
for quantity discounts on official letterhead.' *Panache* is clearly signalling its
status as an example of copyright transgression, as well as a publisher of
obscenities: 'cunt' and other billingsgate words are peppered through the
publication. This wry humour extends to the editorial which is marked by
flippancy: 'send all letters, money (uncrossed P.O.'s Preferred, Knickers, Photos
etc to:– Mick … '. Similarly, there is a self-conscious reference to the name
of the zine in a cut-out cartoon, which contains the following: 'A man must
meet his own final defeat with class. With panache.' *Panache* is obviously aware
of the tensions between subcultural imperative and commodity culture,
observing in the self-deprecating 'Editorial Vomit' section that 'we must be
latter day trend-setters because after we've written about someone they invariably
end up splash-ed [*sic*] up all over the pages of *Melody Maker*, for which we
apologise.' There is an especial irony here, as Mercer himself wrote for *Melody
Maker* in the 1980s and the equally commercial *Record Mirror* from 1978.
Similarly, the editorial is particularly critical of that cornerstone of punk zine
history, *Sniffin' Glue*:

> Too many of you out there are too content to fester on your arses reading …
> nipping down to your punk boutiques etc. Why don't you try listening to

some of the bands. Some of them are absolute crap … and generally get raved about, whereas a lot of them are good, but get totally ignored! You must be Russians![17]

In this short but vitriolic section, the main focus is a preoccupation with authenticity. Ken Gelder has observed that subcultures function with the assumption that 'the "inauthenticity" of music's commercial and industrial features [contrasts] with the "authenticity" of subcultural music tastes – which, rhetorically at least, can claim to be *anti*-commercial.'[18] This extends to an interview with The Rods (formerly Eddie and the Hot Rods). The interviewer asks 'New single's really commercial innit?', to which [Dave] Higgs responds: 'I'd say all new wave was commercial, wouldn't you?' At the same time, this focus on authenticity is also explicitly gendered. The interview opens with an observation that 'the marquee was packed with the usual foreigners, a few punks and mostly young teenyboppers all hoping to touch a member … All the way thru [Barrie] Masters does his T.O.T.P. bit – enticing young girls to touch him.'[19] Indeed, Angela McRobbie has observed that the 'teenybopper' carries connotations of commercial origins and almost exclusively denotes younger, pre-teen girls.[20] While there is clearly a tension here between the underground music scene and that of commercial and capitalist ventures, it is also a gendered designation which distinguishes between authentic (and implicitly male) fans who are serious about music, and the inauthentic (female) fan who expresses sexual desire. Helen Davies has suggested such binary oppositions articulate how women are overlooked as 'serious' fans of rock music:

> The rock music press prides itself on a cool, detached appraisal of its
> performers, even if in reality it rarely practises this, and teenyboppers are
> therefore ridiculed for their deeply emotional involvement with the artists
> they admire, often described as hysteria. In particular, displays of active
> female sexuality are ridiculed by the music press … This is a way of refusing
> the defiance and rebellion inherent in a young girl's assertion of an active
> sexuality.[21]

While *Panache* represents the underground rather than the mainstream music press, it clearly engages with much of the homosocial rhetoric found in commercial magazines. Despite this, much of *Panache* strives to parody such ideas. Issue 5 also contained 'Our Page 3 Girl' (a soft-core pin-up in UK tabloid newspaper *The Sun*), Patti Palladin of Snatch (a New York post-punk outfit with proto-goth undertones, which collaborated with Brian Eno). The photo defeats any expectations of tabloid titillation however: while Palladin is clearly an attractive woman, in the photo she is fully clothed and performing on stage. Similarly, a cut-out photo montage in the same issue features a reclining topless woman, her nipples replaced by an eye. Handwritten words across the model's body identify 'Forehead' 'Neck' 'Bosom' 'Thigh' 'Bikini' (the latter marked by a prohibitive cross), and also boldly state that this is a 'sexist photo'. This is not without self-conscious irony, of course, but it does seem to have different targets: sexism, but also those who seek to censor or otherwise prohibit the sexualised representation of women's bodies. As much as it is using soft-core images and their viewers for humour, it also seems to be using feminism itself as a source of satire. This is particularly important given the context of second-wave feminism, and particularly the so-called 'porn wars', which marked a schism in feminist discourses in the 1970s and 1980s, reflecting chiefly upon how to represent women and sexuality.[22] At the same time, this conflicted discourse emerges in other sections of the zine. The clearly ironic readers' wives section features blurred shots of men, the band Snatch playing the Fulham Greyhound, and Patti Smith 'In Heat'. This latter section is prefaced with 'No, not another *Panache* sexist article … It's another Patti Smith bootleg.' In contradistinction to other sections of the zine, the commentary here is about the music: Patti Smith's voice, keyboards, drumming, etc., rather than the objectification which the running header might suggest.

This wry humour also features editorial reflection on issue 4 (which features in issue 5): 'I suppose I ought to apologise to anyone who was offended by our "Sexist" outbursts in The Slits/Siouxsie review last issue where Su came in for quite a description. I won't go into details … Well the review was written when we were totally inebriated … as we had been at the gig.' The editorial reluctantly apologises, while at the same time casting doubt on how far the material is offensive (the scare quotes around 'sexist' neatly encapsulate this). Siouxsie and the Banshees are a useful band to focus on, as they neatly straddle punk/post-punk and goth aesthetics. Referring to The Banshees in *Gothic Rock Black Book*, Mercer suggests 'Modern Goth started here. (Much to their disgust.)'[23] Given the penchant among goth bands to deny their goth status (Andrew Eldritch of The Sisters of Mercy among them), this is hardly surprising. Issue 4 features Siouxsie on the front cover, with studded cuffs, hallmark make-up and iconic pale skin. In short, Siouxsie espouses, even in her comparatively early career, the visual spectacle which would be a key component of goth. The song 'Painted Birds', from the album *A Kiss in the Dreamhouse* (1982), references this notion of spectacle quite clearly, as the 'painted birds' clearly suggest the over-the-top visual performativity of many goths on the scene.[24]

Dick Hebdige has noted that 'spectacular subcultures ... are precariously placed between the worlds of the straight and the deviant ... They *display* their own codes (e.g. the punk's ripped T-shirt) or at least demonstrate that codes are there to be used and abused.'[25] Siouxsie's performance of aggressive femininity (studs, heavy make-up) also signals how early goth drew much inspiration from fetish and BDSM culture, in the same way as punk: 'adherents to "Goth" style combined the nihilism of Punk, the perverse sexuality of fetish wear and the graveyard exoticism of nineteenth-century mourning costume to create a macabre aesthetic. Garments were predominantly black, accessorised with "vamp" makeup and memento mori motifs.'[26] Certainly, Siouxsie and the Banshees were very aware of their impact and their complicity in making Siouxsie a spectacle: Steve Severin, bassist with The Banshees, has remarked that 'Goth was reacting much more to how Siouxsie looked' than how she sounded.[27] This also renders Siouxsie a source of desire in a very conventional way, as Simon Reynolds has remarked: 'most girls in Goth bands fell into the traditional role of attractive singer.'[28] As such, the editorial disavowal in *Panache* not only underscores how gender determinants in zines were perhaps not as radical as other aspects of their content and design, but moreover, how punk and early goth was heavily complicit in marketing women as spectacle.[29]

## Whippings and Apologies

The Leeds-based zine *Whippings and Apologies* was one of a select number of zine publications (along with *Attack on Bzag* and *Roar*) in circulation around Leeds in the early 1980s priced 35p (rising to 40p from January/February 1984). While *Whippings and Apologies* represents a conventional zine in many respects, it is unusual in its comparatively glossy print quality. The content was based on news and reviews of bands from the local scene (The March Violets, The Sisters of Mercy, Salvation, The Three Johns and Skeletal Family among others), and maintained a solid focus on many of the bands signed by Merciful Release (the record label founded by Andrew Eldritch in the early 1980s). One of these was The March Violets, who along with The Sisters were the subject matter for issue 6 of *Whippings and Apologies*. This is very much a testament to the Leeds scene at the time: many academic accounts of goth situate it in the Batcave nightclub in London, but the Leeds scene, centring around several nightclubs (Le Phonographique, F-Club, Warehouse and Primo's) and the university, was arguably as foundational (Eldritch was a student of Mandarin at Leeds University and Rosie Garland of the March Violets was an English student at the same institution).[30] *Whippings and Apologies* also represents an exceptional incursion into early goth. Counterculturalism is self-evident in these musical geographies. Dave Russell has commented that London and the BBC retained a 'dominant position' in terms of music coverage, but that in the 1980s 'Manchester and Liverpool … produced a substantial number of the nation's commercially successful and/or musically significant bands, with important contributions too from Sheffield, Leeds, Hull and other cities.'[31] Russell elucidates on this point later in his analysis:

> From the late 1970s, the growth of independent record labels and the emergence of (sometimes) faster and more varied road, rail and air links, allowing for easier movement from a provincial base, has led to a number of groups minimising the time spent in London and in some cases developing a consciously regionalist position.[32]

In many respects, *Whippings and Apologies'* concentration on regional goth and post-punk identity (including a clear focus on gigs and bands from the local area, as well as deriving advertising from local independent shops) reflects the Yorkshire flavour espoused by Andrew Eldritch himself (originally from Cambridgeshire). The Sisters produced a T-shirt bearing the white rose, emblazoned with 'People's Republic of West Yorkshire' (a reference to the 1980s satirical designation of Sheffield as 'the People's Republic of South Yorkshire', a leftist stronghold).[33]

Many of the usual tropes of zine culture can be found within the pages of this publication. There is much less visual chaos on the page here, with clearly delineated columns having much in common with conventional magazine publications. *Whippings and Apologies* introduced colour for issue 6, but there are still elements of self-consciously 'amateur' editorial: the reader is promised interviews with Marc Almond, Siouxsie and the Banshees, Red Guitars and Skeletal Family, but only delivers on the latter in the next issue. The editorial in issue 7 frankly acknowledges that 'Unfortunately we can't bring you the Marc Almond and Red Guitars interviews that we promised last issue. Reasons of tight schedules and the fact that British Rail waits for no man put the dampers on both items, but they should magically appear in time for the next issue.'[34] Similarly, the wry humour of 'Now, who's first in line for the whippings … oops, run out of space. Never mind, we'll be back in March. Bye for now, Steve' suggests both the informality and intimacy associated with zines (this is the sign-off of a friend). It also registers self-reflexivity (*Whippings* clearly refers to the publication's name, presumably derived from the 1972 Sparks song, as well as the ways in which BDSM intersects with goth), and the sense that the editorial process is happening as the text goes to print ('oops, run out of space').[35]

In common with many zines, *Whippings and Apologies* reviewed other zines of interest, and it is especially useful to note here how this zine reflects upon its own format. The 'Small Print' section cites an injunction from *Vague* (1983) which identifies zines as chaotic, free from control, individualistic, witty and contemporary. However, as the writer Mark Johnson suggests: 'try putting it into practice and your [sic] faced with major problems. From the handfull [sic] of recent zines that I've chosen to review, none are able to comply with all the above requirements but never the less are all interesting and informative in their own way.'[36] There is an increased professionalisation in form and content which is in tension with *Panache*'s suspicion of commercial values: Johnson comments 'I'm always a bit suspicious of free magazines because as they're not motivated to <u>sell</u> the magazine, they don't particularly have to worry about how interesting the articles are.'[37] This shift to increased professionalism and use of marketing strategies is also evidenced in the advertisements, carefully targeted to include local music shops and vintage shops (stores like Cheap Thrills, a clothing store on Boar Lane in Leeds, and Priestleys in York), as well as zine contributors including a layout designer, fashion editor and other editorial staff.[38]

While *Whippings and Apologies* is emphatically post-punk and indie in terms of its music coverage, perhaps by contrast with *Panache*'s more ambivalent reflections on gender, it is overtly politicised in its coverage of feminist issues. Issue 7 documents the opening of The Pavilion in 1983, described as 'the country's first feminist photography centre.'[39] Situated in Leeds, on Woodhouse Lane near the university, its main objective was to record 'women's specific position in society, such as the representation of women as workers, as objects in pornography, and as portrayed in domestic life.'[40] Arguably, this more positive view of feminism is also reflected in the ways female performers are characterised and discussed within the zine. The March Violets interview opens with several assumptions which are promptly disavowed: 'In many peoples [sic] estimation, the March Violets fit into a very well-defined category; "Cult Heroes", "Black-leathered elitists", "Gothic arrogant popsters" etc., call it what you will. Admittedly, before meeting the band, even we were guilty of such assumptions. These were soon dismissed, however.'[41] Although this is noteworthy for an early appearance of 'Goth[ic]' as a music subculture, and a discrete genre, as well as the tension between authenticity, credibility and commercialism ubiquitous in zine culture ('popsters'), most importantly, unlike the features in *Panache*, the commentary is distinctly gender-neutral. While Si Denbigh seems to take centre stage for much of the interview, Rosie Garland (vocals) emerges as an artist and performer rather than a source of objectification – she is represented as a musician rather than on the basis of her gender alone.

Similarly, the front cover of the issue features a close-up of Si Denbigh rather than a more titillating image of female singer as pin-up. In part, this is certainly a testimony to the visibility of masculine lead singers in much goth music. Catherine Spooner observes that documentations of goth performers in the media 'are visibly dominated by images of men', whereas the fans are usually represented by pictures of women.[42] The fact that Denbigh features on the front cover is a testament to this gendered representation. However, it is also refreshing that despite Garland's obvious charisma, she isn't foregrounded as a sexual object for the gaze of machismo readers. Part of this may be related to The Violets' own political agenda. On the 1984 track 'Steam', the lyrics 'Doxy Dog-Box Drag Mag Queen/This is the place queer street scene' positions goth alongside a radical queer agenda, patently underscored by Garland's lesbianism and later incarnation as 'Rosie Lugosi, Lesbian Vampire Queen.'[43]

The Violets' own fanzine, which ran to a single issue, presents a cut-and-paste compilation of interviews from the music press and is useful as a point of comparison with the *Whippings and Apologies* coverage. Johnny Waller writes of 'Sex and Violets', reproduced in the band's zine, which offers an insight into how the band came into being. Denbigh and bassist Lawrence (Loz) were already in a band, and Lawrence explains he fell in love with Rosie and wanted to marry her. At which point Waller describes Rosie as 'the long-haired songstress [who] flutters her eyelids and feigns mock indifference.'[44] During a different interview, Garland is distinguished from Denbigh in the following terms: "The contrast is severe. Rosie, soft and shaking, Simon slick and slaking. He is sharp and sometimes demonstrative, but she rarely moves from simpering to shrill. It's weird.'[45] There is an implicit gendered register here. Garland is 'simpering', 'soft' and 'shrill', clearly feminine designations which construct her as nonthreatening, insecure and vaguely hysterical, while Denbigh is designated with masculine adjectives such as 'slick' and 'sharp'. Indeed, as Helen Davies observes, such remarks are not 'demonstrative of the prejudices of individual journalists, but as part of what is regarded as the only appropriate discourse for pop music writing.'[46] It is possible to see *Whippings and Apologies*, in both the coverage of The March Violets and of The Pavilion, as a potentially more progressive zine than its competitors, who are uneasily complicit with the language and idiom of the mainstream music press.

## Propaganda

In *The Goth Bible*, Nancy Kilpatrick identifies *Propaganda* magazine as 'the only subculture publication known to just about every goth on the planet.'[47]

Beginning as a zine in 1982 and finally ceasing publication in 2002, its subject matter often centred on taboo iconography: as a challenge to mainstream conservatism, it included fetish, BDSM, queer and religious imagery alongside classic literature features and music reviews/interviews with goth bands such as The Sisters of Mercy, Specimen, Siouxsie and the Banshees, Christian Death and Xmal Deutschland. In many ways, the magazine also represents a useful referent back to the proto-goth magazines of the 1960s and 1970s.

The zine's editor, Fred H. Berger, has explained how the publication was initially founded:

> When I graduated college I applied to several magazines but it was hard to get hired – almost two years later, I hadn't landed a job. So I said, 'Why don't I start my own?' – a lot of people were doing that in the early 80s, it was the zine revolution. It was DIY – all you needed was rubber cement, some blue pencils, an X-ACTO knife and access to a photocopier. It started in 1982, at which time I was very interested in the hardcore punk movement – I went to the shows in Downtown Manhattan and started photographing the scene, parties, clubs and streetstyle, and that's how *Propaganda* began.[48]

It was initially sold in Manhattan records shops and independent bookshops, and made the transition from hardcore punk to goth when Berger first watched *The Hunger* (1983). While the first issue was limited to 300 copies, by the end of the 1980s it became a much more polished magazine with a distribution of about 10,000. One of the cornerstones of the *Propaganda* aesthetic was the intersection between goth and fetish iconography. As with the earlier instances of zine culture referenced above, the zine provided a sense of solidarity and community: Berger suggested 'Goths came to see *Propaganda* as a sanctuary and a source of inspiration.'[49]

*Propaganda* certainly represented a much more glossy and professionalised type of goth media. It also reveals the subtle distinctions between different types of goth practice. Part of this distinction may be attributed to the fact that it arises from North America and, as such, embraces a scene that has much in common with 'death rock', perhaps encapsulated most emphatically by the iconic and androgynous image of Rozz Williams, founding member/singer with Christian Death, who committed suicide in 1998. In many ways, death rock forms a subgenre of goth, and was to provide an influence for later bands like Nine Inch Nails. Micah Issitt has explained that Christian Death 'led the music in a slightly different direction' with a more 'aggressive take' on the sound.[50] It also had a geographical inflection, of which *Propaganda* was a part. Van Elferen and Weinstock note that Los Angeles and the West Coast 'demonstrate a more pronounced local character of subcultural music

prior to digital media.'[51] This distinction is confirmed by UK readers of
*Propaganda* themselves: 'there was nothing else like it. I mean, there were
zines but this was a cut above, like you'd spent your whole life reading chat
mags and somebody suddenly gave you a copy of *Vogue*. It had articles about
literature and the US scene, which before the internet was pretty much an
unknown quantity … it knocked everything else into a cocked hat and made
the US scene look really cool.'[52] In this way, *Propaganda* might be read as one
of the first zines which emerged to articulate a translocal shared sense of
identity. Indeed, as Hodkinson has maintained, 'local identities and traditions
interact with relatively coherent translocal frames of reference.'[53] *Propaganda*
acquired such distinctiveness through its photographic representation of fetish
fashion and BDSM practice, as well as its reflections on the scene, music and
literature. Unusual in a subculture which is predominantly white, several images
are featured of Black American goths and punks. For instance, 'She's in Parties'
(1984) features a Black American sporting a mohawk and a Bauhaus t-shirt,
marking a departure from the pallid waifs of many goth magazines.

On occasion, the themes of fetish and literature intersected, as issue 17
(1991) demonstrates. Rather than the collage and cut-out aesthetic of zine
culture, this photographic feature and accompanying poem makes use of
stylised Gothic lettering and takes as its subject matter 'The Martyrdom of
St. Sebastian.'[54] As per the legend of the saint, Sebastian is bound to a tree,
with arrows piercing his naked torso. A crucifix is also suspended on the tree
trunk. He wears black tape in the form of crosses, suggesting both a target
for arrows and also an inverted form of Christian iconography, while his
commonly androgynous appearance is Gothicised by heavy eye make-up and
pallid complexion. The inversion of Christian iconography (specifically
Catholic) is a common feature of the magazine. A photo shoot from *Propaganda*'s
1990 issue shows a 'Gothic Pieta' in Los Angeles – an androgynous male
figure is cradled in the arms of a statue of the Virgin Mary. The peroxide
Mohawk, alongside heavy make-up and the taboo gesture of wearing the rosary
implies a challenge to established faith as much as a sartorial gesture. This is
very much a cornerstone of goth: it is simultaneously a romanticisation and
critique of religion. Goth fashion, including the use of the crucifix as jewellery
or adornment, pertains to irony and also homage:

> Goth style offers many opportunities for the mixture of sacred and profane
> signifiers. Goths often 'profane' traditional religious iconography by using it
> for flagrantly stylistic rather than religious purposes.[55]

A similar negotiation of religion is discernible in *Propaganda*.

The homoerotic overtones to Saint Sebastian in these images can be
associated with this very same parodic homage to conventional faith, and this

has a long history in relation to the saint. Oscar Wilde referred to Sebastian in a poem about John Keats, stating he was 'Fair as Sebastian, and as early slain.'[56] The homoerotic cult of beauty which Wilde espoused, and which was a hallmark of the late nineteenth-century Decadence, is both referenced and adapted here:

> Because nineteenth-century writers viewed Sebastian's arrow-ridden body in far more than religiously symbolic terms, as that of a penetrated male who is beatifically ecstatic and not merely submissive, Sebastian would seem to render flagrant the tacit masochism evident in a certain strain of Victorian masculinity.'[57]

This nineteenth-century tradition of the saint as a masochistic and feminised martyr directly influences *Propaganda*'s Sebastian, which in turn is a testament to how far goth derives inspiration from the Victorians. It is also implicated in the broader frame of BDSM culture that *Propaganda* frequently characterises. This appeal to non-normative sexual practice is very much in accord with influences on goth fashion, which date back to the 1970s and the punk appropriation of fetish style: 'The punk "style in revolt" was a deliberately "revolting style" that incorporated into fashion various offensive or threatening objects like dog collars and chains that were designed to horrify straight observers.'[58] Hodkinson notes that the fetish scene and the sex industry were popularised in the 1990s, with the result that 'Goths of both sexes were increasingly likely to be seen in black and sometimes coloured PVC and tuber trousers, skirts, leggings, corsets, tops and dog collars.'[59] Certainly, *Propaganda* represents this overlap between goth and fetish at various points: an interview with the band My Life With The Thrill Kill Kult from 1991 features bondage queen Bettie Page in her trademark leopard-print lingerie, while a 1985 edition of *Propaganda* offers coverage of a Fetish Fashion Show at Danceteria in New York. By the mid-1980s, fetish had moved from its subcultural affiliations in punk and, later, goth, and into the mainstream, in many ways mirroring the trajectory of *Propaganda* as a small-scale zine production to a much larger enterprise. This co-option reflects a broader trend: as Valerie Steele notes, the glossy fashion magazines of the 1980s borrowed fetish motifs, but this was characterised less as BDSM (which remained threatening) and more as 'sexy' fashion or power dressing, itself a common feature of the 1980s.[60] The major distinction between goth and fetish fashion, as Steele notes in an interview, is one of context: 'A lot of the things that are meaningful, the idea of sexuality being dangerous or taboo and all of that, appears in both of them.'[61] At the same time, *Skin Two*, the publication which would define the BDSM and fetish community, was launched in the UK in 1984 with a similar aesthetic to *Propaganda*: 'Pin-up magazines were sleazy and serious art magazines were nervous about sexuality ... We put the first issue together on the kitchen table and printed a thousand. It was produced by fetishists for fetishists.'[62] *Propaganda* by comparison, presents the intersection between fetish and goth, and like *Skin Two*, registers an overlap between 'serious art' photography and sexuality.

*Propaganda*'s Saint Sebastian is emphatically feminine, and his androgynous appearance accords with goth masculinity more generally: 'right from the early days of Bauhaus, the most venerated and fancied males in the goth scene, in terms of appearance, tended to have slim bodies and faces, and minimum body hair.'[63] At the same time, goth is frequently seen to celebrate queer sexuality: 'Goths often display a strong identification with gays, transsexuals and other sexual minorities.'[64] Indeed, for *Propaganda*'s editor, sexual transgression is seen to be a resistant gesture: 'Let's face it, we live in a cultural wasteland where romanticism is considered cornball, imagination is laughable, and anything other than the missionary position is considered pathological.'[65] However, this vaunted radicalism is complex. Women in *Propaganda* tend to be conventional and/or hypersexualised. The article 'From Lilith to Lestat' (1991) is an example of this trend. While the model posing as Lestat, from Anne Rice's novel *Interview with the Vampire* (1976), is a feminised male with long hair, make-up and elaborate ruffled shirt, the model representing Lilith is a very conventional femme fatale.[66] This representation is mirrored by the goth scene more generally. Androgynous women are often absent: curves are accentuated by corsetry, and femininity is invoked by the repeated duplication of pallid, slender, long-haired women.[67] While there are some instances of queer iconography in *Propaganda*, it remains the case that these are more often (but not exclusively) feminised men.

## Conclusion

While offering different definitions of goth subculture, these various publications also testify to the heterogeneous nature of goth identity and music in the UK and the USA, including death rock, post-punk and so forth. They emphasise disparate versions of goth, with the UK scene showing the distinctions between Leeds and London as goth locations, as evidenced through *Panache* and *Whippings and Apologies*. *Propaganda* emphasises the importance of death rock as an aesthetic in US goth more generally. Paradoxically, these zines also emphasise the translocal possibilities inherent in subcultures, with a codification of goth aesthetics and values through zine reading. They reveal a clear tension between subcultural resistance to capitalist values and the evolution of the zines' visibility as mainstream commodity – this is very much the case with *Propaganda*, and this mirrors the trajectory of goth in its increased mainstream visibility in the late 1980s and 1990s. The publications also reveal the instability and fluidity of fanzine culture: in contrast to *Panache*, by the 1990s, *Propaganda* could be found in mainstream bookshops and stationers with emergent glossy production values. These zines also identify that it is critically problematic to ascribe blanket radicalism to goth as a subculture: certainly this is very much the case with the issue of gender representation. Siouxsie Sioux emerges in zine coverage as a pin-up figure but, at the same time, other zines testify to the more nuanced representation of women musicians on the scene. This is particularly evident with reference to Rosie Garland of The March Violets. At the same time, zines such as *Panache* seem to navigate a suspicion of the rise of second-wave feminism, while at the same time attempting to be satirical of gender inequality. In reflecting upon subcultures as instantiating political resistance, it is useful to note Catherine Spooner's analysis: 'to invest the subculture thereby with a particularly subversive or transgressive potential within the wider culture is problematic.'[68] Both the zine and popular press coverage of iconic bands would confirm this statement, oscillating uneasily between an affirmation of feminist values and an ironic position against these discourses.

## Notes

Acknowledgements: Sincere gratitude to Rosie Garland of The March Violets, for advice during the research of this chapter, and giving me access to her zine collection.

1  Catherine Spooner, *Fashioning Gothic Bodies* (Manchester: Manchester University Press, 2004), p. 159.
2  Paul Hodkinson, *Goth: Identity, Style and Subculture* (Oxford: Berg, 2002), p. 161.
3  Hodkinson, *Goth*, pp. 70–1.
4  Richard Rouska (Captain Swing), *The Black Book* (Leeds: 1977cc, 2014), pp. 78–9.
5  For 'billingsgate humour', see Mikhail Bakhtin, *Rabelais and His World,* trans. Hélène Iswolsky (Bloomington: Indiana University Press, 1984).
6  Simon Reynolds, *Rip it Up and Start Again: Postpunk 1978–1984* (London: Faber & Faber, 2005), p. 420.
7  BDSM is an acronym including practice related to bondage, domination, discipline, submission and sado-masochism.
8  *Twylight,* February/March 1968, p. 2.
9  Stephen Duncombe, *Notes from the Underground: Zines and the Politics of Alternative Culture* (Bloomington: Microcosm Publishing, 2008), p. 7.
10  See Duncombe, *Notes from the Underground,* pp. 12–13 for further information.

11   Rosie Garland, 'Here be Tygres – my life & fanzines', 8 February 2017, http://rosiegarland.com/news-and-events/item/947-here-be-tygres-my-life-fanzines.html, accessed 9 February 2017.

12   Duncombe, *Notes from the Underground*, p. 22.

13   Alison Piepmeier, 'Why Zines Matter: Materiality and the Creation of an Embodied Community', *American Periodicals: A Journal of History and Criticism*, 18:2 (2008), 213–38: 214.

14   Teal Triggs, 'Scissors and Glue: Punk Fanzines and the Creation of a DIY Aesthetic', *Journal of Design History*, 19:1 (2006), 69–83: 77.

15   *Panache*, 5 (c. 1977), p. 15. Original spelling and punctuation.

16   Duncombe, *Notes from the Underground*, p. 14.

17   *Panache*, 5 (c. 1977), p. 2.

18   Ken Gelder (ed.), *The Subcultures Reader* (London: Routledge, 2005, second edn), p. 433. See also Sarah Thornton's *Club Cultures: Music, Media and Subcultural Capital* (Cambridge: Polity Press, 1995), where she discusses the notion of subcultural capital, itself influenced by Pierre Bourdieu's notion of cultural capital.

19   *Panache*, 5 (c. 1977), p. 4.

20   Angela McRobbie and Jenny Garber, 'Girls and Subcultures', *Feminism and Youth Culture: From Jackie to Just Seventeen* (Basingstoke: Macmillan, 1991), p. 12.

21   Helen Davies, 'All Rock and Roll is Homosocial: The Representation of Women in the British Rock Music Press', *Popular Music*, 20:3 (2001), 301–19: 312.

22   Lisa Duggan and Nan D. Hunter, *Sex Wars: Sexual Dissent and Political Culture* (London: Routledge, 2006).

23   Mick Mercer, *Gothic Rock Black Book* (London: Omnibus Press, 1988), p. 10.

24   Siouxsie and the Banshees, 'Painted Bird', from *A Kiss in the Dreamhouse* (Polydor Records, 1982).

25   Dick Hebdige, *Subculture: The Meaning of Style* (London: Routledge, 1979), p. 101.

26   Spooner, *Fashioning Gothic Bodies*, p. 162.

27   Simon Reynolds, *Totally Wired: Post-Punk Interviews and Overviews* (London: Faber & Faber, 2009), p. 157.

28   Reynolds, *Rip it up and Start Again*, p. 436.

29   John Berger, *Ways of Seeing* (Harmondsworth: Penguin, 2008), pp. 40–1: 'Men look at women. Women watch themselves being looked at.' See also Laura Mulvey, *Visual and Other Pleasures* (Basingstoke: Palgrave Macmillan, 2009).

30   Catherine Spooner, *Fashioning Gothic Bodies* (p. 171) identifies the importance of Leeds: 'Goth's initial phase of cultural production … corresponds exactly to Thatcher's period in power, and in 1980s Britain was associated geographically with Leeds, another northern city similarly depressed in economic terms.'

31   Dave Russell, *Looking North: Northern England and the National Imagination* (Manchester University Press, 2004), p. 214.

32   *Ibid.*, p. 225.

33   This intersection of disaffected North and goth is comedically documented in the comic strip, 'Great Pop Things', by Colin B. Morton and Chuck Death (Jon Langford

of The Mekons). See *Great Pop Things: The Real History of Rock and Roll from Elvis to Oasis* (Portland: Verse Chorus Press, 1998), p. 126.

34  *Whippings and Apologies*, 7 (1984), p. 2.

35  *Ibid.*, p. 6.

36  *Ibid.*

37  *Ibid.*

38  *Ibid.*, p. 2 lists 'Editorial Staff: Steve Trattles, Mark Carritt and Mark Johnson. Fashion Editor: Sue Hollington. Layout and Design: Steve Trattles.'

39  *Ibid.*, p. 11. Such political coverage was rare in the zine, but does suggest the potential for political investment in Leeds subcultures.

40  *Ibid.*

41  *Whippings and Apologies*, 6 (1983), p. 9.

42  Spooner, *Fashioning Gothic Bodies*, p. 178.

43  March Violets, *Natural History* (Rebirth Records), 1984.

44  *The March Violets* fanzine, n.d., p. 7.

45  *The March Violets* fanzine, n.d., p. 2.

46  Davies, 'All Rock and Roll is Homosocial', 304.

47  Nancy Kilpatrick, *The Goth Bible: A Compendium for the Darkly Inclined* (London: Plexus Publishing, 2005), p. 17.

48  *Dazed*, 'The Cult Mag that Pioneered Goth', by Emma Hope Allwood, www.dazeddigital.com/fashion/article/28734/1/the-cult-magazine-that-pioneered-goth-propaganda, accessed 27 April 2017.

49  Kilpatrick, *The Goth Bible*, p. 17.

50  Micah L. Issitt, *Goths: A Guide to an American Subculture* (California: Greenwood, 2011), p. 21.

51  Isabella van Elferen and Jeffrey Andrew Weinstock, *Goth Music: From Sound to Subculture* (London: Routledge, 2016), p. 45.

52  Marie 'Queenie' McGowan Irving, Facebook correspondence, 28 March 2017.

53  Hodkinson, *Goth*, p. 27.

54  *Propaganda*, 17 (1991), pp. 34–5. 'Sebastiane' had also been a single for Sex Gang Children in 1983, its cover a stylised depiction of the saint pierced by arrows.

55  Anna Powell, 'God's Own Medicine: Religion and Parareligion in U.K. Goth Culture' and Jessica Burnstein, 'Material Distinctions: A Conversation with Valerie Steele', in Lauren M.E. Goodlad and Michael Bibby (eds), *Goth: Undead Subculture* (Durham, NC: Duke University Press, 2007), p. 361.

56  Oscar Wilde, 'The Grave of Keats' (1881), *The Ballad of Reading Gaol and Other Poems* (London: Penguin, 2010), p. 121.

57  Richard A. Kaye, '"Determined Raptures": St. Sebastian and the Victorian Discourse of Decadence', *Victorian Literature and Culture*, 27:1 (1999), 269–303: 270.

58  Valerie Steele, *Fetishism: Fashion, Sex, and Power* (New York: Oxford University Press, 1996), p. 37.

59  Hodkinson, *Goth*, p. 51. See also Gavin Baddeley, *Goth Chic: A Connoisseur's Guide to Dark Culture* (London: Plexus Publishing, 2002), pp. 225–31.

60  Steele, *Fetishism*, p. 42.

61  Burnstein, 'Material Distinctions', p. 265.

62  Tim Woodward, 'Foreword', *Skin Two – Retro 1: The First Six Issues* (London: Tim Woodward Publishing, 1991), p. 1.

63  Hodkinson, *Goth*, p. 53.

64  Djuna Brill, *Goth Culture: Gender, Sexuality and Style* (Oxford: Berg, 2008), p. 122.

65  Kilpatrick, *The Goth Bible*, p. 17.

66  See Brill, *Goth Culture*, p. 49, for ideas of conventional femininity in goth: 'Despite their dark edge and sometimes confrontational display of female sexuality, subcultural beauty norms (e.g. dresses or skirts, make-up, long hair, sexy outfits) are mostly in accord with current cultural ideals of youthful feminine beauty.'

67  See Joshua Gunn, 'Dark Admissions: Gothic Subculture and the Ambivalence of Misogyny and Resistance', in Goodlad and Bibby (eds), *Goth: Undead Subculture*, p. 53.

68  Spooner, *Fashioning Gothic Bodies*, p. 166.

# 7

# The evolution of an anarcho-punk narrative, 1978–84

RUSS BESTLEY AND REBECCA BINNS

From its inception, punk, as articulated through its fanzines, was anti-elitist; positioning itself against self-indulgent, outmoded rock stars and the pretentions of rock journalism.[1] Pioneering punk zine *Sniffin' Glue* (July 1976) and those that immediately followed[2] sought an authentic form of expression to relate directly with 'disaffected kids' who comprised the demographic of punk subculture. Against the hierarchical structure inherent in mainstream media, punk zines showed their egalitarian approach by encouraging readers to submit work or start their own fanzines. Readers were urged to be active participants rather than passive consumers.

Punk zines – and fanzines more generally – were liberated from many of the marketing constraints associated with commercial magazines and as such they could foster alternative forms of communication and editorial content. This enabled their creators and readers to define their identity, political leanings and culture autonomously rather than in response to consumerist dictates. In particular, fanzines encouraged individuals and groups otherwise excluded from the cultural decision-making process to be actively engaged in the creation of alternative culture. Mark Perry set a precedent, writing in 1976: 'All you kids. Don't be satisfied with what we write. Go out and start your own fanzines … flood the market with punk writing.'[3] Other fanzines, such as *Panache* and *Sideburns*, then helped to embed this sense of autonomous production as a practical ideal. Interestingly, however, while early punk zines engaged with underground punk culture and, in the process, helped to define it, there was no wholesale rejection of the music industry and record labels. These zines were often in favour of (or at least ambivalent to) the bands they backed signing to established record labels, though they simultaneously expressed contempt for those perceived to be inauthentic or 'sell outs'.

By 1978, punk was being redefined in light of the commercialisation of many first-wave bands. An article in *Panache* read: 'There aren't many bands around, true punk, not on the major scene anyway. The real punk bands are underground or small bands that aren't commercial or corrupt!'[4] Punk was fragmenting into competing subgenres, with new, underground variants, including what would later become known as Oi! and anarcho-punk, each making claims to an authentic reinterpretation of the subculture's initial promise.

From 1978 onwards, punk zines were essential in the evolution of a specific discourse merging anarchist ideologies with a new model of punk identity and practice based around what can be loosely termed an anarcho-pacifist identity that set its advocates apart from their punk precursors and peers. This anarcho-punk discourse was also articulated reciprocally through a conversation between the zines and bands such as Crass and Poison Girls. The concerns expressed in Gee Vaucher's designs for Crass were embodied in the aesthetic accompanying the subgenre; the younger punk demographic of zine creators and authors further built on an established audience and ready-made distribution and manufacturing networks that were pioneered by the previous punk generation, who in turn had been supported by their subcultural predecessors.

## ANOK4U

The notion of drawing up a creed by which to live your life was seemingly anathema to earlier zine creators. Crass, as a punk band and collective, promoted anarchistic ideas and put their beliefs into practice in various ways throughout their duration, using a multiplicity of media and methods. The release of Crass's first record, *The Feeding of the Five Thousand* (1978), coincided with the second wave of punk, and the group subsequently held great sway in the direction and content of a broad range of punk zines, particularly those whose readership comprised largely young, disaffected punks seeking renewal after the perceived death of the first wave. Crass disseminated their anarchic philosophy on alternative life choices within their music, graphics and written tracts in a way that was distinct for a punk band.[5] This transition was captured by Tony D, writing on the release of *The Feeding of the Five Thousand,* for *Ripped & Torn:*

> This record is an assault on all the phonies and liggers who've built up around the original concept of punk, free-loading and sucking vital energy away into their own pockets. This record blows them all back to their nests and rat holes, clearing out all the preconditioned crap that's been insulting our minds and calling itself 'revolutionary'.[6]

Crass actively engaged with underground punk zines, declaring them the 'real' voice of punk in comparison to mainstream outlets and conducting an enormous number of interviews.[7] In turn, many punk zines were receptive to the group's ideas. The emerging anarcho-punk discourse was communicated through verbal and visual strategies, with Crass proving to be highly influential in both the philosophical debate and its corresponding aesthetics.[8] Graphic design, typography and illustration styles employed by Crass to communicate their ideology – largely created by Gee Vaucher and Penny Rimbaud, both trained and experienced designers – fed into an evolving set of visual conventions that would be adopted and mimicked by other fanzine producers.[9] Some of these conventions drew upon established punk graphic styles, while others used the emergence of a stereotypical punk 'canon' as a counterpoint to signal a more 'authentic' direction.[10] Like the precedents to punk independence and 'do it yourself', however, it should be noted that many of these visual strategies were not strictly new. In many cases, they drew on samizdat and agitprop artistic practices going back more than sixty years, from Futurism to Dada, Surrealism and the twentieth-century artistic and political avant-garde.[11]

## The politics of independence

Specific actions taken by Crass, such as the addition of 'pay no more than … ' instructions to their products, paralleled the already well-established punk fanzine practice of producing publications independently and selling at cost, together with a number of direct precedents within the nascent independent punk scene.[12] Some punk histories erroneously suggest that the 'cheap as possible' ethos to record pricing began with anarcho-punk. However, a maximum price ('70p Maximum Retail Price') had been included on the cover of the Desperate Bicycles' third EP, *New Cross, New Cross,* released on their own Refill Records label in February 1978, and other low-pricing strategies had featured on a range of punk and new wave releases between 1977 and 1979, notably on the Good Vibrations and Stiff labels. The cover of Crass's self-released debut single 'Reality Asylum', released in late 1979, codified an arguably more 'political' reading of the minimal-profit approach, with the instruction 'pay no more than 45p' emblazoned on the front.[13]

In setting up an independent record label, Crass also built on the shared experience of earlier do-it-yourself punk labels, including New Hormones, Refill and St Pancras Records, together with higher-profile independent labels with distribution and retail connections such as Rough Trade and Small Wonder. Crass pushed the 'underground' aspect of punk into more overtly ideological territory, however, in marked contrast to the general situation post-1978, when the wider punk subculture was morphing into new wave, with its mainstream pop appeal, or branching out into what would become known as post-punk.[14] Post-punk bands retained varying degrees of independence from commercialism, with a loose-knit community forming a distinct do-it-yourself, independent avant-garde, largely based around a number of independent labels and record shops including Rough Trade, Small Wonder, FAST Product and Beggars Banquet.[15] Crass, and the subsequent bands that would come to be called anarcho-punk, were to take this model of autonomy in a new direction, foregrounding an overtly ideological and political discourse as an inherent principle within their independent stance and committed radicalism.[16]

The more successful early punk fanzines had been forced to adopt commercial models of production and distribution, though their editorial content was liberated and their design aesthetic often remained distinctly DIY. By the time anarcho-punk had established its own champions within the zine market, such models of large-scale print production and distribution were already well developed. This isn't to say that, like earlier punk fanzines, a range of smaller, low-key, do-it-yourself publications were unimportant, but that the more established punk zines with greater distribution (*Sniffin' Glue, Ripped & Torn, Panache, Chainsaw*) had paved the way for a second generation of zine producers in terms of production knowledge as well as audience and market (*Toxic Grafity, Kill Your Pet Puppy, Vague*). Anarcho-punk zines can, then, be seen as an extension of an already established punk fanzine milieu, tapping into existing networks and practices in relation to manufacture and distribution, for instance, while at the same time attempting to present a break with the past in content and aesthetics. This set them at times in opposition to the wider zine market, particularly in relation to contested notions of authenticity and subcultural identity.

Former Pink Fairies roadie Joly MacFie's Better Badges enterprise was to take a lead in supporting the emerging punk independent producers, initially manufacturing pin badges then extending their services to support the print production of punk zines after investing in litho-printing equipment. As MacFie notes:

> You could make metal offset plates for approximately 75p. I priced it out and came up with a rate of 2p per double-sided sheet for 'zines. But if we dropped in a BB ad, I'd drop it to 1p. And we took pretty much all comers. You paid for what you took, and we'd distro the rest. I always saw my role as empowering the voice of the fans vs. the industry. With style.[17]

A number of underground and counterculture magazines, including *Black Flag*, were printed by Little@ press, based in the former dockyard warehouses at Metropolitan Wharf, Wapping in London. Andy Martin of anarcho-punk group The Apostles worked in the printshop and helped to facilitate access for like-minded producers. It is also notable that the Autonomy Centre, a punk-centered anarchist community space, funded in part by proceeds from the Crass/Poison Girls split single 'Bloody Revolutions'/'Persons Unknown' (1980), was established in early 1981 within the same building as Little@. As Alistair Livingston recalls:

> The Crass and Poison Girls benefit single for what was to become the Wapping Autonomy Centre was released in May 1980 and raised £10,000. The money was used to convert a space in a Victorian warehouse beside the Thames at Wapping into a social centre. After discussion, the more neutral 'Autonomy Centre' was chosen over 'Anarchist Centre' as its name. It opened in early 1981 but was a rented space without an entertainment or drinks license.[18]

Tony D has acknowledged the debt paid to Crass in punk zines, many of which became increasingly politicised following *The Feeding of the Five Thousand*. He recalls:

> Crass were the first to really push the idea of anarchy as a lifestyle not a theory. Crass and the subsequent anarcho bands were a shot in the arm to the fanzine world and it became a bit like the outpouring of fanzines in 1977, some just an 'I am' one-off statement and others continuing for many issues and developing ideas of anarchy, such as veganism and what that entailed.[19]

Alan Rider, who produced the Coventry fanzine *Adventures in Reality*, also notes that this ideological shift mirrored something of a generational divide:

> One of the biggest things I noticed was how young many anarcho-punk 'zine writers were. Many were at school; some were just 12 or 13. The fact that they could do things at a very basic level and it was still fine really opened things up for them to express radical opinions without needing to seek

permission or having to spend a lot of money. In many ways, the music was secondary to the freedom to challenge and express different views and zines were actually a better and cheaper way for lots of people to do that.[20]

Indeed, the newly evolving anarcho-punk narrative encompassed a range of interrelated and sympathetic ideological positions, ranging from anti-war statements (often aligned with the resurgence of CND, the Campaign for Nuclear Disarmament)[21] to emerging forms of what might be termed anarcho-feminism, animal rights,[22] attacks on organised religion and key debates on the nature of resistance and models of anarchism in theory and practice.[23] Content concerns were also reflected in the choice of images. In some cases this resulted in a shift away from the earlier punk fanzine aesthetic that combined handwritten and typewritten text with photographs of bands toward more directly political concerns and the use of alternative visual strategies (collage, illustration, reportage, appropriation of images from contemporary newspapers and magazines).[24] Some of these choices reflected a deliberate attempt to move away from music-based fanzines to more politicised (and serious) zines, while others were driven by necessity; photographs of bands were relatively simple to source or produce, but more ideological or political themes required a more sophisticated, or at least more abstract and less directly representational, visual accompaniment.

## Anarchy and peace

By the early 1980s, punk zines were increasingly focused on exploring lived forms of anarchy, including the rejection of conventional work and squatting.[25] The Puppy Collective, which produced *Kill Your Pet Puppy*, emerged from the punk-squat scene in London. Alongside *Vague*, *Kill Your Pet Puppy* regularly included essays on punk as an alternative life-choice, writing on revolutionary movements as well as covering a range of post-punk bands.

Although Crass's ideas were complex, the band played a significant role in disseminating a pacifist take on anarchism that was subsequently debated in punk's fanzines.[26] *The Feeding of the Five Thousand* had focused on an alliance of anarchy and peace, where previously anything other than anarchy as a rebellion against societal norms – or anything other than peace as 'hippie' – had been absent from punk discourse. The track 'Fight War Not Wars' introduced one of several slogans to be pillaged within punk culture, and the group outlined their beliefs on anarchy's compatibility with peace in an article published in the first issue of *Kill Your Pet Puppy* in 1980. In this, they criticised violence as the corruption underlying political affiliations of both left- and right-wing persuasions. Crass's drummer and songwriter Penny Rimbaud made specific reference to events at a gig held at Conway Hall, where militant anti-fascists had attacked skinheads regardless of their political affiliation.[27]

Initially at least, other contributors were critical of Crass's position. One *Kill Your Pet Puppy* writer complained that pacifism was an inadequate response to state violence, while Tony D commented that Crass's pacifist stance meant they were effectively ignoring or even sanctioning violence perpetrated by racist skinheads against their own supporters.[28] Following this, Tony D was invited to Dial House to discuss the matter. He later remembered:

> Leigh and my-self went to see Crass at Dial House to discuss our views about their pacifist stance, which was printed in the first issue ... A few days later we received a letter from Penny Rimbaud, a long review of their philosophy. This has to go into the next issue I thought, which meant creating a new issue and not faffing about.[29]

Despite providing ample space in issues 1 and 2 for Crass's anarcho-pacifism, an article in issue 4 by Alistair Livingston (1981) stated: 'Violence is not totally evil, but can be used as an energy source. It's just that in our society it has become a negative thing – that violence by the state against people is okay, but by people against the state it's not ... what we call self-defence, the state will call violence.'[30] In a similar vein, an editorial for *Chainsaw* in 1981 stated:

> Although anarchy is a good ideal to aim for, it would not work because in an anarchic society it would be the easiest thing in the world for any fascist group to arm themselves and take control – although it would be impossible to bring about anarchy in this country without a well-organised military coup, which would be neither anarchic or pacifist.[31]

Others interpreted anarchy as psychological and creative transformation rather than politicised action. Such a position was succinctly summarised by Alan Rider for *Adventures in Reality*. Following on from a description of society as an elastic band that snaps back into shape after people stretch it due to the force of 'conventions, morality, tradition, social, political and sexual condition-ing' or the forces of law, surveillance and harassment, Rider continued to give anarchy this definition:

> Anarchy is an apolitical state of mind, an attitude and once that's achieved, no conventions can influence it. Indeed, they seem very crude and clumsy attempts at control once you realise they are there and can spot them. The

elastic band can be broken if it's stretched hard enough, the result won't be painful, but a relief, a sudden realisation of freedoms that no one had before, but didn't realise what they were.[32]

Such an individualised take on anarchy was prevalent in *Kill Your Pet Puppy* and the more esoteric *Rapid Eye Movement*, and was distinct from the collective movement commonly advocated in punk fanzines of the period. Nevertheless, the relationship between anarchism and pacifism remained a point of tension. Punk zines such as *Toxic Grafity*, *Fack* and *Enigma* provided material that debated whether or not lived anarchism entailed direct confrontation. One verse in *Enigma* read:

Give your aggression any name
And I will call it war
Call yourselves anything
And I will call you an elite
Give your violence any justification
And I will show you the blood
Offer any speech you like
And I will shout you down.[33]

By the early 1980s, too, the punk zines emerging from within the anarchist Autonomy Centre – including *Scum* and *Pigs for Slaughter* – began to challenge Crass's narrative. The introduction to the first issue of *Pigs for Slaughter* (1981) read:

We want to express a belief, tendency, call it what you will, that, as yet, we have not seen in any anarchist punk publications. So much time and effort has been given in the stream of what we'll call 'Crass anarchy', including all the fanzines that have sprung up in it; long stodgy bits on 'mental liberation'; existentialism, anarchy and peace and so on.[34]

The article went on to promote direct action to speed up the state's disintegration. Subsequently, *New Crimes* – from Southend – acknowledged the contribution made by the new 'anarcho-militant' movement through 'opening up squats, setting up housing co-ops, printing magazines and leaflets, graffitiing and getting involved with animal liberation'. However, it was also noted that 'throughout the philosophies of the new militants there is an aggressiveness and dare I say machismo which I personally find disturbing.' The article argued that zine authors promoting militancy were naive and wrong to believe their anarchism was reflective of wider society. Instead, their approach confirmed to many people that 'anarchists are no more than a bunch of fanatical bomb throwing cranks and lunatic minded terrorists.' As such, it concluded that 'anarchism must work to prove that society can exist without government

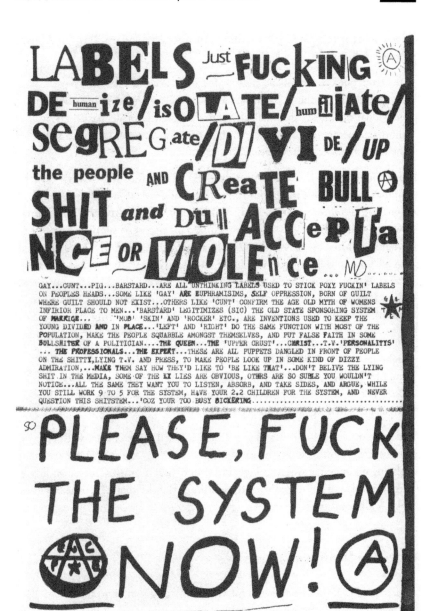

**7.1** *Toxic Grafity*, 5 (1980) © Mike Diboll

and that the alternative, based on trust, co-operation and mutual respect are in-fact better than what exists today.'[35]

While punk zines were invigorated by debates on the concepts of anarchy and pacifism, punk identity was also derided for becoming tired and clichéd.

One article for *Infection* (1984), titled 'Another Redundant Term of Abuse', commented:

> The term 'punk' is redundant; it's sick, feeble ... dead ... Punk may have once meant all the things I associate with it; rebellion, freedom of expression, individuality, honesty and an all alternative culture free of all restrictions; in short an environment that we can truly run wild in. Present day 'punk' shows the exact opposite of these ideals.[36]

The author blamed the music press, chiefly 'Gazza Bullshit' (Garry Bushell at *Sounds*) and 'Carol "tone deaf" Clark' (Carol Clark at *Melody Maker*), and wider business interests for stifling and categorising creativity within punk. However, the stagnant situation for punk was also seen as the fault of the movement spurred by Crass. According to Tom Vague, 'standards [had] dropped to an all-time low. So long as you had a Mohican and leather jacket and sung about state oppression and not eating meat, you were alright.' He continued to slate a wide range of anarcho-punk bands, including Poison Girls, Flux of Pink Indians, Rubella Ballet, Conflict and Subhumans, adding:

> This whole neu-punk thing stinks even more than Bushell's Oi punk nightmare in a way. It's got all the predictable talk, but no bottle. Once alive and fresh. Now dead and un-fresh. Like rotting fruit. Don't fit into rules. Don't follow expected dogmas and stereotypes. Take risks. Show some originality and imagination for god's sake.[37]

Discourse on various aspects of anarchism infused punk culture with energy, purpose and seriousness. By the early 1980s, however, Crass's anarchic pacifism was being reiterated unquestioningly in a proportion of zines. Correspondingly, anarcho-punk as a genre was seen to be stifling and dogmatic by others within punk's wider culture.

## Anarcho-feminism

Ideas from the Women's Movement viewed through an anarchic prism also permeated the anarcho-punk subculture of the early 1980s. Punk fanzines in the late 1970s had attempted to grapple with issues of misogyny, racism and inequality in a manner unseen in their 1960s predecessors, such as *OZ* and *International Times*. Despite sometimes displaying inherent sexism, early punk fanzines provided space for debates on female emancipation and the subversion of traditional gender roles. Overall, the force of women within punk was recognised in the fanzines, though it took those created by women to prioritise female musicians and take an anti-sexist stance. *JOLT* (1977) was involved from the outset, using grainy photos along with typed text and handwritten scrawl to feature female musicians alongside the personal views of its editor, Lucy Toothpaste. Interviews in punk fanzines produced by women, such as *JOLT* (1977) and later *Brass Lip* (1979), focused on what female musicians had to say rather than the way they looked and allowed the expression of views often overlooked in the male-dominated music industry and press.[38]

While the years 1979 to 1981 saw an escalation in the coverage of feminist issues in punk fanzines, the focus on female subordination by institutions of 'the system' (including the family and Christian church) was not reflected in punk fanzines – including specifically feminist ones – at this time.[39] Vi Subversa played an instrumental role in bringing anarcho-feminism to punk with her band Poison Girls, who worked closely with Crass between 1978 and 1980. Subversa directed her message against societal oppression of women and war from her specific perspective as a middle-aged woman within the predominantly young, male milieu of punk. Crass similarly linked misogyny to all institutional oppression through their music and lyrics, and notably in Gee Vaucher's striking images that were reproduced as record sleeves, posters and ephemera.[40]

Vaucher had already developed her 'anarcho-feminist' critique through the graphics she produced for *International Anthem* (1977–81). This publication was anarchic compared to other feminist magazines in its portrayal of female oppression as just one facet of societal control. She produced the first (of three published issues) on the theme of education while living in New York (1977).[41] In it, her painted collages combined news footage, advertising and pornography to critique education in its wider sense, encompassing familial, institutional and societal conditioning. Women's subordination through domesticity or as sex objects, as propagated in the mass media, was a predominant theme. *International Anthem* featured Vaucher's painted collages together with poetic texts by Penny Rimbaud. Subsequently, after returning to the UK to live and work as part of Crass, she published issue 2 in 1979 and issue 3 in 1980. The Poison Girls' magazine, *The Impossible Dream* (four issues between 1979 and 1986) shared some similarities with *International Anthem* in containing montages of images taken from various places – including advertising – spliced with Poison Girls' lyrics denouncing power. Both publications were distributed via radical bookshops and alternate networks by post. *The Impossible Dream* was also sold at gigs, which enabled it to be circulated more widely, particularly among a punk demographic.

The early 1980s saw an escalating amount of space in punk zines dedicated to anarcho-feminism. Zines, including *Acts of Defiance*, *Anathema*, *Antigen*, *Fack* and *New Crimes*, all engaged with feminist politics from an anarchic point of view. The views of Crass and Poison Girls on this theme were often featured through lengthy interviews and opinion pieces.

## Anti-Thatcher/anti-state

In the early 1980s, the new political agenda of the Conservative government had a massive impact on the UK, and was widely perceived to be both authoritarian and discriminatory towards the working class. Unemployment soared, while a major overhaul of the welfare and tax system had a direct impact on young people and the poor. It was natural therefore that Margaret Thatcher should take on a central role as a negative figure of authority within oppositional politics and satire, and within punk's language of protest. Conservative Secretary of State for Employment Norman Tebbit put forward a range of new, hardline rules regarding access to unemployment benefits with the aim of forcing young people into work – a move that also resulted in attacks from both the opposition and protest groups across the country. The 1982 Falklands War resulted in a rift between pro- and anti-war activists, and these attitudes were also played out within the punk scene. Thatcher and her cabinet provided a common enemy for many punk groups and fans, and their iconic status as the *bête-noire* of the political underclass was utilised in countless song lyrics and record sleeves. In much the same way that the Silver Jubilee of 1977 had provided the Sex Pistols with an iconic image to attack, the early 1980s punks took Margaret Thatcher as a figurehead for their collective anger.

An oppositional, politicised rhetoric flourished within underground, punk culture during Margaret Thatcher's first term as Prime Minister (1979–83). Crass's fourth album, *Yes Sir I Will* (1983), was a virulent retaliation against four years of Thatcherism and the Falklands War. The insert to the Crass single 'You're Already Dead', released the following year, featured an illustration by Vaucher commenting on the 'special relationship' between Thatcher and the US president Ronald Reagan. Here Vaucher shrunk the figure of Thatcher into nappies to emphasize the UK's dependence on the USA, symbolised by Reagan's depiction as a hybrid founding American mother and bird of prey nursing Thatcher while shitting on the world.

Visual representations of themes such as this were more explicit within anarcho-punk zines. Thatcher's acute divisiveness exacted a bitter response from a wide range of people and anarcho-punk provided a forum in which a visceral, anti-Thatcher rhetoric developed. The image of Thatcher appeared with increasing frequency in the zines as a locus for vitriolic opposition. Indeed, the content of punk fanzines increasingly became engaged with contemporary

**7.2**   Gee Vaucher illustration, *You're Already Dead* (1984), Crass Records. Gouache. ©
Gee Vaucher

political developments such as the miners' strike, government cuts, the Falklands War, the anti-apartheid movement, Rio Tinto zinc and the UK and the USA's funding of troops, in particular death squads in Latin America.[42]

There was a surge in production of (post) punk fanzines in the early 1980s, which fostered a hardening critique against the Thatcher government while eschewing traditional politics in favour of anarchic solutions. These fanzines provided an outlet for a more oppositional, anarchic polemic pitted against all aspects of societal control. While Thatcherism provoked a strong response, the ire of anarchic punk culture more widely was directed against all forms of government and state control. Crass's accusation of political authoritarianism on the left equating that on the right found a receptive audience among a youthful demographic that was increasingly disillusioned with both mainstream and far-left politics.[43]

## Religion

The church was another institution decried by anarchists as alienating and oppressive. From an anarcho-feminist perspective, Christianity subjugated women in particular due to its patriarchal history, structure and functioning. Crass's preoccupation with organised religion appeared in tracks such as 'So What' and 'Reality Asylum', and in the subsequent album titles *Stations of the Crass* (1979) and *Christ – The Album* (1982). It was also an ongoing theme in Rimbaud's poems and Vaucher's images. Rimbaud, who was the dominant voice in terms of articulating Crass's ideas, has spoken candidly about the impact Christianity had on him during his formative years in his autobiography, *Shibboleth: My Revolting Life* (1998). Crass's attack on religion as an oppressive, aggressive institution, despite its declarations of peace, was reiterated in the content of punk zines in the early 1980s. So, for example, an article in the third issue of *Acts of Defiance* (1982) read: 'The Jewish religion encourages the myth that men are superior to women – it's fucking pathetic. The Catholic religion disgusts me the most … millions in the world live in poverty … while the church spends thousands on visits for the Pope.'[44] An article in *Chainsaw* stated:

> A recent opinion poll by one of the national daily papers showed that if you are an atheist you are more likely to be a pacifist than you are if you believe in God. Which tends to make a mockery of the 'love thine enemy' messages that the God squad tend to preach. Do you think that Maggot Thatcher, Ronald Reagan and Co, leaders of the western world, orderers of cruise missiles, believe in God? Of-course![45]

**7.3**  *Toxic Graffitti*, 3 (1979) © Mike Diboll

The article went on to argue that a religion's belief in its own superiority and subsequent divisiveness made it analogous to fascism, while *Enigma* featured discussion on how morals were used to enforce patriarchy and provide justification for suffering. It added:

> Christianity is responsible for 'the system's' morality and mentality, the two things that oppress us most. The morality of murderers; the mentality of sheep. Adherence to a rigid morality is a terrible slavery because no one can react without referring back to it, nor can go beyond its definite limitations. If you've got a set of values like that then you cannot act with free will.[46]

Such views were contested. *In the City* questioned Crass about their attack on the figure of Christ as opposed to acts carried out in the name of religion. Rimbaud responded by saying they were trying to get people to question their unthinking acceptance of religion. He argued that to just attack the actions of Christianity left the institution as a whole intact. Crass's response was directed at the guilt Christianity induced in believers. They argued this was a tool that subordinated people into acquiescing to the control of this institution. The interviewer asked 'are you then denying that your songs are of a blasphemous nature?', to which Rimbaud responded:

> I don't consider the statements we make are blasphemous as such. They don't deny anything. They say, well, so what if Christ died on the cross! What's that got to do with me? Why should I have to carry the burden of everyone else's guilt? I wouldn't put anyone on a cross and certainly, having put someone on the cross, I wouldn't then burden other people with the responsibility of that … So what we're attempting to do with those songs, is not to be blasphemous, but again to demythologize, to rid people of the guilt that they've been forced to carry through other people's prejudice.[47]

Interestingly the zines also drew a correlation between the belief system of anarcho-punk and that of organised religion. In *Enigma*, Matt Macleod commented: 'to make a dogma out of anarchism is a contradiction. It's like turning it into Christianity.'[48] Crass were seen to display religious traits in their position as (unwitting or unwilling) leaders of a movement who disseminated what was sometimes seen as an ideology. In an article for *Zigzag*, Tom Vague wrote:

> Another criticism that is often given of Crass is their attitude towards religion. I always thought Christ was alright. It was the people who came afterwards that corrupted what he said. In the same way that you can't blame Johnny Rotten for The Exploited, Crass view Christ differently. They believe that anyone who sets himself up like he did, as an individual authority; stand

to be criticised on the effect. That leads me to the obvious conclusion – have Crass set themselves up for more than they can handle and are they good enough? That's up for you to decide. Take it or leave it. Crass are there if you need them.[49]

## Animal liberation

While Crass focused exclusively on releasing their own materials in 1979, from 1980 onwards their focus was not just on releasing their own output but on applying the model to other like-minded bands.[50] The ideas and priorities of these bands were channelled through their music and imagery. Single-issue politics emerged as a focus for more generalised opposition to globalised, hegemonic capitalism. Correspondingly, fanzines reacted, not only through the dissemination of Crass's ideas into the wider anarcho-punk sphere, but also through the bands' various focuses on issues such as vivisection, nuclear energy, war and organised religion.

The commitment to animal liberation shown by bands such as Flux of Pink Indians, Conflict and Subhumans helped to entrench this as an issue within anarcho-punk circles.[51] Their concern was expressed through music and the design of their record sleeves and inserts. Releasing their music on independent labels gave anarcho-punk bands the opportunity to express their views without the expectation of censorship or compromise. In addition to the focus of their music and associated graphics, Flux also gave out thousands of leaflets on vivisection, anarchy and pacifism at their gigs.[52] Such strategies built upon an already well-established animal advocacy and animal rights counterculture, where leafleting and flyers were commonplace at demonstrations and other gatherings.[53] The bands' views were also disseminated via interviews in punk fanzines, live performances and the example they set through personal choices such as vegetarianism. The fanzines explored concepts of animal liberation and veganism from an anarchist philosophical perspective in in-depth articles. Such tracts articulated a moral or political standpoint regarding the exploitation and commodification of animals within a contemporary, capitalist society.

While Crass, Poison Girls and various other key anarcho-punk bands had a strong influence on the evolution of a specifically anarcho-punk discourse between 1978 and 1984, debates were also to move on independently from them. The notion of autonomy and empowerment, and the rejection of authority figures and 'leaders', led to the emergence of a more critical stance in relation to the aims and influence of anarcho-punk's major figures. At the same time,

many of the original anarcho-punk zine producers were moving on to new
territory. Some followed influential bands within that scene, including Conflict
and Subhumans, into a new era of anarchist activism, while others reflected
on the self-styled limitations of the scene. Mike Diboll of *Toxic Grafity* notes
the ways in which the medium of the anarcho-punk zine itself became
restrictive:

> I wanted to go further, but resources and my then skills set held me back
> from completely transcending the 'fan'-zine format. Later TGs hint at the
> direction I sought to go in, which was to capture the ethos, attitude, aesthetic
> and politics of that scene at that moment in prose, free verse, prose-poetry,
> image and collage.[54]

## Evolution and discourse

Anarcho-punk needs to be understood in relation to the wider evolution of
the punk subculture. Many concerns expressed by anarcho-punk groups and
zine writers predated any kind of 'year zero' punk stereotype, drawing upon
political philosophies dating back more than a century together with many
of the ideologies revitalised by the late 1960s and early 1970s counterculture,
including sexual liberation, animal rights, pacifism and mutual cooperation.
Anarcho-punk should also be viewed as a (sometimes contentious and disputed)
continuation of internal discourse within the punk subculture itself. Through
the evolution of subcultural networks (and the establishment of an audience
and market), punk, in its broader sense, facilitated the emergence of the more
radical politics of anarcho-punk. Equally, lessons learned by zine producers
within the earlier punk fanzine market would directly enable a new generation
of anarcho-punk zine-makers through both tacit knowledge and access to
now-established 'DIY' networks of production and distribution.

Crass had originally picked up on the debates articulated in zines on punk
as a grass-roots movement and an unmediated form of expression, and in
turn fed back their own anarchist-pacifist philosophy. From around 1980,
Crass had a significant input into the evolving rhetoric and aesthetic adopted
by the zines. The underground media that enabled debates (and internecine
rivalries) to flourish are exemplified within the do-it-yourself punk zines and
independent punk voices away from the mainstream. Punk's model of anarchism-
in-practice, rather than just rhetoric, was a ground-up model of political
discourse, where ideological positions were debated and argued by participants
in the scene themselves, with anarcho-punk zines at the forefront of those
debates.

# Notes

1  In seeking to express the 'real' voice of punk, punk zines criticised music journalism in mainstream publications such as *New Musical Express* (*NME*), *Sounds* and *Melody Maker* for being pretentious, simplistic and elitist respectively.

2  Notable examples from 1976 to 1977 include *48 Thrills, Bondage, Chainsaw, Jamming, JOLT, London's Outrage, Panache, Ripped & Torn, Stranded* and *Strangled*.

3  Mark Perry, 'No Doubt About It', *Sniffin' Glue*, 5 (1976), p. 2.

4  'The Message', *Panache*, 10 (1979), p. 19. See also the interview with Jimmy Pursey in *Temporary Hoarding*, 6 (1978), where the Sham 69 singer suggests that the commercial death of first-wave punk means that those involved for emancipatory reasons can carry the movement forward.

5  While Crass proved distinct in disseminating what can loosely be termed a philosophy, several other post-punk bands, including Gang of Four, The Mekons and The Pop Group, espoused political ideas within and alongside their music.

6  Tony D, 'What Potent Force Blows … ', *Ripped & Torn*, 17 (1979), p. 21.

7  George Berger, *The Story of Crass* (London: Omnibus, 2006), p. 120; Tom Vague in *Vague*, 6 (1980), http://tomvague.co.uk/vague-6/, accessed 20 October 2015.

8  Ian Glasper, *The Day The Country Died: A History of Anarcho Punk 1980–84* (London: Cherry Red, 2006).

9  Russ Bestley and Ogg, *The Art of Punk* (London: Omnibus Press, 2012).

10 Jamie Reid and Jon Savage, *Up They Rise: The Incomplete Works of Jamie Reid* (London: Faber & Faber, 1987); Johan Kugelberg and Jon Savage (eds), *Punk: An Aesthetic* (New York: Rizzoli, 2012). For models of authenticity within popular music, see Hugh Barker and Yuval Taylor, *Faking It: The Quest for Authenticity in Popular Music* (London: Faber & Faber, 2007).

11 Robert Hughes, *The Shock of the New: Art and the Century of Change* (London: Thames & Hudson, 1991); Sadie Plant, *The Most Radical Gesture: The Situationist International in a Postmodern Age* (London: Routledge, 1992); Stewart Home, *The Assault on Culture* (London: AK Press, 1991).

12 It should also be noted that major labels were equally involved with this practice, albeit perhaps driven by the pursuit of profit as much as any engagement with the punk 'zeitgeist' of street-level politics and value-for-money. Several employed loss-leaders to promote their acts, with notable examples including The Flys (EMI Records), The Stranglers (United Artists) and The Clash (CBS).

13 Crass's debut release, *The Feeding of the Five Thousand* EP, was initially released by Small Wonder and did not feature any price stipulation. The reissue on Crass Records in 1981, *The Feeding of the 5,000 (The Second Sitting)*, stated 'pay no more than £2.00'.

14 Simon Reynolds, *Rip It Up And Start Again: Post Punk 1978–84* (London: Faber & Faber, 2005).

15 Alex Ogg, *Independence Days: The Story of UK Independent Record Labels* (London: Cherry Red Books, 2009).

16   Crass, *A Series of Shock Slogans and Mindless Token Tantrums* (London: Exitstencil Press, 1982).

17   Email correspondence, 12 December 2016.

18   Alistair Livingston, 'Everyone was an Anarchist', in Greg Bull and Mike Dines (eds), *Tales from the Punkside* (London: Active Distribution, 2015), p. 33.

19   Email correspondence, 15 December 2016.

20   Email correspondence, 18 December 2016.

21   Matthew Worley, 'One Nation Under the Bomb: The Cold War and British Punk to 1984', *Journal for the Study of Radicalism*, 5:2 (2011), 65–83.

22   Francis Stewart, 'This is the A.L.F. – Anarchism, Punk Rock and Animal "Rights"', *Punk & Post Punk*, 5:3 (2016), 227–45.

23   It should be noted that counterpoints to the emerging anarcho-punk ethos were equally prevalent, ranging from the ongoing evolution of punk and new wave to post-punk, hardcore punk, Oi! and what was termed New Punk in the early 1980s.

24   Typographic approaches tended to remain relatively standard, even with the shift in content within anarcho-punk zines and the adoption of more overtly politically charged images. Blocks of typewritten text were still common, though often utilising a tighter grid and featuring much lengthier texts – in part reflecting the conventions adopted by Crass and other anarcho-punk groups within their record sleeves.

25   An article in *Acts of Defiance*, 7 (1983), p. 20, ends: 'To wear a Mohican/to have your face tattooed is to burn most of your bridges. In the current economic climate, when employers can afford to pick and choose, such gestures are a public disavowal of the will to queue for work, defying the right to work … ' On squatting, see 'Squatting: Why Not Squat Now', *Fack*, 6 (1981), p. 10.

26   Berger, *The Story of Crass*, pp. 249–61.

27   *Kill Your Pet Puppy*, 1 (1980), pp. 13–15.

28   See Buenaventura Makhae, 'Peaceful Pro-Crass-tination', *Kill Your Pet Puppy*, 1 (1980), p. 16 and Tony D, 'Another Direct Hit by Crass', *Kill Your Pet Puppy*, 1 (1980), p. 7.

29   http://killyourpetpuppy.co.uk/news/kill-your-pet-puppy-issue-2-febmarch-1980/, accessed 14 October 2015.

30   *Kill Your Pet Puppy*, 4 (1981), pp. 9–10.

31   *Chainsaw*, 11 (1981), p. 21. Conflict became central to the establishment and dissemination of this position.

32   Alan Rider, 'Within Certain Limits', *Adventures in Reality*, issue J (1981), p. 13.

33   *Enigma*, 4 (1982), p. 26.

34   *Pigs for Slaughter*, 1 (1981), p. 2.

35   'Anarchy, Violence and Freedom? One "Wet Arsed Pacifist" Reflects on the Anarchist Youth Federation and their Propaganda and Tactics', *New Crimes*, 7 (1983), p. 7.

36   'Another Redundant Term of Abuse', *Infection* (1984), p. 4.

37   Tom Vague, 'Those Not So Loveable Spikeytops', *Vague*, 14 (1983), p. 29.

38   See interviews with The Slits and Poly Styrene in *JOLT*, 2 (1977) and *JOLT*, 3 (1977) respectively. See also *Brass Lip*, 1 (1979), which featured extensive interviews with

female musicians who adopted a more androgynous look, including the Au-Pairs, The Raincoats, The Mekons and Poison Girls.

39  Articles in *Brass Lip* (1979) focus on male oppression and misogynistic violence, both in the music industry and in wider society. An interview with The Raincoats discussing women in bands trying to break the sex symbol stereotype features in *Allied Propaganda*, 3 (1979/80), p. 3. 'Welcome Women', by A Male in *Don't Dictate*, Issue D (1980), recognises the shift in punk music towards female-orientated bands in the late 1970s.

40  For example, 'Women' and 'Asylum', on *The Feeding of the Five Thousand* (1978). Crass's take on the issue of misogyny was highlighted in the lyrics for their album *Penis Envy*, for which they were prosecuted under the Obscene Publications Act.

41  Images from issues 4 and 5 on *Ireland* and *War* respectively are in circulation, although they were not published due to a lack of funds (email conversation with Vaucher on 16 May 2016). Vaucher also commented more directly on female objectification in pin-up magazines in work she produced for another self-produced magazine, *Pent-Up* (1975).

42  See, for example, *Time Bomb*, 1 (1984), which took in the miners' strike, cuts and the politics of Central America.

43  See the lyrics to 'Bloody Revolutions' (1980) for Crass's take on leftist politics.

44  *Acts of Defiance*, 3 (1982) p. 15.

45  'This is Religion (Your Religion)', *Chainsaw*, 12 (1981), p. 26.

46  Matt Macleod, 'These are the Right Morals', *Enigma*, 4 (1982), p. 4.

47  Interview with Crass, *In the City*, 10 (1979), p. 23.

48  Macleod, 'These are the Right Morals', p. 4.

49  Tom Vague, 'Crass', *Zigzag*, 122 (February 1982), pp. 38–9. See also an interview in Belfast's *Blast*, 3 (1982/83), p. 10, where Gee Vaucher refutes an accusation that Crass were merely 'preaching as clergymen do'. Interestingly, an article by Tony D ('Another Direct Hit by Crass', p. 7) used religious terminology to ascribe status to Crass as 'leaders'. He describes the persecution of their 'followers' by British Movement skinheads as an attack on their 'faith'.

50  Crass Records produced 21 albums and 36 singles, of which 12 albums and 25 singles were by other bands, predominantly released between 1980 and 1984.

51  It should be noted that concern for animal rights was established as an issue relatively early in the development of anarcho-punk culture. This led to something of a two-way dialogue between bands and participants rather than the top-down imposition of an ideological agenda, which was perhaps more the case with other issues once anarcho-punk became more widely recognised as a specific punk sub-genre.

52  Hammy, 'Flux', *Roar*, 7 (1983), p. 4.

53  In fact, this led onto other debates concerning the use of inks or photographs that hardline vegans objected to in relation to animal products such as gelatin (in film), chemicals in dyes and inks, and even the use of paper as a negative environmental impact.

54  Email correspondence, 21 December 2016.

# 8

# 'Don't do as you're told, do as you think': the transgressive zine culture of industrial music in the 1970s and 1980s

BENJAMIN BLAND

Of all the musical subgenres that emerged in the immediate post-punk era, industrial may be seen as that which most readily transcended the traditional confines of a musical movement. Industrial stood out as a result of its strong focus on aesthetics and ideas, even in a musical landscape that was widely concerned with rejecting tradition and which interpreted 'punk as an imperative to constant change'.[1] S. Alexander Reed highlights three areas of particularly significant influence on the genre: Italian Futurism, the American counter-cultural author William S. Burroughs, and twentieth-century art music.[2] The prominence of the former two sources of inspiration may be seen as differentiating industrial artists from many of their contemporaries in the wider post-punk milieu. This is particularly true of Burroughs, whose ideas were of fundamental importance to the industrial scene, especially in its foundational period (the late 1970s and early 1980s).

These avant-garde touchstones made the industrial subgenre an intimidating one to outsiders. This was a movement that was transgressive not only in its musical form but also in its philosophical outlook. As Christopher Partridge has noted, industrial artists took seriously 'their role as the damned in society and enthusiastically excavated what the modern world had rejected – including occult thought, far-right political discourse and sadistic criminality'.[3] This ensured that the industrial scene stood out as a particularly anarchic and nihilistic force in the post-punk musical underground. Unsurprisingly, then,

Matthew Worley emphasises that industrial zines also stood out: largely due to their focus on 'systems of control and the darker corners of the human condition: murder, fetishism and the abject'.[4] Before these zines can be analysed in any depth, however, it is necessary to provide some further background to the industrial genre and – in particular – to its most influential artist. Throbbing Gristle (TG)'s central importance to the original industrial music scene is hard to dispute, and not only because the genre's name stems chiefly from the band's own independent record label: Industrial Records. Officially 'activated' on 3 September 1975 (a date specifically chosen to match the anniversary of Britain's entry into the Second World War), this Hackney-based quartet evolved out of the controversial performance art collective COUM Transmissions.[5] TG's most prominent early performance, in fact, took place at the Institute of Contemporary Arts during COUM's *Prostitution* exhibition in October 1976. The moral panic created by this event – and specifically its overwhelming focus on pornographic images of COUM/TG's Cosey Fanni Tutti – was such that Conservative MP Nicholas Fairbairn spoke of the group as 'the wreckers of civilisation', and accused them of wanting 'to advance decadence'.[6] Although TG were not necessarily the first band to play what would become known as industrial music (Sheffield's Cabaret Voltaire had been active since 1973), they were the first group to set in place many of the scene's defining extra-musical characteristics, and particularly the interest in transgressive ideas and imagery highlighted by Partridge. As the band's contemporary and confidant Jon Savage notes, despite being made up of 'aesthetic utopians – who believed in the liberating power of communications and technology', TG played from the beginning of their career with 'extreme aesthetics' and engaged in 'totalitarian exploration'.[7]

This was not simply the result of a desire to shock, but instead was part of the band's attempt to participate in what Burroughs thought of as an 'information war', based on his belief that the manner in which information was disseminated by institutions and social structures was a form of oppression.[8] TG aimed to take part in Burroughs' campaign against the forces responsible, referred to by Burroughs as 'control machines'.[9] As Michael Goddard has correctly highlighted, this was more important to the band than their musical output.[10] The centrality of this participation to TG's work prompted their experimentation with extreme aesthetics. These transgressions were a necessity for, as Reed notes, 'where there is transgression, there is law, and where we reveal law, we reveal external control'.[11] TG's cavalcade of unusual (and often, by the times, extreme) aesthetics was their own equivalent to Burroughs' cut-up technique: a tactic designed to subvert hegemonic control over information. As Genesis P-Orridge (the band's de facto leader), who handled almost all of TG's interviews, revealed in a highlighted passage in 1983's influential *Industrial Culture Handbook*: 'We're interested in information, we're not interested in music as such. And we believe that the whole battlefield, if there is one in the human situation, is about information.'[12] This belief informed every aspect of TG's work, from their music and lyrics, to album artwork and live show visuals, to what would – in a traditional music industry sense – be described as promotional materials (flyers, press photographs and the band's zine-style newsletter, *Industrial News*). The majority of TG's aesthetic productions were deliberately lacking in context, leaving the interpretation up to the reader/viewer and thus seeming to embody the libertarian-anarchist mantra of the 1980 live track 'Don't Do As You're Told, Do As You Think'.[13]

This may, at first, appear to conflict with what, in interviews, P-Orridge was happy to assert as the 'sole reason' for TG's existence: to act 'as a platform for propaganda'.[14] Any contradiction here was, however, limited. Alongside Burroughs, one may detect the influence of Joseph Goebbels in TG's propagandising, and indeed Z.A.B. Zeman's classic tome *Nazi Propaganda* appeared in the TG reading list in the *Industrial Culture Handbook*.[15] The group may, in fact, be seen to have followed what David Welch has cited as Goebbels' revisionist reading of Gustave le Bon's *Psychologie des foules* (*Psychology of Crowds*) in looking to reach their audience 'both as individuals and as a group'.[16] The idea of 'don't do as you're told, do as you think' should, therefore, be read on two levels. TG aimed to promote individual expression, through catering to a wide variety of outsider interests, but they wished to coalesce these interests into something approaching a loose subcultural identity. The creation of such an identity would then prompt engagement in the information war.

*Industrial News* was a critical part of that strategy, and the first half of this chapter shall focus on this publication as a route into analysing the wider nature of industrial zine culture in the late 1970s and early 1980s. Such an approach consciously interrogates industrial more as a quasi-political ideology rather than as a musical genre. Such a perspective has two clear benefits. Firstly, it enables a clearer distinction to be drawn between industrial zines and zines from the wider post-punk milieu. This distinction would be less clear, for example, by examining industrial-related titles primarily as material artefacts.[17] Secondly, it allows for a more thorough dissection of the transgressive mentality found in industrial publications. Given the importance of this mentality to industrial music culture, I would suggest that such an examination tells us more about both industrial zines and the industrial subculture more generally.

## Industrial News and the information war

To readers with a wide knowledge of music zines of the punk and post-punk eras, *Industrial News* may, at first glance, seem wholly unremarkable. TG used many of the same visual techniques as several of the most influential punk zines, and the introductory note to the first issue did not appear to connote a radical new approach. First it emphasised that the zine was intended both as a newsletter and as a potential 'mini-library of image [*sic*] and information, idea and possibility not normally found in more accessible publications'. It also encouraged the involvement of readers: 'We feel very strongly that an active role of participation should be taken ... and to this end we have suggested various things which you can do to further work in our field and to help us identify the form which this interest currently takes.' The most important aspect of the introduction, however, came at its conclusion, in which it is asserted that TG's 'ideas are usually implicit in [their] choice of content'.[18]

While this introduction would seem to be setting *Industrial News* up to be – much like Jon Savage's *London's Outrage* or Crass's *International Anthem* – a mixture of scene building and cultural-political critique, the first issue as a whole offset its introduction. Approximately a third of the issue was as may be expected, for example in the inclusion of catalogue-style Industrial Records information and a letters page. Meanwhile, in an amusing parody of the inane artist profiles published in the mainstream music press, Tutti revealed, among other things, her favourite foods ('My spaghetti; Cornish pasties; Bakewell tarts; School dinners; Chinese'), her favourite colour ('Blue'), her favourite actresses ('Jane Birkin; Sissy Spacek'), and her enjoyment of 'listen[ing] to Radio 4 on [her] own.'[19] The rest of the issue, however, consisted of a collection of disconnected imagery. TG lyrics and artwork were included, as was a collage by the band's friend Monte Cazazza. There was also a small clipping from the *Evening Standard* (bearing the heading 'A message thieves just cannot resist'), information on riot control copied from an unidentified book, and two context-less photos, one seemingly of a naked woman's dead body in a field.[20] The template established here provided a stark juxtaposition between the clearly defined, but relatively inane, tone of most music-based publications and the comparatively extreme avant-garde leanings offered by TG.

The purpose of such contrast was twofold, allowing *Industrial News* simultaneously to subvert both the traditional dynamics of the mainstream music periodical (a subversion inherent to all independent music zines) and the supposedly transgressive dynamics of much of the alternative media generated by punk. Whereas most of the contemporaneous radical-leaning punk zines offered a (nominally) cohesive viewpoint, from its first issue *Industrial News* established that it would provide anything but.[21] This fitted perfectly with TG's Burroughsian outlook. After all, as Robert Genter has astutely emphasised, the extreme core of Burroughs' rallying cry of 'smash the control machine' called 'not [for] a form of liberated discourse but the end of discourse itself'.[22] This desire for the destruction of communication conflicts with the traditional core purpose of zines which, following Stephen Duncombe, usually exist chiefly to discuss 'the intricacies and nuances of a cultural genre' (often from an intensely personal socio-political perspective).[23] More fundamentally, Chris Atton suggests, even if the zine is usually 'monological in practice', it is 'dialogical in intent'.[24]

This was only partially true of *Industrial News*. The publication did, as much through its very existence as through its letters page, have a dialogical function. This dialogue was, however, directed towards a form of what – to refer playfully to Jon Savage's five-point plan of industrial practice in *RE/Search*'s influential *Industrial Culture Handbook* – may be termed anti-communication, geared around two of Savage's foremost points about the industrial genre: 'ORGANIZATIONAL AUTONOMY' and 'ACCESS TO INFORMATION'.[25] Read in this light, the first issue's aforementioned introductory claim that the band's 'ideas are usually implicit in [their] choice of content' makes perfect sense. The absence of any clear and obvious perspective in *Industrial News* was the whole point, and the zine was purposefully compiled so as to indicate an equivalence of disconnected – and wildly variable – types of information, from Tutti's food preferences to techniques of riot control. The subcultural identity that TG looked to promote in their work was not centred so much on shared interests (even if an appreciation of the band's work was an obvious prerequisite to any engagement within it) as around a shared distaste for the hegemonic traditions of communication. This was reflected in P-Orridge's rather grand statement, distributed on 4 August 1979, that it was 'through information being made available' that people could 'set up their own structures'.[26]

The second issue of *Industrial News*, which was the work of Cazazza and his artistic partner Tana Emmolo, was the only edition entirely devoid of traditional music zine content. A collage of images focused around the topic of mind control, this edition's ostensible highlights included information on 'neutron monkeys', an article on the use of sound and light to control crowds, and what appear to be diagrams illustrating the process of conducting a lobotomy.[27] Issue 3 must be seen as more noteworthy, however, in that it clearly built upon the stylistic choices made in the first edition of the zine. Through the band member profiles TG fans could now learn Pete 'Sleazy'

Christopherson's favourite drinks ('Milk; Perrier water'), Chris Carter's favourite cars ('Minibus; Range Rover; My dad's tractor'), and that P-Orridge liked 'Uniforms, Self-Discipline; Jackboots; Leather ... Voyeurism [and] Cats', but disliked 'All dogmatic Politics and Religion [and] Russian Bureaucracy.'[28] One collage featured an image of child strangulation alongside the infamous 'I murder so that I may come back' quote from Mary Bell, the young girl convicted of strangling two younger boys in Newcastle in 1968.[29] Another page was dedicated to Burroughs and radical painter Brion Gysin's concept of the Third Mind and, just to further emphasise the related information disruption tactics TG were using, a section on 'Magazines & Fanzines of Note' concluded with the assertion that 'Between the ages of 5–14 the average American child sees 13,000 human deaths on TV.'[30]

Crucially, by the third issue of *Industrial News* the various strains placed on TG by their place at the forefront of a new movement were starting to show. The introduction to this issue emphasised the overwhelming amount of correspondence TG were receiving by this point. More interestingly, however, a previously unpublished interview transcript with P-Orridge (originally intended for the punk zine *Dirt*) was included in response to numerous queries received about the band's views on Charles Manson.[31] The interview itself largely reflected the claim, made in the issue, that TG had relatively little interest in Manson – although P-Orridge also suggested that ultimately Manson was successful, in a Warholian sense, 'because he wanted to be remembered and be a star.'[32] More interesting than the content of the interview, however, was its inclusion in the first place. If the chief purpose of *Industrial News* really was to break up conventional modes of discourse, in a Burroughsian sense, then responding to inquiries about a topic supposedly of little interest to TG represented a contradiction of the zine's philosophy. The tensions inherent in TG's desire to simultaneously encourage a sense of subcultural identity among their followers *and* follow the path of information warfare were becoming obvious.

The fourth and final issue of *Industrial News* – published more than a year after its predecessor, in November 1980 – represented the band's most thorough attempt to deal with these tensions. Aspects of the zine catering to the band's fanbase were kept to a bare minimum and, for the first time, clearly superseded by what the band considered more important: scraps of information. To emphasise this point, the band even included a blunt rejoinder to the many people sending them cassettes: 'The first IR NEWSLETTER asked for tapes of conversations, locations, interviews ... In other words raw material to work with. We never wanted musical works by other people.'[33] While a list of those who had sent them tapes (running to three pages in length) was included, it was emphasised that this was to enable contact between interested parties and 'to encourage the development of a self-controlled, independent scene' (i.e. one not reliant on TG's involvement).[34] A slightly more conciliatory tone was struck in responding to 'requests from guys wondering about where to get magazines featuring Cosey modeling nude', although it was stressed that the band could only offer limited help in the 'quest for TG erotica'.[35]

The overall tone of the issue was heavily influenced by a militaristic survivalism that was also increasingly dominating TG's aesthetic, especially through the adoption of camouflage uniforms. Followers of the band were now largely being referred to in terms of cult membership, often with a paramilitary edge. In place of an introductory note there was a list of 'T.G. Armed Forces Recruiting Centres', and the names of those operating affiliated 'T.G. & I.R. Appreciation Societies' were given alongside the rank of 'Commander'. All this information appeared under a heading indicating what, by 1980, had become one of the band's chief mantras: 'Nothing short of a total war'.[36] Elsewhere in the issue, readers were encouraged to become fully-fledged members of the cult, one advert reading:

> Do you want to be a fully equipped Terror Guard? Ready for action? Assume Power Focus. NOTHING SHORT OF A TOTAL WAR. NUCLEAR WAR NOW! Then send for a catalogue of available weaponry and regalia, survival kits and clothes ...[37]

That TG considered this approach linked to Burroughs' philosophy was made acutely apparent through a quote, taken from his address at the 1962 International Writers' Conference in Edinburgh, in which he professed to being 'primarily concerned with the question of survival'.[38] Burroughs was also interested in the notion of extending the information war into cult paramilitarism. In a section of 'The Revised Boy Scout Manual', published in RE/Search in 1982, he even appeared to directly call for the beginning of a terrorist campaign – composed of a mix of assassinations, bombs and biological warfare – in his name.[39] While neither this nor the idea of the TG Terror Guard need be taken entirely seriously, the radicalisation of rhetoric from both Burroughs and TG in the early 1980s is significant – as is the clear fetishisation of paramilitarism. No doubt, in TG's case, it was also largely the result of P-Orridge's own increased radicalisation of thought, partly indicated by a newly developed obsession with occultism. So, despite the lack of interest in Manson proclaimed in the previous issue, this edition of Industrial News included a request for material related to Manson to be sent to P-Orridge, now described as 'collect[ing] anything to do with the family'; a collage of Manson-related newspaper covers also formed the issue's centre spread.[40] This tied in with what, as Simon Ford notes, was now P-Orridge's chief priority: 'to develop TG into a tribal organisation' that would cater for individuality while presenting an ironic front of subcultural uniformity.[41]

In *Industrial News*, the focus stretched mainly to encouraging a certain mindset among readers, whether through the reprinted 'Instructions by the Director of Operations for Opening Fire in Northern Ireland' or the insinuation that all readers should suspect their phone of being bugged.[42] Epitomising the approach of this issue, page 30 (see Figure 8.1) utilised the header 'National Strategy Information Center' for a collage of unusual juxtapositions. References to Manson and to the discovery of two dead bodies in a farmhouse in Jersey sit alongside information on riot control (that favourite *Industrial News* topic), a dictionary definition of camouflage and a satirical comment that the tapeworm represented a breakthrough for the organisation Weight Watchers. Featuring twice is the assertion that 'The post-industrial society is now becoming an information society where the strategic resources are knowledge and data.'[43] For TG this transition obviously held great significance: an information society provided the landscape for a total information war to be fought, weaponising the fragments of knowledge distributed throughout *Industrial News*.

Further issues of *Industrial News* would undoubtedly have taken this post-industrial approach further. A little over eight months after the fourth issue was published, however, TG ceased to be active (at least until their 2004 to 2010 reunion). Their split, officially dated 23 June 1981, was communicated to followers via a postcard bearing the message 'The mission is terminated.'[44] As the *Industrial Culture Handbook* – published in the aftermath of TG's split – emphasised, the band were not simply influenced by the idea of the information war, they wanted to 'revolt against the obedience instinct' by making 'deliberate attempts to *apply* the cut-up techniques of William S. Burroughs and Brion Gysin.'[45] *Industrial News* was an important part of this, but its anti-communication strategies were not fully formed until the final issue, meaning that TG's primary objective – to promote engagement in the information war – was only partially achieved during the group's lifespan. As the industrial scene expanded and diversified during the early 1980s, it was primarily those influenced by TG who inherited the responsibility of continuing the band's mission.

## The development of industrial zine culture post-TG

Despite the clear sense, in the wake of TG's split, that the group's work was unfinished, many of the industrial zines produced in the early 1980s appeared

### NATIONAL STRATEGY INFORMATION CENTER

**NOT FOR THE SQUEAMISH:** *Manson* is a sensationalistic documentary that includes footage the murderous family shot to record their own activities for posterity. I saw it years ago on 42d Street and am still haunted by some scenes: one family member tosses another in the air like a rag doll to demonstrate their trust in one another. This is your chance to become haunted downtown. *Manson* unspools at Club 57, 57 St. Mark's Place at 9 and 11 on Thursday, brought to you by the *Sleazoid Express.*

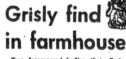

# Grisly find in farmhouse

Two decomposed bodies, their flesh apparently eaten by cats, were found in an isolated farmhouse at Carneys Point, New Jersey, yesterday.

Police found between 75 and 100 cats when they entered the white, two-storey house and said the cats apparently had been eating the bodies. Witnesses said some of the cats were also eating each other.

The bodies were discovered on the first floor by an acquaintance of a woman who rented the home, police said. They were so badly decomposed that authorities could not immediately determine their sex, race or age.

Garbage was piled two feet deep throughout the house, located in a desolate area about 400 feet from a dirt road. Police refused to speculate on how long the bodies had been in the farmhouse or the cause of death, but have labelled the deaths suspicious.

## Riot Control

An armored van that blasts green-colored water while blaring disco music is the latest anti-riot vehicle in use in South Africa.

Harry Breisford, manager of Hotline Equipment in Johannesburg, says, "The idea of combining water and music came from South America, where police found that bursts of music and water help defuse the violence and antagonism of rioting crowds."

## Weight Watchers

have a new friend from the animal kingdom in the tapeworm (*Cestoda Taenioidea*). These friendly flatworms are parasites which dwell in the intestines of higher vertebrates, living off whatever ingested food comes their way. Thus, the host organism (you!) can eat its fill, while the tapeworm picks up the calories! Available in coiled or extended forms from

1. The post-industrial society is now becoming an information society where the strategic resources are knowledge and data. Information occupations claimed only 12% of the work force in 1959, but now account for more than 50% of total employment. At the same time, the number of employees in the industrial sector has declined from 65% to 35% of the total work force.

**Weight Watchers** have a new friend from the animal kingdom in the tapeworm (*Cestoda Taenioidea*). These friendly flatworms are parasites which dwell in the intestines of higher vertebrates, living off whatever ingested food comes their way. Thus, the host organism (you!) can eat its fill, while the tapeworm picks up the calories! Available in coiled or extended forms from Annelid Industries, $10.

Broadcasting Bunker, the BBC wartime emergency control centre at Wood Norton, near Evesham. A relic of World War 2, TV studios 5 storeys below ground have been added for the run-up to World War 3.

Ploog/Hartmann/Pociao (Ed.)
**AMOK/KOMA**
Ein Bericht zur Lage
A-4 Format, ca. 200 Seiten
Subskriptionspreis DM 23,- incl. postage

Texte, Photos und Grafik von:

Burroughs, Wilson, Jenny, Breger, Rufmann, Pott, Liana, Plymell, Gysin, Throbbing Gristle, OAF, Weissner, Diazentrale Ost, Minus Delta T, Hübsch, Beschung, Hartmann, Ploog u.v.a.

Ich habe den Betrag von DM 23,- unter dem Stichwort AMOK auf PS Köln 30668-506 (Pogorzalek) eingezahlt.

Datum:

Unterschrift:

Auslieferung ab Ende September

Sylvia Pogorzalek
Horwarthstraße 27
5300 Bonn
Tel. 0222 21/ 65.58.87

1. The post-industrial society is now becoming an information society where the strategic resources are knowledge and data. Information occupations claimed only 12% of the work force in 1959, but now account for more than 50% of total employment.

cam.ou.flage (kam'a fläzh), n. v. -flaged, -flag-ing. — n. 1 a disguise or false appearance in order to conceal protective coloration. The white fur of a polar bear is a natural camouflage; it prevents the bear's being easily seen against the snow. Its giving soldiers, weapons, vehicles, planes, or ships a false appearance to conceal them from the enemy. Camouflage may cause an object to blend with its background or to appear to be something different from what it actually is. b the materials or other means by which this is done: *The guns were hidden by a camouflage of earth and branches.* — v.t. to give a false appearance to in order to conceal; disguise: *to camouflage a piece sponge cake with frosting. The hunters were camouflaged with branches so that they blended with the trees.* (Figurative.) *The boy camouflaged his embarrassment by laughing.* — v.i. to engage in camouflage; conceal by or as if by camouflage: *We camouflaged in the bushes and no one saw us.* (< French *camouflage* < *camoufler* to disguise < Italian *camuffare*] — sam'ou.flag'er, n.

cam.ou.fleur (kam'a fler), n. a person skilled in military camouflage; camouflager. 1 < French

"Let me through, I'm a necrophiliac!"

"War injuries left me incapaced, but I'm making a living in Locksmithing. Of course, Word of mouth is enough..."

**8.1** *Industrial News,* 4 (1980) © Industrial Records / Throbbing Gristle (by permission of Cosey Fanni Tutti)

only moderately influenced by the approach of *Industrial News*. In analysing these, it is possible to identify a distinction between zines produced, ostensibly, by fans of industrial and zines produced by artists or labels. While artist or label zines were, as a general rule, more similar to *Industrial News* in tone and style, there were stark differences in intent and approach. Industrial fanzines tended to conform to more standardised zine formats. It should also be stressed that relatively few of the fanzines discussed in this section focused exclusively on industrial music, although this is hardly surprising given that the genre – as it is understood today – was nowhere near as densely populated as it became in the 1990s. In line with this fluidity of scene culture boundaries, this section shall also refer to some zines that were not explicitly industrial zines in terms of musical focus, but which nonetheless may be categorised alongside the other industrial zines under discussion due to their content and style.

Of the various industrial fanzines that began to appear in the early 1980s, a small handful stands out because of their clear relationship to TG. *Nanavesh* and *T-GASM Organ* both started while the band were still active, and were run by coordinators of TG appreciation societies. These two publications were clearly intended to continue the work carried out in *Industrial News*. *T-GASM Organ* (T-GASM stood for Throbbing Gristle Appreciation Society of Minneapolis) clarified this in the introduction of its first issue. 'Music and its practical application will be a large part of T-GASM's discussions', the editorial stated, but more fundamentally it emphasised that 'T-GASM wishes only to communicate and exchange ideas with followers of Throbbing Gristle. We like information.'[46] The fourth issue derided those subscribers to the zine who read but did not contribute. 'You are of little use to us and none to yourselves', railed Stefan Hammond's editorial, going on to emphasise that non-contributors would soon not be able to read the zine at all: 'IF WE DON'T HEAR FROM YOU YOU WON'T BE HEARING FROM US.'[47] To Hammond, being an acolyte of TG was impossible without being an active participant in information warfare.

*Nanavesh*, produced by South London-based Dave Farmer, took this aspect of TG less seriously at first. The first two issues focused simply on providing fans with information about TG's activities.[48] Once TG had run its course, however, *Nanavesh* moved on to acting as one of numerous communiqués produced on behalf of Psychic TV and Thee Temple ov Psychick Youth, P-Orridge's post-TG band and associated cultic network.[49] Issue 5 of *Nanavesh* followed closely the template provided by the final issue of *Industrial News*. Some direct information related to Psychic TV's activities was provided, including a selection of lyrics and a request from P-Orridge for readers to send in 'ANYTHING to do with wolves'.[50] Several of the themes present in the issue were continuations of previous TG obsessions, such as phone tapping,[51] but the focus was tipping ever more into the realm of the occult and the arcane. Numerous collages indicated P-Orridge's increasing interest in ritualistic spirituality, Austin Osman Spare's influence was heavily apparent, and the number 23 appeared at steady intervals (a reference to Burroughs' observation that the number regularly appeared in his investigations into coincidences).[52] Given P-Orridge's genuine interest in turning Psychic TV into a cult-like organisation, much of the issue was also devoted to encouraging some form of participation. On one page the group's approach is succinctly summarised, emphasising the notion that it was through the subcultural rituals of Psychic TV (PTV) that control could be shaken off and individualism could break free:

> PTV is intended to trigger and be adapted until you create and discover your OWN mythology, and through that your destiny and thee methods to achieve it to thee greatest degree possible. PTV must never be taken too literally … 23 [sic].[53]

*Nanavesh*, while an intriguing insight into the development of the information war tactics begun in *Industrial News*, ultimately provides relatively little insight into the wider development of the industrial scene – an insight necessary to gain a true appreciation of the evolution of industrial zine culture. More helpful are zines such as *Stabmental*, which had similar origins but was never intended to be solely devoted to TG (or latterly Psychic TV). This zine was started in 1979 (with the band's assistance) by a young convert to the cause: Geff Rushton, who would later become (under the name John Balance) a legendary figure in the industrial scene in his own right, due to his work with Christopherson in Coil (both were also involved in early Psychic TV). The first issue of *Stabmental* – then co-edited by Rushton and Tom Craig – emphasised the zine's adherence to the industrial philosophy in its introduction: 'Sharing information is continuing education and is necessary for the step forward.'[54] The zine's content, however, tended to conform to that of other post-punk zines of the time. Indeed, with the exception of features on TG and Monte Cazazza in the first issue, *Stabmental* mostly consisted of fairly routine interviews with both industrial and non-industrial acts.

In this regard, *Stabmental* set the tone for the majority of industrial-focused fan-produced zines that appeared in the early 1980s: titles such as *Concrete Beaches, Discipline, Flowmotion, Interchange, Subvert* and *Tone Death*. These publications would, by nature of a general focus on industrial artists, touch upon the ideological aspects of the scene promoted by TG, although they did not define themselves along these lines in the same manner as *Stabmental*. Exceptions to this general rule were more on an issue-by-issue, or even feature-by-feature, basis. So, for example, the fifth issue of *Subvert* was more clearly industrial – in an ideological sense – because of its near-exclusive focus on Psychic TV, and the eleventh issue of *Concrete Beaches* owed a clear debt to the anti-communication stylings of *Industrial News*.[55] One article in *Flowmotion*, meanwhile, asserted that 'No one' other than Burroughs 'has done more to expose the machinations of those who wish to control human destiny for their own ends.'[56] Despite these examples, however, there was often little separating these publications from titles that were more focused on the post-punk scene but which overlapped to some extent with industrial, such as *Idiot Strength*, *Rapid Eye Movement* (which later adopted a far more esoteric and occult-leaning focus), and *Vox*.[57]

This is less true of zines produced by artists, such as Australian industrial luminaries SPK, and power electronics acts such as Whitehouse, Ramleh, and Consumer Electronics. SPK (originally named after the West German Marxist movement *Sozialistishces Patientenkollektiv*) were initially signed to Industrial Records, and they elected to celebrate the release of their 1981 debut album *Information Overload Unit* by producing a zine – *Dokument* – to be distributed with copies of the record. Only two issues of this zine were ever produced; the second was largely distributed via 1982 sophomore LP *Leichenschrei*. A similar approach was utilised to that found in *Industrial News* or *Nanavesh*, supposedly designed – in this case – to reflect SPK's overall goal: 'to express the content of various psycho-pathalogical [*sic*] conditions, especially schizophrenia, manic-depressive psychosis, mental retardation and paranoia.'[58] In keeping with its associated album, the first issue of *Dokument* was an exercise in information overload, mostly related in some way to four alternative meanings of the SPK acronym: Special Programming Korps, Surgical Penis Klink, System Planning Korporation and Selective Pornography Kontrol.[59] The information disruption on display here was clearly important to SPK. In the *Industrial Culture Handbook* one member of the band expressed his 'hope that this whole "Industrial Counterculture" can have the ability to become ... a propagandist guerilla movement, instead of just another little set of ideas.'[60]

This desire can be contextualised somewhat by the précis at the beginning of the second issue of *Dokument* (focused on a range of the band's favoured subliminal audio and visual tactics), in which SPK acknowledged that they were '"politikal", but not in the accepted sense of the term.'[61] TG had always denied being a political group but, of course, the information war was an inherently political concept even if – as befitted its postmodern Burroughsian origins – this politics was post-political in its attempted subversion of conventional discourses of power. SPK's greater openness about the political elements of industrial was, unfortunately, left undeveloped. Conflict about the band's musical style (which co-founder Graeme Revell ultimately won, leading to the synthpop approach of third album *Machine Age Voodoo*), and the suicide of co-founder Neil Hill in February 1984 meant that SPK never truly progressed along the path set out in *Dokument* or their section of the *Industrial Culture Handbook*. With Psychic TV's engagement in information warfare leading in ever more occultist directions and much of the industrial milieu being increasingly absorbed into the wider post-punk scene, the post-politics of industrial culture became increasingly associated with the power electronics subgenre.

Power electronics (essentially a harsher, noisier variant of industrial) was, in many ways, a natural outcome of early industrial, both musically and ideologically. TG had always played with noise, and acts like Whitehouse, Ramleh and Consumer Electronics simply looked to push this aspect of the genre's musical personality to its limits. The fact that power electronics has 'been more consistently grouped by its politics and iconography than by its music' is both a reflection of the music's alienating extremity and the fascination with taboo imagery that naturally accompanied its musical viscerality.[62] This was 'a deliberately violent sound form' looking to 'attack the senses' by any means necessary, including by generating controversy through its visual – as much as its sonic – content.[63] Whitehouse, led by William Bennett, were the most notorious of these groups. London listings paper *City Limits* even accused Bennett of being involved with underground British fascist organisation the League of St George (largely because Come Organisation, Bennett's record label, shared the same PO Box address as the group).[64] Whitehouse were prevented from performing at the University of London on the basis of their supposed political extremism, and there were disagreements at Rough Trade over whether Come releases should be distributed by the company.[65]

*Kata*, the zine produced by Whitehouse, illustrated much of what was problematic about Whitehouse's approach. *Kata* tended to be more minimalist than most industrial zines, and more extreme. The second issue specifically criticised *Industrial News* for pandering to the mainstream, suggesting that the band member profiles indicated that TG 'obviously had frustrated ambitions of being new beatles [*sic*]'.[66] Early issues of *Kata* consisted of simply-typed text blending Come catalogue information, violent sadist fiction, letters, reviews, Whitehouse lyrics, and extracts on taboo topics. The increasing comfort with which *Kata* dealt with violence was indicated by a shift between the fourth and fifth issues. The former featured a page-long excerpt from *The 120 Days of Sodom*, while the latter included a lengthy quote from serial killer Peter

Kürten.[67] While *Industrial News* and the other titles discussed above generally did not prescribe a position, and attempted to embody the 'do as you think' mantra, *Kata* was clearly geared around the notion that the only means of transgression that mattered were those of a sadistic nature. Issue 7 featured a call for contributions that made this quite clear: 'If you enjoy or fantasise about any perversion or refinement please write and tell us in detail as we would be most interested and we will print the most obscure/extreme refinements in kata 08 and 09.'[68] Even if this overwhelming focus on more perverse interests was satirical, it was unavoidably prescriptive.

1982 saw Whitehouse, and *Kata*, push things further than ever before. Bennett had, by this point, supposedly formed an organisation called the New Party, and the new Whitehouse album, *New Britain*, came housed in a sleeve featuring a new logo (which clearly aped a Swastika).[69] This logo also appeared on the back cover of issue 11 of *Kata*, replete with the text 'Under the Victory Banner', while the front cover bore the name not only of the new album but also one of its tracks – 'Kriegserklärung' (declaration of war) – under a grainy image of a dead body.[70] The same issue featured the first of a two-part piece on extermination camps (focused on Sobibór and Treblinka respectively) contributed by Come artist Maurizio Bianchi. As with *Kata*'s tendency to quote serial killers – or indeed Whitehouse's tendency to offer dedications to them – these pieces appeared to revel in the horrors of the Final Solution rather than condemn them.[71] The lack of contextualisation provided in *Kata* for any of this material effectively saw Bennett openly accept charges of extreme right sympathies, despite his attempts to laugh off such accusations in interviews in other publications.[72]

Bennett's determination to transgress as viciously as possible reached its unpleasant nadir in the first issue of Belgian industrial zine *Force Mental* in June 1982. Bennett's page-length contribution saw him claim that Whitehouse was at the forefront of 'the struggle against unhealthy Negroid influence and Jewish exploitation in popular music'. He also called for a '"... New Musical Culture" to appeal to the Anglo-Saxon youth of Britain'.[73] Today Bennett claims that his work was satirical,[74] but even if that were true there is little doubt that he fostered something deeply unpleasant in the power electronics scene of the time. Ramleh (named after the Israeli prison in which Adolf Eichmann was incarcerated) not only released numerous dubious titles through the label Broken Flag but also produced zines *King, Krown & Kountry* (or *KKK* for short) and *Farben* (clearly a reference to Nazi collaborators IG Farben). *Intolerance*, run by Philip Best of Consumer Electronics, Iphar Records and later Whitehouse, featured – in its third issue – an advert for the British Nationalist & Socialist Movement.[75] The fifth issue opened with a dedication to serial killer Colin Nickels for his 'glorious actions' in strangling his third wife on New Year's Eve 1981.[76] The sixth – and final – issue of *King, Krown & Kountry*, meanwhile, featured a page on American neo-Nazi leader George Lincoln Rockwell (described in the heading as the 'St. Paul of Nazism'). The main text began: 'Our hearts belong to National Socialism, to the Aryan white man more than they belong to any national boundary or any artificial creations of man.'[77]

As Ramleh's Gary Mundy later admitted, 'this all fitted in with the audience-baiting and obnoxious attitude of the band ... but this kind of game is ultimately futile and childish ... we made an error in judgement in testing out the bounds of offensiveness.'[78] The power electronics faction can, ultimately, be seen as having misunderstood the fundamental idea behind industrial culture. Cultural resistance, in the industrial case, was a process of deconstruction that largely utilised extremes alongside banalities to emphasise the liberating potential of Burroughs' radical postmodern countercultural philosophy. As zines such as *Kata* demonstrate, acts like Whitehouse simply forced extremity (rather superficially) down the throats of their followers.[79] This only further emphasised that the message embedded in *Industrial News*, and central to the early industrial movement, was – even relatively early on in the subculture's history – being misinterpreted or even misused.

## Conclusion

Power electronics marks an appropriate stopping point for an analysis of the early development of industrial zine culture, as much as anything because it is largely artists such as Whitehouse that cemented industrial's forbidding (and in some ways rather unfair) reputation as being primarily interested in extremes above all else. One might also say that titles such as *Kata* illustrate the limitations of an approach fundamentally geared around ideas of transgression. Whitehouse and their ilk took transgression purely in a Sadean (or perhaps, depending on one's transgressive preferences, Artaudian) manner, without recognising that the simple build-up of extremes both gradually eroded the power of extreme imagery and proved severely alienating. 'WAS THE MARQUIS DE SADE A LIBERATOR?', asked one early 1990s issue of industrial zine *FIST*.[80] In this case, no, as the overtly Sadean approach these groups adopted contributed nothing to the subversion of control (not that this is something power electronics acts explicitly expressed an interest in). In fact, the attempted transgressions of power electronics strengthened hierarchical discourses of information control by reasserting the distance between the extremes and the mainstream.

That industrial should have so rapidly taken such a turn is not surprising. The surface nihilism of TG's work left itself wide open to such misinterpretation. Their failure to go further in the direction of transgressive extremity practically goaded others into doing so. This does not in itself render the transgressive strategies pioneered by TG a failure, but it does indicate that industrial – as a 'culture of resistance' (to borrow George McKay's term) – was flawed. Industrial's Burroughsian philosophy was ultimately more successful in an artistic sense than anything else. The fan-produced industrial zines referred to earlier demonstrate this perfectly. Their predominant focus on industrial as a musical movement, rather than something philosophical (or at least fully cross-disciplinary), was continued in titles that appeared in the 1990s, such as *Impulse* or *Music from the Empty Quarter*. As Simon Reynolds has pointed out, despite TG's 'rather disdainful attitude to music *per se*' they gave birth to what has since become one of the more 'densely populated fields of post-punk music'.[81]

Some more recent titles – *Datacide, Electric Shock Treatment, FIST, Gneurosis, Noise Receptor* – associated with industrial have taken up the mantra of 'Don't do as you're told, do as you think', blending together music and ideas in a manner somewhat removed from *Industrial News* but nonetheless clearly indebted to it. Predictably, some titles (the Finnish zine *Special Interests* springs to mind) have steered more in the direction of *Kata*. It certainly is not true, then, that the industrial zine culture of the 1970s and 1980s has not had a significant influence on subsequent generations of zine producers (although there has been a noticeable swing from artist or label-produced zines to fanzines). These developments, I would suggest, indicate that the industrial zines discussed in this chapter were ultimately powerful vehicles for the gestation of a subcultural identity, but they were not necessarily the mediums needed to prompt – in a subversive manner (i.e. without direct instructions) – the application of industrial's ideas. The control machines were challenged by industrial, but they were not vanquished.

## Notes

Acknowledgements: My thanks go to Matthew Worley and archivists at the British Library, National Art Library and at Tate Britain for their assistance in sourcing materials for this chapter, and to Cosey Fanni Tutti for personally giving her permission for the reproduction of *Industrial News*. This research was aided by a TECHNE AHRC Doctoral Studentship.

1 Simon Reynolds, *Rip It Up and Start Again: Post-Punk, 1978–1984* (London: Faber & Faber, 2006), p. xvii.

2 S. Alexander Reed, *Assimilate: A Critical History of Industrial Music* (Oxford: Oxford University Press, 2013), pp. 19–55.

3 Christopher Partridge, *The Lyre of Orpheus: Popular Music, the Sacred, and the Profane* (Oxford: Oxford University Press, 2013), p. 81.

4 Matthew Worley, 'Punk, Politics and British (Fan)zines, 1976–84: "While the world was dying, did you wonder why?"', *History Workshop Journal*, 79:1 (2015), 94.

5 Simon Ford, *Wreckers of Civilisation: The Story of COUM Transmissions and Throbbing Gristle* (London: Black Dog, 1999), p. 5.16. Note that Ford stylises all page numbers in this book to refer to chapter and page (so 5.16 is page 16 of Chapter 5).

6 Nicholas Fairbairn, quoted in 'Adults only art show angers an MP', *Daily Mail*, 19 October 1976, p. 17.

7 Jon Savage, 'Foreword', in Ford, *Wreckers of Civilisation*, pp. 0.8–0.10.

8 Jason James Hanley, 'Metal Machine Music: Technology, Noise and Modernism in Industrial Music, 1975–1996' (Ph.D. thesis, Stony Brook University, NY, 2011), p. 12. Burroughs discussed many of the fundamental ideas of the information war in conversation with Daniel Odier in *The Job: Interviews with William Burroughs* (London: Penguin Classics, 2008).

9 Reed, *Assimilate*, pp. 28–9.

10 Michael Goddard, 'Sonic and Cultural Noise as the Production of the New: The Industrial Music Ecology of Throbbing Gristle', in Simon O'Sullivan and Stephen Zepke (eds), *Deleuze, Guattari and the Production of the New* (London: Continuum, 2000), p. 168.

11 Reed, *Assimilate*, pp. 10–11.

12 Genesis P-Orridge, quoted in 'Throbbing Gristle', in V. Vale and A. Juno (eds), *RE/Search 6/7: Industrial Culture Handbook* (San Francisco, CA: V/Search Productions, 1983), p. 9.

13 Throbbing Gristle, 'Don't Do As You're Told, Do As You Think', *Heathen Earth* (Industrial Records, 1980).

14 Genesis P-Orridge, quoted in 'Throbbing Gristle interview', in V. Vale and A. Juno (eds), *RE/Search 4/5: William S. Burroughs, Throbbing Gristle, Brion Gysin* (San Francisco, CA: V/Search Productions, 1982), p. 87.

15 'Throbbing Gristle', in *RE/Search 6/7*, p. 19.

16 David Welch, *The Third Reich: Politics and Propaganda* (Abingdon: Routledge, 2002), p. 26.

17 Such an approach would inevitably necessitate a sustained engagement with Walter Benjamin. For a brief Benjamin-ian perspective, see Erich Hertz, 'Rethinking Aura Through Temporality: Benjamin and "Industrial Otherness"', in Institute of Cultural Inquiry (ed.), *Benjamin's Blind Spot: Walter Benjamin and the Premature Death of Aura with the Manual of Lost Ideas* (Los Angeles: Institute of Cultural Inquiry, 2001), pp. 100–8.

18  'A Note of Introduction from the Management of Industrial Records', *Industrial News*, 1 (1978), p. 1. This introduction was signed 'Tony Goldstein', but this was simply a pseudonym for the collective members of TG.

19  *Industrial News*, 1, p. 12.

20  *Ibid.*, pp. 5–11 and 14.

21  Generally, if not exclusively, punk zines that may also be seen to have acted against traditional media's role in the control of information still promoted at least a vaguely discernible message. See Worley, 'Punk, Politics and British (Fan)zines', pp. 87–8.

22  William S. Burroughs, *The Soft Machine* (London: Penguin, 2014), p. 91; Robert Genter, *Late Modernism: Art, Culture, and Politics in Cold War America* (Philadelphia, PA: University of Pennsylvania Press, 2010), p. 274.

23  Stephen Duncombe, *Notes from Underground: Zines and the Politics of Alternative Culture* (London: Verso, 1997), p. 6.

24  Chris Atton, *Alternative Media* (London: Sage, 2002), p. 67.

25  Jon Savage, 'Introduction', in *RE/Search 6/7*, p. 5.

26  Genesis P-Orridge, 'Real total war has become information war; it is being fought now', quoted in Ford, *Wreckers of Civilisation*, p. 9.6.

27  *Industrial News*, 2 (1979). I have been told that there were two different editions of this issue produced, with one being the work of Cazazza alone. The edition co-produced with Emmolo is, however, the only one I have encountered.

28  *Industrial News*, 3 (1979), pp. 8, 16, 23. This issue is not explicitly numbered, but it was the third issue to be put together. Confusingly, not to mention incorrectly, the fourth issue was numbered 'N3', but – for narrative ease – I have chosen to refer to it as the fourth issue in notes and in the text.

29  *Industrial News*, 3, p. 11.

30  'Magazines & Fanzines of Note', *Industrial News*, 3, p. 9; *Industrial News*, 3, p. 12.

31  *Ibid.*, p. 9.

32  Genesis P-Orridge, quoted in David George, 'Thoughts on Charles Manson', in *Industrial News*, 3, pp. 18–19.

33  'The Problems of Cassettes Sent to Industrial Records', *Industrial News*, 4 (1980), p. 14.

34  *Industrial News*, 4, pp. 9–11.

35  'Girlie Magazines Featuring Cosey Fanni Tutti', *Industrial News*, 4, p. 8.

36  *Industrial News*, 4, p. 1.

37  *Ibid.*, p. 3.

38  William S. Burroughs, quoted in *Industrial News*, 4, p. 6.

39  William S. Burroughs, 'The Revised Boy Scout Manual: excerpt (Cassette 1)', in *RE/Search 4/5*, pp. 5–8.

40  *Industrial News*, 4, pp. 15 and 17–18.

41  Ford, *Wreckers of Civilisation*, pp. 10.24–10.25.

42  *Industrial News*, 4, pp. 22 and 29.

43  *Industrial News*, 4, p. 30.

44  Ford, *Wreckers of Civilisation*, pp. 11.13–14.

45 'Throbbing Gristle', in *RE/Search 6/7*, p. 9.

46 Stefan Hammond, *T-GASM Organ*, 1 (n.d.), p. 1

47 Stefan Hammond, *T-GASM Organ*, 4 (1981), p. 1.

48 *Nanavesh*, 1 (n.d.); *Nanavesh*, 2 (1981).

49 Many of these titles only appeared for a brief time. Among the most prominent were *Occulture, Ov, Subvert* and *Thee Infernal Templer*.

50 *Nanavesh*, 5 (1983), p. 31.

51 *Ibid.*, p. 30.

52 *Ibid.*

53 *Ibid.*, p. 64. Original spelling and punctuation.

54 Geff Rushton and Tom Craig, *Stabmental*, 1 (1979), p. 1.

55 *Subvert*, 5 (1983); *Concrete Beaches*, 11 (1984).

56 Peter Scott, 'W. S. Burroughs', *Flowmotion*, 4 (1982), p. 4.

57 *Rapid Eye Movement* later morphed into a series of book-length publications, not dissimilar to *RE/Search*.

58 *Dokument*, 1 (1981), p. 3.

59 *Ibid.*, pp. 4–9.

60 'SPK', in *RE/Search 6/7*, p. 98.

61 *Dokument*, 2 (1982), p. 2.

62 Reed, *Assimilate*, p. 147.

63 Philip Taylor, 'The Genesis of Power Electronics in the UK', in Jennifer Wallis (ed.), *Fight Your Own War: Power Electronics and Noise Culture* (London: Headpress, 2016), p. 18.

64 'Come Organisation: Whitehouse (the most violently repulsive records ever conceived)', *Flowmotion*, 4, p. 8.

65 'Come Organisation', *Flowmotion*, 4, p. 8; Neil Taylor, *Document and Eyewitness: An Intimate History of Rough Trade* (London: Orion, 2010), p. 232. Among the early Come Organisation releases was the 1982 compilation *Für Ilse Koch*, which included among its tracks a speech by Heinrich Himmler. Koch herself was the sadistic wife of Buchenwald commandant Karl-Otto Koch.

66 *Kata*, 2 (1980), p. 4.

67 *Kata*, 4 (1980), p. 4; *Kata*, 5 (1981), p. 5.

68 *Kata*, 7 (1981), p. 4.

69 Whitehouse, *New Britain* (Come Organisation, 1982).

70 *Kata*, 11 (1982).

71 Maurizio Bianchi, 'Entrance for a Punishment', *Kata*, 11, pp. 8–9; Bianchi, 'After the Entrance, the Final Solution', *Kata*, 12 (1982), pp. 11–12.

72 'Come Organisation', *Flowmotion*, 4, pp. 7–8.

73 William Bennett, 'The Struggle for a New Musical Culture', *Force Mental*, 1 (1982), p. 9.

74 William Bennett, 'Personal statement', *William Bennett*, 19 March 2013, http://williambennett.blogspot.co.uk/2013/03/statement.html/, accessed 20 April 2016.

75 *Intolerance*, 3 (n.d.), p. 6.

76  'Moment of Triumph', *Intolerance*, 5 (1982), p. 1.

77  'Lincoln Rockwell – The St. Paul of Nazism', *King, Krown & Kountry*, 6 (n.d.), p. 8.

78  Gary Mundy, quoted in Reed, *Assimilate*, p. 147.

79  Goddard, 'Sonic and Cultural Noise and the Production of the New', p. 169.

80  'Inside Four Walls', *FIST*, 5 (1994), p. 28.

81  Reynolds, *Rip It Up and Start Again*, p. 240.

# 9

# Are you scared to get punky? Indie pop, fanzines and punk rock

PETE DALE

This chapter will argue that fanzines played a crucial role in the formation of a perceived genre (or, arguably, sub-genre) called, variously, indie pop, cutie, C86, twee, jangle-pop, shambling or anorak. For the purpose of discussion in this chapter, the scene in question is referred to as '1980s indie pop' or just 'indie pop'. In the twenty-first century, the descriptor 'indie pop' is sometimes applied, in vernacular contexts, to post-1980s 'indie' music which is qualitatively and somewhat ideologically different from the 1980s indie pop discussed here. It should be clarified, therefore, that I am not simply referring to any pop music which can be identified as indie, but rather a particular (perceived) genre within a particular time frame.

The indie-pop genre (or perceived genre, and perceptions among a broad public surely give some substance to the idea of a collection of songs and bands *as* a genre) continues today but in an 'underground' way. This contemporary scene, which clusters around events like Indietracks in the UK and NYC Popfest in the USA, is essentially a 'retro' scene with the 1980s indie-pop fanzines and bands being canonical for most participants. Such was not entirely the case as indie pop emerged in the 1980s, however. There were retro elements, certainly, with bands such as Primal Scream clearly invoking specific 1960s bands (the Byrds, in the case at hand); but there was also something distinctively fresh about 1980s indie pop, at least from the point of view of a large micro-audience.

Where did this felt-to-be-new scene come from? In short, I argue that the 1980s indie-pop movement formed in a fairly 'organic' way, in the sense that it formed from not only the performance aesthetics of bands but also the consumption preferences and discursive negotiations of audiences. Fanzines were crucial to these discursive negotiations among audiences, alongside the written correspondence between individuals which was a vital correlate of the fanzine scene of the era. This can be described as organic because limited mainstream media influence (e.g. *NME* and the other weekly music papers of the mid-1980s) came to bear upon the emergent scene – initially, at least. Instead, fanzines were commenting on certain tropes which were only really being discussed *by* fanzines, particularly c. 1980 to 1984. However, around the time of the *C86* cassette issued by the *NME* in 1986 (featuring a selection of new indie bands of the period and issued in conjunction with Rough Trade), corporate forces, such as the 'major' record labels and the mainstream music press, broke into the organic scene in significant ways. Some fanzine writers were able to become staff writers at that time, but in the following years great hostility would break out between the music press and the indie-pop scene and its fanzines.

Overall, the chapter suggests that the 1980s indie scene was not by any means the apolitical ghetto that the music press of the day would eventually label it as. Indie-pop fanzines often had a consciously political agenda and a fiery way of writing; they were typically committed to the punk rock scene which indie pop grew from. Due to the ephemeral status of fanzines and their limited print runs, coupled with the overt hostility and misrepresentations of the corporately owned music press of the 1980s and 1990s, this political character and link to the punk tradition has been obscured. It is also the case that the importance of the *C86* compilation has been greatly exaggerated. Note, for example, the suggestion by Keith Creighton on the *Popdose* website on 2 May 2016 that indie pop is 'the movement *NME* started 30 years ago'. If one examines fanzine archives in the British Library or the London College of Communication, or if one is able to track down personal collections (as I have done in order to research for this chapter, having been too young to collect fanzines during the period in question), a different picture emerges. One can clearly see that the genesis of the movement/genre in question very much predates the *C86* cassette – and, furthermore, that fanzines were crucial to this genesis.

## The emergence of indie-pop practices and aesthetics, 1980 to 1984

Contemporary indie-pop fanzine *Last Train to Eastleigh* (2015) is on very steady ground when it proposes that: 'It is an undeniable fact that there would be no indie-pop scene without the influence and spirit of punk rock'.[1] What is the link? Indie pop has always tended towards 'DIY' (self-publishing, essentially), not only as a practical preference but also as an aesthetic option. By aesthetics, I mean that the fanzines and record sleeves in indie pop, as well as the music itself, often appear to have been consciously 'unprofessional', hastily assembled and to have revelled in amateurism. At a practical level, meanwhile, indie-pop emerged within a context where upholding DIY values and being 'independent' from the major labels was assumed to be of importance.

*Born Yesterday*, from 1981, demonstrates that such practical concerns were always discursively significant alongside aesthetic preferences. The writer sketches out the particular selection of punk/post-punk aesthetic influences which would become canonical for indie pop: '1977 – The Ramones, 1978 – the Buzzcocks, 1979 – the Undertones ... and this year it took a while but I finally fell ... Orange Juice!'.[2] However, *Born Yesterday* is simultaneously concerned as to whether the Postcard label (home to Orange Juice before they signed to Polydor) 'stays independent'. Given that 'an independent audience is a very limited one', the fanzine writer appreciates to some extent why Orange Juice have aimed for 'change from inside'. Yet, he also worries in this regard given The Freshies' then-recent major label deal.[3]

One can see much the same combination of aesthetic and practical priorities in an essentially nameless fanzine (one side of the A6 pamphlet reads *Orange Juice: 'A' side*, while the other reads *Josef K: 'B' side*) which appears to have been written in 1980. The fanzine writer was finding the punk/post-punk music of 1980 'a bit overwhelming' and 'almost a chore' to listen to, whereas Orange Juice offered 'cheerful, light pop songs ... just what we needed'.[4] Also emphasised, however, is that Postcard Records (home to Orange Juice and Josef K and in many ways the prototype indie-pop label) had 'no middlemen scraping off the profits, no simple churning out of useless product'.[5] That said, Postcard's label boss Alan Horne rejects the idea of being 'a trendy little independent putting out records for the smug elite clique'; rather, 'we want our music to appeal to everyone, while keeping it totally independent of the music industry's businessmen'.[6]

The particular lineage (Ramones, Buzzcocks, Undertones, Postcard Records) as emphasised by these fanzines, and the practical and aesthetic priorities they encouraged, would appear to have either tapped into or, arguably, to have led a distinctive and thus essentially new trajectory in post-punk music. The more harsh and angry side of punk, it is fair to say, was beginning to be eyed sceptically by some in the period in question. Consider, for example, Pastels-related fanzine *Juniper Beri-Beri*'s remark that: 'It's the end of 82 and it's pretty grim ... punk – the original spirits long since dead' and, therefore, perhaps 'we should start a new culture)much smaller I don't know) ... punk's certainly pretty sick [*sic*]'.[7] We can also note the complaint in *Especially Yellow* (1983) that: 'There are still people who believe PUNK holds the key, and cream their pants when they get within two miles of "HARDCORE"' and yet: 'The spirit of PUNK ... has been tainted by a second generation who are nothing but pantomime peacocks'. 'Conflict and Baby Jesus manage to retain true vitality', the fanzine argues: 'But I just can't help feeling that something is happening with bands like James ... and The Smiths'; he also mentions the Kitchenware label (and by implication Hurrah!, an influential group for 1980s indie pop) and *Juniper Beri-Beri*. 'For me things are looking up, but why is everybody else looking down?'[8] *Especially Yellow*'s coverage of Strawberry Switchblade and Orange Juice's song 'Falling and Laughing' gives us an indication that the fanzine was tapping into the then-emerging 1980s indie-pop aesthetic/genre.[9] This essentially canonical (for indie pop) set of bands and songs were beginning to be prioritised by the fanzines at a time when the weekly music papers were failing to 'join the dots'.[10]

Fun 'n' Frenzy, from 1983, also covers The Smiths, alongside more obvious indie-pop progenitors such as Hurrah! and Josef K. We can also note that Morrissey, in what will have been one of his first interviews, criticises major labels and praises Rough Trade 'who truly care about what we do'.[11] In fact, The Smiths had made certain efforts to strike a deal with EMI while relations with Rough Trade are known to have soon deteriorated. So what, though? The salient point, for our purposes, is that The Smiths initially fitted with an emerging practical priority: remaining independent ('indie', that is, in the sense the word was applied at that time) but also seeking 'to be heard ... We will grab every avenue and use it.'[12] Aesthetically, meanwhile, the jangly guitars and flowery, 1960s-influenced appearance of The Smiths would seem an obvious precursor to the indie pop that would blossom in the coming years.

After co-producing *Fun 'n' Frenzy* and *Sun Connection*, and gaining significant praise for the former in mainstream music press, including *NME* and *Sounds*, Kevin Pearce produced the first issue of his celebrated *Hungry Beat* fanzine in 1984. Although the Creation Records related fanzine *Communication Blur* (1983–84) was important for its emphasis on key progenitors of indie pop, including the Television Personalities, it was *Hungry Beat* which more strongly distilled the formative elements of early 1980s fanzines ready for the codification of indie pop in the mid-1980s. Musically, *Hungry Beat* is quite a bit more restricted in taste relative to the fanzines which came later; the writer is more picky about contemporary music than almost any 1980s fanzine I have seen.

The single most important thing about *Hungry Beat* is its unflagging emphasis upon 'pop' as well as punk. In *Hungry Beat #1*, for example, Pearce declares that 'in September '84 we are closer to having the right ingredients for the ultimate pop explosion than perhaps at ANY other time – EVER!' This, he goes on, is because 'we know our pop history; the inspired/inspirational parts have all been absorbed and past mistakes will be avoided at all costs', thus 'the future starts here' with Biff Bang Pow, Hurrah!, the Loft and Jasmine Minks.[13] That said, even though 'everybody and their pet monkey seems to be going gaga over The Pastels these days', 'this pop/punk phenomenon' should not include said band, Pearce argues, because 'I think they're dreadful'.[14] New Order/Joy Division, meanwhile, are tarred as 'Mancunian hippy hooligans'.[15] This is fairly typical of *Hungry Beat*: a palpable sense of excitement leaps from the pages (for example, Pearce emphasises the importance of Creation because 'Creation Records is NOW!'), but the writer's absolute faith in the excellence of his own judgements seems unshakeable; in short, what he doesn't like he *really* doesn't like. Not only mainstream music papers but also all other fanzines aside from *Communication Blur* and *Adventures in Bereznik* are snottily dismissed.

By 1985, when indie pop became a more identifiable and popular movement, *Hungry Beat* would become more hostile to the scene which the same fanzine had arguably played a vital part in kindling: 'I feel a terrible insidious nausea creep over me when I witness grubby, naive enthusiastic fun fun funsters playing at being the Ramones/Buzzcocks … '[16] In 1984, however, the fanzine still reads as if the writer feels himself to be on the verge of a great discovery. Pearce's key revelation, as it were, reduces to this: 'pop music/punk rock – it's the same thing, right?'[17] Other important innovations include an emphasis upon 1960s groups such as Love and The Byrds, as well as 'Northern' Soul (more readily available at that time due to the Kent compilations for which Pearce shows notable enthusiasm), which earlier punk-orientated fanzines would doubtless have been unlikely to discuss.

Looking at these fanzines from a twenty-first-century standpoint, *Hungry Beat* sticks out among early 1980s fanzines in comparison with the scrappier and more 'noise'-fixated likes of *Rox* and *Attack on Bzag*.[18] A 1984 issue of the latter (written by James Brown who would go on to write for *NME* and, eventually, to be the founding editor of the 1990s 'lads mag' *Loaded*) shares some of *Hungry Beat*'s disdain for The Pastels, admittedly. However, this appears to be mainly because these Scottish indie-pop pioneers allegedly needed to 'get the R'n'R machine working!' Indeed, Brown's greatest fear seems to be that 'no-one will ever believe me to be HARD when they read this'; precisely the kind of perception which, again, would lead indie pop to be denigrated in the coming years.[19] The crudely drawn image of a man blowing his own head in two with a shotgun which adorns issue 10 of *Attack on Bzag* (1985) is a world away from the visual feel of *Hungry Beat*. The latter is not quite the most canonical indie-pop fanzine, however; arguably that title should be reserved for *Are You Scared to Get Happy?* among the fanzines of the more full-fledged 1980s indie-pop era.

## Indie pop's halcyon days, 1985–87

It is worth pointing out, before we go any further, that the whole indie-pop scene developed in the context of the ten-year anniversary of the first wave of UK punk. This comes through very strongly in *Are You Scared to Get Happy?* (*AYSTGH?*), six issues of which were published between 1985 and 1987. In issue 1, for example, it is suggested that 'Punk-Rock is returning to its rightful owners, whether you like it or not!' while great hostility is shown to 'rebel pose' punks: 'for "politically sound" substitute dumb, humourless and drowning in dogma'.[20] Punk, in other words, still loomed large in the mid- to late 1980s as the paradigm in which 'indie-pop' music (not that this couplet was yet in use, or at least not in the fanzines of the era) needed to be framed; but there was a strong sense of going back to perceived roots. Writing in the closing days of 1985, issue 2 of *AYSTGH?* proclaims that 'In four days' time it's 1976, Happy New Year', and then mimics the famous (even back then) 'here's a chord … ' statement from *Sideburns* fanzine (1977), adding 'Grandad, what's a guitar?' The latter remark is arguably a criticism of the old punk scene and a demand for a new one: 'Wake-up, <u>look</u> up … FORWARDS … upwards and onwards'.[21] Such optimism is commonly tempered with disappointment in *AYSTGH?*, however: '10 years, and we're right back where we started … '[22] And yet, 'Punk-rock is alive and kicking in 1986 … ARE YOU?'[23]

Comparable to *Hungry Beat*'s criticism of the (bluntly leftist) Redskins and praise for the (more subtly left-leaning) Jasmine Minks, *AYSTGH?* is generally critical of left-leaning but noisy 'monochrome monstrosities' such as The Three Johns and The Membranes.[24] 'I DON'T WANT TO BE TOLD HOW HOPELESS EVERYTHING IS – I WANT TO BE SHOWN HOW GOOD IT CAN BE', the fanzine proclaims, for which reason it demands colourful pop rather than 'drab' noise.[25] This does not mean that the fanzine is apolitical, however: on the contrary, fear of nuclear holocaust is indicated on the next page of the fanzine in question, while 'certain government policies' are (rather vaguely) nodded toward.[26] The writers also ask 'what will happen when the Tories do depart and things maybe don't improve'; prescient words, one might add from a post-Blair perspective. Clearly it would be a mistake, then, to assume that fanzines like *AYSTGH?* had no political concerns; but it is also clear that something different from the anarchistic fanzines of the early 1980s had emerged by this point. It would appear that such tendencies were not entirely new: note, for example, that *The Brick* (1984) proclaims coverage of 'anarchism + good music' on its cover and goes on to declare itself 'the fanzine that sets out to prove that anarchists aren't all mohicans or people clad in leather jackets adorned by the Crass logo'.[27] Indie pop had some links to anarcho-punk: note, for example, Stephen 'Pastel' McRobbie's revelation that he booked The Pastels' first gig at Bearsden Burgh Hall precisely 'because he'd seen Crass play the same venue'.[28] We can also note The June Brides' early appearance on a bill with The Mob at the Anarchy Centre in Islington and the original title they had planned for their 1985 album: *Destroying Capitalism With The June Brides*.[29] Matt Haynes of *AYSTGH?*/Sarah Records has said that he 'suspects' Crass had a 'subliminal' influence upon 'the incorporation of politics into Sarah's releases and literature'.[30]

These links to anarcho-punk are not insignificant, and yet there are clear and strong differences between indie-pop and anarcho-punk. For one thing, the politics tend to nestle within a 'cute' context and, generally speaking, to be socialist rather than anarchist. *Adventures in Bereznik* (1985), for example, has an article on Milkybars (the popular confectionery, that is) but also encourages readers to go to the Tate Gallery and criticises '[Norman] Fowler's Welfare State "Reforms"'.[31] *Especially Yellow* (1984) recalls some anarcho-punk fanzines by writing 'Time For Action!' at the top of a page about the importance of CND; but the music the fanzine writes about is considerably less dark than one finds in anarcho-punk.[32] Likewise, *Trout Fishing in Leytonstone* (1985) has pro-animal liberation and anti-vivisection pages but the music covered is mostly upbeat indie pop.[33] Visually, meanwhile, indie-pop fanzines tend to be highly colourful, picturesque and fairly pretty; descriptors which can rarely be applied to anarcho-punk fanzines in particular and other punk fanzines more generally.

None of the indie-pop fanzines of the mid-1980s typifies this new visual aesthetic better than *AYSTGH?*, the design of which remains beguiling some thirty-years later. Indeed, *AYSTGH?* built on the work done by the fanzines mentioned in the previous section (especially *Hungry Beat*) to carve out a very clear set of aesthetic preferences and tendencies which essentially codified 1980s indie pop as a genre. If one looks at the tracklisting of Rough Trade's 2004 compilation *Indie Pop 1*, for example, barely any of the bands featured were included on *NME*'s *C86* cassette (the exceptions being The Pastels, Shop Assistants, Primal Scream, the Wedding Present and McCarthy). However, nearly all of the 46 featured groups (with the exception of a handful of post-1980s bands) were enthused about in the pages of *AYSTGH?*: The Razorcuts, Talulah Gosh, The Clouds, The Sea Urchins and so forth. Despite non-inclusion on the actual *C86* cassette, these last-named bands (and their type) have come to be called 'C86 bands' by many; the aforementioned list (Pastels *et al.*) which *were* featured on *C86*, meanwhile, go some way to explain the common association of indie pop with the cassette compilation in question. We should note, however, that *C86* also includes groups with more in common with The Fall and Captain Beefheart than Orange Juice: groups like bIG fLAME, A Witness, Bogshed and Stump.

It is odd, therefore, that a popular discourse exists which imagines that *NME* in particular and the music press in general more or less invented indie pop. Actually, the movement appeared largely because bands were mining a particular musical trajectory and fanzines were talking about those bands and their records while promoters were booking them and getting good crowds at gigs. Several fanzine writers were able to become staff writers at the music press on the back of their fanzine writing: 'The Legend!' (as he called himself in the early to mid-1980s, before taking the nom-de-plume 'Everett True' c. 1987), for example, and Simon Reynolds, who had previously edited *Monitor* fanzine/magazine. The fact that such employment occurred suggests strongly that the press felt they needed to keep up-to-date with the emerging scene: indeed, The Legend! wrote several pages for *NME* on the new wave of fanzines in late 1985, while Reynolds wrote an extensive piece on fanzines for *Melody Maker* in January 1987. The Legend! (or Jerry Thackray, his real name which he now often uses) expressed amazement to me when he showed me the clipping of the 1985 piece because he had not mentioned *AYSTGH?*: this shows us, perhaps, that the latter fanzine had not yet become canonical in late 1985.[34]

Simon Reynolds, writing about fanzines in the *Melody Maker* issue dated 24 January 1987, by contrast, firmly acknowledges the influential position of *AYSTGH?* by that point. With the cover of the second issue of the fanzine reproduced among the text, Reynolds prefaces his comments about *AYSTGH?* by remarking that: 'The best fanzines are written by monomaniacs, with no sense of proportions'.[35] 'The bloke behind "Are You Scared To Get Happy?" is exemplary', he goes on, 'with his Luddite crusade against 12-inch singles'. The crusade in question was waged because *AYSTGH?* and fanzines which followed it believed that the 7-inch single was a perfect format for (punk) pop whereas the twelve-inch was simply being used as a marketing ploy to allow supposedly 'indie' (and thus ostensibly faithful to a certain conception of punk) record labels to make more profit per unit. *AYSTGH?* certainly did

**9.1**   *Are You Scared To Get Happy?*, 2 (1986) © Matt Haynes (original cover is in colour)

militate against the relatively new record format in question, and the bands and labels which used it, complaining that one band had issued 'a 3-track 12", for which they deserve to be spat at in the street'.[36]

Reynolds was well poised to say something about fanzines and indie pop in 1986, having covered the emerging scene in *Monitor*. Although David Stubbs had complained therein that leading indie-pop band The June Brides 'would always be grey at heart ... A lump of lead is tied to their legs', Chris Scott (of Talulah Gosh) noted more enthusiastically that: 'The example of the TV Personalities has been taken up' by a generation of groups such as Shop Assistants, Pastels and Woodentops – but also, interestingly, the Membranes.[37] The latter were slated in *AYSTGH?* with alarming regularity but actually, many of the fanzines of the period happily covered the 'noisier' side of the mid-1980s indie scene at large (as opposed to the indie-pop scene more narrowly). From c. 1986 *Big and Bouncy, Tambourine, Pure Popcorn, The Legend!, Slow Dazzle, Return to Bereznik, Bludgeoned, Lemonade, Bitter Sweet, Rumbledethump!, Bandits One to Five* and countless others had no problem placing the likes of Bogshed, Stump and Age of Chance alongside The Pastels, Talulah Gosh and The Chesterfields.

It would be unfair to paint *AYSTGH?* as a narrow and 'purist' indie-pop fanzine, however. Admittedly, issue 2 (issued in early 1986) declares a dislike for Sonic Youth and also, more pointedly, A Witness, Bogshed and UK bands of that type who would soon appear on the *C86* tape. 'John Peel's lumped them all together as "Shambling Bands", he meant it as a compliment ... Bands shouldn't "shamble", Mr. Peel, they should burn in bright colours and go POP!'.[38] We can note that the writers also praise Hüsker Dü, however; not a band which would normally be classified as indie pop.[39] Issue 3 (1986), meanwhile, covers The Flys, Patrick Fitzgerald and even The Cure. In Issue 4, the writer proclaims that 'SOMETIMES I just crave NOISE and VIOLENCE', going on to name check noisy American bands such as Meat Puppets, Black Flag, Squirrelbait and, again, Hüsker Dü. By contrast, 'POPmusic as some big docile baby, this worries me, this sort of atmosphere breeds crap like the Wishing Stones and fucking Weather Prophets, y'know, sit-down-and-listen-to-our-songs-boys-and-girls because we are Master-Craftsmen-Songwriters and-you-are-very-priveliged-to-be-watching-us' [sic]. In *The Sun Shines Here* (1985, classified as issue 1.5 of *AYSTGH?* by Matt Haynes), the fanzine writer had decided that he did like bIG fLAME despite his objection to the 'shambling' bands in general.[40]

*AYSTGH?* was a somewhat contradictory fanzine, then. For example, the issue of *AYSTGH?* entitled *The Sun Shines Here* complains that 'the indie scene these days is as sterile as the majors were in '76'.[41] Complaints about major labels and, indeed, indie labels ripping off the fans are consistent in the fanzine. However, we are told that Microdisney are 'fucking CLASSIC' despite, as the writers note, being on a major label.[42] We can also note, in *The Sun Shines Here*, that Haynes declares that 'THE WORST THING I CAN THINK OF WOULD BE TO SEE HURRAH! RECORDS IN THE RACKS IN WOOL-WORTHS ... IT'D BE GREAT FOR THE BAND – FINANCIALLY AND

FAME-WISE – BUT SO MANY DREAMS WOULD BE BOUND TO DIE WITH IT TOO.'[43] This is an odd argument since he also has said he wants them to be on *Top of the Pops* and selling huge numbers of records, just like The Jam and Undertones had (who, of course, had their records sold in Woolworths). That said, an irrational and hate-filled rant follows this, arguably suggesting that the writer had either been drinking or was in a state of near hysteria at the time he wrote it. Perhaps hysteria and irrationalism was an intentional element within this, and other fanzines – part of the style of the time.

By 1988, the major labels (which had signed, directly or indirectly through 'schmindies', groups such as Primal Scream, Stump and the Shop Assistants in 1987) were looking away from the indie pop which, in 1986, the music papers had briefly lauded. The fanzines of this period are rather distinct from the 1985 to 1987 period: many concern themselves with the tags 'cutie', 'anorak' and so forth and most attack the music press vociferously. Some distance themselves from indie pop; some look back forlornly and some try to stay true to some kind of 'original spirit'.

## Years of decline, 1988–92

*AYSTGH?* was immediately influential upon many fanzines during the years in which it was published. *Adventure in Bereznik* declared in 1986, regarding *The Sun Shines Here* issue of *AYSTGH?*, that 'every fanziner should read this, decide which side they're on or rip it up and start again. Reassess! This is the best fanzine of 1985.'[44] We can note with interest, furthermore, that where *AYSTGH?* had complained bitterly about the mundanity of John Robb's *Rox* fanzine and *The Legend!*, by 1987 *The Dream Inspires* fanzine would be complaining of fanzine writers feeling they had 'got to say what John Robb, The Legend!, Matt Haynes etc. would like us to say'.[45] Other fanzines were certainly important in blazing the trail for the proliferation of interest in indie pop around 1985 – *Adventure in Bereznik* was already highlighting '[a] guitar sound that can only be described as "jangly"' in 1985, for example.[46] Indeed, the likes of *Adventure in Bereznik*, *Trout Fishing in Leytonstone* and *Simply Thrilled* were more 'fellow travellers' than followers of the selection of bands/songs/sounds and visual elements that *AYSTGH?* developed.

*AYSTGH?* was influential, then, but it was not the only important fanzine of the mid-1980s.[47] By the end of 1987, however, it was the fanzine most likely to be lauded by other (and newer) fanzines. *373 Miles is a Very Long Way* (1987), for example, gives 'Thanks to Matt who made all this possible (so blame him!) ... '[48] *Disposable But Happy* (1988) clearly takes titular inspiration from *AYSTGH?* and is unabashed in its praise of the latter zine.[49] Leading late 1980s indie-pop fanzine *Woosh* is effusive in its praise of the Sha-la-la flexi-disc label (co-ordinated by *AYSTGH?*, alongside several other mid-1980s fanzines).[50] Such examples of praise are innumerable, but we should note that there is also dissent: *But That's Downbeat and Ridiculous, Sharon!* (1987) complains about 'All these CRAP fanzines just trying to hit the peak that AYSTGH did ... It was great, it made me goa [*sic*] and buy 3 records I'd never heard'. 'Yes I loved them', the writer goes on, 'but it was that writing that made me do it. Now on issue 349316, it is has passed the limit it's BORING now [*sic*].'[51]

There is a noticeable turn against indie pop from within the fanzine ranks from late 1987 onwards, in fact. 'Compare the lack of good debut singles this year to 85/86', complains *Simply Thrilled*.[52] 'Do you remember what it was like 2 years or so ago ... sat in our teen angst bedrooms distributing flexidiscs with a conspiratorial smirk ... ?', writes *Far Out and Fishy* in 1990.[53] Most of the fanzines of the post-*C86* period show a strong resentment that they and their bands ('the scene', as we might put it today) have been packaged by the music press as 'cuties' and 'anoraks'. For example, *Pop Eats Apathy* complains in 1989 about 'cutie-bashing' and people being 'venomous' towards him and the cutie bands. 'I'm not a cutie. In fact I'm really nasty and horrible. Meet me at the bar at any gig after a pint of Tetleys and I'll prove it', writes *Waaaaaah!* in 1991, with a humorous article about 'outing cuties' ('we want YOU to name anyone you believe to be a closet cutie ... ') in the back pages.[54] By that time, the indie-pop scene was much diminished in size, partly due, perhaps, to the negative labelling which the music press had developed. Indeed, indie pop dwindled by 1990 to the extent that *Far Out and Fishy* speculated whether Heavenly might have been 'the beginning of the cutie revival?' We should note, though, that *Adventures in Bereznik* was already grumbling about 'anoraks [because] you'd never get me into one' in late 1986; 'it irritates me because when the trend dies, the bands who are unfortunate enough to be associated with anoraks will automatically become "old hat" in the eyes of nme/sounds/mm. TWATS!'[55]

In this post-*C86* period, the music press turned venomously on the indie-pop/cutie/anorak groups and, in turn, much of the public and some of the bands did the same. In a 1989 issue of *Woosh* fanzine, for example, The Brilliant Corners reveal their perception that association with 'every "jangley [*sic*], love torn, poppy, wipsey dipsey do-dah band"' has brought them bad press through association.[56] In an issue of the same fanzine from the previous year, Remember Fun suggest that: 'You've got to try and rise above that indie ghetto ... Talulah

Gosh, Vaselines and most of that Sarah Records type shit'.[57] Interestingly, Talulah Gosh, Vaselines and the Sarah label are remembered as 'legendary' by many in the twenty-first century, while Remember Fun are almost completely forgotten. More important for our purposes, however, is the perception at that time among many bands that, if a decent audience and the ear of the music press were to be gained, a step away from the indie-pop sound would be necessary.

Sarah was an exception to this, very much staying with the indie-pop sound and visual aesthetic style post-1987. Matt Haynes of *AYSTGH?* co-ran Sarah Records with *Kvatch* editor Clare Wadd from 1987 until 1995. In this period, Haynes and Wadd became particularly aggressive towards the music press and the music industry. For example, Haynes had been initially inspired by Alan McGee and Creation but in the later issues of *AYSTGH?* he became increasingly critical. By the time of the *Sarah 4* fanzine his hostility had become vitriolic.[58] 'We mustn't criticise [1988 low budget compilation album] *Doing It For The Kids* because Alan McGee lost lots of money … ', Haynes suggested in his *Cold* fanzine (issued by the Sarah label), sarcastically asking 'what's a full page ad. in the NME cost, Alan..?' immediately afterwards.[59] The complaint is that Creation were working the system with a 'loss leader' as we would say today: a cheap 'sampler' compilation would advertise the label's other products and the money lost on manufacturing (due to the album's retail price being equivalent to that of a seven-inch vinyl single at the time) would be regained through full-page articles in the weekly music papers. Haynes also asks 'why the sleeves [of the low-budget 7-inch singles which Creation issued around the time of *Doing It For The Kids*] had to proclaim their cheapness when all one colour layouts cost the same'.[60] Was McGee attempting to retain a low-budget image while his label was in fact edging towards the mainstream? Haynes clearly thought so, and we can note that McGee would sell a majority share of Creation to Sony within a few years.

Sarah struck a note of punk rock principle at the very point where the likes of Creation were selling shares to the majors and former indie-pop bands were getting into the 'indie dance crossover' sound of c. 1989–91. The label stuck up for the indie-pop scene: 'bands … get scorned as "cutie" just 'cos folk haven't the guts or imagination to think for themselves'.[61] The cause of the problem was perceived as the music press: NME, *Sarah 4* argues, have 'enough bigotries and prejudices to fill a whole year of newsprint, repeat after me: cutiesanoraksshamblingcutiesanoraksshamblingcutiesano …' Bigotry and prejudice are reasonable words to describe the UK's weekly inkies' attitude towards diehard cutie groups in general and Sarah in particular at this time: the music press frequently offered vitriolic abuse and hostility, as Michael White's excellent book on Sarah amply demonstrates. One example, chosen almost at random, would be a Blueboy review from 1992: 'Acoustic strumming, feeble, breathless posho whining about being sad ... Everything about this song is as irritatingly twee as the name of the group suggests. The vocals are particularly pathetic.'[62]

Why this intense hatred? One possible answer is that the music was simply of a poor quality and that this fact annoyed the journalists in question. Such a position is somewhat unsatisfactory, however. For one thing, as White shows, reviews for innumerable releases on the Sarah label were positive in the extreme; as a rule, though, these positive reviews would be prefaced with an assertion that the music was atypical for Sarah. The truth is that the label released quite a variety of musical styles across its catalogue, including electronic music of different kinds and some quite polished pop music as well as the 'shambolic' stuff with which it was generally associated. The label hoped that reviewers would not treat its releases 'as a "Sarah album" or an "indie album". Just review it as an album, full stop.'[63] For whatever reason, though, the 'cutie' reputation stuck (although, by the early 1990s, journalists were more prone to calling such music 'twee') and the reputation of the label always seemed to override the reputations of individual bands, with the possible exception of Heavenly. Bands released by Sarah were perceived as 'Sarah bands', in short, and the label was certainly highly unpopular with a significant chunk of the music press.

Elements of the antipathy were mutual, we should note. For example, an early 1988 press release from Sarah informed the reader (journalists at large, that is) that they were 'stupid and jaded and sweetly bereft of all wit'; 'You're a jerk basically ... We think you're a real fuck-up.'[64] Their fanzines, meanwhile, never tired of criticising the music papers: *Sarah 4* complains of 'papers like the NME – so priggishly moral, so intolerantly "right-on", yet no original thought or IMAGINATION ever informs what they say'. Perhaps, then, the inkies' attacks on Sarah were as much a retribution for such hostility as they were an outright attack. This seems hard to believe: if the press really wanted to damage Sarah, the best option would surely have been to ignore them. Moreover, the music press looks to have been slightly threatened by the 1980s indie-pop movement, probably in large part because it was fanzines rather than the weekly papers which were so central to the scene.

Another possible reason for the music press's vehement hatred in the 1990s of 1980s-recalling indie pop is a base homophobia and/or sexism/masculine-supremacism. For example, Clare Wadd of Sarah draws our attention to a review which complained of 'Yet another twee Sarah record with twee girl vocals' which was in fact Sarah's thirtieth release but its first with a female vocal.[65] Michael White, who is himself gay, points out in his book on Sarah that the press would describe the music 'as twee or fey or slack-wristed, or [offer] characterisations of the bands themselves as sissies or virgins or remedials'.[66] At this time, Heavenly (featuring Amelia Fletcher of core cutie group Talulah Gosh) were singing about date rape, implying lesbianism and promoting pro-choice in various different songs. Sarah's self-proclaimed 'pro-gay band' Blueboy are a particularly interesting case: 'the oppressiveness of sexuality, the fluidity of gender and desire, the simultaneous thrill and sadness of romantic and sexual thrill-seeking' were central themes for the band in question, White suggests.[67] In punk-recalling fashion, Blueboy 'didn't want fame. We didn't want money'; rather, they wanted to challenge government legislation such as the homophobic 'Clause 28' of the period in question.[68] The *Sarah 70* fanzine (1993), which came with a free flexi by Blueboy (or, one could say, the fanzine came free with the flexi), supports the impression of Blueboy as a revolutionary band for homosexuals: 'I can walk down the street holding some boy's hand and we're REVOLUTIONARIES ... Bloody minded enough to turn this fucking country's lazy spineless bigotry to our own advantage ... '[69]

Some of these themes went back to the emergent/classic indie-pop era of the early to mid-1980s. We can note, for example, *Hungry Beat*'s complaint that disliking stuff for being 'wimpy' is 'what's expected of you in this society'.[70] In *Big Bad Fire Engine* (1986) The June Brides are asked: 'Are you annoyed about being branded as wimps?' They answer, 'No. Annoyed that wimp is a derogatory term? Yes.'[71] *Diana Rigg* (1986) complains about 'chicken dancers' who go 'punching forward violently' when, for example, Shop Assistants play 'Safety Net'; 'Oh aren't they hard men? Of course, I'm not a real man because I only get hot and sweaty by jumping around (punk rock pogoing anyone?) and smiling'.[72] Such issues would become central to the Riot Grrrl scene of 1992 to 1994, much of which (in the UK, at least) had links to the 1980s indie-pop scene, as I have discussed elsewhere.[73] By then, however, the fanzines of indie-pop's halcyon days were hard to find and rarely remembered.

## Conclusion

1980s indie pop was largely forgotten by the mid-1990s, with 'indie' in the Brit-Pop era being a very different beast. Eventually, some of the twenty-first-century generation looked back in interest to the 1980s cutie scene, probably thanks to the rise of Belle and Sebastian in part (and other, less famous bands such as Comet Gain, arguably). *The Cuckoo Press* (2006) from Newcastle upon Tyne, for example, devoted a lengthy article to the *C86* tape in which the young writer marvelled that the groups on the compilation 'reminded me of Umlaut, The Long Blondes, the Research, Art Brut' and other younger bands of the era. 'All the records I buy at the moment seem to have been jumbled together in some way on someone's bedroom floor, hand stamped, hand numbered, or even hand drawn', the writer remarks, and she clearly feels that this makes it comparable to the 1980s indie pop era.[74]

There should be no question that indie pop relates to punk, as this chapter has tried to show. It was also a political scene, to an extent which has been insufficiently recognised in much writing on 1980s indie pop. Much of the politics of indie pop comes through most strongly in fanzines. We should not overstate the political strengths of indie-pop in particular and (as some scholars tend to do) of DIY in general: Scott Plagenhoef is right to point out that 'C86 was inclusive for the same reason it's restrictive – so long as you were interested in the music, you were welcome'.[75] This restriction means that elements of the indie-pop scene which we might value politically, such as its DIY inclusivity, need to be considered in the context of larger factors certainly including ethnicity, gender, class and so forth.

In summary, fanzines were crucial to the emergence of indie pop in the mid-1980s. The mainstream music press of the day came to the party a little later, and fairly quickly became hostile to indie pop. Fanzines kept something of a scene going for several years, however. By the mid-1990s, the indie-pop scene was virtually non-existent, with many former participants getting involved in riot grrrl or, in some cases, dance music and other generic areas. Indie pop has, however, had a resurgence in the twenty-first century, with groups like Martha and Allo Darlin' sharing many aesthetic and/or political interests with the 1980s scene. Fanzines remain contributors to the new scene around indie pop, up to a point, but whether the fanzines which are being published at present could (in the future) attain the level of allure and excitement which the 1980s fanzines retain today is open to question. Clearly, though, indie pop is not yet entirely finished; indeed, many of the 1980s indie-pop bands have reformed in recent years and played to crowds which are probably bigger than any they earned 'back in the day'. The records and fanzines from the 1980s fetch quite high prices among collectors, furthermore. Perhaps, then, indie pop was less frivolous and throwaway than it appeared at a time when fanzines proudly displayed a 35 pence price tag.

## Notes

Acknowledgements: Thanks to Fearghus Roulston and Ruth Collingwood for help in accessing the fanzine archives at the British Library and the London College of Communication respectively. Thanks are also due to Amelia Fletcher, Jerry Thackray, Clare Wadd, Matt Haynes, Sean Price, Tim Neave, Christopher de Coulon Berthoud and David Feck for sharing with me their personal archives of 1980s indie-pop fanzines for this research.

1   *Last Train to Eastleigh*, 1 (2015). The fanzine is formed of a single sheet with multiple folds.
2   *Born Yesterday*, 1 (1981), p. 7.
3   *Ibid.*, p. 11, p. 20 and, as regards the writer having 'swallowed my pride' after the Freshies major label deal, p. 4. By 1981, a pro-indie/anti-major orthodoxy was common to many fanzines, hence the 'worry' in question.
4   *Orange Juice: 'A' side*, 1 (c. 1981), p. 3.
5   *Josef K: 'B' side*, 1 (c. 1981), p. 4.
6   *Ibid.*, p. 5.
7   *Juniper Beri-Beri*, 1 (1982), p. 19 (odd punctuation retained).
8   *Especially Yellow*, 1 (1983), p. 9.
9   *Ibid.*, p. 14.
10  Another example of the emerging canonisation of indie-pop influences is represented in *Slow Dazzle*, 5 (1984), pp. 26–7. In an interview, Stephen Pastel emphasises the importance of The Undertones, Buzzcocks, Television Personalities, Clare Grogan (Altered Images) and Postcard Records.
11  *Fun 'n' Frenzy*, 1 (1983), p. 4.
12  *Ibid.*, p. 6.
13  *Hungry Beat*, 1 (1984), p. 4.
14  *Ibid.*, pp. 4–5.
15  *Ibid.*, p. 16.
16  *Hungry Beat*, 2 (1985), p. 25.
17  *Hungry Beat*, 1 (1984), p. 14.
18  *Rox*, 26 (1985) does feature The Pastels and Buba and the Shop Assistants (p. 18). However, the bulk of the coverage is 'popular/noise combos': The Three Johns, Bogshed and so forth.
19  *Attack on Bzag*, 7 (1984), p. 18.
20  *Are You Scared To Get Happy?*, 1 (1985), pp. 4–6.
21  *Are You Scared To Get Happy?*, 2 (1986), p. 5.
22  *Ibid.*, p. 29.
23  *Ibid.*, p. 35.
24  *Hungry Beat*, 2 (1985), pp. 20–1; *Are You Scared To Get Happy?*, 1 (1985), p. 3.
25  *The Sun Shines Here*, 1 (1985), which is essentially *AYSTGH?*, issue one and a half, was written solely by Matt Haynes (with the acquiescence of his writing partner in *AYSTGH?*). The fanzine was essentially a stop gap before the second *AYSTGH?* was ready for publication.
26  *Ibid.*, p. 9.
27  *The Brick*, 1 (1984), p. 2. The writer professes enthusiasm for Poison Girls, Conflict and The Three Johns but mostly covers what will come to be known as 'indie pop': June Brides, One Thousand Violins, Television Personalities, The Pastels and suchlike.
28  *The Guardian*, 1 March 2016.
29  Private correspondence with the June Brides' vocalist Phil Wilson; the *Destroying Capitalism* … title got far enough that Wilson mocked up cover art, which this author has seen.

30  Michael White, *Popkiss: The Life and Afterlife of Sarah Records* (London: Bloomsbury, 2015), p. 31.

31  *Adventures in Bereznik*, 2 (1985), pp. 6–7.

32  *Especially Yellow*, 4 (1984), p. 16.

33  *Trout Fishing in Leytonstone*, 1 (1985) pp. 12–14.

34  Alternatively, Jerry 'The Legend!' Thackray may have been hostile to *AYSTGH?* at the time and subsequently forgotten his antipathy: note that in *The Legend*, 4 (1986), he suggests that one should only buy "'Are You ... " [Scared to Get Happy?] after getting *Hungry Beat*'; the attacks on his fanzine in *AYSTGH?* may have rankled more 'back in the day' than they do in retrospect, therefore. Thackray was certainly unambiguous about the salient influence *AYSTGH?* held in the 1980s when I spoke to him in late 2016.

35  *Melody* Maker, 24 January 1987 (page number unknown).

36  *The Sun Shines Here*, p. 26.

37  *Monitor*, 5 (1986), pp. 6 and 12.

38  *Are You Scared To Get Happy?*, 2 (1986), p. 4. 'A Witness and Co' represent 'a cul-de-sac', he adds on p. 5.

39  *Ibid.*, p. 26.

40  *The Sun Shines Here*, p. 22.

41  *Ibid.*, p. 21.

42  *Ibid.*, p. 18.

43  *Ibid.*, p. 14 (capitalisation retained).

44  *Adventure in Bereznik*, 5 (1986), p. 7.

45  *The Dream Inspires*, 1 (1987), p. 3.

46  *Sarah 4* (the fourth item issued by the Sarah label) for this and all other quotes in this paragraph.

47  *Adventures in Bereznik*, 2 (1985), p. 3.

48  *373 Miles is a Very Long Way*, 1 (1987), p. 2.

49  *Disposable But Happy*, 2 (1988), p. 12.

50  *Woosh*, 3 (1988), p. 14.

51  *But That's Downbeat and Ridiculous, Sharon!*, 1 (1988), p. 54.

52  *Simply Thrilled*, 4 (1987), p. 4.

53  *Far Out and Fishy*, 3 (1990), p. 6.

54  *Waaaaaah!*, 3 (1991), pp. 2 and 25.

55  *Adventures in Bereznik*, 6 (1986), p. 16.

56  *Woosh*, 4 (1989), p. 3.

57  *Woosh*, 3 (1988), p. 14.

58  *Sarah 4* (1988).

59  *Cold* (1989), catalogue number Sarah 14AA.

60  *Ibid.*

61  *Sarah 4* for this and the next quotation.

62  White, *Popkiss*, p. 186.

63  *Ibid.*, p. 190.

64  *Ibid.*, p. 75.

65  *Ibid.*, pp. 171–2.

66  *Ibid.*

67  *Ibid.*, p. 191.

68  *Ibid.*, p. 183.

69  *Sarah 70* (1993), p. 8.

70  *Hungry Beat*, 1 (1984), p. 22.

71  *Big Bad Fire Engine*, 1 (1986), p. 6.

72  *Diana Rigg*, 1 (1986), p. 27.

73  Pete Dale, *Anyone Can Do It: Empowerment, Tradition and the Punk Underground* (Aldershot: Ashgate, 2012), p. 177.

74  *The Cuckoo Press* (2006), issue and page number unknown.

75  Scott Plagenhoef, *If You're Feeling Sinister* (London: Bloomsbury, 2007), p. 53.

# III

# Memos from the frontline: locating the source

# 10

# Vague post-punk memoirs, 1979–89

TOM VAGUE

*Vague* covers a boring Salisbury–Bournemouth sort of area with enthusiasm.

Kris Needs, *Zigzag* (1980)

At the end of the 1970s, as punk rock became post-punk and Margaret Thatcher came to power, *Vague* fanzine was founded at Salisbury College of Technology and Art (now Wiltshire College) by Perry Harris, Iggy Zevenbergen and me. Perry's '*Vague* beginnings' cartoon illustrates the idea's conception with us saying: 'Salisbury's boring. There's nothing to do ... Let's start a fanzine ... What shall we call it? ... Let's base it on a real magazine.' Thus began *Vague* as a provincial post-punk DIY spoof of *Vogue*, anti-style magazine for the 1980s, also involving a certain amount of vagary and vagrancy.

*Vague* wasn't a 'punk rock fanzine', historically speaking, but it had authentic, irreverent punk attitude, DIY design and semi-literate, stream-of-consciousness reports. Described as 'a huge and interesting pub anecdote in print' (*NME*, 7 May 1983) and 'a sort of disjointed autobiography, with special attention to how drunk he got' (*Sheep Worrying*, February 1982), *Vague* epitomised the punk principle that anyone could produce a magazine or form a band, even if they didn't have any journalistic or musical ability. It was, at the same time, an attempt to keep the spirit of punk going and a post-punk quest to find something new. We didn't use the term post-punk then, but we were into groups that were experimental or unusual in some way and critical of nostalgic, traditional punk rock.

The first few issues were co-edited by Perry, Iggy and me, before I assumed more or less total editorial control and adopted 'Vague' as my punk nom de plume (though it is a real surname found in Cornwall). The editorial staff included my girlfriend Jane Austin (not Austen), Chris Johnson, Sharon Clarkson and Christine Nugent. *Vague* was largely based in Mere, a small town to the west of Salisbury, where some of us lived. Previously, I had kept scrapbooks of punk gig tickets, flyers and press clippings, as we went on expeditions to Bournemouth, Bath and Bristol to see The Clash, The Damned, Buzzcocks, X-Ray Spex and so on. The idea of doing a fanzine began to evolve in 1978, inspired by *Sniffin' Glue*, *Ripped & Torn*, the Salisbury art college fanzine *Ignite* and Tim Aylet's *Channel 4* (from Corsham). The *Vague* interview technique developed from ligging with the likes of The Jam, Sham 69 and The Pop Group. I first went backstage at Bournemouth Village Bowl to lig with Eater when they played with Slaughter and the Dogs. This could be seen as the first *Vague* interview, but all I remember of it is somebody asking 'Have you got any more badges?' and one of them saying 'No.'

The first *Vague* editorial meeting took place after a Siouxsie and the Banshees, Spizz Oil and Gang of Four gig at the Village, during which Chris Johnson and I took speed for the first time. As we talked rubbish about punk till dawn, we started planning to do a post-punk fanzine featuring Adam and the Ants, the Banshees, Joy Division and PIL. Chris began *Vague* merchandising, screen-printing dayglo-green John Lydon shirts and posters at the art college. We were particularly into Adam and the Ants in their pre-pop post-punk prime, when they described their music as 'the new new super heavy punk funk'. At this stage, they were reviled by the mainstream music press as decadent S&M/Nazi art school posers, which enhanced their appeal as a hip cult somewhere between the Sex Pistols and the Velvet Underground. After first seeing them in Salisbury during a bikers' riot, we became part of their cult following and got involved in more aggro on the 'Young Parisians' and 'Zerox' tours.

*Vague* was launched on the world in the wake of the first Futurama science-fiction/post-punk festival in Leeds featuring PIL and Joy Division. As Perry puts it in his forthcoming *Vague* graphic novel, 'We began writing reviews of gigs in Salisbury and Bournemouth, doing interviews with local bands, a few drawings, photos and jokes, which were cut and pasted together with scissors and glue.' From my point of view, *Vague* was an anti-art production, although it started as an art school fanzine: I was at the technical college doing building studies but most of the other punks in Salisbury were art students.

*Vague* 1 consisted of two offset litho-printed A3 sheets, one green, one black, folded and stapled, designed and printed by Mark Cross from the art

**10.1** *'Vague* Beginnings' by Perry Harris (supplied with permission of Tom Vague)

**10.2** '*Vague* Beginnings' by Perry Harris (supplied with permission of Tom Vague)

**10.3** *'Vague* Beginnings' by Perry Harris (supplied with permission of Tom Vague)

college, who went on to design album sleeves. The early issues featured reviews of gigs by the Ants and the Banshees, the Two-Tone and Rough Trade tours, the Mere Youth Club punk festival and our first interviews with Gang of Four, Red Crayola, Joy Division and The Clash. There was also some reggae coverage and pieces on such local post-punk heroes as Program, Animals & Men, The Kitchens and Stalag 44. By issue 3, the *Vague* printers had become Skittles in Gillingham, Dorset, run by a hippy couple – Rob and Sue – from London. They produced the rest of the colourful offset litho issues and the first *Vague* annuals. Most of the typing, cutting, pasting, folding and stapling was done in Mere, in my bedroom and The Ship pub.

At the height of the post-punk fanzine boom, as Simon Dwyer wrote in *Sounds*: 'Every day the seditious seeds planted by *Sniffin' Glue* and *Ripped & Torn* bear some unlikely fruit. Every day another young editor staggers proudly under the Westway with a new bag of radical reading matter, making the three minute trip from one bright spark of the current explosion, Better Badges, to the other, Rough Trade … In every corner of the country there seems to be something going on … (including) Wiltshire's *Vauge* [*sic*].'[1] To begin with, *Vague* was fairly typical of the fanzines that began to pile up in the Rough Trade shop. On our first trip to west London with a consignment of issue 2, we were initially discouraged by the better produced fanzines on display at 202 Kensington Park Road, but encouraged to keep doing *Vague* by Mayo Thompson of Red Crayola, Sue Donne, who coordinated the Rough Trade fanzine distribution network, and Joly MacFie's Better Badges at 286 Portobello Road (who printed fanzines on a 'pay-as-you-sell' basis).

As I left college and signed on in the summer of 1980, the *Vague* 5 'Ants Special' came out, featuring an interview with Adam Ant and an 'Ants Invasion' tour report – including skinhead trouble at High Wycombe, anti-southerner aggro in Middlesbrough and our first expedition north of the border. This was as Adam relaunched the Ants with Marco Pirroni and two drummers. In the wake of being managed by Malcolm McLaren, who went off with the old Ants to form Bow Wow Wow, Adam started to go in a more commercial direction. He advised us to do likewise and be more like the glossy 'professional'-looking *In the City* fanzine than 'Tony D, of *Ripped & Torn* and *Kill Your Pet Puppy* fame. He used to have a sense of humour, now it's worse than the worst political hippy magazine. Keep politics out of art.'[2] Disregarding Adam's advice, the next issue featured The Pop Group and Crass.

*Vague* sales peaked with issue 7, which doubled as the programme for Adam and the Ants' pop breakthrough 'Kings of the Wild Frontier' tour. This was basically a reprint of issue 5 with a different colour cover; pink rather than green. The 'Antzine' was sold on the tour merchandising stall and presented to the Antperson of the night at each gig as Antmania took hold of the nation. At this time, Tony Fletcher wrote in *Jamming* that 'Vague is growing a deserved reputation as one of the best about. In fact, could prove to be the eventual successor to *Ripped & Torn*. It's frequently scruffy, badly printed and incomplete, but must be the most regular fast-growing fanzine about. It's got that hard punk attitude, lots of colour and plenty of spirit. Suffered even more than *Panache* from being an Antperson to the extent that it sold 4,000 copies of an Ants special on their last tour, and then spent the whole of the next issue slagging them off'.[3]

At the end of the Ants tour, I jumped ship to Bow Wow Wow and got their thoughts on sun, sea and cassette piracy, the recession and World's End. After that *Vague's* fortunes went into decline: my Ants book failed to find a publisher and the *Vague* Promotions gig by Martian Dance in Bournemouth was a financial disaster. Then we were evicted from our flat in Bournemouth which doubled as the *Vague* office and I was dumped by Jane Austin. I spent the rest of the early 1980s pretty much as a real vagrant, hitching around the country following tours of Siouxsie and the Banshees (featured in *Vague* 10 and *Zigzag*), Bow Wow Wow, Classix Nouveaux, Theatre of Hate and Wasted Youth, selling fanzines, T-shirts and badges. In retrospect, this seems like typical Thatcher youth activity; but at the time we thought we were rebelling against it.

By *Vague* 11 the office was at its most prestigious address, 34 The Paragon in Bath. This issue featured Crass, CND, the Brixton riots and the Charles and Diana royal wedding, *Viz Comics* and the Velvet Underground. *Vague* coverage of Crass and anarcho-punk fluctuated from critical and dismissive to quite enthusiastic. I don't mind being called an anarcho-punk now but at the time it was as bad an insult as new romantic – *Vague* was somewhere between the two dubious early 1980s sub-cults. In the Ants versus Crass, sex/anarcho-punk schism, we were with the former and against the 'cult of Crass', responsible for inspiring hordes of identikit bands and fanzines, when the whole point of anarchy/punk was to be yourself/individual. But I had some sympathy for their political stance, if not their style or music, and was won over to the cause after putting on a Crass gig in Salisbury and interviewing them for *Zigzag*. The £1 ticket sell-out gig at the Fawlty Towers-esque Grange Hotel was *Vague* Promotions' finest hour, featuring anarcho-punks camped out in the trees surrounding the venue and biker and skinhead kids united.

Not everyone fell for *Vague's* anarcho-romantic charm. According to *Sheep Worrying* fanzine: 'As a review of the would-be street credible music scene *Vague* is irritating, affected and superficial, but as an unwitting expose of the kind of parasite Tom Vague is, it is sometimes fascinating. Tom Vague spends a very small proportion of his lengthy articles writing about the gigs or records he purports to be reviewing … The clever title/cover design lead you to expect some wit, but *Vague* is mostly humourless, the only laughs come from some cartoons that turn out to be cribbed from a Newcastle fanzine called *Viz Comics*.[4]

*Vague* was summed up more favourably by Ray Lowry in *The Face* as 'an above average, funny collection of opinions and bitcheries about post-sporran music trends. In issue 13 there was a really amusing cartoon section (by Perry), a William Burroughs primer (by our counterculture columnist Pete Scott), a hippy-bashing Glastonbury piece, WOMAD report and pieces on *Vague* faves Death Cult and Sex Gang'.[5] After featuring such post-punk/proto-goth bands as Bauhaus, Theatre of Hate, UK Decay and Danse Society, we got into Southern Death Cult and Sex Gang Children, who were seen as successors of Adam and the Ants and attracted similar cult followings. The former took Adam's Indian thing further and more seriously; the latter picked up on the dark decadent sex imagery.

In 1983, the *Vague* office relocated from Bath to squats in Brixton, Elephant and Castle and Islington. *Vague* 14, the first London issue, contained the last interview with Southern Death Cult and the first with Death Cult, as Ian Astbury was staying at our Islington squat on New North Road when he teamed up with Billy Duffy from Theatre of Hate. At the height of the positive-punk/goth scene and the revival of *Zigzag* magazine under the editorship of Mick Mercer (of *Panache* fanzine and *Melody Maker*) – the nearest I got to being a proper music journalist – *Vague* became an annual publication. As I subsequently distanced myself from goth, normal music coverage was largely ditched in favour of general countercultural stuff. The 1984 issue, *Vague* 15, featured the anti-capitalist Stop the City protests and *The End of Music* pamphlet (1978) by the Wise brothers, which began the *Vague* obsession with the situationists and psychogeography, along with Charles Manson and the Church of the Sub-Genius. That year I ended up in Stoke Newington as the area became a hotbed of cider-drinking anarcho-punk crusties with dogs on bits of string.

After a few more address changes, I spent most of the mid-1980s at 7 Evering Road – opposite where the Angry Brigade were busted and a couple of doors along from where Jack 'the hat' McVitie was bumped off by the Krays – reading situationist texts, conspiracy theories, Vietnam war books and watching cult films. Out of this period came the first perfect-bound journal double issue with a spine, *Vague 16/17 Psychic Terrorism Annual* (1985). This was a DIY English attempt to emulate San Francisco's *RE/Search* manuals (formerly *Search & Destroy* fanzine) and revive *IT* and *Oz* hippy underground press ideas, featuring the Lindsay Anderson film *If ...* , the situationists' influence on Paris May 1968, the Angry Brigade, King Mob and the Sex Pistols, Psychic TV, Berlin and Xmal Deutschland's European tour (on which I sold T-shirts), the JFK assassination and the miners' strike.

I attempted to explain the situationists in a 'hip streetwise style', summarising Gordon Carr's book *The Angry Brigade* (1974), which was going around the Stoke Newington squatting scene; linking up the Situationist International and the *enragés* of May 1968 with the hippy terrorists, the radical Notting Hill graffiti artists King Mob, Malcolm McLaren and punk rock. In the epic Psychic TV interview, Genesis P-Orridge talked about TV, sex, mind control, Charles Manson and Jim Jones; accompanied by a feature on the German film *Decoder* about muzak starring P-Orridge, William Burroughs and Christiane F.

*Vague*'s evolution from a fanzine to a countercultural compendium was captured by Robin Gibson in his review for *Sounds*. 'No longer just a thoroughly self-defining fanzine at some kind of odds with the establishment, [*Vague*] has become a complete, confident, but still eminently accessible, outsider. It's also still funny, egotistical and constructively nasty. It brags and nags while the ideas flow, but it has a continuity which intensifies its genuinely anarchic spirit rather than stifles it. *Vague* has a lot in common with the late 60s/early 70s underground press, while its starting point is the most dangerous inquisitive and inspiring area of punk. It doesn't fit into (doesn't need) any clear context, and it's essential because of that'.[6]

*Psychic Terrorism* was followed by *Vague 18/19 Control Data Manual of Programming Phenomena and Conspiracy Theory*, including 'Worldwide Alienation Inc' by Mark Stewart and articles on Freemasons, Hassan i Sabbah and the Illuminati. Issue 20, *Televisionaries*, featured the Baader-Meinhof gang and Perry's 'Apocalypse Now in Stoke Newington' cartoon strip. By the end of the 1980s, ten years on from the first issue, the *Vague* office had relocated to Freston Road, between Notting Hill and Shepherd's Bush, in the ruins of the squatted Republic of Frestonia. Here the *Vague 21 Cyber-Punk Manual* was produced with Jamie Reid's anti-Branson cover artwork and Jon Savage's preview of his Sex Pistols history, *England's Dreaming*.

For James Brown, writer of *Attack on Bzag* fanzine and later of *Loaded*: 'There isn't a conspiracy theory, Gothic hippy band or *Oz* cartoon that Tom Vague hasn't poked his big nose into and exposed in the pages of his annual for Psychic sidekicks. There's no Vietnam book he hasn't devoured and no situationist text he hasn't speed-read. If Tom Vague could wake up to the 1980s he could become both publishing king and cool novelist'.[7]

## Notes

1   Simon Dwyer, 'Stapled Diet', *Sounds*, 29 November 1980, p. 24.
2   Tom Vague interview with Adam Ant, *Vague*, 5, 1980, p. 12.
3   *Jamming*, 12, c. 1981, n.p.
4   *Sheep Worrying*, February 1982, n.p.
5   Ray Lowry, 'Positive Noise', *The Face*, March 1983, p. 46.
6   Robin Gibson, 'Zine Scene', *Sounds*, 26 October 1985, pp. 18–19.
7   James Brown, 'Technofear and Loathing', *NME*, 19 March 1988, p. 7.

# 'Mental liberation issue': *Toxic Grafity*'s punk epiphany as subjectivity (re)storying 'the truth of revolution' across the lifespan

MIKE DIBOLL[1]

All that follows below is data

Alec Grant (2013)

What was I thinking when, in the summer of 1980, I subtitled issue 5 of *Toxic Grafity* the 'mental liberation issue'?[2] As Matt Worley notes, *Toxic* featured 'politically charged collage, essays on anarchy and diatribes against state repression' in which the music coverage was 'all but subsumed within a series of nihilistic ruminations on the inanity of work, the illusion of politics and the stifling abjection of everyday life'.[3] This issue also carried a flexi-disc of the hitherto unreleased Crass track 'Tribal Rival Rebel Revel'.

It is challenging reflecting back 38 years to invoke the subjectivity that was 'Mike D', aged 19; I'm not sure it's possible. The 'mental' was intended as a double entendre: *Toxic*, I fancied, was about 'liberation', and the theme of the issue was the liberation of the mind from the constraining constructions through which socialisation reproduces conformity (I'm retrospectively projecting academic language onto Mike D): an ambitious task for a punk who had not thought to undertake the basic intellectual groundwork of first framing theories of either 'liberation' or the 'mind'. But Mike D was primal enough for his mind not to need 'liberating' from that stuff, the conventions and conformities of academic prose. Yet 'mental' also sought to evoke punk 'chaos': the liberation imagined by *Toxic* was to be 'mental' in the way that the mosh-pit or pogoing was 'mental': chaotic, crazy, primal, angry, 'going mental'; a V-sign; a phlegmy gob; a half-brick Molotov aimed at conformity-constructing socialisation of the sort that (had Mike D known) shaped the working-class subjectivities of Paul Willis's 'lads' in his seminal study *Learning to Labour: How Working-Class Kids Get Working-Class Jobs* (first published in that punkiest of years, 1977). Such socialisation enabled 'self-damnation in the taking on of subordinate roles in western capitalism … damnation experienced, paradoxically, as true learning, affirmation, appropriation and as a form of resistance'.[4] Rejecting such socialisation, Mike D and his ilk were empowered with the agency to flob their gob and lob their bricks at hegemonic structures that were reconstructing Willis's 'lads' as capitalism's 'dummies, dupes and zombies'.[5] This empowerment took place through the countercultural milieu of 'anarcho-punk' (I can't recall the term being used in the day), which shaped Mike D's subjectivity and enabled his agency. In turn, through *Toxic* and related performances, Mike D's enabled cultural agency was able to shape that milieu.

> December 2012, Beachy Head, East Sussex; meet 'Mental Mike':
> The body would be smashed open as it hit the crags as it plummeted, white cliffs stained blood-red against sea of gunmetal, leaden sky. The pounding waves would flush away the mess.
> The phone rings.
> 'It's Richard from Time to Talk … How are you feeling today?'
> 'Is this some kind of tracking app?'
> 'Where are you?'
> 'Beachy Head … It's okay, there's someone with me, I'm just going for a walk … .'
> Still the waves crash and flush: as with the Brighton express that cuts through Mid- Sussex stations at full speed, ending this way would be to stop the pain, not a cry for help.[6]

Mental Mike is 'mental', mentally ill, sick in the head, crazy, neurotic, psychotic, under therapy and on medication, on a therapist's watch list: driven mental through Anxiety, Major Depressive Disorder and Post-Traumatic Stress Disorder (PTSD), he might be a danger to himself, or others.

From the perspective of 2018, semi-retired academic ex-punk Mike ('Old Fart Mike') wonders what the adjective 'mental' might say about the relationship, if any, of those two half-recalled subjectivities – Mike D and Mental Mike – that haunt Old Fart Mike's consciousness as he taps out this paper, pulling on the rusted chains of memory? How might Mike D's 'mental liberation' – '"THE VILEST FORM OF COMMUNICATION" B.U, … @ … O.K. … ?'[7] – inform our understanding, as an exercise in narrative mental health writing, of Mike's mentalness? Moreover, as an investigation into 'the truth of revolution' and the politics of counterculture, how might Mike D's 'mental liberation' help us understand the complex of emotional, military, political, social and vocational forces that drove Mental Mike – with his thousand-yard stare like the GI on the cover of Gee Vaucher's *International Anthem* (1979), his jumps, starts, tics, panic reflexes, anxiety attacks and mind fragmented into a legion of 'characters' (his word) – over the brink into suicidal insanity?

In 2015, Mental Mike recalls 'Higher Education Manager Mike' of 2007–11:

December 2008, Jidd Hafs Maternity Hospital, Bahrain. My daughter's a day old. Just outside the hospital white-helmeted mercenary-police in riot gear confront a small group of shabaab in this most Baharna of neighbourhoods.[8]

My partner asks for baby stuff from my Oxford blue Land Rover Discovery, I leave the ward to fetch. Something's wrong. My eyes, my throat, burn. An ecstasy of fumbling: CS gas canisters over the hospital's perimeter wall. My mucus membranes choke off my throat, I stagger back to the ward. MY DAUGHTER'S NOT IN HER COT!

'SHE'S IN an incubator … ' The jidd hafsy nurse senses my panic. 'We always put the babies there when the gas comes into the hospital … it's just routine … '

Two years, three months later I'll see entire villages carpet-gassed, houses and shops invisible in a thick fog of CS.

Bahrain Teachers College, October 2009: 'Where's Hussein?' The student's missed three classes.

'Don't worry where Hussein is', the senior academic mercenary tells me, 'he's the authorities' problem now, not ours. Make sure his name's taken off the records.'

Bahrain Teachers College, 11 March 2011. I refuse to leave with the mercenary educators. I must bear witness to my students' bid to occupy the campus. They are attacked by baltajiyya: regime-loyalist vigilante gangs who seemed to have turned up on campus by pre-arrangement, police and military out of uniform, sectarian street gangs, jihadist fanatics, gym-bunnies brutalize the students.

Thugs brandish swords, spears, clubs, chains: broke glass, brain-blood.

Builders, fishermen, armed makeshift with the tools of their trades arrive to support the students. The 'police' arrive, shotguns, CS, baton rounds, birdshot.

Then the military, helicopters, live fire. I run and hide ... pools of congealing
blood, scattered handbags, women's shoes, wrecked vehicles. The
counter-revolution has begun.
I arrive in my native UK having lost everything.
I am broken ... .

November 2012. Some Job Centre Plus clown has suggested I take a role as a
Christmas Santa.

Iain Duncan Smith opines that the unemployed are unemployed because of
the moral choices they have made.
Tell me about it.
In anger I say that Bahrain has made me mad. This is unfair. Bahrain and its
people are dear to me.
Bahrain didn't make me mad, the nasty little British-dependent family-state
that runs it did. I'm tougher than that.
No, it was coming back to Britain that pushed me to the brink of that cliff,
the edge of that platform. I felt like a witness to a rape or a murder. I had to
tell the world what I'd seen, felt. But the powers of this world denied it. It
never happened.[9]

'The truth of revolution, brother ... ' is what? 'Mental liberation?' Mental
Mike is more mental than liberated. And yet, standing there, in 'Pearl Square',
Bahrain's Tahrir Square, in February 2011, the young Wordsworth's words
on the French Revolution entered Manager Mike's consciousness: 'Bliss was
it in that dawn to be alive/ But to be young was very Heaven ... '

   In 2009, he had heard about an emerging body of scholarship in 'Punk
Studies'. Writing in his reactionary delusion to the *Kill Your Pet Puppy* website,
treating punk scholarship with snobby condescension, he had written at the
end of a turgid piece about *Toxic*:

   I've repudiated so much of what I used to believe in during those days in the
   late 1970s, but the closing words for Crass' 'Bloody Revolutions' track 'but
   the truth of revolution, brother, is Year Zero' still appeals to the Burkeian
   in me![10]

When the revolution happened, confronted by real, actual revolution, Manager
Mike moved about amid it, smelled, touched, felt revolution 'in the air', in
the crowds. He felt privileged, honoured, to be there. He was staggered to
witness the world that Mike D had once dreamed about, fantasised about,
fanzined about, actually actualise before his eyes: vast numbers of individuals
*en masse* self-organising autonomously, bypassing the state and state structures

to fulfil their everyday needs; becoming one great collective entity expressing powerfully a unified revolutionary will, defying the military, taunting the riot police to occupy public space in the name of the revolutionary overthrow of the detested regime:

> '*Salmiyya! Salmiyya!*'
> [Peaceful protest!]

> '*Ash-sha'b, yureed, isqat an-nidhaam*'
> [The People demand the fall of the system]

> '*Hayhaat minnaa adh-dhilla!*'
> [No more humiliation]

> '*Wa laa khalaas 'illaa tahttaa dhill ar-rasaas*'
> [There's no stopping us unless it's under a hail of bullets!]

Hundreds of thousands of people occupying the so-called 'prestige' social space between the financial and the diplomatic districts, wresting control of the streets from the state with carnival-like creativity – protest as performance and performance as protest – organising autonomously the essentials to maintain bare life while making art and poem and performance and song, graffiti and creative appropriation, mocking humour and creative insurrectionary play: all this in defiance of guns and tanks.

Manager Mike felt himself decentring, fragmenting: an epiphany amid the chanting and the slogans and the singing and the marching, the to-ing and fro-ing, crowds surging, confronting then defending against the riot police: the scales of conformity dropped from his eyes, his public persona, his knowing 'I', his owning 'me' fractured, fell away. An ancient presence emerged into his being; a new-old subjectivity conjured by the chanting from the abyssal depths of the decades. Mike D, newly summoned, saw around him in Bahrain the ancient promise of the Stop the City protests fulfilled in his new present.

As Rich Cross observed, Stop the City was 'imaginative, inspired, subversive and norm breaking'. Organised in 1983 to 1984 without a coordinating committee but with 'willful, passionate utopianism', Stop the City were carnivals of action designed to disrupt the flow of capital and draw attention to issues of arms manufacture, apartheid and exploitation. Targeted first at the City of London, they 'punctured for all of time' (Dave Morris) the 'secrecy and supposed invulnerability' of the state.[11] Many punks were involved. Yet here in Bahrain there was none of the 'marginality' and 'fragility' that Cross noted of Stop the City; rather, the state's *haybat ud-dawla*, the 'fear' or 'awe' that made possible the state's thousands of daily oppressions, the state's projection of itself into the consciousness of its subjects as a God-like entity, all-powerful and enduring, intimidating people from taking collective action against it, here this *haybat*, this toxic charisma, was 'punctured for all time', just destroyed. And Mike D, a living, witnessing link between Stop the City and the Arab Spring grew up again in the punktured shell of Manager Mike.

Few if any of the participants in the Bahrain Revolution would have known of Stop the City, but a genealogy connects them via the anti-globalisation and anti-capitalist protests of the later 1990s to 2000s and the Occupy! movement.[12] Bahrain has a long history of uprising against, firstly, de facto British rule, then the ruling Al Khalifa dynasty during the British Protectorate. This opposition dates back at least to the 1920s, into Bahrain's 'independence' period post-1973. Most recently, the 1995 to 2002 'Bahrain Intifada' forced the regime to make major public life concessions.[13] I knew from teaching radical Bahraini students that young Bahrainis were exploring fresh models of resistance, including those developed by the anti-globalisation and the Occupy! movements. Fellow eyewitness and political anthropologist Toby Mattheisen observes:

> ... we could hear the voices of thousands, the shrieking of megaphones, fanfares, music ... how relaxed everybody seemed to be. There were thousands of people at the roundabout and two had been killed [by state security forces] trying to reach here, but ... it felt like the most natural thing to bring your family to a demonstration in the heart of the capital ... protestors had set up tents, screens, makeshift kitchens, medical centers, mobile phone charging stations and a podium for speakers ... Hundreds of tents and mattresses had been set up in the first two days.[14]

Mike D was resurrected, a living link between Stop the City and the revolution flowering before his eyes. Shortly after, four battalions of military and riot police surrounded the occupation site and cleared it with lethal force. As Matthiesen observes:

> The image that came to symbolize that night's events was a photo of a [protester's] skull, cracked open by a shotgun fired at close range, with the brains spilling out. Counter-revolution is scarier than revolution, especially if the revolution is as velvet as I witnessed at the roundabout.[15]

The events of the counter-revolution and his fleeing from Bahrain to the UK put Mike D back in his Toxic box and Mental Mike emerged in his place. His route to sanity would be to reclaim Mike D – to revisit and restory these events away from insanity-evoking catastrophe to bring to the fore once more that life-giving epiphany, to make it work once more, curatively, therapeutically, in his present. Reflection was painful, but he persevered. Reflecting on *Toxic*, selfhood and revolution on the *Kill Your Pet Puppy* website in 2015 Mental Mike observed:

Looking back from the perspective of 2015, the 'me' of 1978 or 1979 [i.e. Mike D] seems far closer to the 'me' of 2015 [Mental Mike] than does the 'me' of 2009 [Manager Mike]. That 'me' is no more. I hesitate to say 'dead' because I doubt one's earlier selves can ever really be 'dead' to one's present self. Rather, I see that 2009 self as having been distilled away by a kind of alchemy, as dross burnt away in a crucible, as a fragile construct devastatingly deconstructed, shattered, and blasted across the four cardinal compass points by a tsunami of fire.

Stripped of the façade-like persona I had constructed around the 'me' of 2009, I now see a person remarkably like the 'me' of 1978, although I hesitate to say that is the 'real' me: to what extent can any of our constructed personas be 'real' in a fundamental, existential sense? ... Nevertheless, the transformation has been remarkable. The immediate question that arises when contemplating that transformation, then, has to be 'What were the factors that brought it about?' These factors are easy to identify, but hard to write about.

There is the experience of revolution. I don't mean reading about revolution or merely witnessing one, but of experiencing that inexorable movement that draws one – almost drags one, in some ways reluctantly – from bearing witness to a revolution to becoming part of it ... a survival of the 'me' of 1978 lurking about unnoticed among the cacophony of conflicting voices that constitute my consciousness.

Whatever it was, it was able, with a daring and disturbing deftness of touch to take over ... As this happened the part of 'me' that is supposed to direct my actions in accordance with rational self-interest retreated, letting the 'me' of 1978 (or something very like it) dictate my actions, even though 'rational self-interest me' knew in doing so I would be writing the execution warrant for 2009 'me': deprived of the material and professional symbols that announced my 2009 'me' to the social world beyond me, it would wither ... .

[W]hat I was witnessing in 2011 ... was a people, young and old and of all walks of life making history, becoming the subject-objects of their own revolutionary becoming. This was bigger than 'me', of any of the [plural] 'Me-s' that noisily occupied the conscious space of my individuality. I understood how social and political forces flowed through my subjectivity, shaping it and in turn being shaped by it, as a river re-forms the landscape even as its course is determined by it. I saw subjectivity not as a stasis, but as a process, that my 'me' was a construct that would always be a work in progress, never complete. I saw how this transformation of one's understanding of self and society was inherently part of the revolutionary process. That in rejecting the static social and political structures in which both coercion and ideology corral us, revolutionary consciousness, life-as-becoming, is re-initiated.[16]

Old Fart Mike reviews from his experience a rant, 'The Admition', from Mike D's Blakean innocence:

> God is a lie. There is no god, god is a con-trick, death is oblivion ... I reject religion, I reject work, in a system of capitalism (or state capitalism, as in fascism, or communism, the same thing) ... work is slavery, it never sets you free, that's a fucking lie, the 'myth' of capital ... yes, I reject contemporary values and past values ... I see no political solution, for politics left and right is lies ... REALIZE THE INSANITY OF 'CIVILIZATION' AND ITS STINKING OVERKILL, OVEREAT, OVER EVERY FUCKING THING THEN ACT TO DESTROY IT.[17]

There are some familiar 'anarcho-punk' tropes here: 'religion' as an archaic form of oppression enslaving the governed; politics and the state as serving the vested interests of capital; the rejection of political left and right; elements of nihilism and misanthropy.[18] But I'd now say that God is a verb: an eternal and sentient verbal imperative BE!, which we can embody and enact in moments of transformation.

Thinking of Mike's journey across the decades as an autobiographical ethnography, we find here continuities with his pasts and presents: substitute Mental Mike's deconstruction of subjectivity, the 'I', for Mike D's demolition of 'God' and there is continuity; substitute Mike D's undifferentiated rage at politics, left or right, at work, even at 'civilization' itself, for Mental Mike's rage at the Al Khalifa family state's murderous suppression of a popular uprising – a Stop the City writ large – that he witnessed in Bahrain, then there is continuity again. In this, the rediscovery, the re-evocation of his punk subjectivity across the decades allowed him to restory tragedy and trauma; in this lay the cure for Mental Mike's Madness.

My intention above has been to write a 'poststructuralist autoethnography' to explore how a 'punk subjectivity' has endured, sometimes subliminally, sometimes epiphanically across my lifespan, influencing my social and political agency and my action-in-the-world in a range of contexts which are very different to the original 'anarcho-punk' context of *Toxic* and its wider milieu.

By 'autoethnographic' I mean an approach to qualitative research that involves 'research, writing, story and method that connect the autobiographical to the cultural, social and political'.[19] Autoethnography can be seen as 'rewriting the self and the social', as 'a form of self-narrative that places the self within a social context'.[20] It is 'the use of personal experience and personal writing to purposefully comment on/critique cultural practices; to make contributions to existing research; to embrace vulnerability and purpose; and [very punkily] to create reciprocal relationships with audiences in order to compel a response'.[21] It is a contemporary reflexive qualitative research methodology in which 'the researcher and the researched are the same people'.[22]

Yet the 'personal' in experience is problematic, given poststructuralist scepticism as to the existence of essentially discrete and authoritative subjectivities: by calling the above 'poststructuralist', I refer to that approach to autoethnography that deploys 'multiple, de-centred voices to represent fragmented experiences'.[23] Rather than presenting unproblematic 'authentic' or 'lived' experiences, I seek to present the above narrative in a way that problematises the possibility of 'a direct transmission from thinking to describing to receiving' from one holistic narrating subjectivity to a receiving subjectivity.[24]

Insisting that 'the personal is political', I have sought to relate the endurance of my 'punk subjectivity' to my agency in a struggle for social and political justice in the Middle East, using an epiphanic event which 'seizes hold of a memory as it flashes up at a moment of danger' (Benjamin) to 'rediscover the past not as a succession of events, but as a series of scenes … images and stories' (Ulmer).[25] The epiphanic event is the re-emergence of a subsumed Mike D during a riot police assault on a Bahraini demonstration; Mike D having been buried for decades under the conformity-constructing structures of professional academia and the conformities of an academic career (a conformity as constraining as the conformity Willis's 'lads' experienced in their work in a 1970s factory). The text above is 'messy', 'discordant' and 'contrapunctal' to problematise 'my' authority and presence in the text.[26]

I have tried to show how cultural, social and political forces have flowed through and shaped my subjectivity; how subjectivity-as-agency-in-the-world in turn shapes the cultural, social and political forces that flow around us. I've attempted to show how we 'are inscribed within dialogic, socially shared, linguistic and representational practices' across our lifespans, so that our selves can be seen as 'social and relational rather than as an autonomous phenomenon', producing 'difference(s) to be lived with'.[27] Thus, I have acknowledged the crucial agency of revolutionary Bahrainis in rebirthing my subsumed 'punk subjectivity', giving me a new and post-revolutionary perspective on the world, the localisation within the individual of a 'revolutionary consciousness'. This new consciousness survived the Saudi-led counter-revolution that crushed the Bahrain uprising and, since my return/flight/exile to the UK, has enabled me to engage in countercultural, social and political justice movements in ways that are innovative yet grounded in my punk past.

I've sought to acknowledge the therapeutic potential of autoethnographic writing that is 'ethical, vulnerable, evocative' for writers, readers and for those with whom we have shared experiences.[28] Hence, I have foregrounded and personified as 'Mental Mike' my struggle with the multiple mental illnesses resulting from my experiences in Bahrain and exile. To treat this, I have revisited the concept of 'mental liberation', which was the organising theme of *Toxic Grafity* in 1980. I allow Mental Mike to give an open and frank account of his mentalness and allow him to revisit traumatic events, restorying them therapeutically as a positive and empowering epiphany, an evocative epistemology that uses tales of suffering, loss and pain not only to create catharsis, but to spur Old Fart Mike on to reflective, critical, creative action in a socially and politically just praxis. Using paraphrases and quotes from material written between 2011 and 2016, I've traced Mental Mike's 'mental liberation' from potential suicide case to a reauthored and revoiced writer. This has paralleled my experience using narrative in Cognitive Behaviour Therapy and when writing-up ethnography. Thus, the above participates in the genre of narrative mental health writing. As Mental Health practitioner, mental health survivor and autoethnographer Alec Grant notes in *Our Encounters with Madness* (2011): '[An] important function of mental health narratives is that they provide testimony … giving witness to … the experiences of recovery, healing and endurance of sufferers of mental health problems.'[29] Mental Mike wrote in 2016: 'I felt like a witness to a rape or a murder. I had to tell the world what I'd seen, felt. But the powers of this world denied it. It never happened.'[30]

Alec Grant continues: 'in the provision of testimony, both writers and readers are witnesses. This places an onus on both groups to treat stories with care and respect, learn from them as oral history and take the necessary subsequent action in the spirit of social justice.'[31] I've sought to confront these 'powers of the world', Mike D's 'CIVILIZATION AND ITS STINKING OVERKILL', through a storied 'hero', Mike D, my adult self at its most innocent and primal.

This chapter further contributes to studies of the wider 'Arab Spring', and also to critical discourse on higher education: non-elite academics who have struggled through higher education having had diverse life histories are highly likely to end up in out-of-the-ordinary higher education contexts such as the Gulf – how do their life-stories and those of the students they interact with intersect and what are the civil society, cultural, ethical, political and public sphere consequences?

I've suggested new ways of writing about the punk experience, going beyond history writing, discourse analysis and cultural studies-based approaches to reveal how punk pasts can be used in personal-political presents to enable personal-political agency for social and political justice, and to effect therapeutic or curative transformations in a context of a neoliberal mental health pandemic. Important here is the idea of the 'punk epiphany': the sudden and unexpected return of punk consciousness at a life-changing moment: such epiphanies have both ethical and aesthetic aspects. Connecting the personal past with the social, they become almost a kind of pedagogy. For us who were participants 'in the day', these punk pasts seem, when we recall them, purile, simplistic, naive and youthfully exuberant; yet when they epiphanically reshape our presents we restory them, projecting them into our futures they are present to us as ourselves at our most raw, primal and, in that Blakean sense, 'innocent'. This offers new vistas in writing about punk.

The re-voiced Mike D says to the world of 2018: 'The truth of the counter-revolution, sister, is a mental health Year Zero, and today's big issue is "mental liberation" from neoliberal toxicity.'[32] I now see my breakdown as a breakthrough – but back then it was the farthest thing from my mind because I was over-whelmed by flashbacks from complex post-traumatic stress and ... major depression.[33]

## Notes

1 'Mike Diboll' refers to the legal person imbued with citizenship, rights and responsibilities before the law.

2 *Toxic* ran for six issues, 1978–82; each issue carried a different misspelling of 'graffiti'.

3 Matthew Worley, 'Punk, Politics and British (Fan)zines, 1976–84: "While the world was dying did you wonder why?"', *History Workshop Journal*, 79:1 (2015), 76–106.

4 Paul Willis, *Learning to Labour: How Working-Class Kids Get Working-Class Jobs* (Farnham: Ashgate, [1977] 2000), p. 113.

5 *Ibid.*, p. 205.

6 Mike Diboll, 'After 2011 I Lost Everything' (2016), 200 More Stories website, https://200morestoriesbahrain.wordpress.com/2016/06/07/mikes-story/, accessed 21 January 2017.

7 *Toxic Grafity*, 5 (1980), p. 1 (front cover).

8   'Shabaab' is Arabic for 'youth', similar in usage to the Italian 'ragazzi'. 'Baharna' is a
    Bahraini ethno-confessional term.

9   Diboll, 'After 2011 I Lost Everything'.

10  Mike Diboll, 'Toxic Grafity' (2009), on Kill Your Pet Puppy, http://killyourpetpuppy
    .co.uk/news/toxic-grafity-reflections-on-self-hood-and-revolution, accessed 21
    January 2017.

11  Rich Cross, 'Stop the City', in Mike Dines and Matthew Worley (eds), The Aesthetic
    of Our Anger: Anarcho-Punk, Politics and Music (Colchester: Minor Compositions,
    2016), pp. 151–2. Morris was a Stop the City organiser, quoted in ibid., p. 155.

12  Cross, 'Stop the City', pp. 151–5.

13  Christopher Davidson, After the Sheikhs: The Coming Collapse of the Gulf Monarchies
    (London: Hurst, 2012), pp. 205–9.

14  Toby Matthiesen, Sectarian Gulf: Bahrain, Saudi Arabia and the Arab Spring That
    Wasn't (Stanford, CA: Stanford University Press, 2013), pp. 9–11.

15  Ibid., p. 15.

16  Mike Diboll, 'Toxic Grafity: Reflections on Self-Hood and Revolution', Kill Your Pet
    Puppy, http://killyourpetpuppy.co.uk/news/toxic-grafity-reflections-on-self-hood-
    and-revolution, accessed 21 January 2017.

17  Mike Diboll, 'The Admition', Toxic Grafity, 5 (1980), p. 18.

18  Worley, 'Punk, Politics and British (fan)zines, 1976–84', 98–9.

19  Carolyn Ellis, The Ethnographic I: A Methodological Novel about Autoethnography
    (Walnut Creek, CA: AltaVista, 2004), p. xix.

20  Deborah Reed-Danahay, Auto/ethnography: Rewriting the Self and the Social (New
    York: Oxford University Press, 1997), p. 6.

21  Stacey Holman Jones, Tony Adams and Carolyn Ellis, Handbook of Autoethnography
    (Walnut Creek, CA: Left Coast Press, 2013).

22  Carolyn Ellis and Arthur Bochner, 'Autoethnography, Personal Narrative, Reflexivity',
    in Norman Denzin and Yvonna Lincoln (eds), Handbook of Qualitative Research
    (Thousand Oaks, CA: Sage, 2000).

23  Alec Grant, Nigel Short and Lydia Turner, 'Introduction: Storying Life and Lives', in
    Nigel Short, Lydia Turner and Alec Grant (eds), Contemporary British Autoethnography
    (Rotterdam: Sense, 2013), p. 12.

24  Alec Grant, 'Writing, Teaching and Survival in Mental Health: A Discordant Quintet
    for One', in Short, Turner and Grant (eds), Contemporary British Autoethnography,
    p. 34.

25  Walter Benjamin, Illuminations (New York: Schocken, 1968), p. 257; Gregory Ulmer,
    Teletheory (New York: Routledge, 1989), p. 112.

26  Maggie MacLure, 'Qualitative Inquiry: Where are the Ruins?', Qualitative Inquiry,
    17:10 (2011), 997–1005; Grant, 'Writing, Teaching and Survival in Mental Health',
    p. 33.

27  Grant, Short and Turner, 'Introduction', p. 5.

28  Ellis, The Ethnographic I, p. 135.

29  Alec Grant, Francis Biley and Hannah Walker (eds), *Our Encounters with Madness* (Ross-on-Wye: PCCS, 2011), p. 2.

30  Diboll, 'After 2011 I Lost Everything'.

31  Grant, Biley and Walker, *Our Encounters with Madness*, p. 2.

32  This puns on a lyric from Crass's 1980 track 'Bloody Revolutions': back in 1980 both Crass and Mike D were like virgins writing about sex when it came to the phenomenon of 'bloody revolution'.

33  Michael Skinner, in Grant, Biley and Walker (eds), *Our Encounters with Madness*, p. 2.

# 12

# From Year Zero to 1984: I was a pre-teen fanzine writer

NICHOLAS BULLEN

## Approaching Year Zero

Punk smashed into my consciousness like a boot through a television screen. I was 10 years old in 1978, living in a small village located between the cities of Coventry and Birmingham in the Midlands of England. With the exception of a somewhat unwholesome interest in horror literature, my juvenile tastes tended towards the universal – riding bicycles, reading comics, eating ice cream: music played no great role. However, a seismic shift occurred when punk abruptly introduced itself.

By the late 1970s, punk had accrued a visible profile in the mainstream cultural life of the United Kingdom. References to punk often appeared in the television schedules alongside live performances by leading punk bands on music and children's programmes. I watched these programmes with mounting excitement as the energetic urgency of the music united with an intoxicating aura of disobedience that was physically manifest in the direct and dead-eyed stare of Pete Shelley (Buzzcocks), the self-possessed posture of Poly Styrene (X Ray Spex) and the nocturnal thuggery of Hugh Cornwell (The Stranglers). It generated a visceral reaction that seemed to rise from nowhere on a wave of inarticulate emotions: I did not understand what exactly punk *was* or *why* it made me feel the way I did, but I liked it: moreover, I loved it.

For those, including myself, who had minimal prior engagement with the history of popular music culture (and consequently no past to rail against or replace), punk truly was a 'Year Zero' moment. I immediately became obsessed. Records became my default birthday present request and saved pocket money contributed to the purchase of records and copies of the weekly music papers. The discovery of John Peel's late night radio show (providing further and free access to the music) only stoked the fire of my obsession. I also began to cultivate the requisite sartorial style of soap-spiked hair, ripped t-shirts and tight trousers, much to my parent's chagrin.

Isolated with no older siblings or peer group to encourage and inspire, my interest in punk remained a solitary passion until the end of 1978, when the family moved to a new house in the village. I was introduced to my new next door neighbour, Miles Ratledge, a year older than me and as equally obsessed by punk; we forged an immediate friendship and began loitering in each other's bedrooms, playing records and discussing punk. Our mutual interest would later lead us to create our own music (as the founder members of Napalm Death), but it first led us to fanzines.

## Admiring the zine-ery[1]

By the end of the 1970s, many of the bands from the first and second waves of punk had imploded, disbanded or become increasingly inaccessible. As importantly, the more successful artists began to exude an aura of inauthenticity as they became entrenched within the mainstream, creating a disjuncture between themselves and the younger punks. The anarchist band Crass, whose blend of aggressive music and vitriolic lyrics seasoned with a judicious selection of expletives had increasingly gained influence in the punk milieu through 1979, articulated this developing perspective in their song 'Punk Is Dead': 'CBS promote the Clash/ but it ain't for revolution, it's just for cash/ Punk became a fashion just like hippy used to be/ and it ain't got a thing to do with you or me.'[2]

This resonated, and my interest consequently began to turn away from mainstream bands towards others who displayed a keener relevance to my pre-adolescent and earnest perception of the constituent elements of punk. Such exploration not only introduced me to the lower echelons of the second wave of punk bands (The Users, Alternative TV and Desperate Bicycles), but also to the raft of independent labels (including Small Wonder, FAST Product, Rough Trade and Cherry Red) that provided concrete examples of an active application of the 'do-it-yourself' punk ethos. These labels and the bands they released became the indicative representatives of my perception of punk, allowing an expansion of taste that was serviced on Saturday mornings by patronising a wider range of outlets beyond the larger retail chains including exploration of the local independent record shops where, nestled beside the overfilled racks of records and the bricolage of posters advertising local concerts, were a selection of publications called fanzines.

Fanzines possessed an instantaneous appeal, largely due to their coverage of punk music (at both national and local level). They provided a portal into this brave new world, delivering dispatches from a frontline that was being fought at that very moment in the world around me. They also connected on a deeper personal level, speaking to me in a direct manner that was absent from the mainstream music papers and providing communication that forged a relationship – however tenuous – between their producers and myself. Amplifying the excitement of the moment, their animated tone and chaotic presentation only enhanced their appeal (along with the additional bonus that they retailed at an affordable cost, placing them within the economic reach of a pre-adolescent's pocket money).

I purchased my first fanzine in August 1979 (issue 7 of Coventry's *Alternative Sounds)* and developed an urgent addiction, avidly purchasing other local fanzines when each new issue appeared in the local record shops.[3] The Better Badges fanzine listings in the back pages of *Zigzag* and a chance exposure to a compendium of *Sniffin' Glue* further assisted in locating fanzines within the punk continuum, reinforcing the sense that fanzines were something that I could call my own.

## We are *Antisocial*

Often perceived as naive amateurs by critics (and sections of their audience), the vibrancy of expression evidenced by many fanzine writers transmitted itself to me as a positive attribute. The tone of their discourse (conversational, almost conspiratorial, directly addressing the reader through editorials and marginalia) cultivated an intimacy that promoted access, including access to a wider community of loosely aggregated like-minded individuals, indicating the possibility of a cultural narrative situated outside of the common structures.

This direct communication extended to their visual presence: their pages an explosive and pulsating bricolage of text and image where words bled over the page, filling all available space and erupting over multi-layered backgrounds that blended graphic patterns with occluded images. Often wilfully amateur in conception and realisation (and largely designed by producers without formal training), the visual aspect of fanzines acted as a signifier of their difference, imbuing them with a keenly authentic aura of energy and vibrancy. This 'do-it-yourself' approach also provided a contrast to the more traditionally formal graphic design of the weekly music papers and magazines such as *Smash Hits* (despite frequent attempts by their graphic designers to accommodate the energy inherent in punk design).

Miles and I had spent 1979 making a crude and rudimentary attempt at being in a punk band under the name The Mess, utilising the classic instrumentation of detuned acoustic guitar and cardboard tub redolent of much untutored organised music. Despite our enthusiasm, the harsh reality of our technical inability and the barriers placed before us by our age presented a seemingly insurmountable obstacle. We could, however, respond to the clarion call of fanzine editorials that frequently combined admonishments to those who critiqued their efforts with demands to become active: 'This is all to do with independence, demystification & doing something. All this assembled mass of bored humanity on these pages are doing something, which proves that you can do something too if you bother about it. If you already are, then tell us. If you feel like, tell us. No matter where you live ... '[4] This repeated urging to realise the 'do-it-yourself' ethos intertwined with punk from its outset provoked us into becoming active agents. The moment itself was suitably offhand – a simple 'let's do it'. In the early months of 1980, we produced the first issue of *Antisocial*.

The first *Antisocial* appeared through a blur of typing, scribbling, cutting out and gluing over the duration of a week in April 1980. The content reflected our key interest by concentrating exclusively on punk, with a particular focus on the local telegraphed through the front cover strapline: 'A fanzine for Coventry'. Rudimentary articles on local band Criminal Class and our own band The Mess jostled for space with inept record reviews and haphazard collages that cannibalised political leaflets, Sex Pistols advertising copy and content from other fanzines.

Our creative partnership was characterised by a lack of defined roles and hierarchy: we created the content that we wanted to with little discussion or editing, synthesising our desire in the most immediate manner. The visual presentation of the fanzine reflected this approach: influenced by the now common signifiers of punk graphic design (including the almost obligatory 'ransom note' letters cut from existing text), it displayed a chaotic spontaneity that became emblematic of our later fanzines. Typewritten text (produced on a barely functioning antique typewriter) and handwritten scrawls were presented at vertiginous angles against images harvested from a range of print media, combining with our individual customisation of each copy through colouring, handmade stickers and the application of text and image via hand-printing kits.[5]

The strictures of the available budget (governed by what we could save from our pocket money) required the technology used for production to be minimal in terms of cost: the first issue was xeroxed at a local printer near to my school, resulting in a faint reproduction of our master copy as a single-sided A4 publication in an almost negligible print run of 25 copies. Priced at 10p per copy, we added a selection of handmade stickers as a further incentive for purchase. After distributing the copies to local record shops in Coventry, we waited: to our surprise, we sold every copy, recouping enough money to finance a second issue. The sense of achievement we felt was not only palpable but inspiring: we set to work on *Antisocial 2*.

Appearing a month later, the second issue demonstrated an expansion of our ambitions. Beyond the articles on music (The Notsensibles, Dead Kennedys, my fledgling band Destroy) and the scattershot collages, a key innovation was the inclusion of interviews with punk practitioners: a direct result of the sharing of information by another fanzine (via a 'band index' feature in *Alternative Sounds*).[6] The somewhat inept interviews were conducted with local bands The Shapes, Flackoff and Gods Toys, almost certainly to the bemusement of the participants. We also expanded the reviews, moving beyond the record reviews of the first issue to include assessments of cassette releases, fanzines and films.

An unanticipated outcome of our youthful naivety was a sense of possibility in terms of the range of music which we responded to and wished to represent. Absorbing material from fanzines (which often covered a wider range of artists than many critics would later give them credit for), the nascent 'cassette culture' of home-produced tape releases and the expansive musical education provided by John Peel, our field of vision was opened to a range of artists who we felt possessed a unifying quality of independence that fostered the 'do-it-yourself' spirit that inspired us. *Antisocial* not only included material on those bands that represented the ongoing legacy of punk at the turn of the decade (The Slits, Crass, UK Decay, Angelic Upstarts, Varukers), but also local bands with an aesthetic more focused on post-punk and pop (Religious Overdose, Wild Boys, Human Cabbages) and artists operating beyond the conventional structure of the music industry. Issue 2 explicitly highlighted 'cassettes' on the cover and included reviews of such cassette luminaries as the Scottish Polis Inspectors.

While the design aesthetic was maintained from the previous issue, it expanded to include headings etched through plastic stencils, minimal use of

Letraset transfer lettering and the placement of text on backgrounds of pointillist dots and diagonal lines. Printed on the same inadequate photocopier in a print run of 50 copies, this issue embraced double-sided printing and an A5 format, with copies again customised through colouring, ink printing and handmade stickers.

Positive reviews in local fanzines (one of which generously described *Antisocial* as '[An] enthusiastic 'zine from a few very young kids ... It is really refreshing, I think you should buy one')[7] provided further encouragement to continue, and our confidence extended to initiating an increasingly furious correspondence with other local fanzine writers who would good naturedly humour our precocious exuberance at concerts we attended. The optimistic promise of fanzines had delivered, allowing us to gain entrance to the milieu that obsessed us: our evenings after school would be a feverish trawl through fanzines, leaflets, flyers and cassette tapes, with Saturdays spent in record shops and radical bookshops delivering copies of our fanzines for sale and hunting for new items to absorb. Issues 3 and 4 of *Antisocial* appeared in quick succession through 1980, following a similar model of content and design and buoyed by a confidence which saw us paying for the fanzine to be printed via offset lithography in a larger print run of 100 A5 format copies.[8]

The changing nature of *Antisocial* through 1980 was reflected in other ways. Addressing an inchoate but growing desire to redirect focus on our own personal interests (and acknowledging that we both worked at a slightly different tempo), we developed a sideline in producing our own individual fanzines. Miles produced two issues of *Twisted Nerve*; I produced *Discarded* and *Out of Vogue*, which began a personal tradition of changing the title of my fanzine with every issue. Inspired by a series of pocket-sized publications created by another local fanzine editor,[9] these fanzines were produced in A6 format: the simplicity of this smaller format appealing as a medium that could facilitate the fast-and-easy creation of a publication.[10]

*Out of Vogue* appeared in late 1980 and was indicative of the beginning of a shift in the content and tone of the fanzines I produced. Featuring anarchist punk bands (Crass, Discharge, Subhumans) alongside local bands (Delayed Reaction, Varukers), reviews (of records, cassettes and concerts) and collages, the title itself – appropriated from California's The Middle Class, widely regarded as responsible for releasing the first American hardcore record – provided an indication of the future. The fanzine was adorned throughout with the circled 'A' of anarchism and graphics taken from leaflets and pamphlets promoting anti-nuclear and anti-authoritarian messages; symbols of a nascent political consciousness that erupted in embryonic form through a centrespread collage that juxtaposed torn images of Discharge and a raised fist with pasted text saying 'Art Horror'.

## Welcome to 19AT1

This creative divergence led to the fifth issue of *Antisocial* appearing in August 1981 under a new name – *Twisted Morals* – which registered both the end of *Antisocial* as a fanzine and our collaboration in print. The front cover made this rupture manifest, rejecting the listing of contents used for each issue of *Antisocial* in favour of a collage of symbols of oppression (the then prime minister Margaret Thatcher, the police, the union flag of Britain, the statue of the scales of justice at the Old Bailey criminal court, images of family groupings) captioned 'Be warned: Hypocritical crap'. *Twisted Morals* physically embodied the dislocation of its production, mixing three different forms of printing (on both single and double-sided paper) with handwritten annotations. It furthermore demonstrated a disassociation from the content of the recent past: despite the presence of bands representing the lineage of local coverage in *Antisocial* (Attrition and Protégé), the content was heavily weighted towards bands that represented the anarcho-punk genre on a national level (The Eratics, Flux of Pink Indians and The Mob). The remaining content mixed politicised rantings with obsessive collages and a centrespread ridiculing the recent royal wedding.

This shift in content and tone was a direct result of an embrace of radical politics facilitated, in part, by an on-going interest in fanzine culture. Local fanzines would often include information on outlets that stocked fanzines, from record shops and independent retailers catering for the accoutrements of youth culture to the political bookshops set up through the 1970s to promote radical politics on the left of the political spectrum.[11] Tightly packed with often precariously stacked volumes of political tracts and heaps of protest campaign leaflets, these radical bookshops would often take fanzines on a 'sale or return' basis.[12] Visiting these bookshops (in particular, The Wedge in Coventry and the Peace Centre in Birmingham) inevitably led to my exposure to the wide range of radical politics emanating from the left (from anti-militarism and anti-nuclear campaigns to gender politics, animal rights and anarchism).[13]

This exposure on a personal level coincided with an increased visibility of politics in punk as a whole, in particular the development of the anarcho-punk genre through the years 1979 to 1981. The progenitors of the genre were Crass, a band that had ascended into the punk consciousness through 1979. Their committed political stance (which embraced a range of non-affiliated left-wing ideas, notably anarchism as a personal belief system and the anti-war position of the Campaign for Nuclear Disarmament) provided an alternative not only to attempts at infiltration by external political organisations but also the pervading sense of malaise that had descended on punk.

By the end of 1979, fanzines aligning themselves with this politicised viewpoint had begun to emerge, replacing the dominant focus on music with one concentrated on radical left-wing politics and its expression through musical artists who allied themselves to it. Following the example given by the strapline 'The punk rock fanzine for anarchists and revolutionarys' on the cover of *No Real Reason*, these fanzines were initially referred to under a range of terms (including 'anarchist zines', 'anarchist propaganda' and 'anarchy zine') before the adoption of the term 'anarcho-punk fanzine' (or 'anarcho-zine').[14] As they had done at the outset of punk, the fanzines rapidly assumed a vital role in the nascent anarcho-punk milieu, an importance demonstrated by Crass's raising of funds for their production through benefit concerts[15] and the inclusion of contact addresses on the sleeve of 'Bloody Revolutions' (followed by the exhortation 'or start up your own').[16]

From their inception, anarcho-zines placed themselves in opposition to other forms of print media. A critical position towards the content and purpose of the mainstream music media had been a feature of fanzines since punk's early days, but this criticism adopted a more explicitly political tone after the election of Margaret Thatcher's Conservative government in 1979: the anarcho-zines aspired to be 'Not just a fanzine'[17] and thereby provide 'an alternative to the established music press not a copy of it'.[18] They also promoted self-expression ('ZINES ARE ABOUT INDIVIDUALISM AND SELF EXPRESSION, UNLIKE SNOUTS, MNE, SMASH SHITS ETC.')[19] and, in so doing, articulated an aspiration that the fanzine could act as a tool for liberation – that is, 'to give people a broadened view of what life has to offer, to help them liberate their minds and to assist them in their search for personal freedom'.[20]

Anarcho-zines approached this ideal by foregrounding their politics. Lengthy articles and poems on a variety of political concerns were fused with gnomic slogans and visual collages designed to reinforce the messages they wished to convey, with music increasingly presented as a vehicle for the dissemination of political ideas. Many preferred to print lyrics and band statements in place of interviews with musicians[21] and located fanzine and cassette reviews with reference to the political ideas they presented. Graham Burnett's *New Crimes* succinctly expressed this realignment, stating: 'The band (hopefully) should be trying to put across ideas and opinions to make their listeners question the world, and the magazines should be trying to do the same on paper, not simply acting as alternative fan club news-sheets … The bands themselves are not that important, it's the messages they carry that matter.'[22] This approach also questioned the traditional relationship between the artist and the consumer: 'It seems all some zines can do is print the opinions of bands leaving no room for their own. This is just creating a "Them & Us" situation where the bands are people to look up to and you're just one of the gullible masses … '[23]

The ideas expounded by anarcho-zines had a considerable impact on myself and Miles, resonating with our youthful anger at injustice and fostering an optimistic vision that the world we lived in could be radically altered for the benefit of all. This influence coincided with our entrance into adolescence which allowed us greater levels of personal freedom and provided opportunity to travel to attend concerts and demonstrations that further solidified our immersion into anarcho-punk. Under these influences, we were altering the way in which we lived (both becoming vegetarians at the age of 13 and 14) and were inspired to return to making music with an added purpose, renaming our band Napalm Death in May 1981.

In this context, *Antisocial* felt – to me at least – like a relic of another era.[24] After discussion, we made the amicable decision to cease production and concentrate on our own individual publications. While Miles continued to produce *Twisted Nerve* (releasing a further three issues during 1982 and 1983), my first act was to work on a new fanzine called *Autopsy*, completed in October 1981. Produced in a photocopied A4 format and a very minimal print run, *Autopsy* contained a mixture of polemical texts and collages alongside contact addresses for campaigning groups and lyrics by the anarcho-punk bands Disorder, Flux of Pink Indians, The Apostles and Terminal Disaster. In doing so, it represented a new direction.

## I was alive in 1982

In retrospect, 1982 was a particularly fertile year. Immersing myself in the milieu, I continued a feverish level of correspondence with people, fanzines and bands and began visiting my fellow gazetteers across the country. Dodging the fare on the train and always accompanied by a plastic carrier bag of fanzines for sale, I would travel to concerts by anarcho-punk bands, including visits to the 'Anarchy Centres' at Wapping and the Centro Iberico in London. These activities dovetailed with political engagement, attending demonstrations (on one occasion witnessing an early version of the anarchist group Class War disrupt a CND rally) and taking part in politically motivated actions. Despite the dissolution of *Antisocial*, Miles and I continued to collaborate together in

Napalm Death, playing our first concerts and recording demo cassettes that we disseminated to fanzines accompanied by articles on our views and lyrics.

The fanzines I produced at this time – *Black Cross* (March 1982), *Museum Farce* (June 1982) and *Sine Nomine* (September 1982) – demonstrated a committed focus on anarcho-punk and the ideas it conveyed. While the design aesthetic continued to present the material in the chaotic manner that appealed to my sensibility (densely-packed typewritten text jostled for space with handwritten slogans and line drawings, printed at home in my bedroom; the 'do-it-yourself' ethic in action), the music coverage shifted to concentrate on the presentation of band statements and lyrics.[25] The remainder of the content consisted of personal writings on a range of topics, including consumerism and social control (*Black Cross*), animal rights and capitalism (*Museum Farce*), ecologism, religion and the conformity of fashion (*Sine Nomine*). This, in turn, was augmented by contact addresses for campaign organisations and placed alongside a small selection of reviews covering fanzines and cassette releases.


## 1 2 198Bore

1983 marked an endpoint, with the appearance of a single fanzine (*Unreason*, a polemical blend of personal texts and collages) heralding my withdrawal from anarcho-punk. During 1982, an undercurrent had begun to appear within the milieu that perceived anarcho-punk as an increasingly calcified and inflexible form. This sentiment was reflected in a number of fanzines, with editors bitterly describing their own contents as 'more of the same old anarcho-punk bands'[26] and 'another shit zine, same old views and groups'.[27] Both sentiments were echoed on the cover of my own *Sine Nomine*: 'Same old shit'.[28] While this sense of frustration may have been based on an increasingly negative perception of the music of anarcho-punk, the sense of repressive conformity seemed to encompass the movement as a whole. Hemmed in by peer pressure and fragmented allegiances, anarcho-punk had – for some – become a restrictive environment, not only for creativity but also for the very act of living. Miles expressed his own sense of alienation in the final issue of *Twisted Nerve* in February 1983: 'Well, How's life? Don't you just love escaping from reality by reading these fanzines, I mean you are only reading it for the bands, aren't you? … Anarchist is just another label created by the system to stop you from being you.'[29]

My response to this growing awareness of an impasse was a gradual but ultimately decisive withdrawal of my engagement. Retaining the positive outcomes of this period (the recognition of the value of creativity, the energy generated from collaboration and interaction, an awareness of my own political perspective), I moved forwards: by the end of the year, Napalm Death had entered an indefinite hiatus and the written and visual content that I sporadically created through the remainder of 1983 and into 1984 remained unpublished. My time as a fanzine producer had reached an organic conclusion: I ceased making fanzines before I left school.

## Notes

1   The subheading comes from *Damn Latin*, 5 (1980), p. 18.
2   Crass, 'Punk Is Dead', *The Feeding of the Five Thousand* (Small Wonder Records, 1979).
3   Examples included *Private Enterprise* (Coventry), *Adventures in Reality* (Coventry), *Smart Verbal* (Birmingham), *Scrawl* (Birmingham), *Guttersnipe* (Telford) and *Damn Latin* (Nuneaton).
4   Simon Dwyer, 'Editorial', *Rapid Eye Movement*, 1 (1980), p. 3.
5   We used the John Bull printing kits that could be commonly found in second-hand shops at the time. A relic of previous decades, their availability and affordability led to their use in a number of fanzines, including *Surrey Vomet* (1978) and *Pigs for Slaughter* (1981).
6   The 'band index' provided a means of directly accessing bands by publishing their telephone numbers. Martin Bowes, the editor of *Alternative Sounds*, foregrounded his perception of the importance of facilitating communication in the pamphlet he produced to accompany his appearance on the BBC television programme *Something Else*: 'In my mag, I place great emphasis on contacts – addresses and phone numbers, and I think these are very important to get things progressing and get people helping each other out' (Martin Bowes, *Something Else – How to Make a Fanzine*, 1980, p. 5).
7   Martin Bowes, 'Local 'Zines-and-not-so-local', *Alternative Sounds*, 17 (1980), p. 14.
8   The fanzine was printed by the bass player of Coventry's The Wild Boys (who were featured in issue 3 of *Antisocial*). He also printed *Alternative Sounds*.
9   Alan Rider, the editor of *Adventures in Reality* fanzine, produced three of these fanzines: *Sticky Fingers*, *Certain Substances* and *Negative Response*.
10  Both fanzines continued the reproduction approach taken for our previous fanzines, appearing in small print runs as single-sided photocopies annotated with hand colouring and printing stamps. *Out of Vogue* was also housed in a handmade, annotated fold-out envelope.
11  Many cities and towns had their own examples of these bookshops. Examples include Freewheel (Norwich), Grassroots (Manchester), News from Nowhere (Liverpool) and The Other Branch (Leamington Spa).

12 'Sale or return' was a common method of retail, allowing unsold stock to be returned to the producer. Rough Trade used this approach for selling fanzines.

13 I was particularly inspired by Stuart Christie and Albert Meltzer's *The Floodgates of Anarchy*, Colin Ward's *Anarchy in Action*, reprints of the communiqués by the Angry Brigade, David Wise's pamphlet on Situationism and punk music, *The End of Music*, and Larry Law's series of chapbooks *Spectacular Times*.

14 *No Real Reason*, 3 (1979), p. 1. Examples include references to *Enigma* as 'an excellent piece of anarchist propaganda' (*Aftermath*, 5 (1980), p. 9) and *A New Body* as an 'anarchist 'zine' (*New Crimes*, 5 (1981), p. 10).

15 These concerts included benefits for fanzines such as *Toxic Grafity*, *No Easy Answers*, *Cobalt Hate* and *Final Straw*, alongside benefits for other radical publications including *Peace News*.

16 Crass and Poison Girls, 'Bloody Revolutions' backed with 'Persons Unknown' (Crass, 1980).

17 *Nihilistic Vices*, 1 (1979), p. 1.

18 Rob Challice, *So What*, 4 (1981), p. 16.

19 Jah Ovjam (Graham Burnett), 'Doing It Yourself: Some Handy Hints', *New Crimes*, 5 (1981), p. 11.

20 Letters page, *Black Dwarf*, 2 (1980), p. 12.

21 *Toxic Grafity* fanzine presents an example of the development of this approach: issue 5 (1980) contained articles on bands but no interviews and issue 6 (1981) removed all musical content, focusing instead on polemical articles.

22 Jah Ovjam (Graham Burnett), 'Other DIY Magazines', *New Crimes*, 7 (1983), p. 12.

23 Rob Challice, *So What*, 4 (1981), p. 16.

24 In an act that seems prescient, Miles had added the strapline 'Ye Olde Fanzeen' to the front cover image of a nuclear explosion on issue 4 of *Antisocial*.

25 The fanzines were printed on a secondhand Gestetner stencil duplicating machine. In this process, carbon stencils were typed and drawn on to create a single side of an A4 page and were then attached to the ink-covered rotating drum of the printer for printing by hand. Pages were fed through the machine and placed to dry, before a new stencil was attached to the drum and printing continued on the other side of the paper. The fragility of the stencils used to create the page masters and the unpredictability of the print coverage meant the fanzines were often poorly reproduced (with the exception of *Museum Farce*, which was photocopied in order to deliver a faithful copy of the collage content). At the time, however, this seemed a small price to pay for controlling the means of production.

26 *Hell Starts Here*, 1 (1982), p. 1.

27 *The Big If*, 1 (1982), p. 1.

28 *Sine Nomine*, 1 (1982), p. 1.

29 *Twisted Nerve*, 5 (1983), p. 3.

# 13

# *Kick*: positive punk

RICHARD CABUT

In the autumn of 1982, I was living in a punk squat in New North Road, London, N1, a walk from Old Street, unreconstructed and sort of scary/lairy at that time. On one occasion I was mugged for 26½ pence; all I had in my pocket and pretty much all I had in the world. I was on the dole and spent my time conducting a fruitful lifestyle based on what I described in my fanzine *Kick* as 'creativity, individuality and rebellion'.[1]

*Kick 4* had been published at the end of that summer and had attracted a fair amount of attention from other fanzines, the music press and even received mention on the *John Peel Show* – which meant a lot. It was the interaction offered by selling the mag at gigs by bands like Southern Death Cult, UK Decay and Sex Gang Children that had led to an invite to live in the squat. *Kick* was part of, and described, a certain scene. As I wrote in the introduction to that issue:

> Although we are pushing PUNK, I think it's become necessary to define
> terms. For a start, we're not talking about punk in terms of the oi oi, bootboy
> lot who have nothing to say & nothing to offer. It's their brainless, class,
> macho mentality that punk has been trying to get rid of from the start. It's
> 'easy way out' punk that requires a leather jacket for the night and not much
> else. Then for the rest of the week it's work, pub, death. On the other hand
> and at the opposite end of the scale are the 'dead-head' type punx who have

seen punx who have seen a fragment of freedom (thru squatting, no work etc.) but have chained themselves up again thru drug dependence and other fixed dogmas & expectations. Self-destruction has become some sort of punk common denominator in a lot of people's minds. But not in ours. We're still conveying it as a positive way of beating reality rather than escaping it (for a few hours down a pub or club). Punk still means the destruction of the conventions and expectations that society has thrown up. It means working on the preconceptions that surround things like work, parents, school, clothes etc. etc. This is why punk is still relevant and important and if you want it to happen, then make it happen for yourself, don't wait for others to do it for you. 'Do it now'. When you do, natural intelligence, instinct & energy will develop thru repeated indulgence. The rebellious surge will transform 'WORK', REST & PLAY into one single conscious and subconscious experiment in LIFE.

In the second part of the introduction, I imagined punks as barbarians at the gates of 'Rome' – their appearance signalling a crisis in civilisation. Punks, I fancied, were part of one of W.B. Yeats's cyclic turns: they were the rough beast slouching towards Bethlehem to be born. I was sure of this. After all, 'mere anarchy' had been loosed. Although there was nothing 'mere' about it as far as I was concerned. I suggested that the current punk sphere had evolved from the 'caper of the Seventies' on to a 'total rejection of the whole of society'. I wrote about how I and some friends in my suburban hometown had always been barbarians, or at least since being first inspired by punk, and had remained so, waiting for the world to catch up with us, to reach a crisis: 'What that crisis is and why the present generation is reacting to it the way it does is the theme of this fanzine and of the issues following it'.

My own crisis had culminated in the flight from suburbia. Mostly I dreamt of escape. I lived in smalltown, working-/lower middle-class suburbia: Dunstable, Bedfordshire. Thirty miles from the capital. Here, kids left school and went on the track, the production line, at the local factory, Vauxhall Motors. If you could get some qualifications you could join the civil service. Meanwhile, Trevor and Nancy had been going out with each other since Third Form and watched telly round each other's house every night, not saying a word. I didn't know what I wanted but I knew I didn't want any of that shit ever. Instead, I was in love with punk rock. I was in love with picking up momentum and hurling myself forward somewhere. Anywhere. Rip up the pieces and see where they land. I was suburban punk Everykid in pins and zips, with a splattering of Jackson Pollock and a little Seditionaries. In my bedroom there was some Aleister Crowley, a bit of Sartre, *48 Thrills* (bought off Adrian at a Clash gig), Sandy Roberton's *White Stuff* (from Compendium in Camden) and *Sniffin' Glue and Other Self Defence Habits* ( July 1977), of course. If, as the cliché has it, escape from the ghetto could only be achieved by means of sport or showbiz, then either learning three chords or scrawling a fanzine was the easiest way out of the suburbs for bored punk rockers.

I was rubbish on guitar at the time, and so I started planning my first fanzine, *Corrugated Boredom*. For the zine, which was never actually printed, I wrote a review of a local Clash gig (25 January 1978) Steve and I joined a big group of new punks, maybe 30 or 40 strong, walking along the main road. A police car stopped us, and everyone waited his or her turn to be searched. The kid in front of me surreptitiously pulled out a gun, a real revolver that he'd nicked from a party, apparently, and passed it back through the group to a girl who stuck it in her handbag, crossed the road and walked away. I should have done the same. The gig itself was a bloodbath. Different estates slugged it out with each other – Lewsey Farm v Stopsley – people staggered around with axe wounds, blood everywhere, the Wild West. A support band called The Lous were killed, the Sex Pistols' minder English wandered around with a knife. I was backstage and The Clash were worried, popping Mogadons. I was worried, too – that I'd get stuck forever in all this bollocks. I knew it was time to move. Which, I did – to London. The bright lights. 'Don't dream it, be it' (*The Rocky Horror Show*). Yeah.

London was, of course, the traditional refuge for suburban refugees – people who felt disaffected by life in the sticks: the treadmill, the mores, the conservatism, the repressive nature of family life. We wanted to tip all of this upside down, assert ourselves and fathom the world. In the late 1970s and early 1980s, there existed a diaspora centred in London, where punks sought fresh forms of community. Consequently, social spaces sprang up where punk culture could really develop. The Anarchy Centre, first in Wapping, and then on the Harrow Road, provided a place for extraordinary enveloping happenings. And, Ollie Wisdom's Batcave – before the hoo-ha: a multi-media hangout mixing DJs with cinema and a range of live acts in a fantastically expressive atmosphere where reality could be confronted and perhaps subverted a little.

I lived and gallivanted with some of the people who would later become known as the *Kill Your Pet Puppy* Collective, including Tony D, who produced the *KYYP* fanzine, first at the aforementioned squat in New North Road, and then in Westbere Road, West Hampstead. The New North Road squat broke up thanks to petty animosities and personality clashes. The house was later taken over by Tom Vague and friends, and my room was inhabited by Ian, singer of The Southern Death Cult, later The Cult, who drew some pretty funky drawings all over the walls.

The place I moved to in West Hampstead was something of a hub. All kinds of cool and crazy people would pitch up. Bands, writers, vagrants, and a TV crew on occasion. It was a punk rock melting pot of striking creativity and cross-pollination. The interaction fuelled creativity and vice versa. 'Westbere Road was a sanctuary from the changes sweeping punk at the time,' Tony D recalled. 'It was also a catalyst'.

In Westbere Road, and other punk squats, a young, rebellious, open culture began to create (mostly mayhem!) An honourable, self-sufficing and self-sufficient economy – low-level capitalism – began, based on the production of music, fanzines, fashion and art. Squats became hives of activity for a diverse range of people. It was a world away from both suburban restraint and urban bedsit boredom, or from the lifestyle of the aforementioned 'dead-head type punx' in their seedy, down-'n'-out squats. Blood and Roses' Bob Short in his book *Filth* portrays this scene best, perhaps. Bob accurately describes how life was really lived – and death really died – in extreme conditions of debauch and poverty underpinned by a sense of overwhelming stare-at-the-wall-drooling boredom, punctuated only by outbursts of violence and furore, usually fuelled by whatever substances came to hand. It's an underworld of alienation, loneliness, hopelessness and anger. Well, it was either that or get a job ...

Short's London was centred in the Campbell Buildings in Waterloo, a kind of punk annexe to Dante's inferno, a nether place peopled in the main by 'dole bludgers, charlatans, delinquents, drug addicts, petty thieves and musicians'. The worst, of course, were the musicians and therein lies the link between squalor and glamour, I suppose.

A similar hellhole was to be found at Coronation Buildings in Vauxhall, home for a while of *Kick* writer Lill. I remember visiting once to find scenes of devastation after a roving gang of skinheads had attacked the squat and raped some of the female punks. In *Kick*, though, I very much accentuated the positive. I liked the punk scene in the early 1980s. I liked it in the mid-1970s too. The late 1970s, though, were like the third Monday in January, officially recognised by the medical profession as the day on which more UK citizens wake up depressed than any other. The reality of another grinding year kicks in, the horror of the Christmas credit card bill bites, and the misery of another rain-dashed day dawns. It was like that. But the early 1980s were another punk spring. As described, punk at that time became a way of life for an increasingly large and motivated group of people. Moreover, folk were, to paraphrase Malcolm McLaren, creating an environment in which they could truthfully run wild. Instead of just listening to records in isolation and going to the odd gig, people were having life adventures – documented by fanzines like *KYPP* (the biggest and best fanzine), *Panache*, *Vague* and *Kick*.

We wrote about bands like Southern Death Cult, Sex Gang Children, Bauhaus, their predecessors Adam and the Ants and the Banshees, and later Brigandage and Blood and Roses: bands that promulgated the overriding ethic and aesthetic of rebellion, individuality and creativity, with a touch of esoterica, some flash and plenty of glam dash to boot. Having said that, the music was the least important part of the equation – the bands simply provided the soundtrack to a lifestyle.

We strutted our Billy-the-Kid sense of cool – bombsite kids clambering from the ruins – posing our way out of the surrounding dreariness. We were living in our own colourful movie (an early-ish Warhol flick, some of us liked to think), which we were sure was incomparably richer, more spontaneous and far more magical than the depressing, collective black-and-white motionless picture that the conformists had to settle for. But we had a clear understanding of the here and now, and a desire to get out of it – rather than just *get out of it*. We cared with unflinching sincerity, although not many were intellectuals or activists in the traditional political sense. Of more interest were, perhaps, the fantastic slogans. 'They said that oblivion was their ruling passion. They wanted to reinvent everything each day; to become the masters of their own lives.' That kind of thing. And I don't recall many people attending marches or 'political' meetings on a regular basis.

I once wrote a sort of verse, which talked about the 'Romance of Anarchy' becoming 'Reality'. I believed that the romance is grounded in a reality that makes clear that, on all levels, the process of daily life is based on a trade of humiliations and aggro, as the situationists (a big influence, of course) said. I thought that 'alienated work is a scandal', that so-called 'leisure' is an affront, and that 'real life is elsewhere'. Where? Well, the pertinent questions, I thought, are not about restructuring economic systems, although I admit on a day-to-day level that helps, but about how quickly the underpinnings of society – all the givens, great unmentionables, so-called axioms, the fact that it is a closed-loop feedback system which easily sops up and throws back challenges and critiques – could be dissolved. I demanded that this happens. And I felt, to paraphrase the Situ slogan and Malcolm McLaren's shirt, I was entirely reasonable to demand the impossible.

This, I feel, was the overriding, if sometimes coded, message given in the best fanzines of those years. Including *Kick*, I hope. My fanzine, and the scene itself, to an extent, was probably more influenced by someone like Richard Neville and his 'Politics of Play' than party politics. In his 1970 book, *Playpower*, Neville stands aside from the straight Left. We got the memo. The straights were about working hard and supportively, while for us there was no wish to work at all. The straights wanted work for everyone (and this was a time of mass unemployment) whereas we shrugged off the very thought of routine to focus on the exciting stuff, and somehow managed to get by.

We were like kids (hence *Play*power). I was positive that self-empowered, autodidactic, spiky guttersnipes were an upsurge of the future, certain to overcome the old political order – the RCP, the SWP, the stolid Left, the more traditional anarchists even. I remember, later, sneering at the people who supported the miners' strike. Many in our circle did. I remember talking to Fred Vermorel, author of *Sex Pistols: The Inside Story* among other books, who moaned about the Pistols' art director Jamie Reid because he spoke out in support of the strike. We wondered why anyone would want to work underground. I regret this attitude now. We should all have stood firm. This is clearly the downside of the so-called 'cult of individuality' – politically, a liberal dead end, to paraphrase writer Marek Kohn.

Instead, *Kick* and the other fanzines described the punk scene in the same way as, in one episode of the TV show *Bewitched*, the character Endora describes the difference between witches and humans, 'They all look the same to me, noses to the grindstone, shoulders to the wheel, feet planted firmly on the ground, no wonder they can't fly!' She adds: 'It's fine for them but not for us. We are quicksilver, a fleeting shadow, a distant sound that has no boundaries through which we can't pass. We are found in music, in a flash of colour, we live in the wind and in a sparkle of star … '[2]

It was a magical time, in more ways than one. Serious, sometimes seemingly endless conversations were held about occultists like Aleister Crowley, Austin Osman Spare, Kenneth Grant and the possibilities of magic. Use of the tarot and I Ching were a daily occurrence. The inside back cover of *Kick 4* was a hastily drawn Tree of Life – from Kether to Malkuth. 'Magic hung in the air', Tony D recalled, 'life was almost unexplainable and the only way to make sense of it was through people like Crowley and his works and path.'

Few, though, ploughed through the theory. Most were more interested in the mystery rather than the history, I suppose. As Kohn wrote in his 1983 'Punk's New Clothes' piece for *The Face*: 'Two things in rock are really easy to conjure up without trying very hard: a loud noise and an air of mystery. For the latter, you just drop a few hints and your audience fall over themselves to do the rest. A lack of irony, playfulness and humour; a handful of horror

**13.1** *Kick*, 4 (1982) © Richard Cabut

images (both the supernatural and the violent varieties), a need to conjure up an aura ... '[3]

But there was a little more to the association between magic and our punk scene than that, as I myself wrote in the *NME* in 1983:

Nor is it a silly hippy Tolkien fantasy joyride, or even a Killing Joke stench-of-death gloomier-than-thou slice of fanaticism. These groups are aware: UK Decay (positive punk forefathers), using the dark to contrast and finally emphasise the light; Sex Gang Children taking us into the sub-world of the Crowleyan abyss; while Blood And Roses are pushing the symbols a whole lot further, their guitarist Bob being a serious student of the Art. The mystical tide we are talking about here refers, if nothing else, to the inner warmth and vital energy that human beings regard as the most favourable state to live in. The new positive punk has tapped into this current.[4]

I started writing for the *NME* towards the end of 1982. This was probably one of the reasons why *Kick 5* was never printed, although I had already put together much of that issue. Echoing the 1960s/1970s exodus of writers from the underground press to the mainstream, I jumped on the music press bandwagon, as did many of the main punk fanzine writers: Tom Vague (*Vague–Zigzag*), Mick Mercer (*Panache–Melody Maker*), Alistair Livingston (*The Encyclopaedia of Ecstasy–Punk Lives*), Tony D (*Kill Your Pet Puppy–NME*), Robin Gibson (*It Ticked and Exploded–Sounds*). Why? The consensus among ourselves was that we had 'sold out' in order to further push 'our' bands and 'the revolution'. We felt that we were, with our undying passion for punk, attacking orthodoxy and challenging those in power, sometimes in volatile ways. We thought we were encouraging the overground music press to tackle concerns that they would otherwise have ignored – for instance, I wrote about the Black Sheep Housing Co-op, which grew out of the squatting movement in Islington (I was a member). Tony D wrote about international anarchist organisations for the *NME* and Alistair Livingston wrote about the Anarchy Centre for *Punk Lives*.

But we also revelled in the attention and status that an *NME* byline attracted and afforded. I remember the moment I decided I would try to join the *NME*, during a conversation with Tony about the merits of some LP. Tony, who had already taken the IPC shilling, countered my no-doubt excellent argument with, 'Pah, *you* don't write for the *NME*'. I soon did – Tony was to blame. Despite the fact that we had all sniped at the *NME* in our fanzines, we regarded it, in truth, with no little respect.

I wrote the positive punk article for the *NME* in January/February 1983. Really, it reiterated much of what I had previously written in *Kick*, and what other fanzines had reported, too, about the state of the punk scene in the early 1980s. At that time there were three distinct groupings. The Oi-sters and 'herberts', who were basic and gumby-ish in their music, fashion and behaviour; the anarchos, who were a mass of black, in terms of clothes and demeanour; and our loose, nameless collection of punks and former punks who were colourful and full, it seemed, of vim and go-ahead spirit. We tended to go to see roughly the same bands and attended the same sort of clubs. I wrote about many of the bands and places, ranging from the Batcave and Specimen to The Mob (who were sort of anarcho-plus). I liked the make-up-break-down, safe-when-dangerous, follow-the-heart-and-unconscious-mind, heaven-and-hell-and-kiss-and-tell bands like Bauhaus, Wasted Youth, Flesh for Lulu and Psychedelic Furs. Groups that promoted sensual style and re-action:

> With wild-coloured spiked hair freezing the eye, and even more vivid clothes to spice the imagination – faces, thoughts and actions – the atmosphere's infused with a charge of excitement, an air of abandon underlined with a sense of purpose. Something stirs again in this land of fetid, directionless sludgery, this land of pretend optimism and grim reality. Theory and practice are being synthesised under the golden umbrella of a 24-hour long ideal. Welcome to the new positive punk … a re-evaluation and rejuvenation of the ideals that made the original outburst so great, an intensification of and expansion of that ethos of individuality, creativity and rebellion.[5]

The positive punk article garnered a reaction. *Melody Maker* wrote an amusing pastiche; *The Face* replied with its own piece complete with photos of all the key participants; there were myriad mentions in the fanzines; LWT's Friday night arts and leisure series, *South of Watford*, devoted an episode to the 'movement'. Host Michael Moorcock came to Westbere Road one morning to conduct interviews and, seeing that we were all worse for wear after a late night at the Tribe Club, gave us some (extremely potent) speed to encourage the chat. It worked … perhaps all too well – *Private Eye* contacted me afterwards to ask whether it was true that the presenter had given drugs to his obviously over-refreshed interviewees. I denied everything.

But Positive Punk was a disaster. Once something is named, it becomes easy to attack. Bands like Sex Gang Children refused to become involved – because they couldn't control it. Their noses had been put out of joint. The bigwigs in the scene, Sex Gang, Southern Death Cult, *et al.*, had suddenly been usurped, or so they thought, by upstarts like Brigandage and Blood and Roses, who had received most coverage in the piece. Overnight, the atmosphere changed from togetherness to suspicion, jealousy and loathing. This would probably have happened in any case, but the article greatly accelerated the process. As far as I am concerned, positive punk described the 'Passage of a few People (wearing makeup and top hats) through a Rather Brief Moment in Time.'[6] I think it was accurate. In hindsight, the music wasn't great but, as aforesaid, that wasn't really the point. And then it turned into goth, with even worse music.

The Westbere Road house also finished – many of the *KYPP* collective went off to become New Age Travellers. I, meanwhile, joined Brigandage and continued to write for the music press and, later, various national media organisations. Nevertheless, I maintain that *Kill Your Pet Puppy*, *Vague*, *Kick* and the other fanzines of that time and space, revealed our particular genre of 1980s punk to be remarkable in its essence – creative, spirited and progressive. Full of, yes, individuality, creativity and rebellion.

## Notes

1  *Kick*, 3, 1980, p. 4.
2  *Bewitched*, Series 1, Episode 2, 1964. BBC.
3  Marek Kohn, *The Face*, April 1983, p. 18.
4  Richard Cabut (writing as Richard North), 'Punk Warriors', *NME*, 19 February 1983, p. 14.
5  North, 'Punk Warriors', p. 14.
6  This sentence is obviously a nod to the title of a film by Guy Debord, *On the Passage of a Few Persons Through a Rather Brief Moment in Time* (1959).

# 14

# 'This is aimed as much at us as at you': my life in fanzines

CLARE WADD

It was the summer of 1984 and I lived in Harrogate, was sixteen and was doing – or had just finished doing – my O levels. I'd been really into music for a couple of years by that point, but hadn't yet made it to many gigs, nor bought many actual records. I'd gone from obsession with the charts – finger poised over the pause button during Sunday dinner – to taking a little transistor into school on Tuesday lunchtimes to hear it first, trying to work out how things got in the charts if you didn't hear them until they were in the charts, to evening Radio One. It wasn't long since David Lees at school had explained what 'indie' meant one lunchtime when he brought in the first music paper I ever saw, nor since Rosie Cuckston (later of Pram) had lent me *Transformer* and it had fairly much blown my mind. Rosie had older half-brothers who listened to John Peel, so she told me about him too, but he wasn't on until 10p.m. and that was bedtime, so I was only really supposed to hear him say hello. Mostly I settled for Kid Jensen, whose music I liked better at that age too.

This particular night Kid Jensen was talking about fanzines. I'd never heard of them before, but I loved writing and loved music so I decided I was going to write one. It never occurred to me that being sixteen, living in a town not a city, not really knowing anything much about music, nor, frankly, anything else, and never having seen a fanzine, would be any sort of barrier. Neither did it occur to me that being a girl would be a barrier either. Ever since I'd understood that my brother could do stuff I couldn't because he was two years older, not because he was a boy, I'd just assumed I could do anything. There was sexism at school of course – the uniform, sports, woodwork vs. cookery – but I didn't really understand that it existed as a real thing in real life, that when there weren't actual rules there was still the ability to patronise, put down, make fun of, bully – and that that worked nearly as well as rules to exclude girls and women. Writing a fanzine just seemed like it would be right up my street.

I wrote off for some fanzines, mostly other Yorkshire ones, as I was looking for community too. Once you got one, you had the addresses for others, and a whole new world opened up. Coins taped to bits of cardboard whizzing round the country, letters exchanged. At this point I was an enormous fan of The Alarm. I liked the music, I liked the politics, I liked the down-to-earth-ness, the way they hung around after gigs to talk to fans, the decentness of them. I'd barely seen another band play, except them and the bands supporting them. That summer I went on holiday to Tenby and was thrilled to go to a Radio One Roadshow there (Peter Powell!), which I saw as both hugely exciting and slightly naff. I just wanted to be near music.

Then suddenly the house was full of *Rox* and *Tongue In Cheek*, and I was reading about The Membranes, The Legend!, Chumbawamba, music I'd never heard, and had practically no way of hearing. I saw fanzines and I studied them and emulated them. James Brown from *Attack On Bzag* (later *Loaded*) kindly met me in Leeds and spent an afternoon showing me how to make paste-ups, explaining what would and wouldn't copy or print well, about shadow lines, and WH Smith's Letraset equivalent.

In common with most middle-class households back then, we had a typewriter which was used for official letters and job applications, or my dad's occasional articles. I commandeered it. I understood that fanzines were meant to be about not just music, but politics, life. I might have been living in Harrogate, but it was still 1984 and Yorkshire, and the miners' strike was the defining political event. At sixteen, battle lines were drawn – you were either for the miners or you weren't – and I was for them. The local news – Yorkshire in the living room, Tyne Tees in the kitchen – was factory, shipyard and chemical works closures day after day after day, job losses after job losses after job losses. I decided to do Economics A level.

The first issue of my fanzine, *Kvatch* (featuring Rosie as the cover star) included an interview with John Peel, reviews of books I'd been reading, interviews with several local bands, an article on youth hostels, a note that Leo's 'is the best nightclub' in Harrogate, and a page and a half of fanzine reviews. 'Zines!' it proclaimed on the cover, so clearly I thought a good reason to buy a fanzine was to link into other fanzines: *Raising Hell, New Youth,*

*Halitosis* (I had to ask my mum what that meant), *Total Nonsense, Yet Another Rag, Idiot Strength, Stability Ink, Sugar Beat, Primitive Patriot's Last Stand, Viz, Edition* and *Roar.*

I'd become aware of Richard Rouska, a ranting poet who did a fanzine and ran a copy shop in Leeds, and he printed up the early *Kvatchs*. I think both John Peel and Kid Jensen plugged the first one, and so the orders started to arrive. That autumn, there was what turned out to be a one-off York Rock Festival, with The Chameleons, Sisters of Mercy, Echo and the Bunnymen and Spear of Destiny. I went on my own and sold fanzines – having something to do between bands made going to gigs on your own OK – and proclaimed in issue 2 that Richard Rouska was the best act of the day.

My interests expanded into long-arm staplers and golf-ball typewriters – I had *two* fonts – and I had my first experience with prices quoted ex-VAT. I'd started making national-rate calls after school – thankfully, then, no itemised bills to give me away – to arrange interviews and talk to record companies. I came to love the smell of fresh printing. I hung out at the Entwhistle Thorpe copy shop on Cold Bath Road. I nipped out of school at lunchtime to call the printer – I was now using one on a trading estate in Scarcroft, East Leeds. I started to buy black-and-white film for my camera and took some terrible pictures of bands looking very grey and contrast-less. It all felt very worldly and incredibly grown-up compared with what my school friends were doing.

I was now in Sixth Form and had friends with driving licences who liked exotic bands like The Birthday Party, and I started to go to more gigs, where I could sell more fanzines. Over the next two years I produced a fanzine around every six months, growing the circulation each time to about 1,500. I got to understand what and where the independent record shops were that would sell them for me, and continued to get them mentioned on the radio. Looking back they're an eclectic mix, but I was a small-town kid, not really part of any scene, busy with A levels and the Saturday job in the library which paid for me to up the circulation, and then, with number 5, the size to A4 and add spot colour on the cover. As well as bands – Terry & Gerry, New Model Army, Half Man Half Biscuit, The Pogues, The Alarm, Faith Brothers and the Harrogate 'scene' – I wrote about Greenpeace, Traidcraft, Amnesty, The Ecology Party and Union Carbide. I printed other people's cartoons and poetry – there's one by Henry Normal and some by Chris Cooper, later of The Pale Saints. Surprisingly, looking back, there were also adverts for mail-ordering records, which I presumably must have been paid to run.

When my friends from the Upper Sixth left home, my horizons expanded, and I travelled to Birmingham to visit them. I drove all of us over the M62 one night to the Hacienda to see The Pogues. Matthew Eaton (later of Pram) drove us to Bradford to see The Smiths. In the summer of 1986 I went to stay with someone in London I'd met through the fanzine, and who had sent me a reading list opening my eyes to Capote, Salinger and Plath. I stayed with another friend met through fanzines in Darlington, Newcastle and Nottingham – he was a vegan, a kind of anarchist, and taught me to cook (and how to make a bong). I interviewed Ivor Cutler at the Ilkley Literature Festival and he rang up and (as I was in the pub) told my mum she should be proud of me. There was a lot going on in Leeds – The Wedding Present, Pink Peg Slax, The Sinister Cleaners, Age of Chance, Cud. I didn't like all of it, but it being there, just down the road, was exciting. And at home in Harrogate my friends formed Friends of the Family and released a record on Red Rhino. Everything was happening.

I went to art galleries and to Menwith Hill peace camp. I become a vegetarian and started eating funny food like chickpeas and tahini, and drinking herbal tea. This doesn't sound weird now, but this was North Yorkshire in the mid-1980s – a month before, the only vegetable I'd even liked had been peas. I started going round barefoot in summer, my feet getting so hardened I could walk the gravel path that took me to school. I went to jumble sales and bought a big grey men's overcoat and I made myself a skirt out of an old sheet.

A band called The Housemartins had sent me a demo I liked, and I arranged to interview them when they were playing at Warwick University – a friend's elder sister was at Poly nearby, so we could stay. By the time we got there they were number three in the charts and I was back in the mainstream. I watched soundchecks and met famous people.

University crept up and got less and less appealing. I was having too much fun. I'd only been to Bristol once, for the open day and, though it was a decent-sized city and nicely far away from home, I didn't really know anything else about it. In the weeks before I moved, I wrote off for three Bristol fanzines, hoping to make some friends, hoping to link into something like the scene I was a little bit part of in Leeds. *Are You Scared To Get Happy* (*AYSTGH*) suddenly seemed to be getting great reviews everywhere, although somehow that put me off and made me not want to like it; when it came it wasn't like anything I'd ever seen before and it left me a bit baffled.

Finally, I lived in a city with gigs that were easy to get to. Subway Records was taking off and was run from Martin Whitehead's parents' house, which wasn't far from where I was living in student halls, and looked not unlike my parent's house and made this world feel accessible. I was selling *Kvatch* 5 at gigs and by mail order, trying to keep up with my degree and my friends from home – and to make new friends, which wasn't really going so well. My friend Matthew was at Birmingham University and started talking about a band called The Sea Urchins, whose singer (Jamie) he knew and introduced me to. A lad in my student halls suggested I put a flexidisc with my next fanzine: everyone was doing it, he said. I'd met Matt from *AYSTGH* when I'd tried to sell him a fanzine at a gig, Primal Scream supporting Julian Cope, and he was part of the Sha-la-la flexi label with *Simply Thrilled*, *Baby Honey* and *Trout Fishing in Leytonstone* fanzines. As I walked virtually past his front door every day, I dropped a note through, wanting to know how heavy and bulky 1,000 flexis would be – could I get them home from London to Yorkshire on a National Express coach?

One thing that strikes me in retrospect about the community was how easily we trusted the other people in it, and how little, so far as I've ever heard, anyone got ripped off or abused. Matt was taking tapes up to London to make the new Sha-la-la flexis, so offered to take mine too (The Sea Urchins and The Groove Farm), along with my cheque (my entire savings) to get them made. They were making 2,500 copies of several flexis at once, to be distributed across various fanzines, by people they'd barely even met – they must have sent each other cheques, or perhaps delivered the flexis first and trusted the others to pay. We made friends through the post in the way that people now make friends through the internet. We had total strangers to stay, and we invited ourselves to stay with total strangers. In my first year at university, Dave from *Wake Up* fanzine drove me to see Billy Bragg in Cardiff and slept on my student halls floor for a couple of nights. I'd never met him before and have never met him since. We were a community and we trusted each other, but logically there must have been times when that trust was abused and things went badly wrong – perhaps they just weren't talked about.

At this point I don't think I'd ever met another female fanzine writer, and the only girl or woman I can remember corresponding with back then was an older (meaning mid-twenties) Alarm fan who, after a couple of months, was sending me thrice-weekly 45-page letters which, even as a teenager, I realised was a bit weird. I remember other girls doing fanzines from 1987 onwards but nothing before that – though there must have been some, even if very few.

*Kvatch* number 6 in 1987 turned out to be the last, because that summer Matt from *AYSTGH* and I got together and set up a record label, and everything we did after that was under the Sarah Records name. We both, in different ways, and coming from different directions, were deeply involved in the fanzine scene, so there was no question but that fanzines would play an integral part in the label. The bands were obscure, the music press was temperamental, and whether or not you could get played by John Peel or Janice Long involved a lot of luck. But we knew we could promote the first record through fanzines, and through people we knew through fanzines, and that gave us the confidence to set Sarah up and press an initial 1,000 Sea Urchins singles. We never had any doubt that we could sell them.

When we went to see Revolver in Bristol to ask for a manufacturing and distribution deal – meaning they would pay to press the records and would ensure they got in the shops, taking their money back from the proceeds – we got it because Sha-la-la had had 'singles of the week' in the music press, and because they knew we were part of a scene, which meant they weren't really taking such a big risk on two kids, one of whom was only 19. Inspired by Factory, we wanted our catalogue numbers not to be just for records, and we wanted the fanzines to be considered as important as the records. So *Sarah*s 3 and 4 in 1988 were a flexi and fanzine package. We each wrote half of the fanzine, working in from two different coloured covers, red and blue, two different ways up, with the flexi in the middle. We were nailing our fanzine colours firmly to our record label mast from the start. We weren't, and were never going to be, in bands – but the fanzines were our artistic contribution to the label's output and the thing that made us in it together with the bands.

*Sarah*s 13 and 14 were a flexi and two fanzines (14A and 14B) printed in brown; they were much less about music, and were more free-form writing. Mine featured a picture of an anonymous cute boy on the front and opens with: 'This is a fanzine for girls which means it won't be full of terribly drippy tales of wet Sunday afternoon girls on bicycles … ' The very male indie scene was getting to me clearly. It says: 'About once a week a letter arrives here addressed to "Clare & Matt". About 30 times a week a letter arrives here addressed to "Matt & Clare" (the rest are plain old SARAH). Irrelevant in itself, and certainly not worth getting worked up about – except that, surely, it must be indicative of something greater? Of the way people think: *man* and *then* woman … ' This is late 1988, and I'm calling myself a feminist and talking about the lack of female representation in parliament, equal pay and the tampon tax, and linking national politics back to indie-music politics. 'I hate you because you phone and say "Is that Sarah Records?" and I say "Yes, hello" and I can tell what you wanted was for me to say "Just a moment, he'll be right with you" and I WON'T I WON'T I WON'T. I hate you for that, for dismissing me, for thinking oh just some girl, his girlfriend.'

The next fanzine was *Sarah* 32, just mine, printed in pink (as a feminist statement), 10p, and hardly really mentions music at all – or just in passing as something that occupied our lives as people who ran a record label full-time. It was written in late 1989 and the back cover has a dedication 'to the writers of the only three fanzines left: Akiko, Big Maz from California, and Anne' – indicating a new internationalism, because these were respectively Japanese,

American and French. It seems to mostly be about the Berlin Wall coming down, Tiananmen Square and a little-remembered health scare involving hazelnut yoghurt.

We didn't do another fanzine until *Sarah* 70 (although we did write a lot of fanzine-esque inserts for the singles). *Sarah* 70 is so slight it's barely a fanzine at all – it's 6" square and 16 sides, not stapled or bound, wrapped around a Blueboy flexi and in a plastic bag. I had 4 sides, as did Matt and our friend Paul, and then Matt and I did one piece together. This is 1993 I guess, riot grrrl is in full swing, and we're on the sidelines of something publicly feminist when we've been feminist in this scene for years, without anyone really being interested. 'Where were you, mummy, when they closed down the NHS? Well, honey, I was busy making photo-collages of Kim Gordon and Anita Hill to stick onto lamp-posts … ' before a comment about 'REAL politics' being 'boing and grown-up' (ouch). 'This is aimed as much at us as at you', we say in a big font down the side for some balance.

Sarah Records continued until 1995 when we reached catalogue number 100, threw a big party and called it a day – it was never about running a business and it was always about being part of something. We took the inclusive anyone-can-do-it ethos of punk rock and fanzines into running what was ultimately a very successful record label, and which operated and supported us for eight years. We priced records cheaply, crammed lots of tracks on, didn't do limited editions or special versions, and exchanged huge numbers of letters with our record-buying public – many of whom also wrote fanzines, ran record labels, were in bands, or otherwise part of this whole thing. The whole point was that there was no divide between us as producers and the consumers, you couldn't have one without the other, and nobody was better than anyone else. And we knew that today's consumer would be tomorrow's producer – perhaps not everyone has a book in them, but certainly everyone had a fanzine in them.

# Global communications: continuities and distinctions

# Punking the bibliography: RE/Search Publications, the bookshelf question and ideational flow

S. ALEXANDER REED

Since 1980, San Francisco-based RE/Search has published zines, compendia and significant texts of western subculture. These publications contain hundreds of interviews with underground artists, intellectuals, collectors and scenesters, and throughout RE/Search's history, editor V. Vale (Vale Hamanaka) and former editor Andrea Juno have repeatedly asked these subjects some version of the 'bookshelf question': *What do you read?* When reading lists appear in the context of interviews and in the imprint's recognisable visual branding, RE/Search positions literature as epistemologically 'upstream' from inter-viewees' creative work in other media and indeed from their personalities – 'upstream' in the sense that literature apparently precedes and makes possible other expression. RE/Search is noteworthy in punk culture for privileging literary ideation, but far from rendering other expression simply lesser, literature's 'downstream' flow in this model becomes the lived actualisation of its ideas.

RE/Search (and its offshoot imprints V/Search and Juno Books) brands itself foremost as a punk publisher: it was born as an outgrowth of the punk zine *Search & Destroy* and, more recently, Vale has referred to punk as 'the final, terminal philosophy which encompasses the ideas, ideals and methods of all past undergrounds.'[1] RE/Search's publications cover industrial music, swing, retro and exotica aesthetics, pranks, DIY filmmaking, third-wave feminism, medical oddities, sadomasochism, the works of William S. Burroughs and J.G. Ballard, paganism and zine culture – and no matter how apparently unbookish some of its topics may seem, the bookshelf question insinuates itself, having simply become part of the interview process. 'We'd interview someone, and I'd go to their house and I'd see all their books. It was a little bit later that I got smarter, and I'd say "Can I take pictures?" That's so much faster than writing them down', Vale recalls.[2]

In 1979's *Search & Destroy* issue 8, an interview with punk band The Offs concludes with a section labelled separately as 'Vinil's Volumes', listing over twenty books from lead singer Don Vinil's bookshelf: a mix of Lovecraft, Gorey, Lautréamont and nonfiction works on film, art and horror.[3] When *Search and Destroy* metamorphosed into RE/Search's self-titled tabloid in 1980, among the interview subjects of issue 1 are Octavio Paz (who would win the 1990 Nobel Prize in Literature) and UK industrial band Cabaret Voltaire, with whom this exchange occurs:

> R/S: You've seen a lot of interesting films that have come out – the Cronenbergs, Romeros, THE CRAZIES ...
>
> MAL: Films are quite an important input that we feed off ... we have to go out of our way to see them.
>
> CHRIS: Actually a lot of my inspiration comes *through literature*. One of the really great things that Burroughs has said is – *The only true creative writing comes from technical journals and treatises* – and that, no matter how glib it may sound, is very true in a lot of senses. Access to technical information is one of the most important things, to me.[4]

Issue 2, from 1981, offers a separate text box of 'Suggested Reading' in its interview with Survival Research Laboratories' Mark Pauline; his picks include Michael Uhl and Tod Ensign's *GI Guinea Pigs: How the Pentagon Exposed Our Troops to Dangers More Deadly Than War*.[5] Full pages of references follow every interview in issues 6 and 7 (collectively *The Industrial Culture Handbook*) and, from then on, various entries in the *RE/Search* series contained a bibliography. In the postmillennial Real Conversations series, interviews wrap up with a page or two of 'Recommendations'. And so the bookshelf question extends across the imprint's whole history. 'Right from the first issue of *Search and Destroy*, we were asking people what they read. It's the internal life that matters', Vale affirms.[6]

Dominating interviewees' varied responses to the bookshelf question are trade paperbacks, nonfiction exposés, textbooks and works of philosophical or political argument. Consistently we encounter authored works of intention that, while perhaps offbeat, are primarily *books* – in a way that RE/Search publications themselves are typically not, as we shall see.

RE/Search volumes are germane to the study of zines on several fronts. First, two of RE/Search's popular publications (1996's *Zines!* volumes I and II) expressly collect interviews with zine writers and archivists from various generations and locales. Second, those earliest RE/Search tabloids were typewritten zines before the brand expanded to use professional bookbinding. This occurred when Juno and Vale launched a typesetting company in the early 1980s, RE/Search Typography. And third, RE/Search's publications have continually blurred the line between media categories including catalogues, coffee-table books, academic volumes and, yes, zines.

Even on the rare occasions when Juno and Vale reprinted fiction, the house style of oversize formats and intentionally gaudy graphics branded the physical products as sensationalist: the way RE/Search publications *look* places them outside easy belletristic categories. Juno says, 'In *Incredibly Strange Films*, we had this quote, "the enemy of creativity is good taste". That's what guided how the early projects were designed: hand-done, with full quotes – that kind of funky design, not super slick. Some of our friends published with lovely minimalist clean design, and I just felt like I just wanted to destroy that with bad taste, something that would maybe pull in the eye – something earthy.'[7] The specific aesthetics of these publications' look and layout serve important functions: following familiar zine practices, a page's disjunction opens to readers juxtapositional spaces that suggest depth beyond the actual text – spaces whose nonstandard reading and writing metaphorically extend to nonstandard ways of being and thinking; this is part of why zine aesthetics are so tied to cultural undergrounds. Furthermore, this design compels rereading: a nonlinear pass through a zine or a RE/Search book can leave a reader asking: 'Did I see everything there was to see?' Obsession beckons. Scholar Joanne Murray writes of RE/Search's zine-like layout (in the context of its Ballard publications),

> This radical non-linear narrative structure, one that encourages the reader to engage with the text like a media product or a collage, is encouraged not just by RE/Search's inclusion of actual illustrations and photographs, but also through the interplay that is set up between text and image. On a basic level, the images create another platform for associative links to take place, but the way in which RE/Search actually label the images also intensifies our experience of the text ... and [the aesthetic] also finds its way into the RE/Search Conversations and Quotes books.[8]

RE/Search may no longer use mimeographs as an authorial tool, but their aesthetic medium – in all its debt to zine practice – is of a qualitatively different stuff than the 'proper' books they list in their recommendations.

## The bookshelf question

A quote from John Waters' 2007 stand-up movie *This Filthy World* has become a social media meme in recent years: 'We have to make books cool again, you know? If you go home with somebody and they don't have books, don't fuck 'em.'[9] Part of the joke's power derives from the unspoken assumption that *you are what you read*. Juno puts it: 'The question of what someone reads is really important. That's the window of your mind. That's the great "Is this person interesting?" question.'[10] To RE/Search and John Waters alike, literature bears a specific primacy: Waters caps his gag: 'And DVDs don't count either.'[11] By publishing titles from the alleged library of an interview subject (often a celebrity), editors can set in motion a surprising number of power plays. Let us step momentarily outside the RE/Search corpus and closely read two examples.

First, the year is 1900, and the 18 August edition of London's *The Academy: A Weekly Review of Literature and Life* features a brief about the supposed reading habits of famous men. For the prime minister, Robert Gascoyne-Cecil, 'One book has always fascinated me, and on more than one occasion has drawn me out of bed very early in the morning. This is Dumas' *Monte Cristo*.'[12] The Archbishop of Canterbury Frederick Temple has meanwhile apparently traded in 'the noble ancient classics' for Kipling.[13]

These anecdotes are reprinted from a contemporary magazine, *The Gem*, and were sensationally viral, being published again two weeks later in the *New York Times* and, for the next three years, in various newspapers across the USA. *The Academy* noncommittally questions their authenticity ('Qualms of incredulity – we know not why – mar our enjoyment of some stories')[14] but publishes them nonetheless. The stories humanise their lofty subjects while advertising to readers a humbly populist new canon. By quoting *The Gem*, *The Academy* establishes participation and membership in a contemporary written dialogue, but by critiquing the stories' veracity, it takes a jab too. Most curiously, the article primes readers for recommendation and then – in the very same column, and separated only by a horizontal rule – is immediately followed thus: 'It is not often that we see a catalogue of such out-of-the-way literature as one which has just been issued by Messrs. Maurice, of Bedford-street, Covent Garden. It is a catalogue of "The Literature of Occultism and Archæology"; and it is divided under such awesome headings as Alchemy, Astrology, Chiromancy, Magic and Witchcraft, Mystics and Oracles, Platonism, &c.'[15] Whether by bizarre chance or subversive design, this juxtaposition is provocation: when you've exhausted the great leaders' disarmingly boyish libraries, here are the strange tomes to lead you down winding paths.

Second, fast-forward to 2007: *Control* is a biopic about the post-punk band Joy Division and their doomed lead singer Ian Curtis, who committed suicide in 1980. Directed by punk photographer Anton Corbijn (who had known and photographed the band), the story begins in 1973, and its first scene, both in its filmic construction and in the teenage reality it believably portrays, is a case study in the power of the bookshelf.

Here's what happens: Curtis, sixteen or seventeen at the time, enters the family flat in Macclesfield to the soundtrack's strains of David Bowie's 'Drive-In Saturday', the lead single from that April's *Aladdin Sane* LP. Media choices indicate identity in this scene: Bowie's lyric 'lend us a book, we can read up alone' arrives as Curtis rushes silently past his father, who sits at the breakfast table reading a newspaper – *his* world of black-and-white factuality. Curtis then heads to his bedroom, a space whose first identity comes from our glimpse down the hallway, where through the door we see three full bookshelves on his wall, along with a picture of Lou Reed. The difference between Curtis's media and his father's newspaper underscores the apartment's geopolitics: the rulers and the information flow differ from room to room.

A moment later, the camera has joined Curtis in his room and pans slowly across the walls to show off the boy's pre-punk curriculum: a Jim Morrison postcard, the brightly iconic cardboard sleeve for *Aladdin Sane*, a January 1973 copy of the *New Musical Express* with headlines about Pentangle and Roxy Music, coinciding with Bowie singing 'It's a crash course for the ravers'. And then, within seconds, come the books – a single shelf, its volumes stacked haphazardly as if to suggest their having all been read fragmentarily and at once:

William S. Burroughs's surrealist grotesque *The Naked Lunch*
J.G. Ballard's icy erotic sci-fi *Crash*
J.G. Ballard's experimental microfiction *The Atrocity Exhibition*
Robert Taber's guerrilla guide *The War of the Flea*
Norman Mailer's anti-government takedown *The Armies of the Night*
Allen Ginsberg's banned classic of beat poetry *Howl and Other Poems*
David Cooper's anti-conservative psychiatric work *The Death of the Family*
William C. Schutz's group psychotherapy manifesto *Joy: Expanding Human Awareness*
James Joyce's künstlerroman *A Portrait of the Artist as a Young Man*

And here too are coffee-table histories such as Hilaire Belloc's *Warfare in England*, Christopher Lloyd's *The British Seaman*, J.B.R. Nicholson's *Military*

*Uniforms: The Splendour of the Past* and Ingri D'Aulaire's *Buffalo Bill*. The truly obsessive will note a few post-1973 anachronisms: Burroughs's *Ah Pook Is Here*, Reginald Allen Brown's *Castles: A History and Guide* and Walter Laqueur's *Fascism: A Reader's Guide*.[16] The intellectual territory staked out by the collection matters more to the film than copyright dates.

Merged with the décor of his room, these books are shown to be as much part of Ian Curtis's identity as the mirror on his wall. When his friends visit, they demonstrate Curtis's status as a tastemaker (and by extension a self-maker) to us, the audience. They paw through his records and magazines, absorbing them. Corbijn synchronises the display of this collection with Bowie's ode to teenage discovery as it shifts from film soundtrack to Curtis's diegetic listening: we are the ravers, and this is our crash course. *Control* is not alone in ogling Curtis's bookshelf, but instead it faithfully stages culture's desire to know what books lay upstream of Joy Division's sacred music: just months after the film's release, punk historian Jon Savage corroborated this desire with an article in *The Guardian* devoted entirely to Ian Curtis's reading and book-buying habits.[17]

Portrayals such as those in *The Academy* and *Control* utilise their own form as media to empower their literary recommendations in ways that extend beyond their nominal subjects' endorsement. Layout and bibliographic topicality prime readers for the prurience of *The Literature of Occultism and Archaeology*, and the combined emotional swell of 'Drive-In Saturday' and our foreknowledge of Ian Curtis's eventual suicide illuminates his every artefact with a glow of jouissance and fate.

So to theorise now beyond example, when editors publish a subject's response to the bookshelf question, any or all of the following become possible:

1 Being the alleged contents of a respondent's bookshelf, it acts like a descriptive stand-in for the contents of the respondent's mind; this is the simplest, most tempting and most pervasive implication of the bookshelf question.

2 Following this, not only is the bookshelf list a descriptive stand-in, but taken prescriptively, it is a recipe: an instruction guide on how to become like this person.

3 Not merely does the bookshelf list suggest the contents of what has fed into someone's mind, but it indicates the world in which this person lived such that *these* were the books that they found and latched onto.

4 It affirms or challenges pre-existing suspicions about the interviewee – certainly one's reading habits and potentially

much more, inasmuch as reading may constitute the self or anything else.

5 It is a yardstick by which readers might measure their own progress in grasping or matching the respondents' mind and cultural context.

6 It is duly a yardstick by which readers may judge the respondent: does this person's reading choices mark them as worth paying attention to?

7 When some volumes on a shelf are familiar to readers, the list can create a sense of kinship between the interviewee and fans who have similar tastes.

8 A bookshelf allows the reader to picture the interviewee warmly and relatably as a real person in a real place, reading a real book.

9 It rehearses intimacy by doing with a famous person what readers already do with friends and lovers: look at their bookshelves.

10 It flags future directions of the interviewee's work, functionally asking 'What are your current projects?' by way of 'What are you thinking about now?'

11 Being publicly printed, the bookshelf list becomes not only a guide for a single reader of the interview, but a social syllabus for all such readers who care: via shared knowledge, it sets up future kinships between fans of the interviewee or of the publication.

12 The bookshelf question is almost always a representative one – not all one's books will be listed – and so savvy readers can interpret the list as a performance of self-presentation or editorialising.

13 It is an opportunity for an interviewer's performance of sophistication and intellectualism by claiming to care about what the interviewee reads, broadly reinforcing cultural assumptions surrounding the importance of books.

14 A bookshelf list is convenient publication filler, given that it is easily edited, easily read, information-dense and immediately discussable.

15 It is also an economic class signifier if 'bookshelf' is taken literally to mean books that the respondent actually owns.

16 It is a space for the interviewee or editors to make a particular connection or hat-tip to an author, to give exposure, acknowledgement, pay a debt or put oneself on the listed authors' radars.

17 It allows for seemingly disparate authors and books to be thrown into conversation by their inclusion together.

18 Inasmuch as it assumes that readers do not already own all these books, it duly assumes and suggests that without this list (and the publication containing it) readers would not otherwise have learned of these books' existence, importance, or connection.

19 To someone who has read few or none of the books, it can both suggest (in list form) and actualise (when the books are read) a substantial world of novelty on its own, even without a reader's investment in the interview subject or editors.

20 To someone who has read some or most of the books, it can fill in the odd contextual gap or introduce the rare unheard-of title – an experience increasingly precious as readers grow more erudite or completist.

Certainly, at least the first ten possibilities listed above are relevant to the examples given thus far (regardless of the reality of their subjects' bookshelves), and all these cases broadly position literature as ideationally prior to politics, prior to music. The book's apparent relation to the individual is shown here somewhere between controlling him (bidding the prime minister to rise before dawn) and constructing him (Ian Curtis becomes the sum of his media intake: we search on his shelf for the seeds of his lyrics).

Modern developmental science tells us more about how we become ourselves than the discipline of bibliography ever will, but it is nonetheless profoundly easy and tempting to privilege the written word over other media and categories through which the self is constituted. In torrents, words denote where music and art merely connote; writing is fixed and public where conversation is ephemeral and private. Thus novels become films, but films are rarely adapted back into literature; countless bands, albums and songs are named for books, but nearly no bestsellers derive from 7-inch singles. Even in the novels of Fitzgerald (to pick just one example), the backdrop of jazz is stylistic: more diffuse than specifically adaptational.[18]

To understand in greater detail and context the worldview disseminated in RE/Search's fascination with bibliography we might ask: in what formats does it make the most sense to print bookshelf lists? The answer is: formats outside of the proper 'book' category that the question concerns. It is no mistake that RE/Search volumes themselves are assembled with leeringly adolescent layouts: borders are bold and decorated, text boxes and margins are haphazard, and typeface changes suggest editors going trigger-happy with the font menu. Where Joanne Murray previously noted the layout's ability to propel non-literary readings, Patricia Allmer observes that the publications' semiotic extends to seemingly every aspect of the brand: 'RE/Search is more reminiscent of popular science and curiosity magazines', she writes in her study of volume 13, *Angry Women*.[19] 'Perhaps most of all it evokes ethnographic publications, not least implied by some of the issues' titles such as *Modern Primitives* (1989) and *Modern Pagans* (2001), as well as the publication's own title. RE/Search is perhaps best seen as offering an ethnography of that which is regarded as waste, wasteful, discarded and repressed in Western society'.[20]

The visual carnivalesque of the page is thus in lockstep with the publications' topics: just as Juno loves to flaunt 'bad taste', she consciously foregrounds conceptual ugliness in the volumes she guides. The title of each book was always in place before the interviewing began, she says. 'In the art of editing, everything comes down to the larger issue of what you want to transmit, what kind of information. It's not about journalism, or profiling this or that person – the personality is subservient to the ideas … The interviews were edited. A word-for-word transcription can't do justice to someone's more elaborate thoughts.'[21]

But although we have *Incredibly Strange Music* (vols I and II), *Incredibly Strange Films* and *Deviant Desires: Incredibly Strange Sex*, there is no *Incredibly Strange Books*. Literature remains cordoned off from other media (music or film) and behaviour (sex) – perhaps it is too categorically tasteful. RE/Search's rare fictions also intentionally flout the genteel, but beyond this, they are editorially constructed as somehow secondary to 'literature' – as downstream: Ballard's *Atrocity Exhibition* (which Vale and Juno reprinted in an expanded version) is written as a catalogue, its final pages eliding effortlessly into the back material's mail order forms for old RE/Search issues (the sort of thing found in magazines, not books). Wanda von Sacher-Masoch's *Confessions*, for that matter, claims no small share of its interest from (and guides the reader to) the writings of her partner Leopold von Sacher-Masoch. In their introduction, Vale and Juno reaffirm this current by which life happens downstream of the page. 'Leopold's best-selling novel *Venus in Furs* (1870) provided a *behavioral archetype whose influence persists* to this day', they write, immediately before going on to cite Gilles Deleuze.[22]

## Access to information and RE/Search's history

To put Juno and Vale's bookshelf question – and, indeed, their larger mission – in context, recall the days before our modern informational flood. In his introduction to *The Industrial Culture Handbook*, Jon Savage writes that a central concern of industrial artists' liberating belief system is: 'Access to Information: At this time, the phrase "Information War" – meaning that the struggle for control was now not territorial but communicatory – came into currency.'[23] (He also praises zines that, like RE/Search itself, demonstrate 'a happy marriage of form and content'.)[24]

Early on, RE/Search embodied a specific worry that emancipatory information and perspectives were being withheld conspiratorially by governments, commerce, news media and academia. As John Sears writes of *Incredibly Strange Music*'s opening essay:

> '[Specialized] critics', in particular, are implicitly condemned for the failure of their specialization to provide 'critical attention' to the music under discussion, and later the essay commends items that have 'escaped the eye of the academic, the critic and the antique dealer' (p. 4). Attention and its evasion are thus set into a complex relation: 'specialized criticism' offers a kind of attention too narrowly focused to accommodate that which will constitute the 'incredibly strange', which, by definition, is thus located outside the purview of the specialized critic, and thus privileged.[25]

Juno and Vale's critique is less of academic specialization itself than the apparent discursive monopoly by which it assumes authority. As Juno says:

> I was thinking back then about how a lot of film genres were really ridiculed until somebody in France said they're important. Godard and the new wave were the ones who said film noir is actual art; before that time, no one could take those films seriously. And in the late seventies I was saying something similar – that a lot of these horror and exploitation movies contained incredible gems of art and politics and had a populism that I loved.[26]

Vitally, this attitude is not anti-intellectual – merely anti-elite, and we can trace this back to Juno and Vale's schooling. In the mid-1970s, Juno moved from Mystic, Connecticut to San Francisco to attend college, initially for psychology at Sonoma State, but she quickly transferred to San Francisco State to study film, eventually staying on for a master's degree after her undergraduate work. Throughout, she perceived a disconnect between her curricular education and her own aesthetic and critical leanings: 'I got into postmodern philosophy very early on. I loved everyone from Baudrillard to Baudelaire and the surrealists. We studied Jonas Mekas and Chris Marker, but I didn't learn a lot about what I really loved in film school. It was outside of academia, in the underground, that I found the surrealists, postmodern philosophy and Baudrillard, Walter Benjamin and Donna Haraway. All those books came through the underground scene.'[27]

Vale's college studies left him similarly worried that he was not getting the full story: 'I was a huge fan of structural anthropology and a huge fan of

Claude Levi-Strauss. In my life I wanted to imitate him crossed with Andy
Warhol. But regarding Levi-Strauss, I took an anthropology class in college
and they didn't know about him yet, or at least they didn't teach him. He was
overlooked. His work was all in French still. I actually discovered him through
the surrealists.'[28] Levi-Strauss, Benjamin and Baudrillard may now be standard
reading in western humanities postgraduate programmes, but with these
educational omissions fresh in their minds, the editors understood their
bookshelf lists as part of an evangelist-hacker mission that cut two ways: rescue
hidden literature and empower individuals with its perspectives.

In his 1931 essay 'Unpacking My Library', Walter Benjamin waxes: 'to
a true collector the acquisition of an old book is its rebirth'[29] Preceding this
rebirth (whether by a decade, a week or thirty seconds) is the similar thrill at
learning of a book's existence (as enumerated earlier in the final two functions
of bookshelf lists). Joseph D. Lewandoski explores this typically Benjamin-
ian dialectic in which an esoteric book both constructs a satisfying part of
the collector's selfhood and is itself saved by (and reborn to) the collector:
'Anamnesis is a solidaristic form of historical remembrance or mindfulness.
When individuals collect old and outworn phenomena they actualize an
anamnestic possibility because they rescue devalued objects from the one
historical fate – a consignment to the trash heap of historical progress – and
offer them another fate; they allow the natural history of estranged and decayed
books to show itself in new ways and become recognizable anamnestically.'[30]

But to RE/Search, the fate to be raged against was neither simply the
trash heap of progress, nor even the boringly suffocating surplus of late capitalism, but a perceived force that insidiously did not want these books to be
found: surely they were too powerful, too real. In *The Industrial Culture
Handbook*, a pull-quote from Throbbing Gristle singer Genesis P-Orridge
declares: 'The more you tell the truth, the more camouflaged it is', but the
good conspiracy theorist sees also the converse: the more camouflaged a
source is, the more likely it is to be true.[31]

Reinforcing the paranoia surrounding these books was their universally
post-religious argument, their value in radical artistic and political undergrounds
of the day (perhaps most obviously Situationism), and their common place
of origin: 'We were into the French theorists', says Vale.[32] 'Everyone actually
read books, and we knew who was hip.'[33] France's formidable cultural and
intellectual reputation in the American underground was a fact – Kerouac,
Burroughs, Ginsberg and Ferlinghetti had all spent formative years in Paris.
But it was also personal in this case: since 1968, Vale had worked at Ferlinghetti's
City Lights Books in San Francisco, the American homebase of Beat culture.
Both Ferlinghetti and Ginsberg also provided seed money for him to start

publishing *Search & Destroy*. Furthermore, Vale's own subcultural connections to France were familial:

> I have to give a lot of credit to my beatnik uncle Canan [Takaoka]. He was in World War Two fighting Germans, and afterwards he went to Paris, where he met Ferlinghetti, because there weren't many other rebel ex-GIs in Paris taking painting classes. They were reading Sartre and Camus in French, and Hermann Hesse. This was happening in the forties, hanging out in coffeehouses. So my uncle, being Japanese, knew Shig Murao who was managing City Lights. It was a form of nepotism. I met Shig, I asked for job, and he created a job on the spot for me.[34]

In his 2016 autobiographical collaboration with Kelsey Westphal, *Search for Weird*, Vale recalls: 'I read books all day long – Shig kinda let me do my thing. I didn't know what radical was until then.'[35] Indeed, it was the mission of City Lights to carry new, foreign, small-press and radical books, and so the store's identity meant that an aura surrounded whatever he read there. The fact that many of those books were certainly in nearby university libraries (even if they were not on course syllabuses) did nothing to dispel the perception that they were underground, hidden, or in some literal way, occult.

## A critique of the upstream model

Sears's critique of the 'incredibly strange' category that RE/Search constructs may as well extend to the broader 'search for weird' at its editorial heart. As it turns out, the strangeness and weirdness here, 'when read in relation to avant-garde histories, is conventional.'[36] That is to say, RE/Search positions itself squarely in an intellectual lineage now familiar to anyone who studies the radical margins of western culture – one whose beginning and endpoint are debatable, but whose golden-era dynasty boasts the surrealists, the beats, the hippies and the punks. Vale contextualises: 'Bruce Conner said that all undergrounds are the same: trying to find a way to do art in every aspect of your living, to live a creative life. Undergrounds are always about just one word, and it's freedom. You are seeking freedom – a very complicated word, I know – applied to every aspect of living.'[37] The narrative of generational descent from one 'freedom'-seeking subculture to the next has become so reinscribed over time that alternative histories and nuances of class, education, race, gender, faction and location are often obscured. Thus the 'incredibly strange' in RE/Search's work is not merely the unordinary, but a specific and opulent context of friction with the social, economic, spiritual and intellectual structures that determine the whole category of 'ordinary'.

Since individuals and groups have built their identities around hunting and savouring this particular incredible strangeness for over a hundred years, many weirdos of the last half century have reached a set of realisations. First, since those previous subcultures have excavated so much, plugging into them is an efficient first move in mediating an historically aware radical identity: even in the twenty-first century, teenagers identify as latter-day beats, hippies and punks. Second, those subcultures were successful enough at finding and making their particular brands of strangeness that most of the easily available artefacts culturally marked as 'strange' come from their ranks – and it can be difficult to find or make radical artefacts that don't rely on these subcultures' monopoly of the fringes: hence the peculiar valuing of 'outsider' art and culture that stumbles upon the incredibly strange without assistance from or knowledge of those heritages. Finally, incredible strangeness can foster a manic addiction because it perpetually hints at how it might feel to exist beyond mass culture's banalities, and yet in our lives these banalities never fully recede. Thus the collector's impulse: Ever more! Ever weirder! The rabbit holes open for exploration (microstyles of film, literature, music, clothing) quickly approach the infinitely esoteric, wherein lies not 'freedom' but merely obsession over long-forgotten aesthetics. And loneliness. For a more tragic prognosis, see Paul Mann's famous screed 'Stupid Undergrounds'.[38]

As Sears notes, Vale and Juno themselves recognise that readers' aesthetic tastes (and their own) can stagnate, misreading well-worn subcultural trappings for liberating political potential – scene status for self-actualisation: 'the only barrier to virtually unlimited knowledge and insight remains one's "taste"' (p. 5) they write, not fully (to Sears's liking) avoiding this trap themselves.[39]

Confounding all this is the potential conflict between RE/Search's self-stated impulse on one hand to know 'what the next "big thing" after punk would be'[40] and, on the other, to 'destabilize all the hierarchies in culture creation and knowledge'.[41] Michael Lucas, in an occasionally acerbic article, suggests that by prioritising sales and cultural cachet, RE/Search undermines its own political mission.[42]

But must we read it so? Vale has acknowledged his debt to the situationists, whose leader Guy Debord writes: 'we will be present at, and take part in, a sprint between independent artists and the police to test and develop the use of new techniques of conditioning'.[43] In this mission, finding the 'next big thing' is potentially not so much mercenary bandwagoning as it is a *strategy* for staying on the semiotic and economic frontlines of the back-and-forth that pits grassroots and détournement movements against cooptation and recuperation. Vale verbalises this in Sarah Lowndes's 2015 book. 'My whole obsession has been: how can you keep Punk Rock alive forever? Like, for the really long haul, like hundreds of years, not just some ten-year fad, like the Hippies or the Beats or whatever. So our goal is, how can we *strategize* DIY undergrounds forever?'[44]

One must grant, though, that to model the outrunning of the culture industry is not to outrun it. And although RE/Search for many years seemed to thrive on serendipity – the editors claim to have thought intentionally very little about audience and marketing – this may ultimately have hurt the execution of such strategies. Lucas is correct, then, to question whether RE/Search has successfully cracked the code for keeping punk rock alive. Taking up the *Swing!* volume as an example, he writes: 'Since Vale gives the year of the commence-ment of the "Swing Renaissance" as 1988, a book published in 1998 seems more of an attempt to capitalise on a trend at its height of popularity than to document the novelty of its initial stages', and both Lucas and Sears note the postcolonial trouble inherent in publishing pop ethnography on subculture after subculture.[45] At the very least, it runs the risk of accelerating the recupera-tion of the situationist spectacle – of spoiling an intimate party by inviting gawkers.

The narrow collector mentality that RE/Search both explicitly documents (notably in *Incredibly Strange Music*) and implicitly encourages is the same impulse that drove so many zines in the 1980s and 1990s to compile com-prehensive bibliographies and discographies: the public nature of the published bookshelf commands social interaction (as enumerated above), and so zine writers would crowdsource their information. In Suzuki Shunya's *Interim Report 2*, for example, his hunger for information on Italian noise artist Maurizio Bianchi leads him to track down Bianchi's previous collaborators by international post:

> I tried to ascertain whether Maurizio Bianchi is living at his old address, or not. I mailed a registered mail to his old address (written in English). The result: here is the receipt. Who is the receiver? I don't know. As preview for detailed special article about MB in future issues, Here I quote some letters & infos from kind helpers who had ever contacted with MB in many times [*sic*] ... [46]

There's a whole article to be written demonstrating that the massive amateur project of cataloguing the world was launched and carried out in zines from the 1970s to the 1990s – and that the internet didn't revolutionise it overnight, but was instead taken up as a tool in its early years before it slowly obsolesced the diffuse enterprise; those paperback books of the mid-1990s listing interesting websites to visit – so silly now in retrospect – are evidence.

This warrants mention because it is in part what happened with RE/Search. Initially the editors were utopian about the internet: Vale prints recommended websites at the end of his 2001 interview with Jello Biafra,[47] and Juno had planned an entire book on virtual reality, social networks and the body:

> There were a number of books that I didn't get to do. I had known a lot of people in Silicon Valley working in everything from virtual reality to what became social media, who were interested in what it was going to do to society, culture and community. At first I was swept up in how positive we thought this would be. I'd given a lecture in Austria in 1990 at Ars Electronica. With virtual reality just coming out, I wanted to explore what would happen if you could socially inhabit another body, a black body, a body of another sex, an animal body, an octopus.[48]

But both have grown much warier since. Juno continues:

> When I went to the New School for another master's degree in 2001, I read Marshall McLuhan, who had actually warned about the new media, that it would break down community, and that very ugly things could start happening. I think now we're seeing the ugliness of what happens when people don't communicate with people with any different ideas, or when they don't communicate face to face. I'm on a college campus, and most students are on the phone. And I think there's a physical energy with eye contact that picks up on another person's gestures, their silences.[49]

And so Lucas wonders (with an apparently foregone conclusion), 'whether the internet has provided a more efficient means of transmitting subcultural memes, rendering RE/Search commercially and otherwise unviable as a promoter and popularizer of subcultural trends and tendencies'.[50]

## RE/Search RE/Dux and the downstream

The obvious and the theorisable reasons for RE/Search's receding subcultural profile are numerous; they include the minutiae of the editors' personal lives, the nature of publishing, the morphing role of subculture and the massive postmillennial changes in media sales. But we can imagine too that in an information economy of superabundance and not scarcity, where books account for a progressively smaller share of media consumption, the fundamental assumption that you are what you read no longer holds. Indeed, the search for 'freedom' as coded in the search for books may be flawed both in design and execution – and perhaps this was always the case. But such is the map laid out in RE/Search's work. This chapter, as stated, does not itself suggest that the upstream model of literature is correct or valid – merely that it is an implicit thesis of RE/Search's collected publications and a notable strain in the media epistemologies of zine and punk cultures.

As mentioned at the outset, all of Juno and Vale's interviews have been conducted live with a tape recorder. Likewise, when answering questions themselves, they both shun written communication. Vale says: 'There are a bunch of people who sent me long interviews and I never answered them. I felt sorry for them since they did all the work, but you sit down and start trying to write answers and it doesn't feel like fun. There's a huge difference between speaking and writing: when we're speaking, it's dialogue, which allows the Third Mind to arise.'[51]

Vale here refers to Brion Gysin and William S. Burroughs's mystical explanation for a surprisingly meaningful synergy of collaboration or juxtaposition, which they applied not only to personal interaction but to the collision of texts and ideas, specifically in randomised or 'cut-up' contexts. They introduce the concept in an interview that opens their book of the same name:

GYSIN: when you put two minds together ...

BURROUGHS: ... there is always a third mind ...

GYSIN: ... a third and superior mind ...

BURROUGHS: ... as an unseen collaborator[52]

Vale, who as a child had attended a glossolaliac church in Long Beach, California, continues:

Talking matters because I would never say some of the stuff I've said if you weren't here. I look at all speaking as channeling. You're not thinking before you speak. You are just somehow talking. We don't know where it comes from. You and me sitting at this table forming a third mind that's bigger than either one of us. We are channeling it, tapping it. It's not rational, otherwise it would be linear. It would be me crafting a thought and then saying it, but we don't do that. In other words, if you interview someone live, you have a much better sense of who they really are.[53]

This comes into a potentially paradoxical relationship with any belief that one's reading is 'the window of your mind'. But dissecting this seeming paradox doesn't require, for example, Derrida's work on writing versus speech. As we established early on, RE/Search's editors position themselves through approach, topic and aesthetic outside of the category of the book. But this does not diminish their work: instead, these publications implicitly argue for that hierarchy in which 'literature' – whether vetted by the academy or not – is upstream in the ideational flow. The territories less constricted by 'taste' and fixity – where zines lie, followed by music and art – are just as vital as the written source, even though they are downstream. This is so because the lowlands are where ideas collide in lively manifestation: this kinetic current *is* each interviewee; it *is* the music, the film, the pranks. RE/Search shows the whole river, then, and not merely its source. It models this first in suggesting that interviewees are made up of their books and, second, in locating itself downstream, thereby suggesting that its own efforts – that the big ugly RE/Search volume in your teenage hands – is the dynamic real-world *doing* of ideas that precede it somehow, somewhere.

Vale and Juno admit to laziness: 'We didn't want to actually write the books. It was ultimately about putting ideas onto paper, but without having to write an essay', says Juno guiltlessly.[54] But if RE/Search had conducted its interviews in writing (or if its editors had been essayists instead), might we lose this implied praxis in which ideas become action? And perhaps beyond the presence of any third mind, might the tidiness of writing deny the strange physicality of the interview? As Vale and I spoke, his wife and daughter buzzed about the kitchen. When Juno and I phoned, I was sitting in an illegally parked car, watching the sun set. We gain nothing when we silence these unwriterly realities.

This downstream of lived life and its literary upstream are both part of the same ecology. Patricia Allmer invokes a similar high–low metaphor: 'RE/Search, to use Bataille's terminology, focuses on the big toe rather than the lofty head, demonstrating how this toe, close to the earth and filth, is what carries the head.'[55] These publications were first in bookstores – City Lights was the original distributor – but they show up now more often in flea-markets, subcultural trading posts and oddball garage sales. In a no-man's land between book and zine, between academic criticism and trash, between generations of western subculture – they are the filthy body, the thickening weedy river flow.

## Notes

1   V. Vale, www.researchpubs.com/shop/terminal-punk-zine-philosophy-w-i-p-by-v-vale/, accessed 31 January 2017.

2   Author interview with V. Vale, 13 January 2017.

3   V. Vale, *Search and Destroy 7–11* (San Francisco: V/Search, 1996), p. 52.

4   V. Vale, www.researchpubs.com/products-page-2/xerox-reprints-research-1-2-3-the-shocking-tabloid-issues-excerpt-cabaret-voltaire/, accessed 31 January 2017.

5   V. Vale, *RE/Search*, 2 (1981), p. 30.

6   Author interview with Vale, 13 January 2017.

7   Author interview with Andrea Juno, 12 January 2017.

8   Joanne Murray, 'RE/Search, J.G. Ballard and New Brutalist Aftermath Aesthetics', *European Journal of American Culture*, 30:2 (2011), 151–68.

9   John Waters, *This Filthy World* (Dokument Films, 2007).

10   Author interview with Juno, 12 January 2017.

11   Waters, *This Filthy World*.

12   *The Academy*, 1476 (18 August 1900), p. 125.

13   *Ibid.*

14   *Ibid.*

15   *Ibid.*

16   *Control*, Anton Corbijn (dir.) (Momentum Pictures, 2007).

17   Jon Savage, 'Controlled Chaos', *The Guardian*, 9 May 2008, www.theguardian.com/books/2008/may/10/popandrock.joydivision, accessed 13 April 2017.

18   Exceptions exist, naturally, especially since the 1990s with works by the likes of Nick Hornby. An illustrative unpacking of mutual reference in the writings of Neil Gaiman and the records of Tori Amos can be seen, for example, in S. Alexander Reed, 'Through Every Mirror in the World: Lacan's Mirror Stage as Mutual Reference in the Works of Neil Gaiman and Tori Amos', *ImageTexT*, 4:1 (2008). Eric Weisbard's forthcoming book *Songbooks: The Literature of American Popular Music* will surely illuminate this issue more completely.

19   Patricia Allmer, 'RE/Searching *Angry Women*', *European Journal of American Culture*, 30:2 (2011), 113–23.

20   *Ibid.*

21   Author interview with Juno, 12 January 2017.

22   Wanda von Sacher-Masoch, *The Confessions of Wanda von Sacher-Masoch* (San Francisco: RE/Search Publications, 1990), p. 3. Added emphasis.

23   V. Vale, *RE/Search #6/7: Industrial Culture Handbook* (San Francisco: RE/Search Publications, 1983), p. 5.

24   *Ibid.*

25   John Sears, '"Incredibly Strange": Unlimiting RE/Search', *European Journal of American Culture*, 30:2 (2011), 125–35.

26   Author interview with Juno, 12 January 2017.

27   *Ibid.*

28   Author interview with Vale, 13 January 2017.

29   Walter Benjamin, 'Unpacking My Library', *Illuminations* (New York: Schocken, 1968), pp. 59–67.

30  Joseph D. Lewandowski, 'Unpacking: Walter Benjamin and His Library', *Libraries & Culture*, 34:2 (1999), 151–7.

31  Vale, *RE/Search #6/7*, p. 15.

32  Jack Rabid, 'V. Vale', *The Big Takeover*, 63 (2008), p. 100.

33  *Ibid.*

34  Author interview with Vale, 13 January 2017.

35  Kelsey Westphal and V. Vale, *Search for Weird* (San Francisco: RE/Search Publications, 2016), p. 5.

36  Sears, 'Incredibly Strange', 125.

37  Author interview with Vale, 13 January 2017.

38  Paul Mann, 'Stupid Undergrounds', *Postmodern Culture*, 5:3 (May 1995).

39  Cited in Sears, 'Incredibly Strange', 128.

40  V. Vale, *Swing!* (San Francisco: RE/Search Publications, 1998), p. 20.

41  Author interview with Vale, 13 January 2017.

42  Michael Lucas, 'RE/Search in Context', *European Journal of American Culture*, 30:2 (2011), 83–97.

43  Tom McDonough (ed.), *Guy Debord and the Situationist International: Texts and Documents* (Cambridge, MA: MIT Press, 2002), p. xi.

44  Sarah Lowndes, *The DIY Movement in Art, Music and Publishing: Subjugated Knowledges* (New York: Routledge, 2015), p. 19. Added emphasis.

45  Lucas, 'RE/Search in Context', 92.

46  Suzuki Shunya, *Interim Report*, 2 (1992), p. 25.

47  V. Vale, *Real Conversations Vol. 1: Henry Rollins, Jello Biafra, Lawrence Ferlinghetti, Billy Childish* (San Francisco: RE/Search Publications, 2001), p. 186.

48  Author interview with Juno, 12 January 2017.

49  *Ibid.*

50  Lucas, 'RE/Search in Context', 83.

51  Author interview with Vale, 13 January 2017.

52  William S. Burroughs and Brion Gysin, *The Third Mind* (New York: Viking Press, 1978), p. 14.

53  Author interview with Vale, 13 January 2017.

54  Author interview with Juno, 12 January 2017.

55  Allmer, 'RE/Searching Angry Women', 115.

# 16

# Punks against censorship: negotiating acceptable politics in the Dutch fanzine *Raket*

KIRSTY LOHMAN

Punk took root in The Netherlands in 1977, with scores of new bands forming through 1978–80.[1] As elsewhere, punk's mix of spectacular imagery, nihilism and/or radical politics, shock value and a do-it-yourself approach appealed to young people.

Also in the late 1970s, the port city of Rotterdam was undergoing a process of deindustrialisation and automation. It was still being rebuilt, both literally and figuratively, following near-annihilation during the Second World War.[2] The city's teenagers worked together to create strong subcultural and artistic networks, heavily influenced by left-wing political groups actively vying for attention.[3]

The fanzine *Raket* – Dutch for 'rocket' or 'missile' – was a crucial element in all this, with its creators seeking to support those involved in punk and new wave. The first issue, published in April 1979, was designed as a two-sided informational poster to be put up around Rotterdam. By so doing, its creators announced their presence on Rotterdam's alternative scene and declared their willingness to act as a point of contact for other bands and punks in the city.

Each issue of *Raket* carried a strapline stating the makers' intentions. The first issue read:

> *Raket*'s purpose is to act as a mouthpiece for Rotterdam's New-Wave groups. That is to say, Rotterdam bands can submit lyrics, details of gigs, small

advertisements and similar, but also tales from concerts and other lovely stories. Of course, people who aren't in bands can also submit articles, comic-strips or drawings. ... *Raket* will be released irregularly and pasted around the city of Rotterdam.[4]

As a submission-based publication at a time when new wave and punk were on the rise, *Raket* expanded quickly and gained a central position in the Rotterdam scene. It outgrew its poster format just a few months later, with issue 4 (September 1979) coming out as a more standard fanzine booklet. Overall, the fanzine ran for fourteen issues between April 1979 and November 1980; its gig listings and the plethora of new band announcements in each issue helped chart the growth of Rotterdam – and Netherlands – punk.

While *Raket* remained a Dutch-language fanzine, thereby limiting its potential circulation, its focus and readership expanded beyond The Netherlands' borders, with occasional reports from other countries such as Belgium and Germany. In issue 7 the creators acknowledged the growth of the fanzine's geographical reach by changing the strapline to read: '*Raket* is a fanzine by/ for punks and no/new wavers, particularly in The Netherlands'. Print runs rose to 1,000 copies for issue 2 and for issues 12, 13 and 14. Copies were sold in record shops and squats across the country.[5]

Leonor Jonker has argued that *Raket* quickly became one of the two leading Dutch punk fanzines, despite – in 1979 – being a relative latecomer to the scene.[6] The other was *KoeCrandt*, first created in August 1977 after its makers, based at Amsterdam's Sarphatistraat squat, saw an issue of Mark Perry's *Sniffin' Glue*. Many early Dutch punk fanzines, such as *Braak Maar Raak* and *Pin*, prioritised punk's cut 'n' paste aesthetic of stencilling over text-based discussion. Others, like *Raket*, served as mouthpieces for Dutch punk.[7] Thus, *Raket* was not unique in serving to advertise what was happening in a local punk scene, nor in inviting submissions from readers. However, it was produced by a highly active collective who made connections through gigs across the country, which might explain its rise from representing activities only in Rotterdam to speaking to and for the Dutch punk scene more widely.

*Raket*'s creators were part of the KunstKollectief Dubio (KK Dubio), a collective of artists who met at Rotterdam's art school and were attracted to the aesthetic and political potential of punk. KK Dubio's involvement in punk led to the formation of the band Rondos in 1978. They secured a place to both live and work: the dilapidated Huize Schoonderloo. This provided the artists with a base from which to operate as they embarked on other punk and art projects, including *Raket*, a publishing house and the 'Red Rock' band co-operative which included Rondos, Rode Wig, Sovjets and Tandstick-örshocks. The collective, living at Huize Schoonderloo, thereby positioned themselves as the vanguard of the Rotterdam punk scene, advocating for more practice space in the city and using *Raket* to communicate with other bands.

Rondos and the Red Rock collective took an explicitly political approach to their music and activities, with lyrics and imagery that drew on communism and, in particular, Maoism. *Raket*'s purpose, however, was different. As a 'mouthpiece' for the scene, relying on submissions and with a promise to print everything that was contributed, the fanzine's output was more politically varied. Adverts, announcements and gig listings were present throughout the fanzine's issues; however, it quickly started to attract lengthier political discussions, with conversations between contributors taking place over numerous issues on topics such as anarchism, socialism, communism, capitalism, sexism, racism and fascism. *Raket*, therefore, provides a vivid snapshot of Dutch punk in 1979–80, and particularly the growing political tensions of the time. Politically oriented punk (primarily left-wing) had by this point become an established part of The Netherlands' subcultural landscape, fostered by an organised squatting movement and a tradition of anarchism (including the Provo movement) that had engaged closely with Amsterdam's alternative cultural life.[8] By the late 1970s, there was also a rise in the activities of right-wing political groups, both politically and on the streets.[9] Indeed, the Dutch punk scene was not immune to rising fascism, as this chapter will illustrate.

While *Raket*'s political remit was wide, directed both by its creators and its readership, the fanzine remained firmly oriented to the left. This chapter, however, will focus on the presence of fascist and homophobic submissions to *Raket*. Such pieces were infrequent; nevertheless, their presence provides an important insight into the fanzine's 'no-censorship' approach.

This chapter conducts a close reading of *Raket* to discuss the ways in which these submissions were treated by the fanzine's makers and the resulting response from its readership.[10] In so doing, it frames a discussion of self-censorship and boundary-drawing practices in punk, issues that are of particular importance in a subculture that has, since its inception, witnessed tensions between far left and far right ideology and iconography. This chapter therefore contributes to debate on punks' engagement with the far right;[11] with issues of censorship and anti-censorship in punk;[12] and on the role of the fanzine editor as an influence on their readers.[13] It further contributes to a growing body of literature on Dutch subculture.

## Anti-censorship and punk fanzines: providing a platform to fascists?

*Raket* operated a strict no-censorship policy, a logical extension of publishing a submission-based fanzine to serve the Rotterdam/national punk scene. Mostly, this policy meant it received advertisements, letters, drawings and lyrics from enthusiastic fans. The zine collective took this policy so seriously that on one occasion they felt the need to apologise for having shrunk down some of the submissions in order for them to better fit on the page.

However, there were some less savoury submissions that led the collective to consider how the no-censorship policy was implemented. Issue 8, published in January 1980, was the first time they felt an editorial decision had to be exercised in this regard. They explained their thought process in the pages of *Raket*, writing:

> The following letter was sent to us by the fascist organisation N.P.N.
> [Nationale partij Nederland; National Party Netherlands]. We first
> considered not printing it, because we have little desire to have such fascist
> ideas present in *Raket*. That in the end we decided to publish it, is because
> we do not want to <u>apply censorship to a single thing</u> so you can read this
> letter and make up your own mind what you think about fascism.[14]

The NPN was a small nationalist party. Its letter to *Raket* explained its two principal demands: first, calling for a pay rise for those who worked in heavy industry; second, stating that they wanted to 'help' 'foreigners' return home. The party was not a large force in Dutch politics; instead, the Nederlandse Volks-Unie (Dutch Peoples-Union), the Centrumpartij (Centre Party) and its predecessor, the Nationale Centrumpartij (National Centre Party), were most active on the extreme right of Dutch politics in the late 1970s and early 1980s.

The NPN registered as a political party in 1974 but did not contest an election and left few records of its activity. However, the letter to *Raket* indicates that it was active in 1980 and it may be presumed that the NPN hoped to appeal to the same sense of punk working-class solidarity that was present in many other political submissions to the fanzine. Moreover, a police report to the Head of Homeland Security suggests that there was prior contact between Rotterdam's punk scene and the NPN. The report contained intelligence regarding an NPN demonstration in Rotterdam, which took place on 24 November 1979 (a month *before* the date on the letter). It claimed that the demonstration was attended by some Rotterdam punks and drew attention to tensions within the Rotterdam scene through reference to punk debates about whether or not those who had been to the NPN demo would still be welcome in Kaasee, the local punk venue.[15] The report also contained a copy of the page in *Raket* containing the NPN letter as further evidence of collaboration – and tension – between punks and the far-right party.[16]

In sticking with their decision to publish the letter, the makers of *Raket* drew on a wider trend in punk. Punks in many countries (including Britain)[17] had struggled against state censorship of their output. While record releases could more easily be banned, fanzines' underground nature allowed freedom from this censorship. As such, punk zines became a site to argue against censorship. Engaging with fascists became a strategy in a wider anti-censorship struggle even for punks who were politically opposed to the far right. Andy Martin of the British band The Apostles went so far as to protest against censorship of punk by printing an advert for the neo-Nazi band Skrewdriver in his *Scum* zine.[18] This could be further framed as an attempt to keep lines of communication open in the hope of changing opinions. In this vein, Andy Palmer of Crass stated that they would consider playing gigs for the NF.[19] Fascism, in these contexts, becomes the milestone to test the extent of punks' anti-censorship position.

*Raket* had not itself been subjected to state censorship; indeed it had been the recipient of a local government subsidy designed to foster Rotterdam's cultural creativity. The money was used to support printing costs, details of which were printed in the fanzine along with their work to secure housing, practice space and gig spaces for the city's punks. However, the fanzine's anti-censorship policy and its use in regard to fascist material can be read as part of wider punk approaches forged in opposition to state censorship.

A second fascist letter was featured in issue 10 (March 1980). In this, the street group Utrechts Jeugd Front (Utrecht Youth Front; UJF) proclaimed they had heard that 'you are looking for trouble with fascists'. The letter, which was clearly intended to intimidate punk anti-fascists, asked for someone to share the personal details of 'Joop', 'the scared anti-fascist' who had previously written for *Raket*. The letter signed off with an illegible signature and: 'with regards to the skinheads, SEIG HEIL SEIG HEIL, Our Furher' [*sic*].

Much has been made of links between fascism and punk, particularly in terms of the appropriation of fascist symbols (i.e. the swastika) by early UK punks, as well as punk engagement with fascist politics.[20] Certainly, the rhetoric and deployment of this imagery by early punks opened a space for 'punk and fascism' to become a contested territory.

Roger Sabin argues that a process of 'myth making' by the music and mainstream presses started almost immediately.[21] They positioned punk as *anti*-racist in order to defuse the potential impact of their fascist provocations at a time of heightened racial tensions in the UK. Sabin highlights how this served to paper over the ways in which punks were engaged with racism and fascism and thereby erase any such links from history.[22] However, this myth-making process also had the effect of feeding directly into punk practices around the world, as can be seen by Rock Against Racism, the 'Nazi Punks, Fuck Off!'[23] refrain and much of the discourse and imagery used in *Raket* itself.[24]

Notably, while the fascist letters to *Raket* and the police records on NPN activities provide us with an insight into tensions between punks and 'Nazi punks', neither the NPN nor the UJF letter can be read as coming *from* 'Nazi punks' themselves. There are both addressed *to* punks from an 'outsider' perspective; from organisations trying to reach punks who might be sympathetic towards them, or to intimidate those who are not. However, the fact that both organisations believed that a submission to *Raket* might reach this target group shows how they felt *Raket* had a wide readership, politically speaking.[25] *Raket* was widely distributed and we cannot be certain of the full variety of the readership's political leanings. However, the presence of fascist and racist punks in the Rotterdam punk scene was discussed regularly in *Raket* and, as previously noted, the police assumed that Nazi punks read the fanzine.

Given this backdrop, the 'no censorship' policy might at first seem particularly curious. It provided a platform for exactly those opinions and ideas that the makers of *Raket* were struggling against, along with other punks around the world. However, I argue that the rationale for this went deeper than a liberal discomfort with censoring submissions, and explore this by unpicking *Raket*'s editorialising practices.

## Editorialising fascism

While the makers of *Raket* decided not to censor submissions, a closer examination of the fanzine shows that they did take a strong editorial line with respect to submissions from fascist groups. This can be seen, for instance, in the aforementioned editorial comment that accompanied the publication of the NPN letter in issue 8, which asserted (in a disdaining manner) that the letter would make the idiocy of the NPN's ideas clear to any reader. However, the practice of editorialising with regard to discussions around fascism in *Raket* went further than this.

**16.1** *Raket*, 10 (1980). Reproduced by kind permission of Johannes van de Weert

Firstly, pieces that discussed or pictured anything fascist or racist (which were commonly written from an anti-fascist/anti-racist perspective) were usually accompanied by the same image and text (see Figure 16.1).

The text reads:

> We know that fascism is bad. But why? And moreover what are we doing to counter it? If you wish to write something about [swastika] and [odal-rune] (drawings and suchlike are good too) then send them to us: *Raket*: [address].[26]

This disclaimer functioned to make explicit that the creators of *Raket* did *not* support fascist views, and instead wished to foster debate on taking action *against* right-wing groups.

The editors of *Raket* also made use of their ability to influence readers through the placement of submissions. The NPN letter in issue 8 was one page long, with three pages on either side expressing anti-fascist messages. First was a full-page sketch informing readers that the Nationaal Jeugdfront (National Youth Front; NJF) was fascist, despite claims to the contrary. Then came two pages explaining the inner workings of fascism and its relationship with capitalism. Finally, the NPN letter was followed by a page with anti-fascist lyrics from Rondos, Tändstickorshocks and Rode Wig. This, in turn, was followed by two pages containing more anti-fascist letters, as well as a drawing of a feminised Hitler character 'squashing' some miniature punks that posed a threat to the dream of a militarised Netherlands.

The letter from the UJF was similarly preceded and succeeded by pieces that made anti-fascist arguments. This first of these was a two-page piece on the recent history of fascist political groups in The Netherlands. It focused particularly on links between the politically active Nederlandse Volks Unie (Dutch People's Union) and the Nationaal-Socialistische Beweging (National-Socialist Movement), which had been banned after the Second World War, but also mentioned the NJF and NPN. There was then a reproduction of John

Heartfield's *Krieg und Leichen* ('War and Corpses'), accompanied by lyrics by Rode Wig, before the UJF letter gave way to another two-page essay calling on readers to think independently and critically in the face of fascism. The page featuring the UJF letter itself was subject to further editorialising, not simply with the usual anti-fascist disclaimer, but also with a cartoon encouraging people to 'follow no one, lead yourself'.

The anti-fascist discussion continued into issue 11, with a response to the UJF letter from 'Razzia'. Razzia ridiculed the UJF, not least for their inability to spell 'Führer', and then taunted them to try and track him down too. Unlike other anti-fascist submissions, Razzia's letter – the only direct response to a fascist submission in *Raket* – was not a piece of political critique, but instead a personal attack to undermine the UJF's standing. The letter was designed to defuse the UJF's threat to Joop and other anti-fascists, and to make clear that their views were not welcome in the fanzine.

Practices of editorialising, through the placement of fascist articles next to anti-fascist ones or using anti-fascist drawings and disclaimers to accompany fascist pieces, has a long history, particularly in the cut 'n' paste style of punk fanzines.[27] While the makers of *Raket* favoured a 'cleaner' aesthetic, which included stencilling, typed letters and articles, and only featured a cut 'n' paste style in pieces submitted by others, they clearly engaged in the same practices of juxtaposition through their editorial decisions. Furthermore, *Raket*'s editorialising practices stretched beyond this to include explicit requests with regard to future submissions. For example, issue 10 contains this request: 'In the next issue of *Raket* (no. 11) we would like to shut down further articles about [swastika]. But you can of course still send us anti-[swastika] drawings *et cetera*.'

Such instructions were common, and their use was not limited to discussions of fascism. *Raket* also invited a debate on anarchism (issue 7), which was then shut down again (issue 8). Of course, being a submissions-based punk fanzine with a 'no censorship' approach, these pleas were not necessarily heeded by contributors. While issue 9 is missing from archives,[28] issue 10 features a number of articles on anarchism submitted against editorial instructions.

The way in which the makers of *Raket* engaged with fascism was therefore more complicated than a liberal reading of their 'no censorship' stance would suggest. Practices such as explaining the decision to print the NPN letter, using disclaimers, soliciting or dissuading articles on particular topics and taking a very deliberate approach to the placement of submissions, all served to reinforce the political line that runs through the fanzine. Counterintuitively, it seems that the decision to publish fascist submissions worked in *Raket*'s

**16.2**   *Raket*, 11 (1980). Reproduced by kind permission of Johannes van de Weert

favour as it strengthened the makers' own left-wing political message. The NPN and UJF letters raised the spectre of ties between fascism and punk. This led the fanzine's creators to call for readers to unite behind the aim of keeping punk anti-fascist and anti-racist, spurring responses in later issues. The fanzine's contents exhibited a great deal of disagreement and debate around the form that a left-wing punk movement could – or should – take. However, by allowing fascists a (limited) platform, by carefully managing the use of this platform through editorialising, and by regularly describing the links between fascism and capitalism, the overall left-wing political message of *Raket* was strengthened.

The use of fanzines to simultaneously foster debate through submissions and to promote particular lines of thought is not uncommon. Indeed, this is a criticism that has been levelled at what is arguably the most famous and influential punk fanzine, *Maximum Rocknroll* (*MRR*).[29] Craig O'Hara has argued that: '[too] many Punks now depend on MRR to inform them of who to support and who to boycott, and while I would agree with the majority of their views, their new found power is extremely dangerous and sometimes abused by the columnists and staff whose opinions have a very great influence on younger Punks.'[30] While *MRR* operated in a different time (1982 onwards), place (San Francisco) and punk scene (hardcore) to *Raket*, the 'taste-making' power that it held over its readership allows for comparisons to be drawn.

The power that a fanzine can hold as a tool for influencing opinion, even under the guise of debate, extends beyond the role of those compiling the fanzine to all others who make submissions. As Stephen Duncombe explains with respect to *MRR*:

> Tim [Yohannon, founder of the fanzine] and *MRR* are often slagged [off] for dictating what fits within a very narrow definition of punk ... This definition took place in editorials by Tim, columns by other regular writers, and in scene reports and articles sent in by readers. But the war of definition

primarily happens in *MRR*'s extensive letters section. For over twenty-five years, and over three hundred issues, punks have been slugging it out in the trenches of *MRR*'s letters column, setting up and tearing down the rules of being a punk.[31]

As such, the fanzine forms a site for policing the boundaries of punk, be they the practices of punk, or – as in *Raket* – the politics of punk. While it might seem antithetical for punk to 'police' anything, this is a process with a long history that can be seen from the very origins of punk.[32] This practice is made all the more important in instances where terrain is contested, or contestable. As Sabin highlights with his discussion of 'myth making', the history of punks' dabbling (and/or full involvement) with fascism make this an important contested site, which invites heightened boundary policing within the subculture.

In their editorialising practice, the makers of *Raket* made explicit the ways by which they directed the overall argument presented in the fanzine. As such, the fascists' letters posed no real challenge to the punk scene or its hopes of political unity, with any threat undermined by editorial practice, by ridicule from other contributors, and by appropriation in order to strengthen *Raket*'s argument. The next section highlights the importance of this holistic approach to confronting fascist arguments by turning to another instance in which the limits of 'no-censorship' were tested.

## Homophobia and *Raket*'s no-censorship controversy

It is evident from the large volume of anti-fascist submissions to *Raket* – including those that directly responded to the two fascist groups' letters – that many of the fanzine's readers did not agree with what the NPN and UJF had to say. However, I have not encountered a single submission which critiqued the makers of *Raket* themselves regarding their decision to publish the letters. In instances where there was a direct response to the letters (as can be seen for example in Razzia's reply to the UJF), readers critiqued the content of the letter rather than editorial policy. It seems, therefore, that on the whole the readership understood and accepted the 'no censorship' approach by the fanzine's creators.

One letter, however, printed in *Raket* 12, did result in a questioning of the editors' decision to publish. The letter, written in capital letters, read:

HELLO RAKET! IF I EVER COME ACROSS THE FAGGOT 'RENÉ' THEN HE'S GETTING A THUMP TO HIS HEAD AND A KICK TO HIS

BALLS. DESTROY THE GAYS. PUNX ARE DEFINITELY NOT
FAGGOTS. YOU DIRTY SISSIES. THIS WAS A WARNING. THAT
'RENÉ' DARE NOT MAKE HIMSELF KNOWN. SECRET PERVERT.

The letter was signed 'WHOLESOME HENDRIK.'[33] It was written in response
to an advertisement placed in *Raket* 10 by René, who was organising a festival
in Amsterdam for 'faggot-punks/punk-faggots'. Immediately below the body
of the letter, Hendrik wrote: 'You will certainly not be brave enough to print
this letter'. As is evident, *Raket*'s response to the challenge was to go ahead
and publish it anyway.

Raket 13 featured a reply to Hendrik from a group of punks in Utrecht,
who first quoted Hendrik's threats and then stated: 'I do know that you at
*Raket* don't censor anything, but that you printed a letter like this from some
fascist who thinks he's a punk, I think is going too far'. On this occasion, the
readers' critique is levelled *not* at the content of Hendrik's letter, but instead
at the makers of *Raket* for choosing to publish the letter. While publishing
Hendrik's letter was considered a step 'too far', the publication of the NPN
and UJF letters was not. In considering this incident, a few further comparisons
between the content, treatment and reception of the respective letters are
useful.

To begin with, it is important to note that both Hendrik's letter and the
one from the UJF single out an individual to directly threaten as part of wider
strategy of intimidation. The UJF asked for details on Joop; Hendrik names
René as his target. Given that only one of the decisions to publish was criticised
it seems, therefore, that this was not a decisive factor in marking out the
bounds of acceptable censorship.

I suggest instead that there are two elements that marked Hendrik's letter
as unacceptable for the Utrecht punks. Firstly, and unlike the previous two
examples, the letter from Hendrik purports to come from a punk rather than
an outsider. Hendrik positions himself as 'in the know' regarding punk, as
part of the scene. He attempts to position gay people as *not* part of punk.
Hendrik's letter can therefore be read as engaging in practices of punk boundary
drawing; of debating what might or might not constitute punk, as became
common later in the letter pages of *MRR*. Secondly, in coming from *within*
punk, Hendrik's letter demonstrates that individuals with intolerant opinions
*are* present within the scene, despite the discursive efforts by *Raket*'s creators
to claim punk as (broadly) socially liberal and politically left wing. As such,
the Utrecht punks' criticism targets Hendrik's claim to speak for punk as
'some fascist who *thinks* he's a punk', rather than engaging directly with the
content of the letter itself. In drawing a boundary for punk that does not

include Hendrik and his views, these are dismissed and deemed not welcome in the punk scene.

Furthermore, none of the letters that constituted this exchange had been subjected to the same level of editorialising as the letters from the NPN and UJF. Instead, they were placed in generalised letter/advertisement sections and published without comment from the *Raket* team. It is this that antagonised the Utrecht punks and led to a criticism of the decision to publish Hendrik's letter, as the reader is left unsure of the fanzine makers' opinions. Since there is not a disclaimer, can the reader assume that there is implicit support of Hendrik's views, or not? Given this ambiguity, the need to respond in order to counter homophobia becomes greater, lest other readers be swayed by the letter. In the example of Hendrik's letter and the subsequent response, we therefore see how some believed that *Raket*'s 'no-censorship' rule should be more carefully considered, rather than utilised as an absolute approach.

## Homophobia and fascism in punk

Homophobia (and homosexuality) and fascism were sites of tension for punk more widely in the late 1970s and early 1980s. However, it is important that we do not unquestioningly correlate these two without recognising the wider contextual situation. Sex, including controversial sex, and particularly homosexual sex, was an important part of early punk imagery in the UK, used by some in a liberating manner but also, more commonly, for shock value. The uneasiness present in some punks' engagement with homosexuality was perhaps most notable when it overlapped with play with fascist symbolism. David Wilkinson highlights the 'flirtatious referencing of the historical crossover of fascism and same-sex passion' in regards to the Bromley Contingent's dabbling in both.[34]

Punks in the UK, unwelcome in many (straight) bars, adopted and frequented gay bars such as Louise's in London, Ranch in Manchester and Bear's Paw in Liverpool; there were some prominent punks who were openly bisexual/gay.[35] However, societal norms of homophobia pervaded punk, especially as it became more popular.[36]

Dutch punks certainly played with images and discourses of sex in a similar way to the UK; indeed they played more with sexual imagery than fascist imagery (which was largely only used by Nazi-punks or to express negative connotations). Band names included Coïtus, Dildos, Spoiled Sperm, Masturbation Problems and Tits. Issue 3 of *Raket* (designed as a poster to be plastered around Rotterdam) featured two logos, side by side (see Figure 16.3).[37]

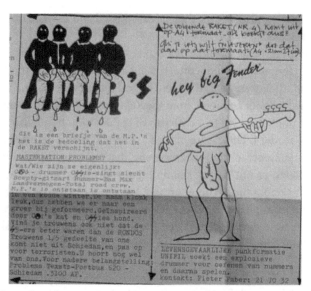

**16.3**   *Raket*, 3 (1979) Reproduced by kind permission of Johannes van de Weert

One of the earliest Dutch punk bands, Tedje en de Flikkers (Ted and the Faggots) were actively involved in the Rooie Flikkers' actiegroep (Red Faggots action group) in Nijmegen. René's organising efforts in Amsterdam highlight that there were a number of queer bands active in The Netherlands in 1980: certainly enough to come together under the banner of 'faggot-punks/punk-faggots'. Moreover, some of the politically progressive essays in *Raket* mention gay rights as one aspect of their fight for a better society.

However, there was also a great deal of homophobia present within punk in The Netherlands, just as in the UK. Homophobic slurs were used casually in a number of pieces in *Raket*, arguably a reflection of the language used within society at large rather than a problem specific to the fanzine's contributors. Issue 3 featured a letter from punk Hans Kok, declaring his resignation from Rotterdam's Rock Against Racism organising committee; he had been physically threatened with violence at Kaasee punk shows for publicly displaying affection with his boyfriend. Wider societal tensions around homosexuality were therefore replicated through these subcultural spaces, despite discursive attempts to draw boundaries around what was and was not acceptable punk behaviour.

*Raket* – and its editorial policy – did not exist in a vacuum from wider societal norms, just as punk did not. The complex relationship between punk and homophobia was (and is today) reflected in the attitudes and behaviours of anti-fascist and anti-racist punks, who were equally liable to hold insidiously racist perceptions. Views that were – and are – normalised in wider society are not always critically addressed in subcultural spaces and it was perfectly possibly for 'pro-reggae punks [to] hold racist/fascist views without even pausing over the contradictions'.[38] Such contradictions further complicate the way in which contested political territory is navigated in subcultural spaces and highlights the important role that fanzine editors hold in boundary drawing and taste-making.

## Conclusion

The pages of *Raket* provide a snapshot of the burgeoning Rotterdam punk scene between April 1979 and November 1980. By inviting submissions from anyone and promising to publish everything that was sent to them, its makers brought together an array of views regarding what punk is, was, could be and/ or should be. As *Raket* grew in size and scope to encompass the wider Dutch punk scene, tensions between different political factions started to spill onto the letters and essays pages of the fanzine.

The makers of *Raket* were – and remain – proud of their 'no-censorship' platform, as a political intervention at a time when punks around the world faced state censorship and regulation.[39] However, as this chapter highlights, the fact that they published everything submitted to them did not mean that they presented everything to the reader in an 'equal' manner. Their editorial practices with regards to fascism served to present submissions from fascist groups as items not to be taken seriously. Furthermore, in printing these letters alongside disclaimers and anti-fascist essays they redeployed fascist words in order to strengthen their own anti-fascist arguments. In doing so, the makers of *Raket* – along with those who submitted letters and essays to the fanzine – were engaged in a process of boundary drawing with regards to the role of fascism in punk, thereby utilising their fanzine to communicate a particular political message to the readership.

From this, we can learn valuable lessons about the implementation of no-censorship strategies in subcultural spaces. Rather than 'shutting down' debate with fascists, *Raket*'s editors created space for a range of different ideas and ways of seeing the world. Fascist submissions were *not* treated in the same way as those from anti-fascist punks; 'acceptable' words were privileged over unacceptable words. However, the (curated) presence of these viewpoints allowed *Raket*'s readership access to understanding the variety of opinions and political stances that were held by members of their punk scene and those on the periphery of punk. This meant the Dutch punks were allowed 'to make

up [their] own mind what [they] think about fascism'[40] – while being guided
to the 'right' conclusion.

The 'success' of this no-censorship approach can be judged by the response
it provoked from *Raket*'s readership. It 'succeeded', with regards to its treatment
of fascism, in that it presented a diverse set of voices in a way that was accepted
by the readership. Conversely, the policy 'failed' in regards to the treatment
of homophobia due to the lack of contextualisation and editorial comment,
thereby prompting a group of readers to make a complaint to the editors.
Success can therefore be read as finding an effective way to navigate punk
boundary management, making the editors' political position clear while
simultaneously allowing a voice to all through not censoring submissions.

## Notes

Acknowledgements: My thanks to Matthey Worley, Ruth Pearce, Katherine Hubbard,
Jo Smith and two anonymous reviewers for their comments on previous drafts of this
chapter, and to Johannes van de Weert, Jos Kley and the International Institute of Social
History, Amsterdam for helping source issues of *Raket*. The writing of this chapter was
supported by a Leverhulme Trust Postdoctoral Fellowship. It is based on data collected
while undertaking research sponsored by an AHRC Doctoral Scholarship.

1  For a history of punk in The Netherlands see Jerry Goossens and Jeroen Vedder,
   *Het Gejuich Was Massaal: Punk in Nederland 1976–1982* (Amsterdam: Stichting
   Popmuziek Nederland, 1996); Leonor Jonker, *No Future Nu: Punk in Nederland
   1977–2012* (Amsterdam: Dutch Media Uitgevers, 2012); Kirsty Lohman, *The
   Connected Lives of Dutch Punks: Contesting Subcultural Boundaries* (Basingstoke:
   Palgrave Macmillan, 2017).
2  Ron Blom and Bart Van der Steen, '*Een banier waar geen smet op rust': De geschiedenis
   van het trotskisme in Nederland, 1938–heden* (Soesterberg: Uitgeverij Aspekt, 2015).
3  See Blom and Van der Steen, '*Een banier waar geen smet op rust'* for a discussion of
   the wider context of left-wing activity in Rotterdam.
4  All translations are the author's own.
5  Print runs for the first three (poster-format) issues were higher than for the first few
   issues that were in a standard zine format. Circulation figures are given in *Raket*, 14
   (1980).
6  Jonker, *No Future Nu*.
7  Examples include Enchede's *Aambeeld* and Amsterdam's *Attack*. Harold Schellinx, *Ultra:
   Opkomst en ondergang van de ultramodernen, een unieke Nederlandse muziekstroming
   (1978–1983)* (Amsterdam: Lebowski Publishers, 2012).
8  Richard Kempton, *Provo: Amsterdam's Anarchist Revolt* (New York: Autonomedia,
   2007); Lynn Owens, *Cracking Under Pressure: Narrating the Decline of the Amsterdam*

*Squatters' Movement* (Amsterdam: Amsterdam University Press, 2009); Lohman, *The Connected Lives of Dutch Punks.*

9   Rob Witte, *Racist Violence and the State: A Comparative Analysis of Britain, France and the Netherlands* (London and New York: Routledge, 1996).

10  Issues of *Raket* often had special supplements; however this chapter focuses on the fanzine itself.

11  James J. Ward, "'This is Germany! It's 1933!" Appropriations and Constructions of Fascism in New York Punk/Hardcore in the 1980s', *Journal of Popular Culture*, 30:3 (1996), 155–85; John Street, *Music & Politics* (Cambridge: Polity Press, 2012); Matthew Worley, 'Shot By Both Sides: Punk, Politics and the End of "Consensus"', *Contemporary British History*, 26:3 (2012), 333–54.

12  Martin Cloonan, *Banned!: Censorship of Popular Music in Britain: 1967–92* (Gateshead: Athenaeum Press, 1996).

13  Craig O'Hara, *The Philosophy of Punk: More Than Noise!* (Edinburgh: AK Press, 1999); Stephen Duncombe, *Notes from Underground: Zines and the Politics of Alternative Culture* (Bloomington, IN: Microcosm, [1997] 2008).

14  Original emphasis.

15  The police's efforts to target fascist punks did not go unnoticed by the rest of the punk scene. Issue 11 of *Raket* contains a warning to other punks that the police were hanging around outside Kaasee.

16  *Het nationaal veiligheids archief* (National Security Archives), www.inlichtingendiensten.nl/groepen/npn, accessed 7 March 2017.

17  Cloonan, *Banned!*

18  *Scum*, 6, p. 10.

19  *Toxic Graffitti*, 3 (1979), p. 9.

20  See Dick Hebdige, *Subculture: The Meaning of Style* (London: Routledge, 1979); Dave Laing, *One Chord Wonders: Power and Meaning in Punk Rock* (Milton Keynes: Open University Press, 1985); Jon Savage, *England's Dreaming: Sex Pistols and Punk Rock* (London: Faber & Faber, 1991); Ward, "'This is Germany! It's 1933!"', 155–85. For fascist attempts to appeal to punk see Matthew Worley and Nigel Copsey, 'White Youth: The Far Right, Punk and British Youth Culture', *Journalism, Media and Cultural Studies*, 9 (2016), 27–47.

21  Roger Sabin, "'I won't let that dago by": Rethinking punk and racism', in Roger Sabin (ed.), *Punk Rock: So What?: The Cultural Legacy of Punk* (London: Routledge, 1999), pp. 199–218.

22  There is more work now dealing with this; see, for example, Stephen Duncombe and Maxwell Tremblay (eds), *White Riot: Punk Rock and the Politics of Race* (London: Verso, 2011), in addition to those listed above.

23  As with the song by the same name by Dead Kennedys.

24  Of course, this myth-making equally served to reinforce the existence and the possibility of neo-Nazi punk, which remains in evidence around the world. See Ward, "'This is Germany! It's 1933!"', 155–85; Michelle Phillipov, 'Haunted by the Spirit of '77: Punk Studies and the Persistence of Politics', *Continuum: Journal of Media*

& *Cultural Studies*, 20:3 (2006), 383–93; Ivan Gololobov, Hilary Pilkington and Yngvar Steinholt, *Punk in Russia: Cultural Mutation from the 'Useless' to the 'Moronic'* (London: Routledge, 2014).

25  This, in turn, raises further questions as to why Nazi punks who might read *Raket* did not contribute anything ostensibly political.

26  There are many identical images in other issues of *Raket*.

27  Duncombe, *Notes from Underground*. For more on the materiality of fanzines and editorial practices see Alison Piepmeier, *Girl Zines: Making Media, Doing Feminism* (New York: New York University Press, 2009); Michelle Kempson, '"I just call myself a DIY feminist": Subjectivity, Subculture and the Feminist Zine' (University of Warwick, Ph.D. thesis, 2012).

28  The issue is missing from both my personal collection and the collection housed in the International Institute of Social History in Amsterdam.

29  O'Hara, *The Philosophy of Punk*; Duncombe, *Notes from Underground*.

30  O'Hara, *The Philosophy of Punk*, p. 67.

31  Duncombe, *Notes from Underground*, p. 67.

32  In *The Philosophy of Punk*, O'Hara discusses this issue. But as a book written by a punk and widely read by punks, it can also be seen as an example of this policing.

33  'Gezonde Hendrik' translates literally to 'healthy Hendrik'. However, 'gezonde' is used both for health of the body and of the mind in a more social capacity. The translation 'wholesome' better encapsulates this social function, in which Hendrik delineates himself from the 'unhealthy' gay people he targets.

34  David Wilkinson, 'Ever Fallen In Love (With Someone You Shouldn't Have?): Punk Politics and Same-Sex Passion', *Key Words*, 13 (2015), 57–76.

35  Including Pete Shelley, Tom Robinson, Bertie 'Berlin' Marshall and Gene October. For further discussion of homosexuality and punk, see Wilkinson, 'Ever Fallen In Love (With Someone You Shouldn't Have?)'; Jon Savage, 'The Conflicted History of Queer Punks', *Attitude*, April 2016, 100–3; Matthey Worley, *No Future: Punk, Politics and British Youth Culture, 1976–84* (Cambridge University Press, 2017).

36  Savage, 'The Conflicted History of Queer Punks', 100–3.

37  Image downloaded from http://rondos.nl/raket_fanzine/index.php?id=raket_3, accessed 19 January 2017.

38  Sabin, '"I won't let that dago by"', p. 205. Indeed, it is important to note that both Rondos and *Raket* took an explicitly *anti*-reggae position, which they argued was based on its links to Rastafarianism and their belief that *all* religion had a damaging effect on society.

39  This is discussed prominently on the *Raket* part of the Rondos website http://rondos.nl/raket_fanzine/index.php, accessed 8 March 2017.

40  *Raket*, 8 (1980), quoted above, p. 267.

# 17

# Contradictory self-definition and organisation: the punk scene in Munich, 1979–82

KARL SIEBENGARTNER

This chapter presents a history from below that draws on fanzines to show the complexity of Munich's punk scene between 1979 and 1982. In so doing, the function of fanzines within a local space will be demonstrated, shedding light on the inner workings of a particular punk milieu. Punk in Munich has yet to be adequately researched. But through this case study, assumptions as to the development and influence of German punk can be reviewed. Methodologically, fanzines offer a crucial resource for constructing a view from within this metropolitan subculture.

The formation of a subcultural self contains the production and consumption of music and literature; the appropriation of spaces; interactions with certain persons and groups; body modification strategies through fashion or direct operation on the body itself. As a product of social interaction, self-formation comprises exclusionary acts and group building activities.[1] In terms of punk, interpersonal communication is important. This can happen directly as well as indirectly; in person or via media like the telephone.[2] In the context of this chapter, fanzines form media that function as a means of communication in the absence of persons. Communication is always dependent on the space where it happens; fanzines provide a means to both describe and create space.[3] Space can, therefore, be related to communication in a threefold manner. Firstly, space can be the object of communication. Secondly, communication always takes place in spaces and thereby feeds back into the spatial perception of the actors. Thirdly, spaces can be produced communicatively and, by so doing, allow punks to individually appropriate spaces.[4]

Munich is the capital of Bavaria, where the conservative Christian Social Union (CSU) has traditionally governed. The *Ministerpräsident* for the period 1978–88, Franz Josef Strauß, was a hated figure for many young people of the time and known as a hardliner. In Munich itself, habitually social democratic territory, another CSU member, Erich Kiesl, was the mayor from 1978 until 1984. Under his mandate, policing changed drastically. Once known for their psychological methods, the city police adopted harsher strategies in the early 1980s. Left-wing terrorism during the 1970s had led to a climate of fear. To this the youth revolts of the early 1980s – where squatters in Munich claimed spaces of self-government in response to rising housing costs – were answered by draconian measures: no building could be occupied for longer than 24 hours.[5] Such a policy culminated in the arrest of seven under-aged persons associated with Freizeit 81, a loose group of young people, including punks, who tried to symbolically appropriate urban space. Forms of protest included squatting, graffiti and the throwing of Molotov cocktails. But although the group could not strictly be classified as a political movement, its members were arrested under section 129a of the Straftgesetzbuch and accused of forming a terrorist association.[6]

Although punk bands played at the Schwabingerbräu and the Alabamahalle in Munich, permanent spaces for punks were scarce. The first was Damage, but other important clubs were found in the Milbenzentrum (Milb), which originated as a centre for multinational left-wing activism, and Lipstick.[7] Munich's punk bands tended to play straightforward punk rock, though there were a few more experimental exceptions (such as Freiwillige Selbstkontrolle). The likes of Tollwut, ZSD, Scum and Dagowops, to name just four, released but a handful of records. In contrast to its relatively limited recorded output, however, Munich boasted a thriving fanzine culture.[8]

## Trouble and DIY

This section will explore how fanzines helped create Munich's punk scene; how fanzines helped constitute punk's character, particularly its association with the motif of 'trouble'. 'Trouble' formed part of many a punk testimonial. In 1979, for example, Conny Wallner wrote in *Molotow Coctail*: 'the Munich punks ... wandered around town, from one pub to the next ... keen on shocking people and sometimes causing trouble'.[9] Besides the shock effect caused by their flamboyant appearance, the punks' actions also served to separate them from society. Wallner noted broken glass and scribblings on walls, markers of group-belonging, and an air of 'trouble'.[10] As long as such aggression was turned against the imagined establishment, 'trouble' functioned as self-description. It was integrated into the scene's DIY logic. Action had to be taken because the punks' surroundings were so unbearable – a strategy that could play out in contrary ways. The authors of *Kakalake* fanzine, which was created in the Milb, made direct reference to this. The autonomously governed district centre had an enormous problem with vandalism. They accused:

> those fucking wankers ... who want to destroy the Milb again and again, always smashing lights, windows, equipment and glasses, or go on the rampage in the streets instead of figuring out that the Milb is a pub that can and should be established, and that the Milb is not a fucking commercial pub ... where a beer is double or triple the price and gigs are ridiculously expensive.[11]

As this suggests, the destruction of objects relating to the local punk scene was vehemently criticised, revealing a break in the self-configuration of Munich's punks. Perceptions within the scene developed and divided fast, with fanzines serving to document these changes.

One fanzine, *Langweil 111B*, had already postulated the death of punk by 1980.[12] On the one hand, the fanzine suggested punk should adopt an individual style that set its members apart from society. On the other, the by then rather homogenous punk style seemed only to suggest a counter-perception. 'The average punk nowadays wears a leather jacket with two safety pins and three badges and feels different – fuck it – every punk just looks the same ... '[13] The apparent uniformity of Munich's punks was thus criticised, so denying their self-formation and sense of belonging to the group. Instead of mutual solidarity, the possibility of belonging was negated through a lack of individuality. Further on, the fanzine stated that punks should concentrate on having fun; that bands should never sign a contract with a major label. If they did, punk would become a job.[14] The aim was to charge as little money as possible;[15] the motto was 'to form your own bands/fanzines'.[16] The idea of DIY therefore became integral to punk's identity in Munich, with fanzines serving as a clear expression of that. Nevertheless, moments of 'trouble' often proved incompatible with such DIY strategies because the dynamics of it helped destroy established structures like the Milb.

'Trouble' was not only turned against objects but also against persons. In *Langweil*, the antagonism between punk and disco[17] was discussed:

> The big battle between disco suckers and punks arguably takes place in Schwabing – but it is almost impossible to talk of a battle, it rather is a beating! ... This is the biggest shame for the Munich punks, when they are

known as fair game that may be chivvied, isn't it? I suggest that we all …
meet up and then walk to Schwabing, punch some disco suckers – if we don't
do it, they will always come back at us! … It has to be possible that punk
kids in Munich can act as they want to without getting their face smashed in
everywhere![18]

The alliance of 'trouble' and group-formation is here further deepened. Disco
represented a majority to contrast against punk's marginality; violence was
enacted against punks by those attending Munich's discos. As a result, an
ambivalent relationship to 'trouble' emerges. 'Trouble' as self-description could
also be turned *against* punk and the formation of punk-as-self constituted
negatively. The visibility of the punks became a problem for the own self.
The use of violence against punks forced them to lose power as their own
self-attribution of 'trouble' was turned against them. Therefore, the confrontation
between disco attendees and punk reconfigured the limits of the latter's own self.

The question of *belonging* was a crucial element of fanzine writing. Conny
Wallner provided the following impression of a gig: 'Amongst the punx scrim-
maged two or three freaks and Simon … bad-mouthed a freak because she
had pomade in her hair and he likes pomade just as little as garlic. Just before
a fight broke out, Heiner (of Desaster) intervened and verbally attacked Simon
as an intolerant square'.[19] In this story, the aggressive atmosphere takes on
different forms. The quote shows the fragility of punk identity. Not only in
terms of problems with other groups, but also within punk's own milieu.
'Trouble' did not exclude supposedly like-minded people. The description of
physical violence is only implied, but it shows that fights over correct interpretations were not always solved on a verbal level. Boris Vankaev described a
similar situation at the Milb: 'I don't need to talk much about the fights among
different punk gangs and nobody was surprised that this was the wrong place
for "If The Kids Are United". No one ever talked about solidarity … '[20]

But his thoughts go further. '[Don't] the political punks understand that
they are being used by the leftist communist mob? If a punk participates
because of trouble or only wants to have fun that's apparently of no interest to
the media, but they always notice the punks that support the CM (communist
mob)!'[21] This self-reflexive quote is notable because the media did sometimes
portray punks as blindly following the left in demonstrations.[22] The situation
of Freizeit 81 certainly played into such interpretation. 'Trouble', therefore,
was here again not only a self-description but also an extraneous one. Equally,
Vankaev's point reveals the punk self to not necessarily be decidedly political.
Vankaev excludes himself from those punks who claimed to be politically
active. But his statement was simultaneously a political act.[23] By declaring

against politics, he commits to a political action. This includes a rejection of, in this case, left-wing politics, but also party politics in general. 'Trouble' could be fun and Vankaev positioned himself against both a conservative society and the political left. Destruction-as-fun was therefore the ultimate means of turning his back on his environment while at the same time acting to provoke it.

## Scene and individual

Beyond the idea of 'trouble' as self-descriptor, fanzines presented DIY as integral to both punk's individual and group identity. Without a scene, there was no punk self. In other words, the individuality of punk was highlighted, but a critical mass of followers was necessary to appear significant within an affluent city. In *Langweil*, an ambivalent attitude towards this paradox was regularly played out:

> The Munich punk scene lives! And how it lives. Every Saturday sixty dressed-up blokes traipse to Damage. Each of them with a black leather jacket, drooping faces and of course 1017 badges – the most beautiful funeral march. And when you're finally in there everybody gets vain, observing each other's dyed hair, the t-shirt which was bought in England's trendiest boutique ... I discover more and more splinter groups and lone punks ....[24]

This quite clearly shows 'scene' to be a relevant term. However, the accompanying expectation of unity is not recognised. The individual always appears outside the group; the elements do not mesh. The author stresses in the fanzine how incompatible these configurations of the punk self could sometimes be. The scene was dressed uniformly. Recognisable characteristics – leather jackets and badges – are noted. But, in turn, these signifiers serve to contradict the individualistic view of a punk-self wishing to attract attention to her/his own stylish body.

A similarly ambivalent comment may be found in *Langweil*: 'And the new generation of punks? We should be happy that we have offspring. But when you see some of these monstrosities. Shit. Do you think it's funny when five punks chase after two little teds to incite them? Do I really have to go to the smelly (hippy) Theatron to meet some punks?'[25] The growth of a scene is generally welcomed; but, in almost the same breath, the young punks are denied any form of subcultural identity. The notion of 'trouble' also comes up again, though in a different form. To construct a scene, other youth cultures are crucial. The punk self, in group form, needs a counterpart. Disco, as already stated, was a culture that was often attacked violently. Followers of disco were deprived of subcultural status and considered 'mainstream'. The groups that are mentioned in this *Langweil* quote, teds and hippies, had status as recognised scenes. As a result, violence directed against them was hindered by bigger inhibitions. Punks needed counterparts to feel relevant themselves. But while disco was a blatant enemy, other youth cultures were granted a degree of negative recognition. The self-formation of punks would not have been complete without teds and hippies to differ from. Fanzines depicted the fragmentation of different subcultures in Munich while simultaneously stressing the need for co-existence.

Attempts were evidently made to solve punk's individual–collective paradox. Thus, from *Langweil*: 'Just because nobody goes outside on the weekends anymore. I don't believe that at all! Munich punks laid off their clichéd clothes (just like I did) so you can't recognize them as punks anymore. By the way, you'll recognize me as ONE OF THOSE. ... We know each other too little.'[26] Within the scene, fixed patterns of clothing soon became dated, indicating the incompleteness of self-formation. Individual style and punk characteristics were never fully compatible, despite their interdependence. As a result, attempts by individuals to integrate into the wider punk scene could lead to conflicts of punk identity. This, in turn, sometimes provoked fights over interpretations of the punk self. The scene was divided as to who was and who was not part of it. Wallner states that:

> [Within] two months ... the Munich punks managed to fragment themselves totally. I can't believe it; everybody acts as if we were at an afternoon tea party in a nursing home. Some bitch about those who have only been punk for a year because they are fashion victims ... Others bitch about punks who run around like teds ... I get the impression that there are many punk squares who run around in the same uniform and don't tolerate anyone who is different from themselves. The one who has got longer hair is a hippie; the one with too short hair is a fucking skin ...[27]

Simultaneously, the exclusion of other scenes became even more explicit, especially as hybrid forms came into play. The fear that punk behaviour mirrored that of wider society became a concern. In particular, the term 'square' suggested incompatibility with the punk self. By 1981, the quarrels within the scene were summarised as: 'intolerance like anywhere else ... cliché+uniform, where's the joke? But rather no feelings+hatehippies.reactionary kidpunx "new wave-idiot", pogo über alles, badges and elitist cool trendies' [*sic*].[28] The confusion of the description underlines the tension between the individual and the scene. A form of elitism was clear. The self as individual unit was no longer compliant within the wider scene, and if the punk self was forever incomplete, then delineation became a strategy not only to keep society away, but also a mechanism to navigate through the scene. Fanzines, moreover, provided a platform to stage these fights within Munich punk.

## Spaces

Communication strategies are important because the punk self was contradictory. Communication within the punk scene also helped realise claims to DIY. Therefore, communication processes were crucial to forming a punk self.

Punks were particularly visible in public; their style distinguished them from casual pedestrians. In fanzines, the dynamics of such interaction were detailed in relation to punk gatherings in public spaces. A letter to *Langweil* complained: 'What do you mean by saying that "the meetings at the Fischbrunnen on Saturdays" were better? We only bummed and hung around there and didn't know where to go. I remember a certain M., E., S. and a P. but no B.'[29] As this suggests, recognised meeting places like the Fischbrunnen at the Marienplatz existed. Once there, punks demonstratively *did nothing* and displayed their hatred for aspects of the city. By so doing, they effectively transformed the public space, codifying it as a space for punk and a transfer point for information.

It is unsurprising that Marienplatz served as a space for punk gatherings. As well as being located in the centre of Munich, it also hosted a spontaneous gig by Lorenz Schröter. In issue 2 of *Die Einsamkeit des Amokläufers*, Schröter described what happened: 'After a couple of days we agreed on it: A STREET GIG! To avoid the constant nuisance of folk music ... we met at the Marienplatz.'[30] The objective was to gain attention by appropriating the public space. Photos reproduced in the fanzine provide visual evidence. The author writes: 'The audience was large but very sceptical+tentative. No pogo, no beatings, no police+not enough punks' [*sic*].[31] As this suggests, the gig did not quite go to plan. Nevertheless, the temporary occupation of the Marienplatz – replete with unapproved street music – served as a platform for communication. The DIY credo was fully realised, even if not enough punks turned up and the expected response of the police did not materialise.

Clubs provided another important punk space. Damage, the first punk club in Munich, may be analysed in such a way, again through fanzine coverage from 1979.[32] The desire for a local punk space had been building for a while. 'After horrible gigs ... there is something going on in this appalling city. SCUM!!! played Damage. ... Pure mayhem. I haven't seen that many punks at a gig in ages. I spotted around 80 punks (who would have thought there were that many).'[33] Thereafter, Damage was recognised as a space for punks: a place where like-minded people could mingle. According to Conny Wallner's account: 'At the command of the singer, three blokes started pogoing, then four, and then more and more ... The room was superbly overcrowded, on the "dance" floor kids pushed themselves around in the whole room ... and soon you couldn't really distinguish the band from the rest of us.'[34] As this suggests, Damage was recognised as a space of equality. The audience and the band were on a level, so realising the conditions associated with DIY. Everyone became part of the performance and, thereby, of equal importance. In the process, Damage functioned as an expression of an independently organised scene built around a Munich band.

Wallner's depiction goes beyond recognising a created space. Nonverbal communication also formed part of the description: 'Most of the punks looked incredibly good, net shirts, bondage trousers, made-up eyes, safety pins, suspenders and crazy t-shirts ... Best of all was the anarchy shirt of Simon (singer) that didn't have a swastika on it.'[35] In Damage, the scene could act itself out, presenting self-made clothes and flamboyant looks. Scene-relevant references were deciphered and valued, further explaining how the band and the audience merged into one. Similarly, in the shared experience of pogo dancing, animosities within the scene no longer counted; they were enveloped by the space and tensions dissolved. As a letter to *Langweil* stated: 'You call the Damage punks "long-faced leather blokes" – OK, that's your opinion. Now mine: The Damage punx say that they are punks ... They like their punk bands and their punk music. ... It is possible that they all kind of look the same but they are punks!'[36] Of course, the tensions of self-formation could not be wholly solved. But cohesive forces could also be played out in this particular space. Criticism of the Damage punks was rejected by the letter writer because they *did something*; practice was more important than critique.

Unfortunately, Damage closed down in the summer of 1980.[37] The licensee, talking to *Mailänder Scala* in April of the same year, stated: 'I like the music myself but as a businessman I have to view it from the business side ... The local administration received complaints and a collection of signatures from residents. These mainly protested against my clientele ... and against noise in the streets, [so] now I have to play music at a low volume and dancing is prohibited.'[38]

Munich's fanzines covered the closure of Damage. Some offered further reasons for its closure. According to *ZLOF*, in an overview of Munich's punk scene: 'Damage annoyed the Munich punks because 4DM is not really cheap for a beer.'[39] But despite all the problems, Damage remained an important touchstone for Munich's punk milieu, signalling the first collective space for the scene. It helped realise the ethos of DIY. A report on the band Tollwut, for example, stated: 'Back then, someone at Damage had the idea to produce a cassette sampler of Munich bands, and so we rehearsed three songs, forgot about the whole thing, and again played just for fun.'[40] Contact with other punks instigated further projects. Although Damage was open for just under two years, it installed itself in the collective memory. A review of Scum in an issue of *Positiv* from 1982 referred back to the 1979 gig that effectively launched Damage as punk space. 'Back then there was a lot going on in the first Munich punk club. The band mainly covered songs by the PISTOLS and CLASH ... Punks of the first hour ('77ers) were joined by a lot of hippies and pseudos. Anyway, Damage was packed for the first time, people were in a good mood and we felt a beginning in boring Munich.'[41] Damage was thus granted the status of pioneer. The space gained a mythical ambience and has been written about constantly over the years. As the first meeting point of punks, it offered a space of communicational exchange where tensions could be resolved and DIY practised.

## Local communication

Fanzines offered information and a means of communication. In the first issue of *Langweil*, Bernhard Schornak noted: 'This is your fanzine, not only mine, meaning if you want a top-notch fanzine, you have to write good articles yourself and send them to me ... We need newspaper cuttings and photos too. You can find my address below!'[42] Almost all fanzines listed an address to write to, presenting themselves as a platform for mutual exchange. This meant, at times, choices had to be made with regard to editorial control. Or, as Schornak put it: 'Criticism is useful for our fanzine otherwise we won't know what you like and what you don't!'[43] Thus, in the second issue, Schornak published the already quoted letter on public spaces that offended his own sensibilities.[44] Clearly, he took the idea of fanzines offering a platform seriously, listing contributors and appealing for freelancers and a 'cheap copy shop'.[45]

Adverts could further stress this approach. In its 110 issue, *Langweil* listed various records for sale; a 'Dieselmotor' wanted to get rid of them.[46] Schornak thereby played an intermediary role in the dissemination of records: 'Interested persons should inform me and I will forward your order.'[47] He also invited people to follow suit: 'If you want to get rid of something, search for musicians or bands, every ad is published for free!!'[48] In this sense, fanzines became

more than *just* a magazine; they became part of the organisation and dissemination of music, particularly records that were hard to come by. Or, as
*Langweil* stated in the quest for an American punk sampler: 'you literally can't
get hold of it. Munich is not small. But I only found one copy in the whole
city ... So if you know where to get more, let us know.'[49] The infrastructure
of the record stores did not cater for punk. Therefore, information on finding
records was communicated through fanzines and word-of-mouth. Again, DIY
provided one solution. 'If needs be, I can tape it on cassette for you for a small
recompense.'[50] Thus, music was dubbed and shared on cassettes, with fanzines
enabling the transmission of relevant content. A rare record could be distributed
across the scene (even if some wilfully made a profit out of it).

The need for record acquisition was ever present. As such, record shops
were important and fanzines provided crucial connections. Two shops were
noted in particular. Stachus-Musik advertised in *Lächerlich*, highlighting its
stock of British and American punk with the slogan: 'WE CATER FOR YOUR
LISTENING HABITS IN EVERY GENRE!!!'[51] By so doing, the shop evidently
grasped the potential of fanzines as a transmissional part of the sales process.[52]
The second shop was Optimal Schallplatten. '[There] is also a new record
shop in Munich, it is called OPTIMAL and has mostly punk and new wave
goods on the shelves. For Munich, it's even cheap ....'[53] Such a shop had long
been desired: a place for punks stocking the right kind of music.[54] Michael
Sailer's *Der Blitz* advertised both Optimal and its associated label, Kein Zurück,
extending punk's DIY network in the process. The 'infobox' on the label listed
its production of 'gigs, records and cassettes' and called for 'contact details of
groups, labels and fanzines'.[55] Such ads allow us glimpses of the Munich punk
scene; capturing the process by which fanzines helped punk realise its own
DIY organisational and informational structures.

Besides those spaces that provided sites of communication, the telephone
also served as a key instrument of organisation. Again, fanzines acted as a
link. The editors of *Punk im Milb*, for example, printed their telephone numbers
to exchange relevant scene information. However, things were not always as
simple as they seemed. Most punks were teenagers or young adults; some
lived at home with their parents. Embarrassingly, perhaps, 'Diesel' had to add
to his contact details that people calling him should ask for 'Daniel', as his
parents wouldn't know who Diesel was.[56] The individual punk self with a
suitably *punk* nickname existed in conflict with the kid at home with his
parents. Not dissimilarly, Wallner, the other editor, asked: 'the best thing would
be to call during the week around 8 p.m.'[57] In her *Vive Le Punk* fanzine she
was even more precise: 'But not after 10 p.m. or before 8 a.m.'[58] Telephone
calls connected the scene but also disrupted domestic routines.

Finally, fanzines were used as media to insult other members who were deemed to undermine the spirit of DIY. In the process of self-formation, both the individual and the wider scene were contested. This often led to defamatory comments. Thus, Lorenz Schröter – in *Die Einsamkeit des Amokläufers* – called *Langweil*'s Schornak 'a big ass'.[59] Schröter himself was also a target; *ZLOF* described him as 'a Bavarian whore'.[60] As this suggests, personal antipathies were just as common in Munich's punk scene as anywhere else, and were fought out in the fanzines. Michael Sailer of *Der Blitz* was at the heart of one particular dispute, during which he was regularly attacked by the managers of the Gruft record label, Schornak and Vankaev. *ZLOF* published documents relating to the feud, while Sailer called Schornak a fascist in a letter to *Sounds* magazine. In response, Schornak's lawyer sent a demand that Sailer pay a required 90.97DM, before a letter of apology from Sailer was published in *ZLOF*.[61] *Akt der Verzweiflung* also criticised Sailer,[62] who published a further letter of apology for Vankaev in his own fanzine and made monetary recompense for the insult made.[63] He wrote dispiritedly: 'I want to add that I think it deplorable that Mr. Vanakev, who also publishes *Zlof* under the name of Jeff Stress, thinks it necessary to solve things in this way'.[64] The DIY ethos could only be lived out partially within the scene. The possibilities of communicating through fanzines had a darker side as well. Therefore, the tensions of self-formation could never be wholly resolved through such communication practices.

## Conclusion

As shown in this chapter, punk was – and is – a fluid phenomenon. A focus on local scenes is crucial because only there can assumptions about punk be tested. This case study of Munich punk around 1980 shows how quickly a unified grouping of the imagination could be dissolved or destroyed. As fanzines reveal, the formation of a punk self was difficult. Every identificatory step had its limits. 'Trouble' as self-description restricted the effectiveness of DIY. Notions of individuality could conflict with a sense of scene. All in all, the 'punk self' and the 'punk scene' were contradictory – any assumed homogeneity is misleading.

Certainly, in terms of the self-formation, there was little unity within the scene. Communication strategies, including fanzines, were applied to partially resolve such tensions. Communication processes in public spaces and punk clubs were essential. Moreover, communication opened up possibilities at a local level with regard to the production and distribution of music. The downside was a disruption of privacy, while insults and feuds soon broke out among participants, suggesting the contradictions of self-formation could not be resolved through such DIY communication. The punk self was fragile and measures of self-organisation had its limits. Punk in Munich was as contradictory as the individual perceptions of each actor. To glance at the scene's fanzines is to reveal the inner tensions, the ambiguities and the sense of the conflicted self that informed the punk subculture.

## Notes

1 Alexa Geisthövel, 'Lebenssteigerung: Selbstverhältnisse im Pop', in Alexa Geisthövel and Bodo Mrozek (eds), *Popgeschichte, Band 1: Konzepte und Methoden* (Bielefeld: transcript Verlag, 2014), pp. 177–90.

2 Moritz Föllmer, 'Einleitung: Interpersonale Kommunikation und Moderne in Deutschland', in Moritz. Föllmer (ed.), *Sehnsucht nach Nähe: Interpersonale Kommunikation in Deutschland seit dem 19. Jahrhundert* (Stuttgart: Steiner, 2004), p. 10.

3 Alexander Geppert, Uffa Jensen and Jörn Weinhold, 'Verräumlichung. Kommunikative Praktiken in historischer Perspektive, 1840–1930', in Alexander Geppert, Uffa Jensen and Jörn Weinhold (eds), *Ortsgespräche: Raum und Kommunikation im 19. Und 20. Jahrhundert* (Bielefeld: transcript Verlag, 2005), p. 20.

4 *Ibid.,* p. 28.

5 Michael Sturm, '"Die Räumung ging zügig vonstatten": Eine kleine Geschichte der Polizeibewaffnung', in Zara Pfeiffer (ed.), *Auf den Barrikaden: Proteste in München seit 1945* (Munich: Volk Verlag, 2011), pp. 105–6; Michael Sturm, '"PASST BLOSS AUF": Militante Proteste in München (1969–82)', in Zara Pfeiffer (ed.), *Auf den Barrikaden: Proteste in München seit 1945* (Munich: Volk Verlag, 2011), pp. 127, 134.

6 Sturm, '"PASST BLOSS AUF", pp. 135–6; Manfred Wegner and Ingrid Scherf, *Wem gehört die Stadt: Manifestationen Neuer Sozialer Bewegungen im München der 1970er Jahre* (Andechs: Ulenspiegel Verlag, 2013), pp. 55, 136.

7 Christian Ertl, *Macht's den Krach leiser! Popkultur in München von 1945 bis heute* (Munich: Allitera Verlag, 2010), pp. 17–18; Wegner and Scherf, *Bewegungen*, p. 134.

8 Frank Apunkt Schneider, *Als die Welt noch unterging: Von Punk zu NDW* (Mainz: Ventil Verlag, 2007), pp. 76–7. The bands mentioned are just a few examples. Schneider gives a good overview of the bands and their output in his discography. For short biographies of some important bands, see https://muenchen-punk.de/steckbrief, accessed 23 March 2017.

9 *Molotow Coctail,* 1 (1979), p. 8.

10 *Ibid.*

11 *Kakalake,* 1 (1980), p. 2.

12 *Langweil*, 111B (1980), p. 5. The fanzine starts with the issues 111B and counts down from there on. The B is included because there was a test print-run before distribution. The majority of the fanzines cited are collected at the Archiv der Jugendkulturen, Berlin. In fanzines with no page number indication I counted the cover as page one and went from thereon.

13 *Ibid.*, p. 13.

14 *Ibid.*

15 *Ibid.*

16 *Ibid.*

17 The term disco is used broadly to comprise its followers, the music and the space itself.

18 *Langweil*, 110 (1980), p. 3.

19 *Vive Le Punk*, 3 (1980), pp. 1–2.

20 *ZLOF*, 4 (1981), p. 5.

21 *ZLOF*, 6A (1981), p. 4.

22 Staatsarchiv München, Polizeipräsidium Presseausschnitte 390, *Münchner Merkur*, 25 September 1981.

23 Detlef Siegfried, 'Pop und Politik', in Geisthövel and Mrozek (eds), *Popgeschichte, Band 1*, pp. 33–4.

24 *Langweil*, 111B, p. 17.

25 *Langweil*, 108 (1980), p. 3. The Theatron was an open-air festival held at the site of the 1972 Olympic Games.

26 *Langweil*, 108 (1980), p. 3.

27 *Vive Le Punk*, 2 (1980), pp. 2–3.

28 *Die Einsamkeit des Amokläufers*, 1 (1981), p. 2.

29 *Langweil*, 110, p. 6.

30 *Die Einsamkeit des Amokläufers*, 2 (1981), p. 3.

31 *Ibid.*

32 Henning Fürst, 'Damage: Der erste Punkladen', in Mirko Hecktor (ed), *Mjunik Disco: Von 1949 bis heute* (Munich: Blumenbar), p. 60.

33 *Molotow Coctail*, 1, p. 7.

34 *Ibid.*

35 *Ibid.*

36 *Langweil*, 110, p. 6.

37 *Musterexemplar* (1980), p. 2.

38 *Mailänder Scala*, 1 (1980), p. 3.

39 *ZLOF*, 4, p. 5.

40 *Lächerlich*, 4 (1981), p. 9.

41 *Positiv* (1982), p. 8.

42 *Langweil*, 111B, p. 5.

43 *Ibid.*

44 *Langweil*, 110, p. 6.

45 *Langweil*, 111B, p. 5.

46  *Langweil*, 110, p. 42.

47  *Ibid.*

48  *Ibid.*

49  *Langweil*, 108, p. 6.

50  Violent Jojo, in *Ibid.*

51  *Lächerlich*, 3 (1981), p. 36.

52  *Akt der Verzweiflung*, 5 (1982), p. 20.

53  *ZLOF*, 7A (1982), p. 4.

54  *Der Blitz*, 3 (1982), p. 3.

55  *Der Blitz*, 6 (1982), p. 7.

56  *Punk im Milb* (1980), p. 7.

57  *Ibid.*

58  *Vive Le Punk*, 3, p. 4.

59  *Die Einsamkeit des Amokläufers*, 3 (1981), p. 13.

60  *ZLOF*, 6A, p. 14.

61  Leaflets inserted into ZLOF, 7A, n.p.

62  *Akt der Verzweiflung*, 4 (1982), p. 21; *Akt der Verzweiflung*, 5, p. 5.

63  *Der Blitz*, 3, p. 7.

64  *Ibid.*

# 18

# 'Angry grrrl zines': Riot grrrl and body politics from the early 1990s

The body was fundamental to riot grrrl politics and performance. In the writing of 'SLUT' on their torsos, unconventional dancing and singing styles, the growing of their body hair, and in encouraging 'grrrls to the front' at gigs; the body was used to subvert expectations of young women's appearance and the spaces in which they could participate. The embodiment of a subversive style was part of a wider ethos of disruption and reclamation within riot grrrl concerning female agency within the music scene and broader structures of oppression surrounding language, sex and the economy.[1] Riot grrrls understood that to reclaim the body they must also retrieve the means of representation. As well as re-educating themselves and each other about the body through music and meetings, the proliferation of cheaply produced and distributed fanzines further provided a textual space for grrrls to foster an increasingly idiosyncratic and reflexive relationship with female embodiment. The issues they addressed ranged significantly from self-image, to fat oppression, sex and sexuality, masturbation, violence, pornography, abortion and menstruation. The approach, however, remained inherently personal, based primarily on the experiences and subjectivity of the writer. This often blurred the lines between author and subject, creator and consumer, and allowed for grrrls the opportunity to be agents in their own constructions of selfhood. In her examination of the riot grrrl zining community, Jennifer Sinor describes how the body and the text became indivisibly linked in the ongoing process of identity-production:

'Through their body, they define who they are and who they are not. By literally taking control of their text, they take control of their bodies, and their writing vibrates with the intensity of those experiences – often shivering on the page.'[2]

The aim of this chapter is to explore how the psychic and the social intersect within riot grrrls' reframing of the gendered body in their zine writing. Elizabeth Grosz has documented how the concept of the body in modern western thought has occupied a semi-public existence: operating as a physical boundary which mediates between messy and emotional inner selves and the '"external" world'.[3] It is possible to identify zines in a similar role occupying a similar liminal, interactive space between the imagined internal and external. This was reflected in many of the grrrls' own conceptualisations of the role of fanzining, such as those recorded in Rosenberg and Garofalo's 1998 study of riot grrrl identity: '"Zines are a way to get into other people's heads" … "Zines are a way of typing how you feel, letting it out. It's another form of crying" … "Emotionally purging the bad stuff"'.[4] This consciousness of a movement of feeling both 'in' and 'out' Sara Ahmed has termed the 'sociality of emotion': connecting bodies to each other and objects as well as shaping our interactions with structures and norms.[5] This sense of fluidity has also shaped the zines themselves. Riot grrrl zines can be seen to inhabit a 'hybridity' of genres, exhibiting crossovers with life writing, political journalism and 'a kind of art practice', as well as becoming vehicles of 'resistance' and 'lifestyle'.[6] Such heterogeneity allowed grrrls to obfuscate the presumed boundaries between public/private, personal/political and mind/body dualisms.

This chapter also highlights how the fanzine context further complicates the relationship between the psychic and social. Spiers reminds us that 'riot grrrl texts connote constructed performances which cannot be read at face value, but rather should be read as modes of politicised self-fashioning'.[7] This study reveals the contentions underlying the performative disclosure of intimate personal dialogues within semi-public texts, as well as problematises the self and others as complicit in furthering conventions of oppression. This has wider implications regarding how we might theorise the precarity and limitations of embodied cultural resistance when enacted within affective communities.

Due to the breadth of fanzine material encompassing matters of body politics, I have selected one theme to examine through two zine publications: the issue of body weight. Firstly, I focus upon the correspondence between Allison and Kathleen Hanna, incorporated in *Bikini Kill #2* (1991).[8] The dialogue between these two friends illustrated how supportive friendship, conceptualised within the movement as 'Girl Love', both helped and hindered Allison's resistance to dominant ideals of body shape. Secondly, I examine the negotiation of body weight in the zine series *Antisocial Scarlet* created by

Sophie Scarlet in the early 2000s.[9] Scarlet's zine is illustrative of riot grrrls' critical engagement with commercialised standards of beauty. Her acknowledgement of the internalisation of these discourses, however, is suggestive of a more complicated relationship between her feminism, body image and psychic well-being.

The two zines reveal a number of parallels in their expressions of resistance and empowerment. Notably they both navigate the paradoxical relationship grrrls had with their female bodies: as sources of tension and anxiety, but equally of pleasure, play and celebration. Pleasure and power are mapped out in fanzine content through discussions of friendship, engagement with cultural icons of the age, and examinations of themselves and their transgressions. As a case study, these zines demonstrate riot grrrl's embrace of the faultlines and contradictions surrounding the volatile female body and of feminism more widely.

Before embarking on this close reading of riot grrrl zining, I offer a short background to the movement itself to demonstrate where this chapter sits within the existing historiography. This will provide a context to explain how kinship networks and intergenerational dialogues underpinned the movement and ensured a sense of collective unity, while also emphasising the importance of grrrls' individual subjectivity. This will assist in our understanding of why the body generally and weight in particular, became the focus of much discussion and contention within riot grrrls' fanzining practices.

## Historicising the movement

Riot grrrls' origins are located in the college campuses and music venues of Olympia, Washington and Washington DC in the USA in the early 1990s. It evolved into a transnational scene and cultural phenomenon based around a vociferous self-publishing creative network, global music conventions, and intimate consciousness-raising style meetings. It became largely popularised by individuals such as Kathleen Hanna, lead singer of Bikini Kill, and by bands such as Bratmobile, Heavens to Betsy and the UK-based Huggy Bear.

Attempts to define riot grrrl and its legacies have preoccupied much of the recent academic and popular scholarship of the movement. Notably, the formal establishment of the Riot Grrrl Collection in the Fales Library, New York in 2009 has also influenced this. Such an archive not only validated the scene as one of cultural significance but has impacted the way in which riot grrrl has been historically reconstructed and interpreted.[10] One particular source of debate has been locating the movement within feminist and subcultural punk/post-punk genealogies. Kate Eichhorn's reappraisal has been crucial in moving beyond the idea that riot grrrl was simply an oppositional or reactionary statement to parental cultures of second-wave feminism and the male-dominated punk scene.[11] Such a model, she argues, obscures its wider intellectual and aesthetic heritage as a 'queer feminist hybrid of punk, continental philosophy, feminism, and avant-garde literary and art traditions'.[12] Michelle Kempson has similarly demonstrated zine creators' uneasiness with locating themselves as a uniformed movement bridging 'second-' and 'third-'wave feminist eras; instead grrrls positioned themselves within their own trajectories of feminist history and grass-roots DIY activism.[13] Duncombe has highlighted how riot grrrls' reluctance to define the movement as a singular entity was a deliberate and conscious strategy of inclusion: a reaction to the rigid parameters of identity that titles such as 'feminist', 'punk' and 'woman' had perceivably procured.[14] Sharing expressions of interpretation, particularly in zine articles such as 'WHAT RIOT GRRRL MEANS TO ME' in *Riot Grrrl NYC #5*, instilled a sense of autonomy and self-determination for individual grrrls, while still maintaining the values of collectivity and collaboration.[15]

Historicisations of riot grrrl have also acknowledged the limitations of this approach to inclusivity, particularly its impact upon the visibility of some grrrls' experiences.[16] Inevitably, the investigation of body politics demonstrates the troubling consequences of exploring nonconformist identities within a movement when it unintentionally reinforces oppositionality. For many differently abled, working-class and minority racial and ethnic grrrls, it was evident that the bodies being discussed did not include theirs. In addition, less evidently interrogated due to the youth orientation of the movement, were issues such as ageing bodies, access to healthcare and motherhood. Grrrl zine-creator and scholar Mimi Thi Nguyen has since discussed the racialised aspect of this exclusion. In one interview she acknowledged, 'I have a hard time relating to most feminist discourses on body and beauty issues, because they originate from a white middle-class "American" context, and I didn't grow up that way and don't see myself reflected in that.'[17] In this respect, frustrations about the exclusivity of riot grrrl generated by the predominantly white and middle-class composition of its community echoed many of the anxieties faced by the Women's Liberation movements in the UK and USA. Kathleen Hanna has since discussed the privileging of certain bodies and experiences within the movement as 'a beauty pageant in reverse'.[18] Despite features in prominent zines such as *Bikini Kill #1* aimed at 'understanding privilege', retrospective accounts of the movement have acknowledged that the grrrls with the greatest access and legitimacy to explore subversive and deviant identities were white, young, able-bodied and middle class.[19] Although this study of the negotiation of body weight will not address these limitations directly, it is significant to note that the two zines selected for this investigation make little acknowledgement of the varied meaning of fat embodiment or weight oppression in relation to intersections such as class, race or sexuality. This does highlight how the emphasis on personal individual experience within the zining community helped to maintain a sense of invisibility and exclusion of certain bodies and voices.

For Hanna, the growing obsession with identity politics was enough for her to take a step back from the movement by the mid-1990s. However, consensus among scholars suggests that the disbanding of original groups such as Bikini Kill did not signal the scene's decline.[20] On the contrary, the Ladyfest music conventions continued to have an international presence into the 2010s and fanzines have continued to evolve, in part facilitated by the embrace of the internet as a means of distributing and cataloguing material without geographical restrictions. *Antisocial Scarlet* creator Sophie Scarlet reflects this sense of a continuing, but also fluctuating interest and engagement with riot grrrl in her correspondence with me in 2017:

> I was too young for riot grrrl the first time around (which I'm still sad about!), but there was definitely a strong second wave in the early 2000s with lots of riot grrrl chapters & bands & zines, and I would say a third wave in the past few years too. I've been playing in bands since I was 16 and it's been great to be part of these queer / feminist / DIY scenes and see them get stronger and bigger, and alongside that there's definitely been a resurgence or boom in zine culture (not that it ever went away).[21]

As one cohort of grrrls moved on, a new generation embraced the body of work that had been produced and developed it in a way that has meant the term 'Riot Grrrl' continues to retain value. This chapter explores zine material from the early 1990s and the 2000s of both US and UK-based riot grrrls. Created approximately ten years apart and in different geographical locations, *Bikini Kill #2* and *Antisocial Scarlet* differ in the cultural and personal contexts in which they were produced. Notably, improved access to home computers, printers and the internet has had a significant impact on style, content and distribution of zines. For instance, alongside the postal addresses in the zine reviews of *Riot Girl London issue 2* in 2001, addresses for email and websites for bands, local groups and e-zines featured frequently.[22]

There are questions regarding the legitimacy of identifying zines from the 2000s as 'authentic riot grrrl' zines. Dick Hebdige has explained the temporal specify of youth cultures such as the Teddy Boys of the 1950s and 1970s, arguing they diverge markedly in their origins, social circumstances and

significations of style.[23] Certainly, the majority of riot grrrl zine writers in the
2000s lacked involvement in producing the original 'canon' of zine material,
as Scarlet's testimony suggests. However, despite changes in production
techniques and distribution networks, riot grrrl zines of the 2000s retained
the self-referential ethos and feminist objectives, the impetus for self-
representation and critical opposition to mainstream commercial print cultures
of earlier riot grrrl zining.

This is not to say that the movement remained static or failed to evolve
in content, style and approach over the decade. A consistent feature of 2000s
riot grrrl zines was a continued dialogue from the previous decade. *Riot Girl
London issue 2* illustrates one local chapter's perception of how the movement
had developed:

> It aint about 'rock music' its not about girls VS boys, or what happened in
> America 10 years ago. It aint about hello kitty and it aint about about [sic]
> pretty dresses and 'girls with gtrs' ... rock music and hello kitty and dresses
> are what might appeal to you individually and that's fine, but as a collective, I
> dontthnik [sic] everyone realises that things have seriously evolved.[24]

This affirmation is suggestive of a complex and overlapping picture of assimila-
tion, criticism and re-articulation of ideas across the generations. Zines such
as *Starlette #3* reflected this hybridity in its coverage of musical influencers:
featuring an interview with Bratmobile's Molly Neuman, a biography of hip-hop
icon Eve, and a review of newly emerging all-girl ska punk band The Cherry
Bombers in a single issue.[25] The ongoing maintenance of a DIY alternative
press facilitated a means for grrrls not only to interact with their past, present
and future selves, but also the movement as a whole. This disrupts the idea
of the movement's linear change over time, rather it illustrates Sam McBean's
assertion of the queer temporality of riot grrrl in which contemporary, locally
specific scenes co-existed and continue to co-exist alongside remembrances
and revisits to historical moments.[26]

## Body weight

The issue of body weight reappeared frequently as a fundamental concern
within riot grrrl zine content throughout the 1990s and 2000s. That dieting,
food and body size generated anxiety among adolescent girls and young
women, Kearney argues is unsurprising 'since body image is such a primary
discursive theme in female youth culture.'[27] But riot grrrl's unpacking of the

socio-psychological tensions tied to body weight was also temporally specific, demonstrating Grosz's contention that body image is a relational awareness, consistently altered by interpersonal and sociocultural contexts.[28] Zines offer traces of these intertextual dialogues, as physical objects from the period and as records of these networks 'built of paper'.[29]

Riot grrrl's discussions of body weight coincided with a burgeoning shift towards DIY publishing culture within the fat activist community in the USA and UK more generally. Closely aligned with queer politics, zines such as *FaT GiRL* and Nomy Lamm's *I'm so Fucking Beautiful* distanced themselves from the perceived exclusionary mainstream feminist movement and shared many of riot grrrl's networks of distribution.[30] As a challenge to the homogeneity of dieting and fitness rhetoric offered by mainstream commercial media at that time, single-issue zines such as *Fat Girl, Fat! SO?, Take it – It's my Body, Fat is not a Four Letter Word* and *Figure 8* would ensure that the cultural production of fat activists and, in turn, a wider diversity of knowledges and readings of fat embodiment were made visible between the 1990s and 2000s.[31]

The motivation to self-publish personal experiences of fat oppression was also a reaction to the development of feminist and psychoanalytical scholarly work on disordered eating, which from the 1970s began to dominate public discussions of body size. Illnesses such as bulimia and anorexia nervosa came increasingly under academic and clinical ownership, most notably in Susie Orbach's *Fat is a Feminist issue* first published in 1978 and in the following decades by Chernin, Wolf and Bordo among others.[32] DIY activists drew attention to how these accounts reinforced a monolithic and pejorative impression of what the experience of living in a fat body must be like.[33] There is evidence to indicate that riot grrrl members knew of and extrapolated from existing feminist scholarship. (Scarlet even used the title 'Fat is a Feminist Issue' in issue 6 of *Antisocial Scarlet*, although she made no mention of Orbach's original work). The emphasis on personal experience within zine content, however, was a political recuperation of the body not only from commercial culture but from the academy and clinic as well.

In providing an alternative to the discursive production of body weight offered by the feminist psycho-social theoretical framework, riot grrrl zines also reworked the victim narrative bestowed upon their generation. Both Chernin and Wolf in their analyses of the relationship between women and hunger in the post-feminist era suggested that the contemporary obsession with ideal body weight was indicative of an identity crisis among young women caused by second-wave feminism's disruption of gender roles.[34] Riot grrrls were by implication part of a generation that experienced increased public freedoms and yet expanding corporeal restraint. According to this hypothesis, they lay at the faultlines of an 'epidemic of eating disorders' in western culture.[35]

More recently, feminist scholars such as McRobbie, Moran, Scharff and Gill have drawn attention to the specific political and economic context of 1990s and 2000s neoliberalism to unpick why body weight became so central to the debate regarding new discourses of patriarchal oppression and female empowerment.[36] By assuming that individuals have and should exercise choice, freedom and personal responsibility, neoliberal discourses posited failure and success as within each individual's mental and physical capacity to attain. The achievement of ideal standards of bodily appearance, particularly for women, has become a key site of this expression of self-mastery and in turn social mobility has become associated with the psychic abilities of willpower and self-motivation as opposed to recognition of structural determinants. Moran has described how 'through this identification of successful femininity with continuous self-improvement ... neoliberalism pressurises women to be dissatisfied with every aspect of themselves and experience perpetual anxiety or "normative discontent" about their appearance.'[37] McRobbie has labelled this as a 'split-self desire for "perfection"' in which competitiveness is directed at the self as well as to other women.[38]

The two zines explored in the remainder of this chapter – Bikini Kill #2 and Antisocial Scarlet #5–7 – demonstrate how riot grrrls have negotiated the neoliberal paradigm alongside their own sense of collective and individual identity. Their discussions of body weight suggest a sense of the ambiguous and permeable margins between subversion of and compliance with patriarchal norms, and both grrrls question what constituted feminist resistance within the neoliberal context of unrelenting self-improvement. Fanzines offered space to challenge the culturally dominant ideals of body shape and explore these complexities through a personalised approach. This was further complicated by the grrrls' sense of the expectations of intimacy and authenticity required by their audiences as part of the zine writing narrative.

## Bikini Kill #2

Handwritten on a mixture of lined and squared writing paper and photocopied onto the pages of Bikini Kill #2, Allison from Wenatchee, WA wrote to her friend Kathleen Hanna about what it is like to be 'an angry fat woman'.[39] The amateurish appearance of Allison's letter juxtaposed the complex interrogation of the social construction of ideal beauty within its content, typifying inversion strategies of punk politics. She began by questioning how resistance might manifest:

> Is being a strong and sexy woman the most powerful form of subversion? Maybe the most powerful for those who are born that way, but being a strong and 'non-beautiful' or 'ugly' and 'fat' woman and declaring openly that you like the way you are is the most <u>defiantly</u> <u>powerful</u> form of subversion.[40]

Subversion according to Allison was not just in the embodiment of non-idealised body type but in 'declaring' your acceptance and even enjoyment of it. This demonstrates an incorporation of the 'coming out' narrative associated with the politics of Gay Pride, utilised as a means to reinscribe and reclaim stigmatised identity from conventional pejorative usage. According to fat studies scholar Samantha Murray, the assumption behind this form of subversion tactic is that 'one's identity is located in one's mind, and that through the act of changing one's mind, it is then possible to change the way one's body is received.'[41] Allison's sense of resistance, therefore, is not simply something enacted but imagined, drawing upon the interconnectedness of mind and body.

The core of Allison's letter presented a post-structuralist critique of beauty ideals in which she explored not only the temporal and cultural specificity of constructions of taste, but also the multiplicity of structures and institutions through which these ideals became dominant. She quoted at length sections of academic research attributed to 'Nancy Barron, Ph.D.', including statistics from a study examining university students' self-perceptions of weight. The amalgamation of the factual with the personal, Duncombe argues, is often characteristic in zine-writing 'as a way to cast off the "preaching" model of persuasion they feel is too common in political discourse.'[42] Instead she speaks directly to her generation through cultural references:

> (Remember how beautiful Barbies were? Or harvest gold w/ avocado green? OR brown tight polyester shirts? Or big wide denim culottes? Or women with blue frost eyeshadow? Well, once big fat gelatinous women were beautiful-ownable-haveable).[43]

References to cultural signifiers such as Barbie and 1980s make-up trends provided an informal, youthful and playful tone in contrast with the previous statistical evidence. Such questioning also illustrates Allison's consciousness of who her audience was and the assumed mutual commonality between them.

The publication of written correspondence was a common feature of riot grrrl zining; alongside reviewing each other's work, contributing artwork and cut 'n' pasting articles from other zines, epistolary fortified the referential nature of grrrl identity and the ever-present conversation with imagined others. In her analyses of second-wave feminist epistolary, Margaretta Jolly has similarly made reference to the relational aspect of identity-building, describing the dialogic exchange of letter writing as a 'a textual looking glass through which women could pass to find themselves again in love with their own kind'.[44] Fanzines similarly functioned as 'textual looking glasses' which allowed grrrls to assert themselves as autonomous subjects, while also cultivating the affective bonds of female relationships and collective care. Allison's contribution to *Bikini Kill #2* exemplifies how 'outsider' identities such as being overweight were negotiated, but also problematised through friendship and community. The practice and form of letter writing is therefore just as significant to Allison's resistance of cultural ideals and renegotiation of the self, as the critical content within it.

The importance of maintaining supportive friendships was encapsulated in riot grrrl's notion of 'Girl Love', and was identified within the movement as a revolutionary kind of politics that challenged the mainstream conceptualisation of girlhood friendships as competitive or trivial. Bearing some resemblances to the idea of 'sisterhood' posited by feminists of the 1970s, mutual trust and care was garnered through a culture of intimacy and the sharing of personal experiences. Hanna's typed response underneath the photocopy of Allison's letter echoes this. She wrote how Allison 'has a lot of fucking guts to speak her mind', applauding her bravery for sharing her experience.[45] Hanna continued: 'Dialogue is crucail [*sic*] and even though it's hard sometimes it is totally worth it. Friends matter. I love you Alleee!!!!'[46] Hanna's response illustrated the inherently multi-dimensional aspect of the zine-writing community, differentiating it from traditional two-way forms of epistolary. Hanna spoke to both her friend and her readers, valuing her relationship with both. The affective bonds of the community were enabled in exchanges such as this: by Allison's exposure of intimate feeling, as well as by Hanna's reciprocal acknowledgement of the effort this entailed.

Allison (or Alleee's) letter to Hanna bears many of the hallmarks of what design historian Teal Triggs has termed the 'graphic language of resistance' associated with the DIY punk-inspired fanzines of the late 1970s.[47] Typographic elements such as the handwritten letterform, the combination of lined and squared paper it rests upon and the muddled use of letter cases, under-linings, crossings out and bolded text, all work as part of the 'aesthetic performance' of Alleee's individual narrative. Visual characteristics such as these are considered to reflect a spirit of democracy and inclusivity cultivated in opposition to the professionalisation of both mainstream media and academic text.[48] Additionally, the scruffy appearance mirrors the visceral urgency and emotional authenticity of Allison herself, 'who cuts through the conventions of manners, norms, and communication and connects to ... her "real" self'.[49] This transitory state of raw, unconstrained emotion is consolidated by Allison in the line 'Now that it's daytime and I'm calm ... ' towards the end of the letter.[50] This implied transition of emotion strikes a chord with Sinor's conceptualisation of diary writing as a process of documentation of a 'discontinuous, changing self (I am not the same as I was yesterday).'[51] Like diary writing, Allison's letter is a performative record of the volatility of her emotions and her consciousness of throwing off the conventions which required their management. This type of confessional writing did not only have therapeutic purposes. The emphasis on showing authenticity, according to Nguyen, was not simply an aesthetic style choice but a political statement in which 'strategic excavation of the true self also becomes an ethical foundation for communion.'[52]

This sense of community, Allison recognised, also caused complications for liberation. She listed the structures and institutions that 'choose the ideal image for a woman' and facilitated the stigmatisation of fat bodies: 'parents', 'teachers', 'governments', 'television', 'kings', 'environment' and 'magazines'.[53] But she also observed that complicit in the maintenance of oppression were her peers. In declaring 'And our SISTERS our GIRLFRIENDS are encouraging us and doing it <u>Right</u> <u>Along</u> <u>With</u> us!!!', Allison began to unfold the complexities of Girl Love and understand how fat oppression must be negotiated alongside the tangled discourse of friendship.[54] Alison Winch has discussed how 'girl-friendship' culture coalesced around mutual body regulation in the neoliberal postfeminist era whereby 'intimate networks of comparison, feedback and motivation [became] necessary in controlling body image.'[55] Fat embodiment as a subversive tactic is therefore complicated by the surveillance of others who have been exposed to the same dominant cultural knowledges and feel the same pressure to conform. This has implications for Allison's notion that simply 'declaring openly that you like the way you are is the most <u>defiantly</u> <u>powerful</u> form of subversion' – even if she came out as openly loving her fat self, would her friends still read her fat negatively? This reinforces Murray's argument that fat liberation through the 'coming out' narrative creates 'a problematic space between the lived and the imagined body'.[56] Simply because Allison had imagined her body differently (and with pride), it did not signify that externally her body was read with any increased positivity. Allison's letter exposed the tensions around the individual in the collective, and the potentiality of this to limit the reframing of the fat body as powerful.

For Allison the textual space of the zine offered an opportunity to reinscribe her relationship with her body and encourage other grrrls to do the same by deconstructing beauty ideals and interrogate what empowerment really constituted. Allison recognised that grrrls were 'not yet rulers of our own waistline', and that although she valued the support and dialogue with her kinship network, the recovery of the fat body was a battle in which they were also complicit.[57] As the next zine demonstrates, these contradictions around friendship echoed the contradictions of living a feminist life more generally. The discussion of body weight in *Antisocial Scarlet* encompasses Scarlet's ongoing negotiation of her punk feminist critical consciousness and her desire to adhere to rigid codes of femininity, while also managing the expectations of her readers.

## Antisocial Scarlet

*Antisocial Scarlet* was a zine series created by riot girl London member Sophie Scarlet in the early 2000s. Unlike *Bikini Kill #2* and the *Riot Girl London* zines Scarlet also co-created, it did not feature many contributions from friends. Instead, each issue of *Antisocial Scarlet* offered a snapshot into Scarlet's 'world' at that particular moment and reflected the perpetual reconstruction of selfhood this provoked. The tagline 'a horribly personal zine' served as a caution to readers that what was disclosed inside would not always be a pleasant read and blurred the conventional boundaries between private feeling and public consumption.[58] Alongside music reviews, interviews and commentaries on recent riot grrrl London gatherings, Scarlet drew upon autobiographical writing to discuss intimate themes such as relationship break-ups, body image and masturbation. The zines appropriated a diary-like aesthetic accordingly: text heavy, using a combination of both handwritten and computer word-processed formats. Images and artwork appeared sporadically other than on the front cover and the heart and star borders with which riot grrrl zining has typically come to be recognised.[59] The choice to construct a diary aesthetic in the semi-public forum of the fanzine according to Nguyen was a political one, used to indicate the disclosure of 'intimate self-knowledge'.[60] Sinor has additionally argued that as a form of life writing, zines allowed grrrls to document their daily lives and represent themselves in a way that was empowering, subverting the notion of girlhood diary writing as trivial or apolitical.[61] Features such as 'Diary of a Vibrator Virgin' which recorded Scarlet's day-by-day experimentation in issue 6 functioned as an important record of sexual experience: a subject matter conventionally seen as taboo for women to discuss publicly.[62]

Weight was a recurrent theme within the confessional narrative of issues 5, 6 and 7 of *Antisocial Scarlet*, all self-published in 2002. Scarlet's exploration was multi-dimensional; she intertwined commentary on the ideals of body size perpetuated by the mainstream media and wrote autobiographically about her own relationship with eating and food. Within these dialogues, body weight was posited as central to Scarlet's sense of personal identity and well-being; it underpinned an ongoing struggle to reconcile her feminist principles with the internalisation of patriarchal norms of appearance and was deeply connected to emotional states of shame and disgust.

This is most evident in *Antisocial Scarlet #5* (see Figure 18.1). The content of this issue was dominated by Scarlet's recent romantic break-up and the disintegration of her band, events which led her to reflect on her anxieties about her current situation and her lack of future plans. 'I really need to change', she wrote in a handwritten passage entitled 'The New Me'. 'Currently I: eat really badly, smoke, don't have a job, have quit college twice … don't really do anything all day, look like shit and feel like shit. Great huh?'[63] Scarlet's negative self-assessment echoes the neoliberal discourse of individualisation and responsibilisation, which Gill argues seeks 'to cajole women into turning inwards to solve external problems.'[64] Scarlet used her zine as a means to publicly confess her transgressions, and through revelation begin the process of transformation into a more desirable version of her self.[65] In this sense, the feminist principles of consciousness raising espoused previously by Hanna in her line 'dialogue is crucial' combines with neoliberal discourse of self-improvement and, in turn, creates ambiguity around bodily empowerment.

That 'eating badly' featured on the list is indicative of the moralising discourse attributed to the consumption of food and the impact of this on Scarlet's own sense of lacking emotional and physical wellness. This is made more explicit elsewhere in the issue:

> And now I've started eating loads. I lost quite a bit of weight (unintentionally) over the past few months and I think thats [sic] because I was getting happier. Not that I've ever liked to admit I have a food/body/image 'thing' going on, but I guess I do. I've just about accepted my size and now I've started eating so much it scares me. Disgusts me. I just eat & eat & eat. I hate being out of control. I don't want to be slim. I don't mind being big, but I do mind not being able to control my eating.[66]

In this instance Scarlet's desire to be 'able to control' her body is not the same as Allison's insistence on the right to be 'rulers of our own waistline'. Scarlet put value on the ability to self-discipline her body as a means of emancipation rather than reinscribe its meaning akin to Allison's 'coming out' narrative.

Shame and disgust Scarlet associated not with physical body size but with a lack of control, evoking the theoretical work on disgust in the policing of

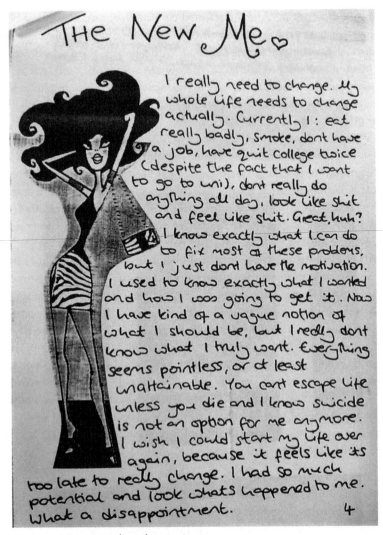

**18.1** *Antisocial Scarlet*, 5 (2002) © Sophie Lawton

bodily boundaries by Douglas and Kristeva among others; her failure to control her eating represented a failure of personal responsibility.[67] Therefore, in contrast to Allison's view that the battle for empowerment was located in opposition to external authoritative structures, Scarlet exemplifies Bordo's assertion that 'the real battle, ultimately, is with the self'.[68]

Through her confession that she did not like to admit she had a 'food/body/image "thing"', Scarlet exposed the double bind of shame she found herself located within – unable to adhere to societal norms of beauty and self-control, but equally unable to fully accept her body and embrace her feminist sensibility. In sharing her own sense of deficiency, Scarlet gave an insight into how feminist resistance to body ideals of weight was complex and often contradictory, recalling McRobbie's notion of a 'double entanglement' in which 'liberal choice and neo-liberal family values, feminist common sense and feminist displacement' have had a discordant effect on young women's conceptualisation of selfhood.[69]

In issue 6, the relationship between weight and feminism was discussed further in a feature entitled 'Fat Is a Feminist Issue' (see Figure 18.2). The entirety of the article was word-processed so that, unlike Allison's letter, emotional intimacy was not conveyed through typography but through content. Indeed, there is little sense of the emotional 'overspill' we get from Allison's handwritten crossings-out and bolded text; only a handful of times did Scarlet use underlined or italicised texts for emphasis. Instead, Scarlet developed intimate reciprocity through directly asking questions of her imagined audience and the collective use of 'we' to denote a shared experience: 'we are brought up to believe that fat is not sexy'.[70] She discussed the stigmatisation of fat bodies within society and the problematic conflation between success, happiness and thinness. Scarlet's honesty is articulated in her confession that although she recognises the structures of oppression, this does not bestow her immunity from them: 'Its all bullshit. I know it is … I can say all that, know it, but that doesn't really help.' She conceded: 'Here's where my feminist side loses: I don't have a problem with other people being fat, but as for myself? I'd rather be a little thinner.'[71] Scarlet exposed the tensions surrounding her own lived experience within a patriarchal system and her understanding of feminist resistance. Her depiction of a lost 'feminist side' is suggestive of an ongoing psychological tussle between acceptance of her body and the internalisation of societal conventions of body ideals.

To further demonstrate this anguish she confessed: 'I have wishes to have the willpower of an anorexic. How horrifying is that?'[72] The 'horror' attached to this admission works on a number of levels. Firstly it referred to the serious extent to which societal norms had impacted upon Scarlet's detachment from her own body. Bordo has documented how the anorexic condition came to represent a 'chance to embody qualities – detachment, self-containment, self-mastery, control – that are highly valued in our culture'.[73] Scarlet's horror therefore could be perceived as her disgust of the way in which society has

## ♡ Fat Is A Feminist Issue ♡

There is a world-wide obsession with thinness. Why? Being thin is promoted as the key to happiness – once thin you will be successful in love, with friends, at work... I believed this once, and have moments when sometimes I still do. Its hard not to when you are bombarded with images of fabulous skinny women and are concurrently shown society's revulsion for fat people. Ever since I was about 9 I have been "bigger than average" – tall for my age and also fatter. Its hard to be comfortable in yourself when you know people are judging you. Its hard when the clothes you want to buy dont fit you. Its even harder going from a size 10 to a 12 to a 14 to a 16 to an 18 and then the occasional size 20. Size 16 is seen as being "too big" (even though 55% of women in Britain are a size 16 or over), so being a 20... Good god. You can get nice clothes in larger sizes, but that doesn't stop you being dissatisfied or even disgusted with yourself.

We are brought up to believe that fat is not sexy, that cellulite is our deadliest enemy, that lose a few pounds and you'll get that man! Its all bullshit. I know it is – I've seen beautiful fat women, cellulite is natural and as for losing weight to get a man... I've never had any trouble with guys because I'm "large". I can say all that, know it, but that doesnt really help. Here's where my feminist side loses: I dont have a problem with other people being fat, but as for myself? I'd rather be a little thinner. I'm not as bad as I used to be, I have come to accept my size a hell of a lot more than I used to, but... When I look at myself in the mirror I wish my waist went in a little more, that I had thinner thighs, more toned arms...

Most women experience this at some point in their lives, so should we accept it as natural? No. I dont think women should lie to themselves and pretend they're happy, but I do think society should get over this ridiculous glorifying of thinness. Women are throwing up their food every day, starving themselves, dying. That is not natural. I have wished to have the willpower of an anorexic. How horrifying is that? Why dont we all step back and shout a big collective NO at the ideas and trends that are destroying women. Maybe not all women are suffering physically from eating disorders, but most of them are torturing themselves mentally. One day I hope to completely love my body, and one day I hope all sizes will be praised.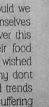

5

**18.2** *Antisocial Scarlet,* 6 (2002) © Sophie Lawton

glamourised and idolised the anorexic body as embodying the ideals of femininity.

The suggestion of horror also demonstrated Scarlet's acknowledgement of the ignorance and distastefulness of wishing to be an anorexic, while simultaneously protecting her from criticism. This type of confession and invitation of approval was common, Nguyen argues, within the framework of grrrl intimacy, as it provided a means of accountability in which they could be 'publicly critiqued for their entitlements'.[74] The articulation of shame was 'proof of good faith' but this did not change the potentiality of Scarlet to deny others who suffered from eating disorders their experience. Scarlet's rejoinder was therefore also a consciousness of fitting with expectations of her audience: her recognition of the potential of being read as 'unfeminist', the acknowledge-ment of her appropriation of patriarchal ideals of corporeal discipline, and the potential disenfranchisement of an anorexia sufferer's experience.

Scarlet appreciated that she was not entirely to blame for her cognitive dissonance. She expressed her frustration with feminism's inadequacy in dealing with issues of body image in issue 7: 'Feminism is good for pointing out faults in society, but how can we fix things when we're up against so many people and skewed mindsets? And I can't even tell you that I'm happy with *my* body, because 19 years of skinny society has done almost irreparable damage to me.'[75] Scarlet illustrated how her experience made resistance to bodily oppression complicated, exposing the limitations of Allison's 'coming out' subversion tactic as simply 'changing one's mind' about the body. She was able to reflect upon the paradoxical situation she found herself in, in desiring a sense of control over her body but recognising how this conformity to patriarchal values was also disempowering. As a result, the faultlines between subversion and submission became increasingly obscured.

## Conclusion

Sociologist Jessica Ringrose has argued that often missing from scholarly debates regarding the sexualisation of young women's bodies in 'postfeminist times' is the understanding of how girls themselves negotiate and respond to commercially constructed ideals of femininity.[76] Self-produced zines offer a means to recognise and interrogate grrrls' active consumption and production of media texts as engaged social actors embedded within communities of consciousness. Riot grrrl fanzines encourage us to re-examine how individual subjectivity and social networks intersect within feminist politics of the neoliberal age.

The aim of the chapter has been to show how zines provided a textual space in which riot grrrls could explore the relationship between the body, self and community. Although we must acknowledge the performative aspect of zine writing, in which subjectivity was carefully constructed and mediated, maintaining a DIY alternative press facilitated a means for grrrls to interact with past, present and future feminist selves and movements, and experiment with identity as producers and critics. In these two examples, *Bikini Kill #2* and *Antisocial Scarlet*, we can observe the multiplicity of readings of stigma, resistance and empowerment with regard to body weight. These were examined in relation to (among other things) dominant cultures of commercialism, kinship networks and grrrls' own expertise as proficient analysts of discourse and experience. Fanzine discussions of body weight exposed feelings of shame, disgust, love, pride and anger and gave grrrls the opportunity to explore how these fluctuating emotions related to their female and feminist identities. The blurring of these public/private narratives formed an important part of the cultural resistance of zining and continued to redraw the parameters of feminist politics and praxis into the twenty-first century. Riot grrrls acknowledged and embraced the messiness, and their zines provide a record of many of these works in progress.

## Notes

1   Feona Attwood, 'Sluts and Riot Grrrls: Female Identity and Sexual Agency', *Journal of Gender Studies*, 16:3 (2007), 233–47; Sara Marcus, *Girls to the Front: The True Story of the Riot Grrrl Revolution* (New York and London: Harper Perennial, 2010).

2   Jennifer Sinor, 'Another Form of Crying: Girl Zines as Life Writing', *Prose Studies: History, Theory, Criticism*, 26 (2003), 246.

3   Elizabeth Grosz, *Volatile Bodies: Toward a Corporeal Feminism* (Bloomington, IN: Indiana University Press, 1994), p. 9.

4   Jessica Rosenberg and Gitana Garofalo, 'Riot Grrrl: Revolutions from Within', *Signs: Journal of Women in Culture and Society*, 23:3 (1998), 822–3.

5   Sara Ahmed, *The Cultural Politics of Emotion* (Edinburgh: Edinburgh University Press, 2014).

6   Michelle Kempson, '"My version of feminism": Subjectivity, DIY and the Feminist Zine', *Social Movements Studies*, 14:4 (2015), 459–72; Sinor, 'Another Form of Crying', 240–64.

7   Emily Spiers, '"Killing Ourselves is Not Subversive": Riot Grrrl from Zine to Screen and the Commodification of Female Transgression', *Women: A Cultural Review*, 26:1–2 (2015), 12.

8   *Bikini Kill*, 2 (1991), pp. 16–17, Kathleen Hanna Papers, MSS 271, 1, 12 (Fales Library, New York University).

9   Sophie Scarlet, *Antisocial Scarlet*, 5–7 (2002), section 3, folder 69 (LCC Library, University of the Arts London).

10  Kate Eichhorn, *The Archival Turn in Feminism: Outrage in Order* (Philadelphia, PA: Temple University Press, 2014).

11  *Ibid.*, pp. 111–14.

12  *Ibid.*

13  Kempson, 'My version of feminism', 459–72.

14  Stephen Duncombe, *Notes from Underground: Zines and the Politics of Alternative Culture* (London: Verso 1997), pp. 68–9.

15  *Riot Grrrl NYC*, 5 (1993), Kathleen Hanna Papers, MSS 271, 2, 23 (Fales Library and Special Collections, New York University Libraries).

16  Mimi Thi Nguyen, 'Riot Grrrl, Race, and Revival', *Women and Performance: A Journal of Feminist Theory*, 33:2–3 (2012), 173–96. See also Laura Cofield and Lucy Robinson, '"The opposite of the band": Fangrrrling, Feminism and Sexual Dissidence', *Textual Practice* 30:6 (2016), 1071–88 for discussion of how individuality undermined collective sense of friendship.

17  Mimi Thi Nguyen interviewed by Janice Radway, 'Girl Zine Networks, Underground Itineraries, and Riot Grrrl History: Making Sense of the Struggle for New Social Forms in the 1990s and Beyond', *Journal of American Studies*, 50 (2016), 20.

18  *Noisey, Kathleen Hanna on Tokenism, Therapy, and Where Riot Grrrl Went Wrong* (2016) [video online] www.youtube.com/watch?v=mLNCCvZ71m4, accessed 26 January 2017.

19  'Understanding Privilege', *Bikini Kill*, 1 (1990), p. 13. For retrospective accounts see Thi Nguyen, 'Riot Grrrl, Race, and Revival', 173–96; Mary Celeste Kearney, *Girls Make Media* (Oxon: Taylor & Francis, 2006), p. 153.

20  Hanna refers to her disillusionment with Riot Grrrl in her personal papers: see *Ideas* [1 of 2], Kathleen Hanna Papers, MSS271, 1, 14 (Fales Library, New York University). See Kevin Dunn and May Summer Farnsworth, '"We are the Revolution": Riot Grrrl Press, Girl Empowerment, and DIY Self-publishing', *Women's Studies*, 41 (2012), 136–57 for discussion of longevity of riot grrrl.

21  Sophie Lawton, *riot grrrl london and zines*; email correspondence with the author, 23 March 2017.

22  *Riot Girl London*, 2 (2001), p. 29, section 3, folder 51 (LCC Library, University of the Arts London).

23  Dick Hebdige, *Subculture: The Meaning of Style* (London and New York: Routledge, 1979), pp. 80–4.

24  Linzy writing in *Riot Grrrl London*, 2 (2001), p. 5.

25  R. Dyer, *Starlette #3* (2002), pp. 6–7 and 20–2, section 3, folder 47 (LCC Library University of the Arts London).

26  Sam McBean, *Feminism's Queer Temporalities* (London: Routledge, 2016), pp. 72–4.

27  Kearney, *Girls Make Media*, pp. 182–3.

28  Grosz, *Volatile Bodies*, pp. 84–5.

29  E. White cited in Rosenberg and Garofalo, 'Riot Grrrl: Revolutions from Within', p. 811.

30  Charlotte Cooper, *Fat Activism: A Radical Social Movement* (Bristol: HammerOn Press 2016), pp. 131–61.

31  *Ibid.*, pp. 68–9. Zines cited in K. Durden, *Figure 8 #2* (Portland, OR: Pony Boy Press, 2003), section 3, folder 60 (LCC Library, University of the Arts London).

32 Susie Orbach, *Fat is a Feminist Issue II* (London: Random House, 1998); Kim Chernin *The Hungry Self: Women, Eating and Identity* (New York: Times Books, 1985); Naomi Wolf, *The Beauty Myth* (London: Vintage, 1991); Susan Bordo, *Unbearable Weight: Feminism, Western Culture and the Body* (Berkeley, CA: University of California Press, 1993).

33 Cooper, *Fat Activism*, p. 22.

34 *Ibid.*, pp. 33–6; Wolf, *The Beauty Myth*, pp. 214–15.

35 Chernin, *The Hungry Self*, p. 17.

36 Angela McRobbie, 'Notes on the Perfect: Competitive Femininity in Neoliberal Times', *Australian Feminist Studies*, 30:83 (2015), 3–20; Claire Moran, 'Re-Positioning Female Heterosexuality Within Postfeminist and Neoliberal Culture', *Sexualities*, 20:1–2 (2017), 121–39; Rosalind Gill and Christina Scharff, *New Femininities: Postfeminism, Neoliberalism, and Subjectivity* (Basingstoke: Palgrave Macmillan, 2011).

37 Moran, 'Re-positioning female heterosexuality', 125.

38 McRobbie, 'Notes on the Perfect', 16.

39 *Bikini Kill*, 2, p. 17.

40 *Ibid.*, p. 16. Original emphasis.

41 Samantha Murray, 'Doing Politics or Selling out? Living the Fat Body', *Women's Studies*, 34:3–4 (2005), 271.

42 Duncombe, *Notes from Underground*, p. 29.

43 *Bikini Kill*, 2, p. 17.

44 Margaretta Jolly, *In Love and Struggle: Letters in Contemporary Feminism* (New York: Columbia University Press 2008), p. 10.

45 *Bikini Kill*, 2, p. 17.

46 *Ibid.*

47 Teal Triggs, 'Scissors and Glue: Punk Fanzines and the Creation of a DIY Aesthetic', *Journal of Design History*, 19:1 (2006), 70.

48 Duncombe, *Notes from Underground*, p. 31.

49 *Ibid.*, p. 32.

50 *Bikini Kill*, 2, p. 17.

51 Jennifer Sinor, *The Extraordinary Work of Ordinary Writing: Annie Ray's Diary* (Iowa City: University of Iowa Press, 2002), p. 49.

52 Nguyen, 'Riot Grrrl, Race and Revival', 177.

53 *Bikini Kill*, 2, p. 17.

54 *Ibid.*

55 Alison Winch, *Girlfriends and Postfeminist Sisterhood* (Basingstoke: Palgrave Macmillan, 2013), p. 2.

56 Murray, 'Doing Politics or Selling out', 272.

57 *Bikini Kill*, 2, p. 17.

58 Tagline on the covers of issue 5 (January/February 2002) and issue 6 (March/April/May 2002).

59 Triggs discusses the significance behind the use of symbols such as hearts and stars as symbolic of 'the space between feminist rhetoric and the riot grrrl who also wants

to be feminine in *'Do it Yourself' Girl Revolution: Ladyfest, Performance and Fanzine Culture* (London: London College of Communication, 2009), p. 20.

60  Nguyen, 'Riot Grrrl, Race and Revival', 177.

61  Sinor, 'Another Form of Crying', 252.

62  *Antisocial Scarlet*, 6, p. 3.

63  *Antisocial Scarlet*, 5, p. 4.

64  Rosalind Gill and Shani Orgad, 'The Confidence Cult(ure)', *Australian Feminist Studies*, 30:86 (2015), 330.

65  Gill and Orgad note in 'The Confidence Cult(ure)' that part of the process of self-improvement is momentary acknowledgement of insecurity, which in being witnessed by others becomes an object which one can now deal with and overcome (338–9).

66  *Antisocial Scarlet*, 5, p. 1.

67  Grosz, *Volatile Bodies*, pp. 192–3.

68  Susan Bordo, 'Reading the Slender Body', in Mary Jacobus, Evelyn Fox Keller and Sally Shuttleworth (eds), *Body/Politics: Women and the Discourses of Science* (New York and London: Routledge, 1990), p. 96.

69  Angela McRobbie, 'Feminism and the Socialist Tradition … Undone?', *Cultural Studies*, 18:4 (2004), 514.

70  *Antisocial Scarlet*, 6, p. 5.

71  *Ibid.*

72  *Ibid.*

73  Bordo, 'Reading the Slender Body', p. 105.

74  Nguyen, 'Riot Grrrl, Race and Revival', 178.

75  *Antisocial Scarlet*, 7, p. 2.

76  Jessica Ringrose, 'Are you sexy, flirty, or a slut? Exploring 'Sexualisation' and How Teen Girls Perform/Negotiate Digital Sexual Identity on Social Networking Sites', in Gill and Scharff (eds), *New Femininities*, pp. 99–116.

# Index